THE
FICKLE
70s

MEMOIRS 1972-79

OTHER BOOKS BY F. S. AIJAZUDDIN

Polari Paintings & Sikh Portraits in the Lahore Museum

Sikh Portraits by European Artists

Aitchison College: The First Hundred Years

Lahore: Illustrated Views of the 19th Century

Historical Images of Pakistan

The Armless Queen and Other Essays

Rare Maps of Pakistan

From a Head, through a Head, to a Head:
The Secret Channel between the U.S. and China through Pakistan

The Bark of a Pen: A Miscellany of Articles and Speeches

The White House & Pakistan:
Secret Declassified Documents 1969–1974

Lahore Recollected: An Album

When Bush Comes to Shove & Other Writings

The Counterfoils of My Years 1942–1971

Commanding Success: Aitchison College, 1886–2011

From a Minister's Journal

The Resourceful Fakirs:
Three Muslim Brothers at the Sikh Court of Lahore

The Morning After: Writings & Speeches, 2006-2014

THE FICKLE 70s

MEMOIRS, 1972-79

F.S. AIJAZUDDIN

SANG-E-MEEL PUBLICATIONS
25, SHAHRAH-E-PAKISTAN (LOWER MALL) LAHORE.

923.5 Aijazuddin, F. S.
           The Fickle Seventies: My Memories,
       1972-79 / F. S. Aijazuddin.-Lahore: Sang-
       e-Meel Publications, 2016.
           xii, 395 pp.
           1. Memories.   I. Title.

2016
Published by:
Afzaal Ahmad
Sang-e-Meel Publications,
Lahore.

ISBN-10: 9 6 9 - 3 5 - 2 9 6 8 - 5
ISBN-13: 978-969-35-2968-5

Sang-e-Meel Publications
25 Shahrah-e-Pakistan (Lower Mall), Lahore-54000 PAKISTAN
Phones: 92-423-722-0100 / 92-423-722-8143 Fax: 92-423-724-5101
http://www.sang-e-meel.com e-mail: smp@sang-e-meel.com
PRINTED AT: HAJI HANIF & SONS PRINTERS, LAHORE.

In Memoriam

TIM & BILL ARCHER

and

DR. M. S. RANDHAWA

This only is denied to God: the power to undo the past.

[Agathon, from Aristotle, *Nicomachean Ethics*, bk. VI, ch.2.]

Authors however enjoy the latitude to rewrite it.

CONTENTS

PREFACE

Writing an autobiography must be one of the subtler forms of narcissism. One gazes into the pool and sees a reflection hopefully not simply of oneself but of a broader backdrop, of the times through which one has passed. That is the only justification I can offer for issuing this second volume of memoirs. They are not only about me but also about the eight tumultuous years in our history, first under Zulfikar Ali Bhutto and then General Ziaul Haq.

The earlier volume of my memoirs - *The Counterfoils of My Years, 1942-1971* – covered the first twenty-nine years of my life, up to the time of Shahnaz's and my marriage in December 1971. The present volume continues the story of my professional and personal life from January 1972 until my departure for the Gulf in December 1979.

During those years, Pakistan went through traumatic convulsions of change wrought by Mr. Zulfikar Ali Bhutto. Even his detractors cannot deny that alive, he was one of the most enigmatic, charismatic, complex, paradoxical, and eventually suicidal of politicians the country has experienced. Dead, his legacy endures still with damaging potency.

He assumed power as President & Chief Martial Law Administrator on 20 December 1971 and after the adoption of the Constitution in August 1973, he emerged from its chrysalis to become our country's 9th prime minister. An admirer of Napoleon, he viewed everyone around him though as a furtive Bonapartist. His insecurity became manifest in this treatment of his colleagues and subordinates, in particular the humiliation he ordered of his Senior Minister J. Rahim. His vindictiveness found an outlet in his appropriation of industries under the guise of Islamic Socialism. The real objective behind this nationalisation was not to strengthen the public sector as much as to cripple those industrialists whose wealth and corporate reputations he envied. The certainty of his own convictions though led ultimately to his own conviction for a crime he did not need to commit.

There was not a day during this eight-year period of my life when I was not aware of Bhutto's existence, or immune to the impact of his decisions, even after he had been removed from power. When I joined the Ghandhara group in the autumn of 1971, I had no idea that I would wake up one morning and find myself the passive victim of his nationalisation. Overnight, from being a corporate executive, I became a servant of the government, Bhutto's government.

For those of us who looked to Islamabad for direction, those initial years of Bhutto's rule proved a period of bewilderment. It never became clear whether Bhutto wanted to follow the Nehruvian path of soft socialism, or Tito's middle road, or the outer inflexible ring of Communist ideology. However, one did not need to read Bhutto's speeches to know what was cogitating in his fervid mind. He was determined that Pakistan should make a giant leap forward economically, industrially and socially. His frustration lay in being reminded daily that he had pygmies as foot-soldiers.

At my level in the public sector, the operational level, I felt enthused by many of his initiatives. I felt a quiet fulfilment in being a part of his effort to standardise and increase the local manufacture of tractors, and the thrust he made to accelerate self-sufficiency in the domestic manufacture of nitrogenous and phosphatic fertilisers. It would be an exaggeration to describe those days as Wordsworthian - "Bliss it was in that dawn to be alive/ But to be young was very heaven", - but I have to admit that there was something exciting for an ambitious professional still only in his early thirties, like me.

I had the opportunity of negotiating with companies of international stature such as Massey-Ferguson, Snamprogetti, and Kellogg International. I sat at a par, across the table, negotiating with IFIs like the World Bank, the Asian Development Bank, Saudi Fund for Economic Development, and OPEC's Special Fund. I could fashion quite literally with my bare hands the organisational structure within the National Fertiliser Corporation itself and then strengthen the umbilical cords between the NFC and its operating subsidiaries and projects.

Where else could I have experienced the challenge of conceiving and then implementing rules, procedures, and pay scales that would find the widest applicability within all the corporations of the public sector? Or where would I have had the opportunity of interacting with joint venture partners as diverse as the Dada Group and the Abu Dhabi National Oil Company?

And where would I have the chance of working with Syed Babar Ali, lauded as one of Pakistan's noteworthy entrepreneurs? His being my father's cousin proved an intangible asset, and after he returned to Packages Ltd. in 1977, a recurring liability.

During those eight years of professional plenty, I managed to travel abroad – to the United Kingdom, Russia, Switzerland, Austria, the United States, and to India – my first there since leaving it as a child in 1947. I was lucky (and devious enough) to synchronise my trips abroad with my academic research. These yielded two publications – both by Sotheby Parke Bernet and Oxford University Press – the first on *Pahari Paintings & Sikh Portraits in the Lahore Museum* (1977), and the second on *Sikh Portraits by European Artists* (1979).

During these years, Shahnaz and I augmented our family by having two daughters Momina (1973) and Mubarika (1976). I can admit now that my decision to seek job opportunities in the nouveau riche Gulf was as much to protect them from Ziaul Haq's suffocating Islamisation, as to escape from the gilded handcuffs of public servitude.

My designation as Director Finance, Planning & Personnel in the second largest corporation in the country (overshadowed only by the Pakistan Steel Mills) did not insulate me from the economic reality that my monthly salary was barely sufficient to meet my monthly obligations. It was humiliating enough not to be able to deflect my landlady's demands for an increase in the rent of the modest two-bedroom half of her house. The surrender of first one servant's quarter to her and then another made me realise that my nostrils would never rise above water-level. Poverty and public service, I learned the hard way, went hand in emaciated hand.

I am not sufficiently narcissistic to believe that my life has been a significant one. The years – 1972 to 1979 - through which I lived however were. Much of what I have written about these years has been culled from memory, refreshed by entries I made in my diary. I have included some of those diary entries to give immediacy to my narrative, and to provide an insight into how I and others viewed events as they occurred. These pages are therefore less about me, a pawn in the hand of time, than about that other author, Time, whom Francis Bacon described as 'the author of authors.'

Let me conclude with expressions of gratitude. Imran Niazi (a former colleague at NFC) was kind enough to read the manuscript and to improve it. To Mr Afzaal Ahmed of Sang-e-Meel Publications, my deepest thanks for bringing out yet another unprofitable book of mine. And to Shahnaz, my love for having shared those years with me, for re-living them while editing this manuscript, and for being there for all the years thereafter.

F.S. AIJAZUDDIN   Lahore, 1 August 2015

CHAPTER 1

CHANGES AT THE TOP

If I were ever to get married again, I would avoid spending my honeymoon nights fearful of an attack by the Indian Air Force.

Shahnaz and I began our married life in the last days of the 1971 war. Our flat on the hill in Bath Island, Karachi, was in a way a haven from the maelstrom through which the country was passing. After the initial air-raids that had destroyed the large oil storage tanks at Keamari, there had been no more direct attacks by Indian aircraft on Karachi. The oil terminals, having been bombed and ignited, burned with a brightness that illuminated the entire city. In addition to affecting the availability of fuel to a city already suffering the effect of a naval blockade, the burning tanks acted as a beacon for Indian aircraft. The next and last air-attack occurred at 8.30 p.m. on 15 December. No bombs were dropped and no damage reported, because for the Indians Karachi was, in a sense, more a psychological target than a strategic one. The actual theatre of war lay a thousand miles away, in East Pakistan.

There, a beleaguered Pakistani army was defending itself against the combined forces of the Mukti Bahini and the Indian army. Despite the bombastic assertions from President Yahya Khan and his government in Islamabad, no one doubted that East Pakistan would soon break away and declare its independence of West Pakistan. The aberration of two parts of the same country separated by a thousand miles of an inimical India had continued for too long. It was, in Kissinger's words, 'a problem whose solution was preordained by history.'

At the same time, on the other side of the world, in New York, a war of words was in full swing in the Security Council, between Pakistan represented by Mr. Zulfikar Ali Bhutto and Sardar Swaran Singh on behalf of India. Yahya Khan, in a desperate attempt to solicit international support, hurriedly designated Bhutto as Deputy Prime Minister and Foreign Minister, and then dispatched him to the UN in New York.

Most of us in Pakistan familiar with Mr. Bhutto's style realised that this had been the moment he had been waiting for, his personal 'tryst with destiny'. Every major event in his meteoric political career until then - his first association with his military mentor President Ayub Khan, the noisy fracture with Ayub's government after the ill-fated 1965 war, his petulant disassociation from the peace agreement with the Indians at Tashkent, the launch of Mr. Bhutto's Pakistan People's Party, its unexpected victory in West Pakistan during the 1970 general elections, his insidious attempts to forestall an Awami League government led by Mujibur Rahman, and his covert encouragement of military action in East Pakistan – seemed to have carried him like an inexorable tide to the chamber of UN Security Council that evening, the 15th of December 1971.

Mr. Bhutto made an impassioned speech before the Security Council, resounding with false bravado and well-rehearsed, pouting defiance. It was in dramatic contrast to the Indian Foreign Minister Swaran Singh's tight-lipped reticence. Bhutto began by saying that he had been in two minds: 'Whether to go to the Security Council to represent the cause of my country, to represent the cause of a people that had been subjected to aggression, or to remain with my people, by their side, while they were being subjected to attack and violence.' He expressed his disappointment at the 'dilatory tactics' of the Council.

Resolving to wage war for a thousand years, he closed his impassioned speech with a dramatic rejection of the Security Council itself. 'Finally,' Bhutto thundered, 'I am not a rat. I have never ratted in my life. I have faced assassination attempts, I have faced imprisonments. I have always confronted crises. Today I am not ratting, but I am leaving your Security Council. I find it disgraceful to my person and to my country to remain here a moment longer than is necessary. I am not boycotting. Impose any decision, have a treaty worse than the Treaty of Versailles, legalise aggression, legalise occupation, legalise everything that has been illegal up to 15 December 1971. I will not be a party to it. We will fight; we will go back and fight. My country beckons me. Why should I waste my time here in the Security Council? I will not be a party to the ignominious surrender of a part of my country. You can take your Security Council. Here you are. I am going.'

With that he stormed out the Security Council chamber. His outburst had been covered by all the major television networks and relayed live to audiences world-wide. Unfortunately, just as Bhutto was reaching the climax of his powerful oration, his aide Rafi Raza sitting behind him could be seen putting his own papers away in a briefcase, as if he knew that Bhutto would make a dramatic walk-out.

I asked Rafi Raza later whether Bhutto had confided to him that he would be making such a dramatic exit. "No," he replied. "In fact, that got me into a lot of trouble with Mr. Bhutto. When he returned to our hotel and saw the re-play of his Security Council speech on television, he noticed what I had been doing. He told me off for 'letting the cat out the bag'. Actually, I was simply putting my loose papers away. In fact, the only person to whom he had revealed his intention was Benazir. She, of course, called her friends to tell them to watch her father's speech at the Security Council as 'there would be some fireworks'."

There were no fireworks, however, in the speech Yahya Khan's made on the night of 16 December. It was preceded by an announcement that he would address the nation at 7.15 p.m., after which his speech would be translated into Bengali. By the time he spoke, Dacca had already been over-run by Indian and Mukti Bahini troops. Heedless of the reality of a hopeless situation, in a slurred voice, he exhorted West Pakistanis to fight an 'all-out jehad' in their own defence. He announced that he would be convening a session of the National Assembly on 20 December and would constitute provincial and a central government drawn from West and East Pakistan.

At 3.00 p.m. the next day, it was as good as over. Radio Pakistan reported that the President had declared a ceasefire on the western border. Mrs. Indira Gandhi had already given the orders for a ceasefire by her troops. The next few days were full of anxiety. Yahya Khan and his generals were only nominally in control. Bhutto was still out of the country, said to be on his way back via Rome where it was rumoured he met up with his friend Princess Ashraf Pahlavi (the sister of the Shah of Iran).

On 20th morning, the news on the radio informed us that President Yahya Khan had decided to hand over power to a civilian administration and to resign. This prompted Air Marshal (retd.) Asghar Khan to demand that Yahya Khan be put on trial. At 3.00 p.m., Mr. Bhutto was sworn in, much to the surprise of everyone except constitutional contortionists, as both President and Chief Martial Law Administrator. The general public including persons like Shahnaz and myself had no knowledge of the furtive negotiations then taking place between a desperate Yahya Khan and a rapacious Mr. Bhutto. According to Mr. Rafi Raza[1], Yahya wanted to remain President with Mr. Bhutto as the Prime Minister. Mr. Bhutto refused. Then Yahya Khan proposed that he remain Commander-in-Chief of the Army and Chief Martial Law Administrator with Mr. Bhutto as the President. Mr. Bhutto had no intention of sharing the spoils. He wanted unequivocal power. He surprised even his closest aides like Rafi Raza by refusing to lift Martial Law. Despite being the head of a political party that had won an electoral majority in West Pakistan, he chose to be sworn in as President *and* Chief Martial Law Administrator.

A rather humorous explanation of this constitutional anomaly appeared in *Dawn* soon after. Sardar Khair Bux Marri (a Balochi leader), when asked to unravel this conundrum, explained that a villager elder was once posed a question: "Does an elephant gave birth live, or does it lay eggs?"

The elder thought for a while and then replied sagely: "An elephant gives birth live … and it also lays eggs."

"How is that possible?"

"An elephant is an elephant," he replied. "If it wants to give birth live, it does; if it wants to lay eggs, it does that too. Who dares argue with an elephant?"

On the evening of 20 January, Mr. Bhutto gave his first address to the nation. He came on the air at 10.00 p.m. Shahnaz and I listened to it. Bhutto spoke extempore, without notes. (Rafi Raza revealed later that Bhutto had refused to allow his aides to draft a speech for him.) Bhutto spent the first ten minutes of his speech explaining why he had not had the time to prepare a written text, and then the next ten minutes giving reasons to his predominantly Urdu-speaking audience why he was not speaking in Urdu. The remainder of his lengthy speech sounded like an unctuous forgiveness of all those who at

---

[1] Raza, R., *Zulfikar Ali Bhutto and Pakistan 1967-1977* (OUP, 1997), p.142.

some time or the other in the past had caused him political anguish.

To the unspoken question whether Martial law would be lifted, he assured his audience: Soon, very soon. The Assemblies? Soon, very soon. A new Constitution? Soon, very soon.

"We have not failed", he told his fellow countrymen. "We have *been* failed. Our generals have let us down." And to prove his point, Bhutto announced that he had sacked seven generals. He went on to explain that he was prepared to negotiate with representatives of 'Muslim Bengal', and as an act of good faith he restored Wali Khan's banned National Awami Party. He distanced himself mockingly from any accusation of nepotism, then showered flattering epithets on his 'talented' cousin Mumtaz Bhutto.

Zulfikar Ali Bhutto knew enough French history to recognise that in a way he had found himself in the same situation as his role model Napoleon Bonaparte and later General Charles de Gaulle, both of whom stepped forward in their time to salvage France from chaos and potential disintegration. Louis XV had famously once said: 'Après moi, le deluge!' A British cartoonist lampooned De Gaulle soon after his take-over in May 1958 by showing him sheltering from the rain under an umbrella, muttering: 'Après le deluge, moi!' In Pakistan, the deluge came both before and after Mr. Bhutto.

Bhutto stepped into a political vacuum of his own making and presented himself as the saviour of the nation. He knew that the army following its surrender in East Pakistan stood discredited. He realised also that it was too early to introduce a parliamentary form of government, a democratic structure however dysfunctional and imperfect. He ignored the protestations of the Pakistani press the day after his address to the nation, in which they deplored that Martial Law was not being lifted. He did not tell the press that it would itself be the next victim of his reforms. General Habibullah was summarily dismissed as Chairman of the National Press Trust, and a respected but controversial journalist Z. A. Suleri removed from the Senior Editorship of *The Pakistan Times*.

That evening, watching heads like these roll, I happened to comment to Shahnaz that Shakirullah Durrani (my former boss at the Investment Corporation of Pakistan) who had been appointed by Yahya Khan as Governor State Bank of Pakistan seemed to have escaped Mr. Bhutto's scythe. Minutes later, almost as if some malevolent spirit had overheard our conversation, the newscaster on television read an announcement that Durrani too had been removed.

Over the next few days, Bhutto took decisions swiftly. He appointed Mumtaz Bhutto as his Governor in Sindh, Mustafa Khar in the Punjab and Hayat Khan Sherpao in the then N.W.F.P. (now Khyber Pakhtunkhwa). He sent U. A. Saied packing. Saied was the Chairman of the National Shipping Corporation but better qualified as one of Yahya Khan's adhesive courtiers. With Saied went some more generals. He abolished the princely perks that Begum Junagadh had obtained with much exertion for her husband from Yahya Khan. To some observers, this was a particularly petty act. Bhutto's father Sir Shahnawaz Bhutto had been the Dewan or Senior Minister at Junagadh State when the present (and dispossessed) Nawab's father had been the ruler. Even the singer Nur Jahan who had benefited from her familiarity with Yahya Khan found herself the subject of a punitive tax demand on her undeclared earnings.

The changes at the political level reverberated within the Ghandhara Group, where I was employed in one of its subsidiaries, Ghandhara Diesels Ltd. (GDL). The project had been conceived to manufacture Bedford Diesel engines. The machinery for making the engines had been ordered from a firm in Germany and the 700 acre plot upon which the factory was to be located had been acquired in Bela, on the Balochistan side of the Hub river near Karachi. The GDL team headed by Muhammad Salar as Managing Director had Saad Hashmi as its Technical Director and me as its Finance Director. No work had begun on the site and therefore GDL continued to occupy offices in the main Ghandhara Industries plant at Hub Chauki, in the commercial area known as S.I.T.E., about an hour's drive from the centre of Karachi.

A Board meeting of GDL had been scheduled for 24 December, ostensibly to assess the status of the project. In reality, none of the directors knew for sure whether General Habibullah was still the Chairman of the company, and therefore no one felt inclined to decide anything. To Hashmi and myself, responsible for implementing the project, nothing could have been more disheartening. We felt no better learning a few days later, the Government had 'reluctantly' arrested General Habibullah, S.U. Durrani, U.A. Saied, and Alvi (Chairman of Standard Bank, which had close links with the Army). They had been placed under house arrest. General Habibullah's wife Marie, according to a close mutual friend, remonstrated at the unfairness of it all. "The twenty-two families[2] have been enjoying themselves for years," she complained, "and now that I have joined their ranks, all the fun is over."

The only reliable reporting came from the BBC overseas broadcasts. Pakistan Television and Radio Pakistan being state organisations parroted the official line. For current information about changes that were taking place by the minute, everyone resorted to hearsay and gossip. "There is nothing about Pakistan in the BBC news," I mentioned to Shahnaz one morning. "Let us see what there is in the newspapers."

"There is even less about Pakistan in the newspapers," she replied, and sure enough the morning papers spouted only propaganda. Occasionally, one obtained a glimpse of the infighting within the new administration. Hafeez Pirzada (the new Minister of information and Broadcasting) lashed out at Nawab Akbar Khan Bugti, calling him 'a hypocrite', for leading a 'peaceful procession' to remonstrate against the appointment of Raisani as Governor of Balochistan, and then hosted a lunch for the same man whom he sought to undermine. Bhutto threatened to remove Khar from the Punjab governorship because PPP gatecrashers had been allowed by Khar to disrupt one of Bhutto's intellectual monologues. Cracks had begun to appear even before the first coat of paint was dry.

Doing my rounds of financial institutions each day in an effort to organise financing for the Ghandhara Diesel project, I found each institution busy calculating not how much it could lend to new projects but how much it had lost in the East Pakistan debacle. The State Bank, for example, lost Rs 250 crores of Pakistani currency that had been left in the vaults at its sub branches in East Pakistan. The Investment Corporation of Pakistan (ICP) had to write off Rs 15 crores on its portfolio of EP securities. PICIC (a development financing agency) lost Rs 63 crores, IDBP Rs 59 crores, the commercial banks Rs 250 crores, the 54 companies based in East Pakistan and listed on the Karachi Stock Exchange Rs 114 crores, the 17 listed companies based in West Pakistan but with assets in East Pakistan another 54 crores. The only industrialist who seemed to have insulated himself against a shock proved to be the canny Mr. Ahmed Dawood. Although many of the companies in which he had a managing interest remained in East Pakistan (for example,

---

[2] In 1968, Dr. Mahbub Ul Haq had analysed that '22 industrial family groups had come to dominate the economic and financial life of Pakistan and that they controlled about two-thirds of industrial assets, 80 per cent of banking and 79 percent of insurance.'

Karnaphuli Rayon, Karnaphuli Paper, Dawood Jute Mills), he had managed to manoeuvre himself into the enviable position of minimizing his stake in these companies whereby his total losses, he claimed, were no more than Rs 15 lakhs.

Meanwhile, the vendetta by Mr. Bhutto against his adversaries continued unabated. Before the end of the month, nineteen sanctions (in those days one needed a sanction from the Government before any project could be started) had been revoked, including one granted to Begum Saifullah (General Habibullah's sister) for the expansion of her textile mill in Kohat. Similarly, other sanctions given to associates of General Habibullah such as Yusuf Shirazi were also revoked. The mood pervading the Ghandhara Group was sombre. Within GDL, it was almost funereal. We wondered whether the project too would be cancelled and its employees sent home.

During all this mayhem, my touchstone with what mattered in my life was personified by Shahnaz. Young as she was, (she had just turned twenty-one), she remained steadfast in her belief that we would survive. Every morning, I would leave her (she rose late) and drive to S.I.T.E.

On one occasion, while I was in the office, she called to remonstrate that I had not kissed her before I left. "That's strange", I replied. "I thought it was you!" And on another, she rang and asked me whether there was anyone else seated in my room.

"No."

"Do you have any PA listening in?"

I assured her that it was a direct line. She then asked me in a hushed conspiratorial tone: "Tell me, how do you roast a chicken?"

Gradually, as we discovered each other anew, we began to depend upon each other for emotional support. She took an interest in my hobby – the study of miniature paintings – and I in her talent for palmistry. We shared books, collected Sindhi embroideries, purchased small antiques. Our first-floor flat reflected our personalities. As one entered its front door, straight ahead hung Shakir Ali's painting *Three Graces*. The dining room was on the left. On the far wall we had hung a Sindhi *chaddar* that had an interesting combination of green and purple embroidery. A door led from the dining room into the drawing room. I had decorated it with sofas (bought second-hand) that were then upholstered with grey velvet. On the floor I had spread a white carpet.

Shakir's large canvas *Lady with a parrot* – a composition in spectacular reds and greens – dominated the room. The corridor connecting the three bedrooms served as a library, with white waist-high bookshelves running the length of it. At the far end of the corridor, in the only place where it could be displayed to advantage, we put Shakir's monumental painting *Man*, inspired by verses from one of Rilke's poems. That is how I had remembered seeing it the first time I visited Shakir sahib's house in Sanda Road when he was still Principal of the National College of Arts.

The carved four-poster bed that Shahnaz and I had bought together during our engagement stood in our bedroom. The base had six yards of a Sindhi embroidered skirt as a valance, and as a counterpane we had another Sindhi embroidered *bochni* or veil. On the wall I had placed the painting that for me symbolised the best of Shakir sahib's work – a study of flowers in a vase, done in rapid strokes of orange, white and Prussian blue paint. I had kept that painting with me ever since I had bought it from him in September 1966. From then onwards it had become such an indispensable part of my life that I took it with me wherever I happened to be living, whether in Lahore, in the wilds of Gambat (Sindh), or in Karachi. I could not bear to be parted from it. I understood then why persons willed that their favourite objects should be buried with them.

It was in this atmosphere of private placidity and public insecurity that the year 1971 ended. Shahnaz and I had been married less than a month. Bhutto had been in power less than a fortnight.

CHAPTER 2

NATIONALISATION

The New Year 1972 had hardly begun when on 2 January we were told that President Bhutto would be addressing the nation that evening at 7.30 p.m. The speech itself was short but seismic in its impact. Bhutto spoke of redeeming his electoral pledge to reform industry, and announced that 'as from today, the control and command of the people over the following categories have been asserted'. The ten categories he listed included basic industries such as iron and steel, heavy engineering, automotive and tractor plants, heavy and basic chemicals, petrochemicals, cement, public utility companies responsible for electricity generation, transmission and distribution, gas and oil refineries. He left it to his Finance Minister Dr. Mubashir Hasan (an engineer by qualification and a university lecturer by profession) to reveal the details.

Bhutto's speech was followed by a hastily summoned press conference during which Dr. Mubashir Hasan read out the names of the industries being taken over. Twenty companies in Punjab and Sindh were identified. None of the major business houses escaped. The Valikas, the Saigols, the Alis, General Habibullah, the Haroons lost one or more units. Even the Hyesons family which had supported Mr. Bhutto during his election campaign lost its steel mill. Many a dispossessed industrialist must have rued not having paid more attention to the PPP manifesto when it was issued in 1970. Had they read it seriously, they would been seen that Mr. Bhutto had stated his intentions more clearly than for example Hitler had done regarding Jewry in *Mein Kampf*.

Article IV of that manifesto contained the unequivocal statement that 'all major industries will be nationalised.' Bhutto wanted to follow (albeit belatedly) a Nehruvian approach to industrialisation, in which all key basic industries that acted as the engine of growth in an economy would remain in the public domain. An Indian bureaucrat some years later explained to me Nehru's industrial philosophy of retaining basic industries such as coal or steel in the public sector. "We wanted to have a radial effect on the economy. If, for example, we raised the price of basic steel by ten paisas, we could foresee that the effect would be an increase of a rupee in the price of a steel *thali* in the retail market. We wanted the public sector to be at the epicentre, the origin of a ripple effect in our economy."

Mr. Bhutto however had less altruistic motives underpinning his decision to nationalise these industries. His victims and many others who knew him well detected an element of personal animus in his actions. It was as if he begrudged these industrialists their wealth. During that first press conference, it became embarrassingly apparent that no one in the PPP had thought through the implications of such mass scale nationalisation. Dr. Mubashir Hasan appeared confused and then, in response to the pointed questions, gave responses that were vague and confusing. He seemed unclear about whether the Government intended to nationalise (i.e. own) or simply control the taken-over industries. Would the Government acquire a majority interest in each of these companies, in which case what would be the mechanism the Government would use to acquire that controlling interest? Would it buy the shares in the open market, or would it acquire them forcibly? Would the owners be given any compensation? The Finance Minister had no answers to such questions.

General Habibullah and Bhutto had never seen eye to eye, and it was no surprise to anyone that Ghandhara Industries Ltd was one of the first units to be nationalised. We in the company waited to know who would be the new Chairman in place of General Habibullah, and if we would be having a change in the Managing Director. The following morning, the newspapers carried announcements of the names of persons who had been appointed as Managing Directors of the taken-over industries. Because I knew many of them, if not personally then by name, I realised that they had been chosen at random mainly from public sector institutions. One, for instance, had been a colleague of mine in the Investment Corporation of Pakistan, another a middle-ranking credit officer in PICIC, a third a loan officer in the Industrial Development Bank of Pakistan. In one case, the man appointed Managing Director had been removed from that very company some years earlier in a management coup and now found himself lording over those who had ousted him.

Not all these appointees had maturity or experience. Ghandhara was fortunate to have as his successor Mr. Naziruddin Mahmood, the MD of National Investment Trust, an open-ended mutual fund. A seasoned banker, he brought a deft touch to what might otherwise have been a tricky transition. General Habibullah had left very large boots to fill. Ironically, NIT already owned the largest number of shares in Ghandhara Industries and therefore technically was already its major shareholder, although no one in Islamabad seemed to be aware of this.

The take-over of these industries had been done swiftly and under cover of darkness. At 5.00 a.m. on 3 January, a Sunday morning, a contingent of police arrived at the Ghandhara factory in Hub Chauki and sealed the premises. The ousted directors met at the house of the senior most amongst them – Humayun Mufti – and discussed what should be their plan of action. The significance of this peremptory nationalization had not full sunk into many of them. One complained that the police should be told to withdraw as their presence was 'affecting the morale of the workers'. Another reminded him sharply that the workers were now the new owners anyway.

Later that afternoon, on 3 Jan, the dispossessed owners of the taken-over industries were called and addressed by Mr. Qamar-ul-Islam, Secretary Industries. Bleary-eyed and haggard after a sleepless night, he battled to field questions from angry industrialists, many of whom were his personal friends. He read out to them the Economic Reforms Order 1972, the authority under which their industries had been taken over. One of them asked whether the Government intended to take over the ghee industry as well. "Certainly not," Qamar-ul-Islam snapped.

"In which case why have you taken over Wazir Ali Industries? It makes banaspati ghee. Did you have Wazir Ali Engineering in mind?"

"Is that a separate company? Oh well, we will have to amend the Order."

Within Ghandhara Industries, the significance of the change had begun to trickle down the corporate structure. All the senior executives were summoned to a meeting in the Board Room. The memory was still fresh in everyone's mind of General Habibullah's domineering presence during the lavish lunches that he hosted for the Army, Navy and Air Force Chiefs soon after I had joined the company. Some felt a shred of loyalty to him but kept it hidden from view. Others were all too quick to acknowledge the change.

When Mufti read out the ERO 1972, and announced that General Habibullah had been removed as Chairman, one of the senior executives – the Parts Manager who had been with Ghandhara for most of his career - raised his hand and asked: "Oh you mean, the Chairman," he coughed, and then continued: "I mean, the *ex*-Chairman will no longer be heading our company?"

The main purpose of the meeting appeared to be to allow the directors to convey the reassurance given to them by Mr. Qamar-ul-Islam that they being professionals would continue as Directors of the company. We returned to our offices but there was little work to be done. We functioned as automatons, unclear about what would happen either to the company or to us as its executives. Would we continue or would we also be screened and winnowed as many bureaucrats were?

I confided my concerns to my dairy. The entry for 5 January read:

'I feel a gnawing apprehension regarding my future. I live in a flat suddenly too expensive for my needs. I do not know whether the GDL project will be implemented at all, for its viability was based on the standardization of the Bedford engine nation-wide, supported by Government protection – both factors possible during the MD-ship of Capt. Gohar Ayub Khan [the son of President Ayub Khan], under whom the project was first conceived. That is unlikely, if not ·impossible now.

My own financial resources are limited, capable of sustaining me for a couple of months or so. If I should be declared redundant, I couldn't for both personal and for financial reasons go back to Williamsons Ltd. That company just could not bear my load as well as that of Ayaz and my uncle Iftikhar. One endures not because one lacks decision, but because there is no decision that can be made.'

Some weeks later, a notification was issued nationalizing Ghandhara Diesels Ltd as well. While that did nothing to resolve the problems inherent within the project, it did bring us unequivocally into the fold of the public sector. Its problems from then on became the headache of the new Government.

In order to have more information about the companies which the government now controlled and managed, a team of consultants were appointed by the Government to do a round of the taken-over companies to assess their situation. Simultaneously the management of each company was required to submit a report covering all salient aspects of its commercial, financial and human resources. The new Managing Director Naziruddin Mahmood relied upon me to draft and after his scrutiny to finalise the report on both Ghandhara Industries and Ghandhara Diesels. The haste with which Mr. Bhutto wanted to implement his reforms made yesterday or a date in the future too late. Information had to be sent to Islamabad as quickly as was inhumanly possible.

While we executives grappled inside our offices with the challenge of revealing to the Government what we wanted it to hear, the labour unions began to assert their power. On 24 January, the local GIL union called on its members to go on strike and then 'gheraoed' the factory. By 5.30 p.m., the strikers were half-inclined to go home and would have done so, had the local PPP MPA Syed Saeed Hasan not appeared to give them a second wind. He ordered the closure of the factory gates, as much to prevent the executives from leaving as the labour from escaping. His speech informed the crowd that the new government was a 'People's Government' and that the new MD being a Government appointee was in fact a 'People's MD'. This seemed to mollify the crowd. He assured the strikers that he would speak to the Governor Sindh and to convey their grievances; the workers promised to double their productivity from tomorrow. Neither believed the other.

The contradictions within the Government in Islamabad did not help to instil confidence in a public battered by all too frequent changes. One moment, Hafeez Pirzada as the Minister of Information dramatically announced the names of those arrested under Martial Law Regulation no. 78, and the next moment, he withdrew the order. In this, as in other things, he seemed to take his cue from Mr. Bhutto who prevaricated over the release of Mujibur Rahman, then in custody in Faisalabad jail in West Pakistan. In an interview Bhutto gave to Peter Hazlehurst of the British newspaper *The Sunday Times*, he disclosed that he was planning to release Mujib. When this news item appeared in the paper, Bhutto pretended to recant and issued a denial that he had said anything of the sort to Hazlehurst.

Bhutto's manipulation of the public became more and more obvious. He made an appeal to the citizens of Karachi as if it was a representative microcosm of the national electorate, and like Mark Antony before the people of Rome, he sought the guidance of the populace. *Should he release Mujib, or not?* He asked the people to decide, when that decision had already been taken by events. He knew he could not detain Mujib – now an international hero. He sought the ephemeral advantage of being seen to be the man who released Mujib from a Pakistani jail. Jails in Pakistan have revolving doors. One inmate leaves, another enters to occupy the space. Mujib left, and Yahya Khan found himself placed under house arrest, as Bhutto put it, 'in the supreme interest of the state and the people of Pakistan'. Stretching the credulity of the public, Bhutto announced that the delay in apprehending Yahya Khan had been again 'in the supreme national interest.' Yahya Khan (whose womanising was legendary) was reportedly shifted, according to the waspish Urdu paper *Jang*, to the former *zenana* or female quarters of the Lahore fort.

If the Pakistani public expected that the new civilian elected government would soothe its nerves, battered after the 1971 war, it was soon disappointed. Bhutto maintained his onslaught against the Armed Forces, the industrialists, the bureaucracy, in fact against every organ of the state and every state organisation. In February 1972, for example, he removed Anwar Qadir (an appointee of Yahya Khan's) from the post of Managing Director of the National Bank of Pakistan. He retired 1300 government officials (Yahya Khan's score had been 303), of whom three had served as Deputy Commissioners at Larkana (Bhutto's home constituency). In March, he removed the two persons – General Gul Hassan, C-in-C of the Pakistan Army, and the Air Force Chief Rahim Khan- commonly regarded as the kingmakers because they had helped him take over the country. Both were exiled into unwanted ambassadorships. In the same month, he suddenly nationalized the life insurance companies and announced revolutionary land reforms. When one of his ministers Ghulam Mustafa Jatoi was asked whether these reforms would affect his considerable landholding, he replied airily that he could not remember how many acres he owned – perhaps 1,500 acres in the Guddu Barrage area?

There was a palpable disconnect between the People's Government and the people, between the leaders and the led. My diary entry for 24 February 1972 gives an idea of the mood prevailing during those days:

'The general mood is short-term and apprehensive. Lawlessness is in vogue. Gheraos [strikes] are continuing, and with each outburst the Government is betraying its inability to control law and order. Of course Bhutto will not dispense with Martial Law. By continuing, at least in the minds of the public, an association between the PPP Government and the Army, he hopes to weaken any authority the Army may like to exercise to wrest control of the State, should the situation deteriorate as it did in 1958 and again in 1969. He shall use the Army against the people, if need be. He is the most dangerous form of autocrat – the civilian turned corporal dictator.'

I had no sooner written these words than the reports came through that Bhutto had ordered the Army to move against the police agitating in Lahore's Tibbi (its red-light area).

Bhutto's strategy had been to foment such a situation whereby anything would be preferable – even an interim Constitution – to Martial Law. Once he had obtained the approval of his rubber-stamp National Assembly, he lifted Martial Law. This was done on 14 April.

Agitation however continued, this time encouraged by another Bhutto – Mumtaz Bhutto, once described by Bhutto as his 'talented cousin' and presumably qualified therefore for appointment as Chief Minister Sindh. Mumtaz was suspected of setting the locals rural Sindhis against the Urdu-speaking urban Mohajirs. In July, language riots broke out in Karachi's Golimar and Liaquatabad areas and soon spilled over into the city of Hyderabad. A curfew was imposed.

The main market in Saddar closed down, and we discovered it was impossible to obtain fresh milk. The BBC reported fighting between Mohajirs and the Sindhis despite the curfew. Censorship had been applied on the news media with the result that many papers resorted to printing blank spaces where a report would have normally appeared.

The upper echelons of Karachi society insulated themselves from these traumas. Many obtained passes which enabled them to travel during curfew hours on the grounds that they were 'an essential service'. I asked one of them what was so essential about his service. He replied that he had to provide feed and water at his chicken farm in Malir. Another friend commented wryly that he had driven through the city and found the markets empty and the jails full.

At the highest level in the troubled province, stories began to circulate about the erratic behaviour of the Sindh Governor Mir Rasool Bux Talpur. One incident I noted in my diary described how, during a meeting convened in Lahore to discuss smuggling, Talpur dozed off. Waking up suddenly, he shouted: "Hang them all, I say!" after which he subsided into another gentle doze. Meanwhile, the Finance Minister Mubashir Hasan commented that 'smuggling, like prostitution, has existed since time immemorial. It is a very fundamental part of our civilization.' Punjab Governor Mustafa Khar asked that if that was the case, then why was everyone assembled to discuss the issue? At this, Governor Talpur woke from his slumber and spoke out with replenished force: "Hanging is the only solution. Hang them all I say!" This proved to be too much, even for the Home Minister, who quickly adjourned the meeting amidst laughter.

At another meeting of the four provincial Governors, Talpur again fell asleep. He woke to find that the cache of toffees placed in front of him had been depleted. He noticed an empty wrapper in the hands of his neighbour the Governor Balochistan, and immediately accused him of poaching the toffees.

Eventually President Bhutto removed him in March 1973 and replaced him by Begum Raana Liaquat Ali Khan (the widow of Nawabzada Liaquat Ali Khan, Pakistan's first prime minister). After his assassination, she had devoted her life to rearing her two sons – Ashraf and Akbar – who were contemporaries of my elder brothers. She was also the founder Chairperson of All Pakistan Women's' Association (APWA). According to her sons, her appointment as governor gave her a fresh lease of life. Her amiable malleability earned her the soubriquet 'Rubber-stamp Raana'. Governors were also appointed in the other three provinces, and Bhutto's ennui could be gauged from the off-camera remark he was heard making during the swearing-in ceremony: "Alright, bring on the next one!"

Gradually, as Mr. Bhutto's attention became distracted by the myriad problems he had inherited, compounded by those he himself had instigated, infighting began amongst the next level in the PPP hierarchy. Old rivalries found new battlefields. Mumtaz Bhutto as Chief Minister Sindh ordered a search of the house of his rival Ghulam Mustafa Jatoi, then Federal Minister of Communications. Jatoi became so incensed at this invasion of his domestic privacy that he sent his resignation to President Bhutto which Bhutto rejected.

In those days, the Minister of Telecommunications had considerable clout. Obtaining a telephone connection through the government-owned monopoly required an allocation by the Minister himself. (Shahnaz and I had to get ours for our flat by sending our application through Jatoi's wife Maria who happened to be a family friend.) The story doing the rounds about the raid on Jatoi's house described how a Sindhi police officer from Jatoi's district had been sent by Mumtaz Bhutto to ransack the house, to enter and also pry into Maria's bedroom. On the way out, the police officer apologised profusely to Jatoi, pleading that as a junior functionary he was duty bound to carry out the orders of his superiors. Jatoi knew the rules of the game too well to hold a grudge against this underling. He forgave him the trespass, at which the police officer produced an application for a domestic telephone from his pocket and asked Jatoi if he would please approve it?

I was told that Jatoi had developed a code with his subordinates that indicated the level of their interest in such cases. 'Please do the needful' was the weakest instruction; 'Please provide a connection, if available' held out some hope to the applicant; the highest was 'I wish to speak the applicant on his new line.'

In time, Mumtaz Bhutto also resigned, and soon he was joined by Mian Mahmud Kasuri, Bhutto's Law Minister and the legal brain responsible for drafting the Interim Constitution. Whatever the overt reasons for their resignations, it was becoming obvious that Zulfikar Ali Bhutto's autocratic attitude and instinctive ingratitude had much to do with it.

My diary entry for Saturday 15 July for example described Bhutto's three-and-a-half harangue in the National Assembly. Having bulldozed the Interim Constitution after only a day's debate, he allowed the parliamentarians to discuss the Shimla Agreement relentlessly without an eye on the clock. It was not as if he valued their opinions or their input. The Agreement had in any case been signed, sealed and delivered to Mrs. Gandhi earlier at Shimla. Mr. Bhutto's treatment of his colleagues and worse still of his subordinates revealed a condescension that I suspect he felt towards all other human beings. He regarded everyone else - except for his eldest daughter Benazir Bhutto (his political heir) - with something bordering upon contempt.[1]

---

[1] A story doing the rounds in Karachi's drawing rooms was his retort to a Cabinet minister who

The speech he gave before the National Assembly members gave one indication of this. He laced his rhetoric with an arrogance imperfectly disguised as false modesty. He assured his party members somewhat disingenuously that he was 'a part of them', that they were not of his making: *He* was of *their* making. After which he attacked the upper crust of Pirs, Khans, Mirs, Sardars, the twenty-two families. It was in the manner of a medieval triumph, when the severed heads of opponents were put on display to demonstrate the strength of the victor at the decimation of his opposition.

Turning to the language riots, he told his audience that there had been accusations that the People's Party was responsible for the unrest and that his Chief Minister and Governor 'should be hanged'. He defended the Sindhi Language Bill he proposed to the assembly on the grounds that the Governor of Balochistan Ghous Bakhsh Bizenjo had advised him to make Sindhi the only official language of Sindh. Bhutto pleaded for an understanding of the historical imperative – after all, Sindh had had a script and a language of its own for over 5,000 years. He maintained that he supported the Bill to prevent Sindhis developing a hatred for Pakistan. If there was any threat to Urdu, he was prepared to be shot in public. And to the criticism that he had betrayed the Punjabis whose support had propelled him to power, he countered with the observation that he was grateful to the people of the Punjab who had elected him from two constituencies, but he never told them that he would renounce his Sindhi heritage.

To those who had heard Mr. Bhutto at any of his public rallies, this was vintage Bhutto. The only difference was that his fiery rhetoric had now been brought indoors into the public's homes.

Gradually, those who opposed Mr. Bhutto began to feel the heat. Air Marshal Asghar Khan's saw his house in Abbottabad burnt to the ground. Yunis Said who had been appointed by Bhutto to head the National Press Trust that 'guided' the policies of newspapers was ignominiously removed. The Government notified that henceforth all advertisements would have to be routed through the Ministry of Information. In retaliation, the Opposition

---

committed the faux pas of addressing Bhutto familiarly as Zulfi. 'Just because I sleep with your wife,' Bhutto snapped back, 'does not give you the right to call me Zulfi!' To another unfortunate fellow-lawyer who confronted Mr. Bhutto at a cocktail party with the observation that they shared a strong resemblance, Mr. Bhutto gave him the withering retort: 'I knew my father was promiscuous, but I did not realise that he was that indiscriminate.'

parties announced that they would organise a strike in protest on 1 August, declaring it a Black Day. Bhutto responded by making the same 1 August a Freedom of Press Day.

S.K. Ghori, writing in DAWN, lampooned this turnaround in a clever anecdote. A king was informed of a revolution in his country:

"How many of my people are part of it?" he asked.

"All your people, Sire," he was told.

"In which case, I will head the revolution."

A fortnight later, Mr. Bhutto used Rafi Raza (his Special Assistant) to refute allegations raised by the Karachi Bar Association against Bhutto. The KBA, in a letter released to the press before it reached the Presidency, accused Mr. Bhutto of reneging on undertakings and assurance he had given its members during the meeting he held with them. Retaliating tit-for-tat, Rafi Raza's letter was also released to the press before it could be read by its addressees. The letter concluded with a statement that 'Administrative changes have been made and are being made. This was the commitment of the President and it is being kept.'

The administrative changes Rafi Raza referred to came with all the suddenness and velocity of the nationalization of industries earlier in January 1972. On the morning of 27 September, bureaucrats throughout the country woke up, opened their newspapers and saw (most of them with horror) two very prominent advertisements. The first announced 'Recruitment to Senior Posts in the Central Secretariat' and invited applications from persons interested in becoming Secretaries (5 posts), Additional (10), Joint (30) and Deputy Secretaries (40). The second invited applications from those who preferred a diplomatic career and were interested in becoming Ministers (10), Counsellors (15), or First (20), Second (20) or Third Secretaries (30) in the Foreign Office.

At a stroke, Mr. Bhutto destroyed the exclusivity of the Civil Service, brushing aside its gossamer invincibility. No longer would its entrants be inducted at the junior-most level and have to spend the rest of their careers working their way upwards. It suddenly became possible for persons even from the non-government and private sectors to join the civil service, laterally at any level. The only qualifications these persons needed were to have been

'Executives in a firm of repute or in a profession.'

There was yet more in store for tenured civil servants. Less than a year later, on 20 August 1973, Mr. Bhutto dismissed a number of very senior bureaucrats, including such prominent officers as Qamar-ul-Islam (Chairman of the Planning Commission), Dr. I.H. Usmani who headed the Atomic Energy Commission, Manzoor Elahi the former Chief Secretary Sindh, and the durable Secretary Defence Syed Ghiasuddin. The latter bureaucrat had served and survived in that crucial post for so long that he had been likened to that other canny survivor - the Russian Anastas Mikoyan. Mikoyan had begun his career with Lenin, outlived Stalin, saw Khrushchev out of the Kremlin, and retired finally under Brezhnev. It was said that if one wanted to know who was in power in the Soviet Union at any time, one had simply to look on either side of Mikoyan.

Whatever opinions people may have had about Mr. Bhutto's style of governance (and there were many other than his victims who deplored his high-handedness), none would have faulted his handling of the issue of the return of 90,321 persons of West Pakistani origin held by the Indian Government jointly with new state of Bangladesh. These prisoners included 73,908 prisoners of war (POWs) because they happened to be combatants in uniform, and 16,413 civilians, described generically as CUPCs - civilians under protective custody. On its side, Pakistan held 639 Indians in Lyallpur (now Faisalabad) jail.

The legal fiction of joint custody enabled the Indian government to plead that it would have been agreeable to repatriating all the West Pakistanis, provided the new Bangladesh government gave its concurrence. And that was not forthcoming. The former compatriots now enemies wanted to exact revenge, however partial or symbolic.

Gradually, Mr. Bhutto increased the intensity of the propaganda that he unleashed using the international media. In May 1972, for example, he gave an interview to a correspondent from U.K.'s Thames Television. Their conversation was carried in the Pakistan newspapers. The correspondent P. Lindley asked Mr. Bhutto a blunt question:

Lindley: Do you think at all, as some of the people I spoke here do, that in the long term India is determined on the end of Pakistan as an independent nation?

President: This has been India's record for the past 25 years. But I would not like to say that now, because I would like to trust India. As much as India should take the risk of trusting us. I would like to take the risk of trusting Indian leaders. And perhaps it would be a long time before they have really swallowed and devoured and digested East Pakistan. So let us hope that we can have a generation of peace.

On Mrs. Gandhi, Bhutto gave an opinion that was at once uncharitable and in the circumstances indiscreet.

President: I have heard that the present Prime Minister [Mrs. Gandhi] says that her father was a saint and not a politician. But she does great injustice to her father. He was an outstanding politician. Perhaps, with all due respect, a greater politician than the present incumbent.

And when asked how did he think he would get on with Mrs. Gandhi, Bhutto slipped in a few softer second thoughts:

President: I hope to get on well and I have respect for her. I never liked it when Yahya called her 'that woman'. She is an elected leader of a big country. We respect a leader of people. We would give her all the respect and all the consideration that is due to a leader of the country and a successful Prime Minister. So we will meet her with reverence and respect, but of course with a sense of equality....

To set the tone for the meeting between Bhutto and Mrs. Gandhi at Shimla, and as a token of goodwill, injured POWs were repatriated on a priority basis.

Interestingly, Mr. Bhutto took with him to Shimla, not his wife Nusrat, but his eldest daughter Benazir. He had already decided that she would in time be appointed as his political successor. Benazir was to be the Indira to his Nehru. He wanted her therefore to meet the prototype.

The drama at Shimla is too well-known to be recounted here.[2] One moment Bhutto was proclaiming that there was 'a deadlock', and then suddenly at 12.40 a.m., in the early hours of 3 July, an agreement was signed. My diary entry for that day read:

[2] For a detailed eye-witness account, see Rafi Raza, *Zulfikar Ali Bhutto and Pakistan1967-1977*, (OUP, 1997), pp.206-216.

'Once the relief had subsided, one wondered what had induced IG [Indira Gandhi] to relent at the last minute. My guess is that she made ZAB beg up to the last and then knowing that his return empty-handed would probably be fatal for him and consequently dangerous for her and for India, she relented, conceding the legally indefensible. The territory on the Western front is being handed back.

Nothing has been said about the POWs. Pakistan doesn't need them at present. ('We are in no hurry', Shahnaz's uncle[3] who was amongst the POWs held in India, had written to us from his prison camp at Ranchi). India, now having disclosed their identities and their number, cannot dispose of them. She daren't hand them over the Bangladeshis because she trusts them less than we West Pakistanis do. The joint acceptance of the surrender on Dacca Racecourse may yet prove a yoke that chafes.

Kashmir has been conceded. Any future debate/negotiations shall have to be bilateral No more the blank cartridges of UN Security Council resolutions.'

At the end of July, Mrs. Indira Gandhi gave a personal interview to Mr. Mazhar Ali Khan, a close friend of the Nehru family and a senior journalist. According to him, Mrs. Gandhi had exhorted him to do his best to create an atmosphere of peace in Pakistan. He had accompanied Mr. Bhutto to Shimla, and his recollection of the atmosphere he had encountered there was stark. According to him, I noted in my diary, the Indians pointedly asked the Pakistanis what they had come for. Had they come to buy time before another bout? If so, then why wait? Have it out now, once and for all! Had they come genuinely for peace, then the Indians were prepared to make one concession: either the land under occupation in Sindh or the 90,321 POWs and CUPCs. Take your pick. Wisely, Bhutto chose the land, because he knew that the Indians and the Bangladeshis could not hold on to the prisoners indefinitely.

Almost every family we knew had one or more members held in captivity. One became aware of this in the most unexpected places. For example, while visiting a firm of lawyers in connection with the registration of

---

[3] Col. Raza Khan, SJ, was Shahnaz's maternal uncle. He had been captured in East Pakistan and then held by the Indians at various locations, including Ranchi and Agra. I corresponded with him regularly. Having been at boarding school in England, I knew how much a letter from home meant.

the mortgage of the land of Ghandhara Diesels Ltd., the senior partner and I began talking about the prevailing political situation. He mentioned that his son was a POW. His last letter from an Indian camp said that 'a shirt would be most welcome'. The father faltered for a moment and looked down with unspoken poignancy at his own crisply starched shirt.

The first POW I met had been brought to our flat in November 1972 by my in-laws. Capt. Pervaze had been in the camp at Ranchi as Col. Raza and had been released on medical grounds. It was only when Col. Raza himself had been repatriated almost two years after the Shimla Agreement in March 1974 that the trauma he and so many like him had endured hit me. I wrote of our reunion:

> 'He rose slowly, still dressed in his khaki POW uniform with a faded but still distinguishable 'X' sign across his chest. He had the same bushy, sandy beard we had expected after seeing his photo in one of his letters, and he looked weary. He spoke gently, and with measured economy – perhaps symbolic of the cautious existence he has been enduring for the past three years.
>
> "May I have an egg?" he asked, almost apologetically, and then added by way of explanation: "It shall be my first in three years."
>
> His account of the EP tragedy, the selfishness of the Army officers, the sadistic humiliations, the shameless betrayal, and the purposelessness and futility of the war made one cringe with remorse that we are too coarse to feel as a nation. The one thing the Government has not been able to nationalize, some wit has suggested, is the country itself.
>
> The 1971 war and its aftermath are clear indications of the pliability of our patriotism, the crudeness of our convictions, the banality of our beliefs, and the selfishness of our spineless society.'

Ten days after meeting Col. Raza Khan, I traced the only Pakistani POW incarcerated within Pakistan: ex-President General Yahya Khan. Bhutto had kept him under restrictive house arrest since December 1971. On 7 April 1974, Shahnaz and I were on a driving tour in the north. We stopped at Abbottabad for a quick lunch at the town's only public restaurant. I wrote a lengthy account of that particular day in my diary.

'At the next table was a young, respectable-looking man, obviously familiar with the local environs. Opposite at another table sat a young lawyer who seemed equally familiar with local politics. I aimed my question at the respectable one. "Would you by any chance know where General Yahya Khan is interned at present?" I asked him innocently. Immediately, the lawyer stopped eating. The respectable one replied: "I am not sure but I think he is in the Guest House." He thought for a while and then shook his head.

The suspense almost choked the seedy lawyer. "He's in the Governor's Guest House, and if you want to meet him, you'll have to get permission from the Deputy Superintendent of Police or from the Assistant Commissioner," the lawyer said hurriedly.

We thanked him, spent some time locating the SP's office and residence (he was out, it being a Sunday), then drove to the AC's office (he too was out), and finally located the DSP's home. He wanted me to make an application in writing. I did not have any paper on hand, and neither did he. So I took the brown paper shopping bag containing fruit we had bought earlier and scribbled an application. The DSP wrote his permission on the other half of the paper bag, which was dutifully torn in half like some medieval title deed. No one at the Guest House asked for it.

We were admitted by the one sepoy on duty at the gate. His main concern was not so much the security as the fact that the family inside may be having a siesta. We were escorted into Ali Yahya's room where we found him, his wife Tabindeh and their young daughter. Toys were scattered everywhere. We moved into the central corridor that bisected the house. I looked down towards the door that led into the verandah overlooking the garden, and saw the General's figure with his back to us, silhouetted against the evening light.

I recalled Compton Mackenzie's description of his encounter with ex-Kaiser Wilhelm of Germany at Doorn, where he lived in exile after his defeat in the First World War. Compton Mackenzie had been waiting with the ex-Kaiserin when suddenly the ex-Kaiser appeared in a doorway and stood beneath a large portrait of him painted when he was emperor. Mackenzie found the contrast startling.

For me, at that Guest House, there was no such reminder of a glorious imperial past hanging above the door, no dramatic sign of the collapse in status. General Yahya sat at a round table covered by a woollen rug, beneath which a small electric fire was glowing. Shahnaz walked up to him and greeted him. It took him a few seconds to place us, but once he had done so, he was all bustle and attention. He asked us to sit, ordered tea, asked after Agha sahib and Aunty Nayyar (Shahnaz's parents).[4]

He was in complete command of his faculties, despite the lengthy period of incarceration with his family. Throughout our stay with him, he was alert, sharp and talkative. His enviable head of white hair had begun to yellow in places.

After a short while, he called for his dark glasses and wore them for as long as we remained with him. During tea, alluding for the first time to anything political or current, he asked me what reaction the nationalization of banks had had on the commercial community in Karachi. I replied that that they were apprehensive and that as a result private investment and activity in the private sector was hardly noticeable. He asked after Rashid Habib[5] and Agha Hasan Abedi[6], and one or two other prominent bankers affected by nationalisation.

We spoke of the removal of the Governor Punjab Ghulam Mustafa Khar, at which Yahya referred to Burney's editorial in *Outlook* magazine. I reminded Yahya of Burney's telling phrase that one casualty (Maulvi Shamsuddin) was beyond pity, and the other (Khar) was undeserving of it. He laughed.'

"Do you read *Outlook* regularly?" I asked him.

"Only if I can get it," he replied, adding: "Who is this Burney anyway?"

I asked General Yahya about Bhutto. 'A *madari* '[7], he replied. 'Nothing but a cheap *madari*.' He continued in this vein with some uncouth epithets about Mr. Bhutto's ancestry. I pointed to the copse

---

[4] Shahnaz's father and General Yahya were maternal first cousins.
[5] Former President of Habib Bank Ltd.
[6] Former President of United Bank Ltd. and later founder of Bank of Credit and Commerce International (BCCI).
' A street conjuror.

of trees at the end of the garden and whispered that he was undoubtedly being bugged by intelligence agencies.

"Let him hear what I think of him!"

By this time, it was almost twilight and I thought it best to take our leave. Shahnaz and I drove back to the house of her uncle Jehangir Khan, then Joint Secretary in the Ministry of Provincial Coordination. He asked where we had been. I told him.

"You met him? Did you ask him whether they were going to hang him?"

CHAPTER 3

RATIONALISATION

With the stroke of a pen, thirty-two key industries in all ordered by Mr. Bhutto under the Economic Reforms Order 1972 had been brought under the control of the state. The consequential imperative was to re-organise their management and bring it to an efficient, productive, and profitable level. That was easier notified than done.

Many of these industries were already being managed by competent professionals. It did not take long though for business tycoons like the Hyesons group to insinuate their own trusted employees into positions they had held before the take-over, or to have them appointed as managing directors in place of those appointed in the first flush by the Government.

There were now two sets of industries in the public sector – those taken-over under the ERO 1972 and those established during the Ayub Khan era by the West Pakistan Industrial Development Corporation (WPIDC, and after 1971, PIDC). As an interim measure therefore, in the first step towards rationalisation, it was decided to create a Board of Industrial Management (BIM) responsible for each category of taken-over industries. A Member was appointed for different sectors - Automotive, Cement, Chemicals, Steel – and to assist them, a Member Finance was made responsible for assessing their financial requirements and arranging finance for them. Mr. Aminullah, a former branch manager of Citibank Lahore and someone known personally to the Finance Minister Dr. Mubashir Hasan, was given this responsibility.

Aslam Khan of ICI became Member Chemicals, Afzal Khan of Burmah Shell Member Steel, and Humayun Mufti of Ghandhara Industries became Member Automotives. No sooner had the notification of the BIM been made on 29 February 1972 than every ambitious professional began sprucing up his bio-data for consideration as a Managing Director in place of those appointed by the Government.

What followed was a game of corporate musical chairs. For example, in the Automotive sector, with which I was directly involved, the senior Directors in Ghandhara Industries and their friends vied with each other to head the better companies. Eventually, Salman Siddique (former Technical Director of Ghandhara Industries) became the MD of Ghandhara Diesels (now renamed Bela Engineers Ld.); S.M.A. Salar (formerly the MD of Ghandhara Diesels Ltd.) took over as MD Awami Autos Ltd. (formerly Ali Autos Ltd.); F. Alfrey (heading Marghzar Industries, the tractor wing of Ghandhara Industries) became the MD of Millat Tractors (formerly Rana Motors); Iftikhar Ahmed (MD of Singer) was appointed as MD Republic Motors (the old Khandalawala Motors company); and Syed Hilaluddin became the Senior Executive Director of National Motors. To anyone in the know, these appointments could not have been more incestuous.

While this distribution of boons was taking place, I remained mired in Bela Engineers Ltd., not because I could not have been useful elsewhere but rather because I was regarded as invaluable to this fledgling project. The project had been conceived in the late 1960s as a means of ensuring a continuous supply of Bedford engines for a market beyond the popular Bedford trucks. The underlying logic had been to import initially the engines from Vauxhall Motors in completely knocked-down condition (CKD). Gradually, imported parts would be deleted as far as practicable and replaced by locally manufactured ones. To make the project viable, it was vital that it should operate at a capacity which happened to exceed the annual demand for Bedford trucks. The Bedford engine, therefore, had to be standardised for trucks other than Bedford and for other vehicles, tractors and marine vessels.

Ironically, now that all the automobile importers/ assemblers/ manufacturers had been brought within the public domain, it should have been possible to replicate the pattern set during the infancy of the automotive industry by Ford in the U.S. and later by the Government in India. Ford offered a car in any colour as long as it was black, and for years the Indian offered any car of your choice as long as it was a locally manufactured Ambassador.

However justifiable standardisation may have been as an economic philosophy, predictably it fell victim to personal ambitions. Each newly appointed Managing Director in the automotive sector wanted to protect his turf. National policies were quickly subordinated to personal agendas.

In Bela Engineers, the appointment of Salman Siddique (formerly Technical Director at Ghandhara Industries) cleared the confusion that had prevailed in the organisation. His predecessor Salar had a number of qualities: he was extremely sociable, quick on the uptake, result-oriented, and with a flair for marketing. His radial style of management was hampered by private insecurities: suspicions made it centralized, sporadic rather than systematic, and flattery became a necessary lubricant to upward mobility. Management was by diktat. Throughout the eight months or so since I had joined the company, for example, there had never been any kind of management meeting.

Salman Siddique changed that. On 19 April he invited three of us senior managers to a meeting. This included the General Manager Technical Saad Hashmi , myself as the Finance Manager, and the Supply Manager T.H. Siddiqui who had begun his career 37 years earlier in General Motors. Saad Hashmi, an engineer, had been in the oil and gas industry for many years. He knew more than he cared to reveal, but his tact notwithstanding, he could not prevent at times Salman Siddique and invariably, always T. H. Siddiqui from feeling professionally insecure in his presence.

I made a note of the meeting because it typified the petty level at which corporate in-fighting often took place:

> THS saw the meeting as a chance of asserting his 'special' relationship with SS, but the SS he knew was a different image to the one he now has to deal with. One illustration shall given an idea of the change. While I was citing the case of the driver who wouldn't sit at my desk until I had ordered him to do so, THS thought this was a capital opportunity to attack.
>
> "In GIL and GM days, we *never* allowed drivers to sit in front of Executives!" THS said, and then looked for support to the new (ex GIL, ex GM) MD.
>
> "'That view is not longer practical," SS replied.
>
> THS looked nonplussed. Suddenly he blurted: "What I meant to say

is that I don't want Aijaz-sahib to become popular with the drivers at my expense."

The confrontation between Hashmi and THS came to a head during an altercation when, fearful of losing the argument, THS hurled what he thought was an ace: "I have more than 25 years of experience in General Motors!" To which Hashmi trumped it with the retort: "No, you have 5 years of experience, multiplied five times."

The GDL / now BEL project had been premised on underwriting financing to be provided by Development Financial Institutions (DFIs). A novel element of the scheme (the brainchild of Mr. Hameed Chaudhri, General Habibullah's financial consultant) had been for the project to have a public offering of its shares, linked with interest-bearing debentures. The subscriber would get a share (for which no dividend return could be guaranteed) and with it a debenture which could be resold on the stock market and which carried an assured rate of return of 12% per annum. Like that, the investor in the years the company declared a dividend, would receive a dividend plus interest, and in those where it had to forgo a dividend, the investor would get interest on his debenture and thereby receive an average of least 6% return on the whole of his investment.

The scheme in ordinary circumstances would have been a flier. In a post-war, post-nationalisation atmosphere, selling it to the DFIs was an uphill task, steep and tiring. It was clear to anyone who had never even bought or sold a share (leave alone a debenture) that the Karachi Stock Exchange was not yet ready for such revolutionary innovations. KSE was the only stock exchange with any depth to its market. Lahore Stock Exchange had been established but was still on a milk diet. Islamabad Stock Exchange was nowhere on the horizon.

My job was to get underwriting commitments for the DFIs and then to borrow from them against those commitments. The loans would be paid off out of the proceeds of the public flotation. In those days, no DFI or bank liked to act on its own. They preferred to act as a consortium, with one – usually the one with either the resources or an acknowledged expertise in project evaluation - to take the lead. I got Investment Corporation of Pakistan (ICP) where I had worked in 1967 to act as the leader of our Consortium.

To give Salman Siddique as the new MD a crash course in project funding (as an engineer, he was used to spending money rather than to arranging it), on 22 April I took Salman on a tour of the all the DFIs who had agreed in principle to be part of the Consortium. On our way to Chundrigar Road (Karachi's Wall Street), Salman noticed that I had a book with me.

"You read a lot?" he asked me.

"Frequently. At the moment I am reading the life of the explorer Sir Richard Burton." I showed him Fawn Brodie's *A Devil Drives: The Life of Sir Richard Burton.* "Have you heard about him?"

"Only what I read in the newspapers."

I knew he had confused the explorer with the actor with the same name. I put him out of his misery: "Actually this book is about his ancestor."

Now that I look back on that period, I recall the sharp desperation I felt at watching the bank account of the project dwindle. On 24 May, I noted in my diary that the project had no money. Almost as if by miracle, I discovered that the bank had credited us with Rs 31,000 on account of accrued interest income, which was enough to pay our immediate bills.

The very next morning, as if in answer to my prayers, Habib Bank Ltd. approved a commitment of Rs 10 lakhs. It took ICP another three months to finalise the Underwriting Agreement. It was completed on 30 August and signed off by all the participating banks and DFIs the following day, on 31 August.

If there was anyone more relieved than I was at this accomplishment, it was Salman Siddique. He paid me a grudging compliment: "Aijaz, I know that you will arrange the money somehow. But could you give me a clue as to how you do it?"

I kept our make-shift solvency a secret from the Board of Industrial Management, especially so after I heard that Humayun Mufti as Member BIM had demanded a contribution from Salman towards the decoration of the plush BIM offices in the expensive National Shipping Corporation building. I decided that we needed the money more than the BIM did, especially since we had shifted our offices from the SITE factory of GIL/NML to Ebrahim Buildings in the West Wharf area. Our new premises had been occupied earlier by Glaxo, the pharmaceutical multinational. It left behind a large empty hall. On a shoe-string budget we built wooden partitions and used desks we 'borrowed' from Ghandhara's surplus.

Our office was very much the poor cousin to the BIM establishment in NSC. There, no expense had been spared. Off-white furnishings, plush sofas, expensive furniture, and wooden partitions inset with glass panels that permitted an uninterrupted view from all sides of Karachi port and of the Arabian Sea. From that height, one felt a heady sense of importance. Although not exactly on top of the world, one certainly sat at the summit of the public sector. The offices, I was told, had cost Rs 2,000,000 to decorate and to maintain it, the BIM intended to levy a contribution of Rs 200,000 from each of the 31 companies under its control.

The BIM's nouveau-riche pretensions were caught out by a visiting Yugoslav whom I took for a meeting with at the NSC building. As we waited for the lift on the way out, he turned to me and commented: "The tendency to avoid in such situations is ... empire building." Coming as he did from a soft-socialist state, he had seen it all before. He could recognise the signs, smelt the temptations, could foresee the pitfalls, and knew that we in Pakistan would be travelling down a well-rutted road.

While I worked as hard as I could to ensure that Bela Engineers had enough money to survive, almost daily the confusion in the PPP Government in Islamabad like river waters reached the lower riparian of Karachi. Mr. J. Rahim as the new Minister of Production took over also as the Head of the BIM. He announced that there was no justification to have the BEL project in Bela and wanted it relocated nearer Karachi, even though it would lose the project the vital tax-free concessions the completed project hoped to harvest, once it came into commercial production.

Because of BEL's lack of importance, it escaped the attention of the new Minister. To register his support for the workers at National Motors whose union had begun a campaign of agitation, he chose to visit its factory at SITE. Acting upon faulty advice (or perhaps responding to pressure from somewhere else) Rahim ordered some executives who had been dismissed at the behest of the union to be reinstated immediately. Orders were issued, the reinstated executives re-admitted, and the workers exhorted to be more productive now that the factory (at least in theory) belonged to them. The workers on their part shouted slogans of support for their People's Government and then waited for its new Minister to leave before locking the gates so that none of the

NML executives could leave the premises.

J. Rahim had been the acknowledged ideologue of the Pakistan People's Party and the spirit behind the nationalization programme. His newly-created Ministry of Production, Industries & Agrovilles added yet another layer in the reporting hierarchy above the BIM.

In order to establish a system of reporting within the units under the control of each Member of the BIM, and then by the BIM to the Ministry, a senior executive who happened to be a fellow Chartered Accountant was assigned the task of developing an Accounting Manual for the BIM controlled companies. Ordinarily, one would have taken a bottom-up approach. Define the reporting needs within each unit, and then build upwards from that. Instead, he took a short-cut. He tried to adapt the Accounting Manual for Coca-Cola on the assumption that if it worked for Coke, it must work for the BIM. I was not surprised to learn later that the BIM Accounting Manual never left his drawing board.

Gradually, as the BIM settled into its shallow foundations, it became clear to all of us at the operational level and in time to the new Minister that there were two parallel public sectors – the BIM and the PIDC – each responsible for promoting industrial growth in the country, each trying to assert a claim to primacy.

In September 1972, a tender was floated for the progressive manufacture of motor cars locally. While Humayun Mufti grappled with the incessant demands of his automotive units - for foreign exchange to finance their imports, for rupee financing to hold stocks of vehicles for sale in a sluggish market, for help against recalcitrant workers - in November 1972, PIDC stole a march by announcing a project for the progressive manufacture of tractors locally. It incorporated a new company – Pakistan Tractors Corporation Ltd. (PTCL) – and much to Mufti's chagrin, bids were invited by PIDC from international tractor manufacturers throughout the world. There was an obvious overlap between BIM and PIDC, and that overlap was the tractor industry.

Mufti on his part had already insinuated himself with Mr. Javed Talat, the new Deputy Secretary at the Ministry of Production. For a while, the Ministry consisted of Rahim as Minister at the top and Javed Talat as the Deputy Secretary at the bottom, with no Joint Secretary, Additional Secretary or effective Secretary in between.

In time I was to have much to do with Javed, first at Bela, then at PTCL, and subsequently at the National Fertiliser Corporation of Pakistan. My first meeting however was memorable – for all the wrong reasons. Soon after he had taken over, he had been invited by Mufti for a briefing on the BIM Automotive sector. On 20 October 1972, Hashmi and I were summoned to the BIM offices in NSC building for a presentation on the plans for progressive manufacture of motor cars. On returning home, I wrote in my diary: 'The meeting itself was rambling and irrelevant [...] It had been convened at 15 minutes notice. Therefore no-one came prepared.'

The Chairman of PIDC – Mr. Faridi (a retired CEO of Pakistan Shell who joined the public sector at a token salary of one rupee a month) – wasted no sunshine in manning the new company. In September, he offered Saad Hashmi the MD-ship of PTCL.

Faridi and Mufti joined forces as members of a Delegation sent to Italy in December 1972 to study the working of the public sector there. Javed Talat represented the Ministry of Production. The report the Delegation submitted on its return saw considerable parallels between what Mr. Bhutto's government was trying to achieve and what the Italians had already achieved. Its assessment was that through a number of agencies such as IRI, ENI, EFIM, etc., the Italian Government 'ensured that economic slumps, which result in the curtailment of investment by the private sector, do not bring about serious repercussions in the economy. Whenever private investment goes down, the public sector starts making major investments to keep the economy going at an even pace. Through this arrangement the State has acquired the ability for large scale intervention in the economy and also for guiding the private sector on socio-economic matters. In addition, the economic power so acquired is used for implementing the socio-economic policies of the Government.'

The recommendations of the Delegation included:

1. The establishment of a Pakistan Public Enterprise Corporation (PPEC), to function as a Parent Holding Company.

2. Under PPEC, there should be 9 Functional Holding Companies:

- Chemical & Fertilisers

- Oil and Gas

- Steel and Heavy Engineering

- Electrical and Light Engineering

- Automobiles and Tractors

- Sugar

- Cement

- Industrial Finance

- Life Insurance

It was envisaged that each Holding Company would have a Board of Directors elected by the shareholders. As the Government would be the majority shareholder, the Board would remain under the effective control of the Government.

All the units existing in the public sector would be brought within the purview of the relevant corporation. It was emphasised that PPEC should be administratively and operationally completely autonomous. Any rules and regulations framed by PPEC would not be subject to Government approval.

All feasibilities for proposed projects would be prepared 'by professionals strictly on economic and financial considerations.' They would be evaluated 'most rigorously' at three levels- by the Functional Holding Companies, PPEC, and the Ministry of Production before being submitted for consideration by the Cabinet and, if approved, for inclusion in the National Five Year Plan.

At least 50% of PPEC's funding needs would be supplied by the Government, and in return, PPEC committed to distribute 80 % of the net profits of its units to the Government exchequer.

The Delegation's report provided the blueprint the Government needed to rationalise the public sector. It accepted the recommendations for the creation of specialised sectoral corporations but put a line through the proposal for a PPEC. The Ministry of Production was not prepared to relinquish direct control over the proposed corporations, and through them over the operating units.

At the close of 1972, the Government was heavy with this brainchild of the Ministry of Production, and Shahnaz pregnant with our first child.

Shahnaz and I learned of her pregnancy on 10 June 1972. I know the exact date because I still have the clinic's report that read 'Pregnancy – Positive.' I kept that as a memento and also as the first paper in a file that was to document the life of each of our children. It was perhaps the accountant in me that made me so meticulous about maintaining such records. (My children dismissed them as embarrassing trivia, until they grew older.) I like to think, though, it was a response to the instincts of an incipient biographer.

Obviously we were concerned to find a good gynaecologist. We made a false start with a gynaecologist who lived in the flat near ours. Her proximity would have been convenient except that Shahnaz found her long manicured nails uncomfortable. We settled on Dr. Stockhausen, a middle-aged German missionary at the Seventh Day Adventist Hospital on Bunder Road. Experienced and efficient, she had a no-nonsense approach, but above all she evoked in Shahnaz a mood of confidence.

From my diary I know that the first response we had from the womb was on 8 October. I am not sure which part of the baby's anatomy moved – the fist or the foot – but it proved a magical, memorable moment for us.

Check-ups continued monthly until the beginning of January 1973 when Dr. Stockhausen asked to see Shahnaz every fortnight, then weekly. The date of delivery, she told us, would be around the end of the month.

On 28 January, the Aghas took us for lunch at the Chandni Lounge – a rooftop restaurant at the top of the Intercontinental Hotel (now the Pearl Continental Hotel.) In those days, the restaurant offered a buffet meal for Rs 10 per head. Shahnaz ate as much as she could in the circumstances, but perhaps a little too much, for when she met Dr. Stockhausen later that afternoon for her regular check-up, Dr. Stockhausen told her that she was going into labour. She wanted Shahnaz admitted immediately, and almost before she knew it, Shahnaz found herself undressed and put into a hospital tunic and loose skirt.

Dr. Stockhausen induced delivery by giving Shahnaz a laxative. I was told to go home as the baby would not be expected until the morning.

I returned to the Seventh Day Adventist Hospital at 5.00 a.m. next morning to find Shahnaz in one bed and her mother as an attendant in the other. Above Shahnaz's headboard hung a print of a fair, blue-eyed, flaxen-haired Anglo-Saxon baby. I could not imagine a more belated or misleading incentive for a mother-to-be about to go into labour.

At 10.00 a.m., Dr. Stockhausen met me on her way to surgery and told me that although Shahnaz and the baby were both in good condition, there seemed to be indications that her contractions were less forceful than she had hoped. The delivery would be later in the afternoon. Shahnaz, meanwhile, remained surprisingly calm and composed, but gradually felt herself losing strength.

At 2.00 p.m., Dr. Stockhausen called me to Shahnaz's bedside to discuss her condition. "The baby's head is in the wrong position," she explained. "Instead of being vertical, facing upwards or downwards, the baby's head is laterally across the abdomen. I can leave her in labour but at the rate her contractions are continuing, it is quite likely that with the delay, the baby will become distressed and she will become too tired to continue. I'd advise a Caesarean."

Shahnaz looked disappointed. "But I have not read anything on Caesareans!"

She was given a spinal anaesthetic and wheeled into the operating theatre at 2.15 p.m. At 2.50 p.m., a nurse rushed out and as she passed me she said: "The baby has been born but I do not know the sex yet!" At 3.00 p.m., Daniel Mall, the Assistant Director of the SDA Hospital, sauntered out. "You know what it is?"

"No," I replied.

"You have a daughter." Suddenly, I felt immortal.

At 3.15 p.m., our newly-born daughter was wheeled out, swathed in a warm blanket. She bawled uncontrollably, her round face creased and red. I noticed a shock of black hair. As she opened her mouth to let out another yell, I dipped my finger in some honey I had brought along and touched her lips, whispering 'Allah O Akbar' three times in her ear. The nurse took her away to the nursery and when I saw her again through the glass partition, she was still bawling.

Shahnaz was brought out almost an hour later. She looked wan and pale. She opened her eyes for a moment, asked how our daughter was, and then fell into a deep sleep. She was able to see our child but only through the glass screen of the nursery.

I should not have been the one to feel exhausted but I did and fell asleep as soon as I reached home.

Early next morning, I rushed to the SDA hospital. The receptionist deflected me by pointing out the prohibition pasted on the wall behind her: 'Husband shall not be permitted to be attendants to their wives.'

I had no option but to return home and to while away the time until visiting hours later in the day. The following day, I made another early start and thought I had discovered an unguarded staircase in the hospital. I ran upstairs, opened a door and encountered Dr. Stockhausen in the corridor. She softened enough to allow me to see Shahnaz.

Shahnaz and our daughter whom we named Momina remained in the hospital for a week, until Shahnaz was fit to return. On 6 February, I brought them home to our flat. We placed Momina in her cot – a beautifully decorated bassinet with lace frills made by Mrs. Kausar Hashmi. I had been advised to keep the head of the cot at a slight incline. So as props I placed two volumes of *Alberuni's India*. When she was six weeks old, Momina indicated her first cognition – she gave me a smile, and in November she uttered her first word – 'aba'.

After we brought Momina home, I regarded every moment I spent away from her as an imposition. However, I had to earn my living and I wished with all my heart that I did not have to do it trying to make an unviable project afloat.

The mantra during the PPP government had been economic and industrial self-sufficiency. The Islamic-socialist government wanted local industry to make everything – steel, fertilizers, chemicals, cement, automobiles and of course tractors. As it had no clear idea how to go about this ambitious aim, it began by first making mistakes.

The plan for the progressive manufacture of a local car faltered when no one in the BIM or the Ministry of Production could decide on which model to make. At a meeting of the Managing Directors of the auto companies held on 2 January 1973, I noted that one of the MDs made a dramatic announcement that his factory had produced a car of which 60% of the components had been made locally. Every other MD in the room looked stunned and defeated at the coup.

"And what is the make you have copied?" Mufti asked the proud MD.

"A Citroen," the MD replied.

"Pity," Mufti retorted. "The Citroen people are the only ones who have refused to participate in the progressive car manufacturing tender. They wouldn't even meet me when I was in Paris."

Unfairly but understandably, the laughter in the Board room that morning was long, loud and derisive.

The new year of 1973 had hardly begun and suddenly I found myself being courted – by Hashmi for PTCL, by Hilal for National Motors, and by my friend Fareed Khan to join the 'M' or Management Section of A.F. Ferguson (one of Pakistan's leading auditing firms.) Of the three, the one that appealed to me was PTCL. Apart from the pleasure of working with Saad Hashmi whom I respected as a consummate professional and regarded as altogether too good for the BIM, I could see more of a future for myself with PTCL.

I anticipated that leaving Bela Engineers and joining PTCL would not be a simple transition from one job to another. Humayun Mufti was both Member Automobiles and a Board member of PTCL. Even before giving Hashmi my CV, I decided to talk to Humayun first. I went so see him at the BIM. Fortunately, he was alone in his room. In my diary I wrote afterwards:

> 'I broached the possibility, in fact the inevitability of leaving GDL. There would have been little point in my asking him point blank to permit me to leave GDL for the Tractor Corporation. His reply would have been frank and negative. I put it another way to him. I told him that in my opinion, the proper time for me to leave GDL would be either now or a year from now. If I were to leave now, my replacement would have a full coffer at least, and the chance of creating a department according to his own designs, as well as having the satisfaction of setting up the project. Alternatively I would have to stay long enough to see the project set up and then leave.

> By diffusing the picture prospects ahead of me at the moment – Tractor Corp'n, Fergusons and NASGAS[1] - I was able to lessen the

---

[1] The NASGAS offer came from Sajjad Haider of Fergusons. I would be joining Sattoo Qureshi's company as its MD and have to put the company right, with a stake in future profits.

shock while at the same time (I hope) leaving open the options to apply for and be considered for PTCL.'

The other contender for the PTCL job, I was told later, was Masud Zain, also a Chartered Accountant. He had been recently retrenched by Standard Bank and enjoyed the support of Hilaluddin.

A week after my meeting with Mufti, I gave Hashmi my CV for review by the PTCL Board. I arrived early for the interview with the PTCL Board. My friend Fareed Khan saw my safari suit and more or less ordered me to go home and change into a dark suit. Fortunately, I was able to go there and be back in time for the interview. For some reason, I was irrationally self-conscious about the frayed cuffs on my white shirt and hoped the Directors would not notice. They didn't. The interview was, despite Mufti's determination to have my application excluded from the agenda, fairly successful. Hashmi was optimistic.

The following morning, I called Salman Siddique to ask whether I could see him. I knew that Humayun Mufti would have told him about my appearance for the PTCL interview and I would have rather he heard it from me directly. He called me the next day. It was not a pleasant session. For most of that afternoon, I had to listen to his harangue. 'He shouted, he abused, he taunted and eventually he wept.' He followed it the next day with another round of recriminations. "I won't let you go," he warned me, "and even if I did, it would certainly not be to the Tractor Corporation."

Salman relented a little the next day. "I don't suppose I can stop you. Shall I speak to your wife?" And then, the coup de grâce: "You, Mr. Aijazuddin, have been an object lesson in treachery and disloyalty for the past four months." By 23 February, his fever had broken. He agreed to my release and to my joining PTCL.

I phoned Hashmi to give him the news we had both been waiting for. He asked me whether the salary he was proposing to give me at PTCL was acceptable. I would receive a Basic Salary of Rs 3,700, plus a House Rent Allowance of 30%, an Entertainment Allowance of Rs 300, Rs 200 towards the telephone, and a fully maintained car. My salary at GDL was not more than Rs 3,500 in all.

"Aren't you giving me too much?" I asked Hashmi.

It took another month for my appointment to be approved by the Board of PTCL, and when it was given a final assent, it was done through a Resolution by Circulation in anticipation of the PTCL Board meeting that took place on 20 March.

Pakistan Tractors Corporation had been created to overcome the chronic shortage of tractors in the country. Bhutto was too sensitive to the needs of a primarily agrarian electorate to ignore their demands for tractors. Their voice in his Cabinet was his Advisor Malik Khuda Bukhsh Bucha, a formidable personality.

In the closing months of 1972, the government had invited tenders for the progressive manufacture locally of tractors. After a series of negotiations with most of the internationally known names in the tractor industry, Massey-Ferguson was selected and a contract for supply and progressive deletion signed with it. The contract was actually with Massey Ferguson Canada, where the Head office was located, although the supply of their popular MF 135 was to come from its plant at Coventry (U.K.).

No sooner had the contract been signed and approvals from the Government and Massey-Ferguson's Board received than it became clear that MF would not be in a position to supply tractors in the quantities they had indicated during the negotiations and committed to send under the agreement. The Government wanted at least 4,000 units. MF prevaricated and offered less. It took months for the first shipment to arrive. It was a disaster. The first consignment consisted of 24 tractors, and even they were unusable because they came with 48 left-hand lights.

An idea may be had of the almost avaricious demand for tractors by the Chairman Agricultural Development Bank of Pakistan that he 'lend' PTCL 10 tractors out of his stock which could then be sold by PTCL for cash to customers identified by him. These would be replaced in time out of the 24 that PTCL was expecting from MF. A simple enough proposal, except that the purpose was to allow political 'favourites' to be allotted tractors out of turn. At the ADBP, they would have to join the end of a lengthy queue of applicants.

There was little Hashmi sahib could do to improve MF's capability to supply tractors, but he found himself the whipping boy. Messages were conveyed to me from Board members, to the effect that Hashmi 'should watch out'. By May 1973, an impatient Government sought to ease the pressure by allowing the import of other makes. On 24 May, I received a telephone call from Javat Talat: "Tell Mr. Hashmi that the Government has approved the import of 1,000 Fiat and 1,800 Belarus tractors this year, and is considering the possibility of importing 1,500 more Fiat and 1,200 Belarus tractors in the next year ... and tell him by telegram." [Hashmi was in London where he had gone for discussions with MF.]

Javed Talat knew that by permitting the import of different makes of tractors, the progressive manufacturing programme of MF tractors would be affected. While it would lessen the pressure on the government, Javed knew as clearly as Hashmi did that import of tractors would not remove MF's supply constraints.

Less than a month later, tractors were put back on the Free List of Imports.

My responsibility at PTCL in a way was no different to that in GDL/BEL. As its Finance Manager, I had to arrange funds. The seed capital was to be provided by the Government. That involved me in endless discussion with the Accountant-General Pakistan Revenue (AGPR) in Islamabad whose reluctance to part with any money was matched only by my determination to extract it from him. In the end, I had to go to Islamabad, sit in the AGPR's office, and type out the release order for Rs 10 lakhs myself.

An attendant responsibility as PTCL's Personnel Manager was to resist attempts by well-placed VIPs to have their sons/nephews/relations accommodated in PTCL.

I suspect the Board Meeting of PTCL held on 17 August clinched Mr. Hashmi's resolve to leave the company. He had called the meeting upon the insistence of the Board members (particularly Humayun Mufti), and on the day, Mufti appeared 45 minutes after the meeting was to have begun and Javed Talat had better things to do in Islamabad.

Hashmi submitted his resignation on 21 September. The notice period expired on 21 October. The Government could not (or would not) decide on his successor and so I was asked to officiate under the benign supervision of Mr. N.N.A Qureishy. He had spent his career in Pakistan Railways and spelt his name differently from his elder brother Mr. B.A. Kureishi, whom I had known as the Chairman of the Lahore Museum.

Shortly afterwards, Faridi called me to tell me that he was bringing S.B. Awan the newly-appointed Secretary Production to PTCL for a briefing. Shaukat Awan's previous posting had been Chief Secretary Balochistan where much to his dismay his daughter got involved romantically with one of Nawab Akbar Bugti's unstable sons.

Faridi and Awan arrived fashionably late. As they settled in PTCL's bright but modest Board Room, Faridi cautioned me: "Aijaz, you have exactly seven minutes!" I had done a number of trial runs and so without wasting a moment, I launched into my presentation, with one eye on the clock. It took just over seven minutes, certainly no more than eight, after which there was a quick tour of the MF tractor's entrails spread out in a display of intention rather than actual performance.

I could tell from Faridi's reaction that he was immeasurably relieved that I had kept my presentation succinct and my briefing on PTCL's teething problems even briefer. He had been apprehensive that in Hashmi's absence, I might not be able to acquit myself. By next morning, I started receiving calls from persons in PIDC telling me that, out of all the forty odd corporate presentations that Awan was made to endure that day, he had found PTCL's the best.

My triumph was Pyrrhic. The night before the PTCL Board meeting scheduled for 22 December, I invited Frank Alfrey (MD of Millat) and Akram Ghauri (Mufti's assistant at the BIM) over for dinner. My diary entry of that evening singes with resentment:

> 'Frank Alfrey arrived just after 10 p.m. and quite embarrassingly drunk. The rest of the evening was a dreadful experience. Like some cringing conspirators, they revealed and then tried to conceal that Mufti was supplanting Faridi as the Chairman PTCL. I let them have it when perhaps it might have been more prudent to have remained silent, but I was so incensed at their pettiness that I really didn't give a damn.'

The fissure between Mr. Faridi and Humayun Mufti in their tussle over the Chairmanship of PTCL at Karachi was paralleled between the Ministry of Production in Islamabad and the BIM. Until S.B. Awan's appointment as Secretary, the Ministry had been headed nominally by the benign Allauddin Ahmed as its Additional Secretary but run actually by Javed Talat, its only

Deputy Secretary with no Joint Secretary in between. Allauddin's strength lay in his formidable and incisive intellect. He camouflaged it by appearing in meetings invariably dishevelled, his greasy tie askew, one cuff with a cufflink and the other without. He would sit through meetings with his eyes half-closed, smoking a Woodbine cigarette which he would balance, in between puffs, on its end on the table. He never felt the need for an ashtray when the front of his shirt was at hand. Allauddin had all the characteristics of a retired physician. He could diagnose with unmatched brilliance but he was just not interested in the tedium of a treatment. He left that to his subordinate – in this case Javed Talat.

Javed Talat by comparison was fastidious and demonstrably efficient. Allauddin took no notes but remembered everything. Javed carried a small diary in his tweed jacket and listed everything he had to do that day and every day. He could be brusque, was impatient with detail, and carried his ambitions on his sleeve.

The absurdity of the MoP/BIM confrontation was exposed when at the PTCL Board meeting held on 22 December, one director arrived at the wrong office, and as soon as the meeting started, Javed Talat announced that he had to leave for Islamabad that very moment. Mufti had already absented himself from the meeting. There was little Faridi as Chairman could do except to postpone the meeting until 2 January 1974.

The reconvened meeting took place on 2 January (I had expected another postponement), but this time Humayun Mufti sat in the Chairman's seat. In the intervening days, he had been appointed in place of A.R. Faridi. The coup by PACO was complete.

Even at the time, most of us involved could see the superior logic of bringing PTCL under the umbrella of PACO. After all, before nationalisation, the then Rana Tractors (renamed Millat Tractors) had been assembling Massey Ferguson tractors for years, albeit at low volumes. Following the progressive manufacturing deal PTCL had concluded with Massey Ferguson, an anomalous situation had been created as only government functionaries can achieve.

PTCL held the franchise but was located at Karachi; Millat owned the assembly facilities but they were located upcountry at Sheikhupura, outside Lahore. Either PTCL would have to establish another parallel plant at Karachi or PTCL would have to be merged with MTL. Hashmi and Faridi had tried to develop a relationship between PTCL and engineering units under Faridi's control such as the Pakistan Machine Tool Factory at Landhi (on the periphery of Karachi) and the Heavy Mechanical Complex at Taxila. Faridi had even gone to the extent of having a small 12 HP tractor fabricated at the HMC to demonstrate the capability of his units to manufacture tractors. He invited the Minister of Production J. Rahim to witness its inaugural performance at the PIDC guest house at Sihala (Rawalpindi). The Minister sat astride the diminutive machine and drove it around the guest house lawns. Everyone present applauded. Only Hashmi after looking at the publicity photographs of the event detected that the machine was useless. He noticed that the rear tyres had been mounted backwards to improve traction.

Had Faridi been less astute, he might have involved himself in a custody battle over PTCL. He could see that PTCL was not worth fighting for, or over. In any case, he had his eyes on the Chairmanship of a much larger prize – the Pakistan Steel Mills, a Russian funded project that promised to be the largest industrial facility in the country.

I doubt whether Mufti anticipated the PTCL Board meeting which he chaired on 2 January would go the way it did. From his point of view, it should have been a formality with his coronation as Chairman and Frank Alfrey's anointing as Hashmi's successor. By some fortuitous accident, he mistook the time of the meeting as 10.00 and arrived at the PTCL offices two hours early. That gave me an opportunity of establishing my own independent equation with him and during those two hours also of insinuating my views on PTCL's prospects, which of course, once the meeting began, he presented with all the confidence of authorship. As it was clear that Massey Ferguson could not supply more than 1,500 tractors until October 1974, PTCL's viability could be ensured only if it resorted to trading in the short-term and – once deliveries for MF increased in the future – through progressive manufacture.

PTCL's dilemma - important though it might have been for me personally - was dwarfed by Bhutto's sudden nationalization of banks. Many saw it as Mr. Bhutto's New Year gift to himself. I recall now the British journalist Kevin Rafferty's observation that for Bhutto's government it was now 'all ...or nothing'.

One of the decisions taken at the PTCL Board meeting which I decided (rather selfishly) to exploit had been to send a delegation to negotiate a revised and hopefully dependable supply programme with Massey Ferguson. It had been agreed that Javed and Alfrey would form the team. I confided to my diary:

> 'Slowly one or two people (J.T. prominent amongst them) thought that a person from PTCL should also go. It was up to me, I realised, to demonstrate that I was the key to the negotiations. Publicly, though, I maintained that the working brief for the tour would be circulated well in time. FA [Frank Alfrey] tried on a number of occasions to obtain a copy of the brief. But I wasn't parting with it under any pretence or pressure. The ruse worked. HSM [Mufti] slowly conceded that perhaps it would be better for me to go as I was 'more familiar' with PTCL's affairs, and then the Finance Minister turned the key by giving permission for JT to leave accompanied by <u>one</u> officer of PTCL'.

My diary exuded optimism:

> 'In my anticipation, I ordered two new suits, and some shirts to be made up from the hoard of uncut materials I have collected over the years, to be used in just such an eventuality. But more importantly, I had Nassé [my secretary] type out the draft catalogue of the miniature paintings in the Lahore Museum, revised in the light of Dr. WGA's [Archer] book[2], and prepared it for discussion with WGA in London. This was more tiring than I had expected, for it required me to read through his voluminous work by evening each day, re-write the catalogue by hand at night, and then checked the typed pages during office hours. The diligence paid off. The draft of the Mughal and Pahari section was ready – tabulated, intelligible and complete the day before I was due to leave. Letters had been sent off to WGA, Mamoo Amjad[3] and the Shis.[4] Shahnaz's shopping list compiled, Fidge's[5] vital statistics measured, my catalogue bound in a presentable folder, my

---

[2] Archer, W.G., *Indian Paintings from the Punjab Hills* (London, 1973).
[3] Syed Amjad Ali (my mother's youngest brother) was serving at the time as Regional Manager in the National Bank of Pakistan's London office.
[4] Shi Siauw Seng and his wife Lan had been my friends during my days as an articled clerk in London.
[5] The pet name we gave to Momina because she fidgeted so much as a baby.

ticket by Pan Am's Jumbo 747 booked, my vaccination papers
obtained painlessly [for a small fee] – in short, I was ready for the trip
to London, to 'return back home'. It would be my first visit to London
since leaving it, almost nine years earlier, in the summer of 1965.

CHAPTER 4

JUMPING SHIP

I left for Luzern and London on 7 February 1974. The programme approved by the Ministry of Production had been that Javed Talat (as a director on the PTCL Board) and I would have meetings with the senior hierarchy of Massey Ferguson at Luzern and then continue to London for a visit to the MF plant at Coventry.

Pan Am had just begun their wide-bodied 747s and it felt strange to see the plane take off with its wings sagging, like some overweight albatross. The interior of the aircraft resembled an elongated airport lounge, crammed to capacity. What did impress me was the efficiency of the American stewardesses, each of whom represented one ethnic grouping in the US – a blonde, a Hispanic, an Oriental, an Afro-American. They handled the passengers with a mechanical efficiency that responded promptly to calls but clearly did not encourage any temperamental requests.

Before leaving I had arranged to meet my friends the Shis at Beirut airport. The last time I had seen the Shi family was in the 1960s. After qualifying from Maurice Apple & Co., Shi Siauw Seng returned to Indonesia to serve out the period of his indenture. He had come to London on a scholarship funded by the Indonesian Government and therefore had given an undertaking that he would work for it for five years. As soon as that period was over, he applied to the UN and got a job at UNRWA, monitoring the Palestinian refugees in Beirut. We had not met for ten years but had remained in touch by post, and it was in one of his letters that he suggested that I might consider working joining him in UNRWA.

In those days, security at airports was minimal, and so it was possible for the Shis and I to spend the transit time having a cup of coffee in the lounge. Neither he nor his wife Lan had aged at all.

From Zurich where we landed, Javed and I were driven to Luzern and accommodated in the Montana hotel overlooking the lake. Early next morning, I took a walk along the lake in the bracing cold air. After breakfast, Javed and I were taken on a tour of Luzern by car to kill time before we were deposited at the MF offices at 11.30 for our first meeting with the MF big-wigs.

The MF team who received us was led by Mr. Vajk, then Executive Vice President (Asia, Africa and Australia). His very seniority indicated the seriousness with which MF treated the Pakistan government's concern over the local manufacturing programme. In essence, when Massey Ferguson had signed the agreement with the Government for the manufacture of Massey Ferguson tractors locally, it held out that it would be in a position to supply 5,000 units annually in CKD condition for assembly within Pakistan. Such a volume was necessary to justify any investment in local manufacturing facilities, whether for major parts by the public sector or for smaller items by the private sector. The premise of such an agreement was that the original manufacturer would maintain a continuous supply of tractors in CKD condition and gradually, as local manufacturing capability improved and a dependable alternative stream became available, the imported components would be deleted until the local tractor could be assembled from parts procured only from local sources.

During their negotiations, MF had touted the example of the Yugoslavs who since the 1950s had developed their own brand of tractor. The Yugoslavs called it the IMT, as they could no longer use the MF brand name.

MF's popularity became its disability. An increase in world-wide demand in the preceding years for MF tractors, particularly the MF 135 model (a middle range horse-power tractor that was especially liked by Pakistani farmers), coincided with a drop in availability, caused mainly by industrial strikes at the main MF plant at Coventry. So, instead of the 5,000 tractors the Government had hoped for, MF could confirm only 1,500 by October 1974, and even that was not a guaranteed figure.

In its keenness to kick-start the local manufacturing programme, Mr. Bhutto's government had not foreseen that we in Pakistan, being the newest entrant in the MF supply chain, would be accorded the lowest priority. MF owed an obligation to those countries which had embarked on a similar local manufacturing programme, such as Spain which had achieved 95 % deletion but was still dependent on MF for critical components. Logically, MF could not divert tractors to us simply because we demanded them.

No matter how hard Javed and I tried, MF remained non-committal. As the person who had been the lynchpin of the negotiations with MF when the original deal was signed, Javed needed to defend his position. He threatened, I cajoled, but we could not get MF to increase the supplies, either in CKD or even PKD (partially-knocked down) condition. What we were able to extract from MF was a price hold on 2,378 tractors which MF had agreed to supply us at the previous year's (1972-73) prices, provided we opened a letter of credit for them by 31 December 1973. On my return to Pakistan later, I managed to get the money from the banks on 30 December and having opened the letter of credit with a day to spare, sent MF a telex message, thereby binding them. MF did not think that, with our foreign exchange situation being tight, we would be able to meet our commitment. It became obvious from their reaction that they had been caught off-guard. They had to supply next year's tractors at last year's prices.

The meeting in Luzern had been to reassure the Government of Pakistan through Javed that it stood by its commitment to the progressive manufacturing programme. All it requested was time.

Discussion on the actual availability of tractors was left by Luzern to its offices in London which controlled the MF plant at Coventry. In London, we were given quasi-VIP treatment by the MF people in London. Dinner at Tiberio's, a sanitised curry lunch at the Oriental Club off Oxford Street hosted by a Mr. Boon (who looked like a waxen effigy of the Duke of Windsor), and a trip to the MF Banner Lane plant at Coventry, where as we entered the gates, Mr. Sjogren pointed out the Pakistan flag which had been hoisted to herald our arrival.

Touching though all these gestures were, they were not enough to satisfy Javed, nor a substitute for actual tractors. After touring the MF plant at Coventry, it became clear that MF was not prevaricating. They had more orders than tractors. They had none to spare.

On many occasions, Javed accused MF of getting what it wanted which was a long-term supply and manufacturing agreement. In return, the Pakistan

Government had received a promise of supplies. Tractors tomorrow, tractors yesterday, but no tractors today.

The meetings with MF occupied less than half a morning each day. For the rest of the day, while Javed was in London for the first week, I had to take him shopping in Oxford Street and accompany him into the shady shops in Tottenham Court Road. London in the 1970s had broken away from the puritanical strictures of the 1960s. I noticed that the soft-porn industry had overflowed into Tottenham Court Road from nearby Soho. An enduring image I have is of an Indian housewife, weighed down by shopping bags, standing cold, patient and disconsolate on the pavement, while her husband went inside the porn shop alone to have his private thrill.

Javed believed rightly that the only way of forcing a commitment from the MF management was to confront them with a questionnaire which would flush out their intentions. I helped him draft it and then was allowed to stay on in London for another week to ensure MF's reply.

For me, that was a God-send. Because I stayed in at the flat of my maternal uncle Amjad Ali (then posted as the Regional Manager of the National Bank of Pakistan), I had money saved from the precious daily allowance the Government allowed for foreign travel.

Shahnaz had given me a list of things she wanted – Mary Quant cosmetics from the new Biba store that had opened in Kensington High Street, and outfits for our daughter Momina from Mothercare. My own longings, after a seven-year abstinence, were assuaged by visits to my favourite haunts – Maggs' bookshop in Berkeley Square, the antiquarian book dealers in Museum street opposite the British Museum, and the Indian Section of the Victoria & Albert Museum, where I refreshed my recollection of its miniature paintings.

From my diary, I notice that I soaked in the latest films – Liza Minnelli's *Cabaret*, Edward Fox's *The Day of the Jackal*, George Segal's *A Touch of Class*, and for some reason linked perhaps to suppressed homesickness, Satyajit Ray's *Company Unlimited*.

My private indulgence was a trip to the theatre, and again my diary jogs my memory and reminds me that I saw Rex Harrison in *Henry IV*, a performance of Bizet's *Carmen* at Sadler's Wells, and my favourite actress Ingrid Bergman in *The Constant Wife*. I went to the backstage door after the performance and waited for her to emerge. She came out, dressed in a mink coat, accompanied by her husband Lars Schmidt. She obliged us clamouring fans by signing our programmes.

"I still remember your performance as Joan of Arc," I gushed, adding: "You made such an impression on me that I almost converted to Christianity."

She smiled and deflected the compliment with: "I am not sure I could have been that good!"

For me, quite honestly, discussions with MF were a means of going to London. The end was to spend time with Dr. W.G. Archer and to have him examine the draft of my catalogue of the miniature paintings collection in the Lahore Museum. Bill had by then retired from Victoria & Albert Museum, London. He and I had maintained a correspondence over the years since I left London in 1966. This had intensified while I was at the Lahore Museum in 1966-67, and continued while he was preparing his monumental two volume survey – *Indian Paintings from the Punjab Hills* (1973) - for which I provided him the information and photographs he needed.

Looking back on our friendship, I realise how sage his advice had been and how supportive he became in my literary endeavours. For example, when I sent him an immature manuscript of some twelve or so Pahari paintings with a commentary on each, he did not dismiss it outright. Instead, he mentioned that it could be published (he mentioned Bruno Cassirer's firm) but that I would have to subsidise it. Both of us knew that was beyond my means. Undeterred, I sent him another careful typed and bound but again superficial manuscript on the *Devi-Mahatmya* folios in the Lahore Museum[1], he suggested that I might perhaps amplify it before submitting it to any publisher.

I struck gold with him with an article on a *Gita Govinda* series painted in Basohli in 1730 A.D. The date (Vikram Samvat 1787) was contained in a colophon on the reverse of the last picture. It was clearly decipherable but it was the only part of the lengthy colophon that was beyond dispute. The rest of the colophon became vulnerable to conflicting interpretations by western scholars like Bill Archer and Basil Gray of the British Museum, and by their Indian counterparts like Karl Khandalavala, Brijen Goswamy and Dr. M.S. Randhawa. Each published his understanding of the colophon. Suddenly, two

---

[1] I had discovered from the concluding lines of a colophon on the reverse of the last folio that this series, painted in Guler, had been completed in 1781 AD, a fact of which most scholars were unaware.

camps emerged – Dr. Randhawa sided with Bill while Khandalavala joined Basil Gray. They attacked each other in print, each group asserting the accuracy of their interpretation of the colophon.

In essence, it contained two key words – *Manaku* and *Malini*. At issue was the identity of each. Was Manaku the painter and Malini the female patroness who had commissioned the ambitious series of 150 folios? Was Malini a hitherto unknown female painter? Or was malini simply the metre in which the inscription had been composed?

I was too much of a novice to enter such a debate, especially as I knew no Takri and therefore was hardly in a position to decipher the inscription myself or to provide an alternative translation. However, I was the only person (so far as I could glean from published research on this set) who had physically examined all the thirty-six paintings in the Lahore Museum. This precious cache of thirty-six paintings was particularly significant because, even though other folios from this series had been dispersed between various public and private collections across the world, the Lahore Museum possessed both the first and last folios in the series. It was possible for me to co-relate the paintings with the text of the *Gita Govinda* poem and then attempt a reconstruction of the series.

Each folio contained not only the relevant text from the *Gita Govinda* poem inscribed on its reverse, but also bore a number in Devanagri. Using the numbers to put them in order was not a problem. Locating the place of the inscription within the text of the poem proved more vexing. I achieved that by memorising the first three and the last three words of the inscription on each folio. Then I scanned visually the entire poem until I located the verses. It took some time, as I was unfamiliar with the Devanagri alphabet.

Having put them in sequence, I then re-examined the paintings. Now that they were in some sort of sequential order, I noticed that there were perceptible stylistic differences as the folios progressed. It indicated that more than one hand had worked on this series, perhaps a family of artists. This reinforced Brijen Goswamy's thesis that he published in his pioneering essay *Pahari Painting: The Family as a Basis of Style*.[2]

I felt this discovery important enough to attempt an article on it. I began

---

[2] *Marg Publications* (Bombay/Mumbai), September 1968.

it on 30 January 1972. It took almost six months of intermittent work (usually in the evenings and on weekends) to complete. When I sent it to Bill Archer, to my relief he thought it good enough to publish. He posted it to Dr. M.S. Randhawa (like Bill, an ICS officer) in Chandigarh. In what I can only describe as an act of courage (I should mention that this was in 1973 when post-1971 relations between India and Pakistan were at an abysmal low), Dr. Randhawa arranged to have it published in Lalit Kala Akademi's journal *Roopa Lekha*.

The article appeared in late 1973. Bill wrote to tell me that Mark Zebrowksi (then researching in Deccani painting) would be bringing off-prints of the article. When Mark did finally land in Karachi, he told me what a narrow escape he had had. He had put the off-prints of my article in his back-pack. En route, his plane had been hijacked in Beirut. The hijackers ordered the passengers to disembark, allowing them to take only portable luggage. Mark scrambled off clutching his back-pack and then had to endure the heart-wrenching sight of the plane containing the stowed luggage, including his suitcase, go up in flames. The only things he could salvage were the clothes he was wearing and the contents of his back-pack – the off-prints of my article on the *Gita Govinda*.

During that first 'homecoming' to London, I stayed with my uncle Amjad and his wife Bano at their flat in Kensington High Street. The two weekends I had available to me I spent with Bill Archer and his wife Mildred ('Tim-bibi') at their house in Provost Road. He and I sat at a desk in their attic which they had converted into a guest bedroom to accommodate their Indian friends like Dr. Randhawa, Karl Khandalavala, Rai Krishnadasa, and Gopi Krishna Kanoria.

He held the two volumes of my draft bound manuscript in his hands while I fed him the black and white photographs for each picture. Systematically and painstakingly, he went through each of my catalogue entries.

Forty years later, I still have the copy containing Bill's pencil corrections. Some of his suggestions I could not argue with. For example, he advised me to use a metric system of measurement. It was easier for the compositor to have running centimetres than fractions of inches. He wanted the dates of the rulers in parentheses after the ruler's name. And he wished me to follow the format he had used in his own book, with explanatory notes appearing under the heading 'Comment'.

His familiarity with Indian miniature paintings was as vast as the subject itself, certainly far greater than mine. I had not seen any of the Indian collections and so relied upon him to provide informed comparisons.

For instance, an attribution to a raja I had identified as 'a Guler noble, possibly Prakaram Chand of Guler', Bill overruled with the information that it was in fact of Raja Amrit Pal of Basohli. A sketch of Raja Anirudh Chand of Kangra (the corpulent son and successor to one of the most famous Pahari patrons Raja Sansar Chand) I had dated to the mid 19th century. Bill disagreed. His comments in the margin of my text read: 'Important as being one of the very few (if not unique) portraits of Anirudh (born 1786? – here looking about 40 (?) as he was in 1826?'

Bill's feud with Brijen Goswamy was still nascent - the older British scholar vs. the younger Indian challenger. In time it would aggravate into a serious rivalry and become a source of deep concern and anguish to them both. In 1974, Bill's comment on my Basohli *Gita Govinda* catalogue entries gave a clue of his state of mind: 'Should you not give in summary form the view of the series which you took in your article? Should you not also say why the series must be given to <u>Basohli</u> (and not to Guler as asserted by Goswamy)?'

Our second weekend together (16-17 February) was all work, with a brief break to go on a trip to Kenwood House, on Hampstead Hill. Although Bill had retired from the Victoria & Albert Museum, being given the honorific Keeper Emeritus, his wife Tim-bibi continued to work at the India Office Library & Records.[3] She reminded me of a sparrow – small and energetic. Her forte was art done by or for the British until 1947. I realised the extent to which she had selflessly subordinated her own literary researches to Bill's when I asked her who had typed the text of Bill's manuscript. The final printed double column volume contained 448 pages.

"Who do you think?" she replied. "The *slave*, of course."

In addition to acting as Bill's amanuensis, Tim had published in 1969 her two volume study of *British Drawings in the India Office Library*. It catalogued a number of drawings and sketches done in the 19th century and

---

[3] It has since been integrated into the British Library.

was of interest to me because it contained work by artists who had visited the areas that are now Pakistan.

I was keen on seeing the originals. I arranged to meet her one afternoon at the IOL's new offices in Blackfriars. Everything there was modern, neat and clean – a vast improvement to the dusty, ad hoc disarray at the old King Charles Street premises which the IOL shared with the Foreign & Commonwealth Relations Office.

Very obligingly, Tim-bibi brought out water-colours by artists such as H. F. Ainslie, A.F. Belassis, Charles Masson, and H. A. Oldfield. Of particular interest to me was the original diary maintained by the British veterinarian William Moorcroft who had visited the Punjab in 1820 before continuing his journey to Bokhara in search of horses. He died there in 1825. Miraculously the journals he maintained of his remarkable journey survived and were retrieved after his death in the wilds of Balkh.

I asked if I could see the album of paintings that Prince Dara Shikoh had commissioned for his wife Nadirah Begum. Tim-bibi brought it out in a velvet-lined box and for a few minutes I stood transfixed, holding it as that unfortunate Mughal couple had done centuries earlier.

I called in at my old firm Maurice Apple & Co, and had lunch with the partners headed by Martin Van Straten. Whether I had changed much since I had last seen Martin in 1965, he had not. He commented on how my public school accent had deteriorated. It obviously still riled him that he - a war-time Dutch immigrant - had never had 'the benefit' of a public school education.

I rang the Rimmingtons at 12 Barcombe Avenue (my former digs) and learned from her husband that Mrs. Rimmington had bought a small house in Brighton and had shifted there. It had been her ambition to have a place by the sea, and all the years she took in lodgers, she squirreled away her savings until she could afford her dream. I rang her and took instructions on how to reach her.

Her dream house, I discovered, was a somewhat grimy semi-attached place, not much different from 12 Barcombe Avenue where she had spent so many unhappy years with Mr. Rimmington. But what mattered to her was that it was Brighton, and her own home, not something rented. We had lunch together and I left, as I had done when I quit Barcombe Avenue in 1965, with her again in a flood of tears.

This extra week allowed me to indulge myself while the Massey Ferguson people worked on their reply to our questionnaire. I collected their letter on 26 February and the next day I caught the Pan Am flight 002 to Frankfurt, Istanbul and Beirut. There I stayed overnight with the Shis as Mr. Shi was very keen that I should be interviewed by his boss Vernon Taylor. On our way to the UNRWA offices, I asked Mr. Shi if he could take me to a camp of Palestinian refugees.

He drove his Volkswagen to an intersection and pointing towards a main street, he said: "That is the Palestinian refugee camp."

"Can't we go in?"

"No," he replied. "That is as far as we are allowed. If we want to meet anyone specific, we asked for him at those crossroads and he is then brought out to us."

Whether this was the reason or the stultified atmosphere in the UNRWA office where I noticed no one could enter an office without permission, despite the touted 'open-door policy', I decided that UNRWA was not for me. Shi remained with UNRWA until he retired and then migrated with Lan to Canada.

Back at the PTCL office in Karachi, I prepared my tour report in time to show it to Javed Talat. It contained no surprises. While we could not obtain any more tractors than the 1,500 MF committed, we had been able to secure tractors at last year's prices.

Conceding that MF would not be able to meet our local demand, the Government's knee-jerk reaction was to permit imports of other brands, even though it knew that a proliferation of tractors of different models would adversely impact the MF progressive manufacturing programme. This gave free rein to the other auto companies like Naya Daur Motors to begin importing and trading tractors of brands other than MF as they had done before the formation of PTCL. In effect the raison d'être of PTCL as the sole importer/regulator of tractors in the public sector was put in jeopardy. I found myself on the bridge of a Titanic doomed even before it left the shipyard.

On 16 March, a meeting took place that made me realise that I was dealing with machinations at a level I could not reach. On my return from it, I made extensive notes of what transpired:

"Have you been ordered to attend the meeting?" Frank Alfrey asked, with customary tactlessness. Remembering the sneaky way the change of Chairmanship had been hidden from me by Frank Alfrey and Akram Ghauri, conspiring together, I could construe from his remark that the possible merger of PTCL and Millat Tractors was to be discussed, and that I was to be excluded from the conclave which was being summoned to elect the new pope of PTCL.

At some time early on Saturday morning, I received a telephone call from Jalil Alam's secretary asking me to send the organizational chart of PTCL to the BIM office. I took the chart personally. Playing on the likelihood of Mufti's secretary not knowing the exact instructions I may have received, I strode into HSM's suite of rooms. The chart was sent in, and with it the pointed information of my presence.

HSM's office has been expensively but ill-constructed. The walls are teak veneered with the ones in his office studded with gilt Grecian urns and rosettes. Fancy, certainly, but not sufficient to keep the sound in, with the result that anyone, but anyone, even the uninvited Finance Manager of PTCL, can hear anything material being discussed (as all material things are discussed loudly) quite clearly and without strain.

The consternation during the meeting within while I sat without was material and loud. First, mutual recriminations for having let the cat out the bag, then muffled arrangements for hiding the bag altogether. HSM padded out of his office and mumbled bravely: "I think there has been some mistake, but anyway I'm glad you came for we may need you later."

'You bet you will,' I thought to myself.

When I did enter Mufti's office, the meeting reminded me of the tiring journey undertaken by Queen Alexandra and her husband the new King Edward VII in 1901. Allocations of the various rooms within Buckingham Palace were the purpose of that tour, but try as hard as the king would, he could not get his charming but single-minded consort to think beyond getting her secretary/confidant Miss Charlotte Knollys 'well lodged'. And so it was with HSM. His prime intention was to see Frank Alfrey 'well-lodged' in PTCL.

"What management structure would you like in PTCL?" I asked HSM.

"On the lines of the Executive Boards, drawn from within the company."

"What designation do you want to give the Chief Executive?" [Hashmi's title had been General Manager.]

"Managing Director."

"And who would you like to be PTCLs' MD?"

There was a pause. HSM coughed and looked hesitant. Jalil Alam, Akram Ghauri, Frank Alfrey, and Wazir Ali Shaikh looked at me. I sat with my pencil poised above the chart to be completed and look steadily at HSM.

"Well, I thought Frank could be the MD."

"Right," I replied. "Now, who would you like at the next rung?"

HSM breathed a sigh of relief audibly. Jalil Alam winked at Frank Alfrey and moved his chair backward, away from the table as if to indicate that his mind also had detached itself from the proceedings. Akram Ghauri lit his pipe. The Holy Trinity looked satisfied as only Gods granting boons to mortals can.'

A week or so later, on 25 March, the lengthening arm of the Government reached the sixth floor of the National Shipping Corporation Building and the offices of the Board of Industrial Management. The free-wheeling and free-spending BIM executives found themselves being harnessed by Government traces. The BIM companies were informed that no projects would be allowed to proceed without the prior approval of the Government, a pre-requisite for which was the PC-I – an abbreviation for the Planning Commission Proforma 1.

They should have known what to expect. Even in Ghandhara Industries before it was nationalised, General Habibullah had trained them to present their capital expenditure proposals in a feasibility report. They were expected to present it personally, to justify it, and then as a twist the General would ask them to argue against it. Like that, he made them flush out themselves the weaknesses that they might have been hidden or glossed over.

The cavalier attitude of these executives when they were told that they had kow-tow to the Government can be gauged from my recollection of the meeting:

'**25 March 1974:**

A mad meeting convened by HSM and Akram Ghauri to expose the automotive companies to the PC-I form required by submitted to the Planning Commission for inclusion of the projects n the National Budget. At just over half an hour's notice, all the representatives of the auto companies were called to congregate in HSM's office. No agenda had been prepared, therefore none communicated. Each MD brought his own team. By the time the meeting was to start, there was a veritable crowd which overflowed from Akram Ghauri's room into the waiting room and finally up to the very doorstep of HSM's office, so that when he opened his door, he was almost swamped by a surging tide of MDs and their Chief Accountants.

It was soon realised that there would not be enough room for everyone, chairs were brought in and continued to be brought in even as the meeting concluded.

The subject of the meeting was the PC-1 Form which Akram read out like a Royal Proclamation, with sterile ceremony. HSM quickly summarized the projects he wanted included – the tyre project, expansion of the Bela engine plant, and the National Motors wheel rim plant.

"The tractor progressive manufacturing project can wait until next year," HSM said airily in my direction.

"Up to you," I replied, "but I would like to mention that in the wheel-rim feasibility report prepared by NML, provision has been made for only 2,500 sets of tractor wheels whereas the target for 1975 imports is 15,000 units. The investment in tooling jigs etc for the tractors is Rs 13 lakhs for an annual output of 10,000 wheels, and Rs 12 lakhs for 22,000 cars and truck wheels. Surely the priority therefore should be for the tractor industry which shall bear most of the cost per unit?"

There was a silence, until Hilal whispered loudly to HSM: "I thought you had taken care of him!"

"So had I," muttered HSM and then laughed nervously.

The multi-million rupee investment plans of PACO for the next year were disposed off in twenty minutes. [This lack of preparation cost PACO dearly. At the meeting of the Planning Commission in Islamabad, Jalil Alam who had been sent to advocate PACO's case found himself being reprimanded for not adhering to Government procedures and had to watch PACOs proposals being rejected. It received a token sum of Rs 5 lakhs with which to conduct a feasibility report.'

April had hardly begun when I was required to be in Islamabad to attend a high-level meeting on the import of tractors. The meeting was chaired by Mr. Feroze Qaiser, then Special Assistant to the Prime Minister on Economic Affairs. Mr. Qaiser, a chartered accountant, had a soft ingratiating manner of speaking and, given a chance, would have accommodated the requirements of everyone around the table. Those most interested in having their demands met and receiving his imprimatur (and because of it, Bhutto's approval) were Malik Khuda Bukhsh Bucha[4] and Mian Riazuddin[5]. Bucha had an interest in the Belarus tractor from Russia and Riazuddin in the IMT from Yugoslavia. The meeting decided that the target for 1974-75 would be 15,000 tractors. 'The lone voice,' I noted in my diary afterwards, was that of Masood Zaman (Joint Secretary, Commerce), who struck a discordant note by asking whether the county could afford so many tractors when it did not have the foreign exchange to import them.

The politics surrounding Frank Alfrey's appointment as MD PTCL had me oscillating between Karachi, Lahore (where Millat Tractors' factory was located) and Islamabad, where Mufti invested his time strengthening his bonds with Feroze Qaiser, much to the chagrin of Frank whom he made wait outside Qaiser's office for hours.

While I was at Islamabad, I received a summons from Javed Talat asking me if I could come to his office in D Block so that he could introduce his younger brother who wanted advice on how to become a chartered accountant. We were still discussing the options when suddenly Syed Babar Ali entered the room. With barely a nod and a perfunctory acknowledgment of my

---

[4] Bhutto's Special Assistant of Agriculture.
[5] Chairman, Agricultural Development Bank of Pakistan.

presence (leave alone of our relationship), he ignored me until Javed Talat handed me a folder on the Baghban tractor project. I opened it, read its contents, and then without a word handed it back to Javed. This indication of a familiarity with Javed and his confidence in me was not lost on SBA. Within a second, he warmed noticeably (for Javed's benefit, if not mine) and became so cordial that he even managed an effusive farewell. Javed then told me that he was leaving the Ministry of Production to join the National Fertiliser Corporation as a Director. He asked me: "Are you surprised?"

"No. I suspected as much when we were in London. I knew the direction you planned to take. I just did not know the destination."

Shahnaz and Momina had joined me in Islamabad and so as soon as our car came from Karachi, we left on 16 April for a tour of the northern areas and Swat. My diary entries for these days were more detailed than usual. I had more time to write.

'Darling N [Shahnaz], Fidge and I left for Nowshera and then on to Peshawar to collect Auntie Nayyar. A splendid vision of Attock Fort from across the river, with the grey silt almost obliterating the broad steps of the disused *ghat* at the riverside. The steps back up the slope to the walls of the Fort, which curve along and then upwards to the right, cradling the barracks and mosque within.

Having come to Peshawar, how could one not perform the pilgrimage to Bara? We drove there and spent a tiring afternoon looking at over-priced articles that the accommodating Afghan government allows to be consigned to it. Most of the stuff shoddy and unreasonable, and useless except to the most determined of shoppers, many of whom seemed to be the types who had made their money fast and therefore did not mind if it left them with an equal velocity.

Called on the Chitrali 'royal' family. First on Malika (the daughter of one of the dispossessed Chitrali rulers who lived in simple discomfort on the wrong side of the railway tracks), and then at Chitral House on Mall Road to meet her brother (and therefore her enemy) Prince Assad – a short, dumpy but sharp man whom Agha-sahib had by-passed when deciding on the succession on the death (murder?) of his elder brother Saif ul Mulk. It seems, according to N, that the ambitious Assad caused to have his elder brother's plane to crash in the hope of becoming the ruler, and secured his claim by quickly marrying the widow (his sister-in-law) before the fortieth of the dead husband. Agha-sahib, having read his *Hamlet,* declared the four year old son of Saif ul Mulk the ruler and appointed someone senior as his Regent. Much gnashing of teeth must have gone on behind those grim Chitrali lips, but not sufficient to render them ineffective for future use.

Uncle Raza, oblivious to this background of intrigue and skull-duggery, blandly asked Assad whether he was the Mehtar. Only the excuse that Uncle Raza had been in an Indian jail and therefore his mind had been seriously impaired as result saved him from Assad's withering expression.

Dinner at the Hong Kong restaurant. Fidge insistent upon eating with chopsticks! We sat *en famille* in a small air-conditioned antechamber. Suddenly, during the meal, the curtains parted and mine host the Chinese owner appeared to ask if all was well. Upon being reassured that we were, he departed and the curtains closed with equal abruptness.

"What was that?" N asked me.

"Obviously the cabaret!"

17 April:

Not quite sure where we wanted to go in Swat, we set off with a full tank and a copy of Aurel Stein's *On Alexander's Track to the Indus* (1929) that I had borrowed from the Archaeological Library for light reading. How useful this proved to be as a guide book!

Drove through Mardan, past the ageing premier Sugar Mills (one thing is for sure – the profits are definitely not being ploughed back into the factory!), then to Jabban Falls, an artificially created outlet of the two mile long canal dug along the Malakand hills from Swat side to the Yusufzai plains. The lift from the powerhouse to the hilltop was out of order, which was just as well for had we used it, we would have missed the pleasant climb along the rushing, cascading waters. A snack of Peshawari white cheese, tangerines and biscuits and then we set along the winding, broad path up to Malakand Fort.

The view that caught Stein's attention of a valley rendered fertile by 'a new river (that) leapt and foamed' was of particular interest to me for, from the height of the road, one could see quite clearly the effect of the steps cut every forty or fifty yards in the canal. From the canal bank, one was aware merely of periodical depressions into which the water lurches, but from on high the pattern and meaning of these depressions was most dramatically visible. The canal looked like a long jade-green ribbon with horizontal bands of silvery tinsel. The effect was quite breathtaking and worth photographing, had I not been so nervous of the drive up the steep road. Fortunately, today there was some sort of strike by the local bus and truck drivers, as a result of which the road was comparatively clear. Malakand Fort was poised like some bald and sleepy eagle on the crest of the hill-top. On the way down, I noticed a prominently located, assertive house on a promontory. We continued into the driveway up to the chowkidar's charpoy.

"Whose house is this?" I asked brashly. Had I read my Stein before the journey, his reply and indeed my question would have been superfluous.

"It's the house of the Political Agent, Malakand," he said, in a tone sagging with tolerance.

Suddenly I recollected the photograph of the view from the Political Agent's house, published by Stein as Fig 1. The greenness of the valley set against the purplish mountains made it seem like a different place in reality.

Lunch we ate in a rather grubby road-side café whose name and fare are best forgotten. Fidge had developed quite a passion for Coca-Cola and refused to allow any bottle to pass her without exacting a toll.

A cool, leafy covering over the road on the stretch to Saidu Sharif, and at the end of this grove the stupa of Raja Uttarasena, visible from the road. It is still in substantially the same condition as when photographed by Stein, except for the addition of an inadequate barbed wire fence. Its location, nestling in the basin of an arc of hills, prominent yet accessible to the pious pedestrian pilgrim, was another 'pleasing example of the care with which ancient Buddhist monks selected sacred spots'.[6]

I took a quick photograph and then drove on to Saidu itself. The Swat Hotel almost swallowed us as we turned up the rise into the main street. The garden was spectacular- roses of almost every colour and shade, all in full and fresh bloom, complemented here and there by the harder hues of vivid red poppies. The weather was clement – sunny and deliciously warm.

We noticed the PTDC office in a hotel room in the old block, built according to a plaque on the central frieze in 1938. The attendant on duty was a smart and presentable young man called Jehanzeb Sohail, who completed bookings for a one night at Madyan and two nights at Kalam.

It was almost 5.30 p.m. when we arrived at Saidu Sharif. By the time we had bathed and dressed, there was little point of doing more than strolling in the rose garden overlooking the south-west of the Swat Valley. Fidge dressed in her bright red frock, red tights and red shoes, and with two red roses to match in her chignon her head. She looked a doll.

During dinner, Prince Amirzeb of Swat passed our table on his way to meet some foreign guests. I remarked to N that I had known him since I was a child (we were both at Aitchison College at the same time), and was just answering a barrage of questions as to why, if I knew him so well, had he not bothered to greet me, when he passed by again, this time on his way out. Spotting me, he stopped to greet us. He insisted that we call on him next morning. I had made a programme with JS to take him with us to Miandam, but now that Amirzeb had asked us, it would have been impertinent to have left without paying our respects to him.

18 April

Ready by 10. Straight to Amirzeb's house, which is just close to the hotel. He was seated in a group of bearded elders and politicians, earning his living. Seeing us, he left them and joined us on the comparatively private front verandah. The bare garden with a

---

[6] Stein (1929), p.17.

suggestion of rose bushes lay before us, to the right an air-conditioned guest-house and surrounding the whole compound a high wall over which the mountains towards Kalam and the north were visible. He hasn't lost any of his nervousness and spoke with a stuttering complacency about ZAB. Having refused all offers to compromise with the PM, lest his people regard his alliance with the PPP as a betrayal, he could nevertheless smooth his conscience by accepting two permits for tractors and another two for motor cars. It was interesting to hear him hold forth on his 'political independence', particularly after he had already told us that he and his wife[7] had been asked for tea by Mrs. ZAB, albeit through her private secretary.

From his house we drove to Marghzar, where the old marble palace or Safed Mahal is being converted into a hotel by Prince Amirzeb. The palace is at the end of a pretty drive but has a somewhat restricted view, being in the armpit of the valley. The central garden still contains its carved marble furniture – broken in places and rooted permanently in the ground. Symbolic perhaps of the treatment by the Swati rulers – you stayed where you were put by them, with no possibility of moving away from your seat.

The hotel I fear may soon after it becomes operational degenerate into either a bordello (if it is kept running) or become another Hotel Shahrazad (if it petrifies). In either case, Prince Amirzeb's interests would have been served admirably.

Lunch at the hotel – a four course meal with more pretension than protein, and then off to Miandam. The drive was extremely pleasant along a firm metalled road. Most of the small hamlets had a school, dispensary and police station each painted in a custard yellow with a red roof, and all clearly identifies in bold English capitals with the year of completion. It was revealing that none of these buildings bore a date earlier than 1959 and none later than 1968.

Miandam lay again like the Safed Mahal at the end of its valley. The rest-house was well-situated, overlooking the steeply terraced cleft below. I was not surprised to learn that this group of rest-houses, out of which two have been retained by the Wali, were built by him.

---

[7] Jamila, a daughter of President Ayub Khan.

Understandably, these Walis chose to live with their backs to the mountain.

Dinner by lantern light as there was no electricity. The generator surrendered by the Wali is not in working order. In fact, according to the Swati attendants still loyal to the Wali, nothing in Swat has been in working order since the 'Gorment of Pakistan' took over the State.

Clear bright starlit night outside, with tiny fireflies of light against the dark hill sides.

19 April

Jehanzeb's pet crony - a lumpy maitre d'hôtel called Khairullah – invited us to his house which lay at the very top of the hill. N & I fortified ourselves with a solid breakfast of *parathas* and fried eggs so that we could attempt the ascent along a barely discernible track. I carried Fidge, who rather thoughtfully did not aggravate her weight by misbehaving.

On the way we passed a chute constructed on shaven logs upon which cut logs were brought down the mountainside. I was full of admiration at the ingenuity of the efficient Swatis until I noticed the logs making their way down the chute were being pulled by a poor labourer down the chute.

The climb was arduous. By the time we reached the top, N & I could have collapsed. The view was worth the effort - to the left snow-covered mountains, to the far right more along the ridge leading to Kalam. Below, the entire valley winding towards the central gorge that is the main Swat valley.

We returned in time for lunch in the garden and then left for Kalam.

The drive after Madyan was stiff, with dangerous unscheduled turns. One spot where a bus containing schoolchildren had plunged from the height of the road in the swirling Swat river below has been marked with a signboard. Past the wooden footbridge spanning the river at Bahrain, up the winding road banked in some places with pockets of glaciers, we motored enjoying each fresh vista as it presented itself.

By 5.30 p.m. we reached the final bend of the road that was the threshold of Kalam. Our initial view was from a lower plane than the one that had tantalized Stein when – almost fifty years earlier - on 26 April 1926, he looked down from the Korumduke ridge above Peshmal and recorded this recollection: 'Nestling below in the amphitheatre of mountains all still carrying snow lies a fertile little plain, which seems to mark the basin of an ancient lake scooped out probably by glacier action. To eyes that had grown accustomed to deeply eroded gorges, this plain looked quite imposing. Above it, only a little over two miles from our ridge, stretched the long lines of houses built in tiers, that form the chief place of Kalam. It looked quite an inviting place from that distance, with dense forest coming down to it over a gentle glacis of the sheltering range. Such might some prosperous little town appear at the foot of the Swiss Bavarian Alps. It was for me a strangely elevating sensation that though further progress was barred by "political consideration", I had sighted land that seemed by comparison next door to Chitral, Yasin and Tangir.'[8]

Our view and our reaction was all of a lower plane, not because there was anything less attractive in the scenery but because it had been altogether much easier to come by to us than it had been for Stein. He had approached Kalam at almost the same time of the year, within days in fact of the same spring month of April, but instead of the warming sunshine that attended us, he endured a temperature a little above freezing point. Because it was now warmer, the snow lay on the prominent peaks surrounding the bowl containing Kalam village. The two cabin PTDC rest-house was mounted next to the Falaksair hotel, overlooking the actual village which was clustered around the Swat river basin. From the verandah of our section we could see - if we stood with our backs to Utrot - the distinctive shark-fin tip of Mount Falaksair.

Instead of the 'political considerations' hampering Stein's progress, we discovered on arrival that early that very morning an army captain and his bride, honeymooning, had been way laid on their way from Gabral to Utrot and had been divested of Rs 950. "At least their honour was intact", the distressed manager of the Falaksair Hotel admitted, taking

---

[8] Stein (1929), pp.96-7.

consolation from this shred of silver lining mentioning in the same breath the tragedy that had befallen one of his European guests. A Dutch girl had been walking with her English husband in the foothills, was stopped by four Swati youths, and the girl raped by them.

I tried to keep a brave face while Jehanzeb proceed to construct plans for a tour of Utrot and Usho the next morning. Shahnaz was wearing her gold bangles, her diamond ring, and I had all our holiday money. We were really sitting ducks in an area where even underfed chickens were at a premium.

If it had not been for our usual indecision which when stretched can be mistaken for extended deliberations, we might have returned to Saidu the same night. Jehanzeb's optimistic assurances, the sight of the PTDC attendants all armed, the cosy fire we ordered (and for a change got) seduced us – dare I use the word? – into staying on at Kalam.

Dinner again by candle-light, and our fare the vegetables we had brought with us from Miandam. Nothing is available here in Kalam. It seems almost incredible and unacceptable that in such a fertile valley with a plenitude of water, sunshine and good earth, they should be a famine of anything edible. With a climate perfect for orchards, the only fruit to be seen were *kinos* selling at 50 paisas each. Eggs were almost a rupee each, and a chicken (if it could be caught) Rs 20. The thing in plenty appeared to be their Swati's' limitless submission to their fate and their environment. Although the Swatis seem to be extremely poor still, for which the evidence of their ragged clothes is proof enough, there is nevertheless an order and neatness in their lives. Their houses are trim, the walls aligned, water-troughs unobtrusively functional, one cannot shake off the feeling that although they may not be much unity or mingling between the valleys, there is an instinctive loyalty to their land and its environs. It is almost as if they have come to terms with Mother Nature and live in some undefined, loose but respectful relationship with her. Their relationship with each other is calmer perhaps than the days of their warring forebears, who crowd the innumerable graveyards one encounters on entering and on leaving every village.

20 April:

Cold, wet night. One blanket below, and two above were still not protection enough. One consolation was that one was able to arrange running hot water. By 9.00 a.m., the sun was up and it became warm. We piled in the car – N, Fidge, Jehanzeb Sohail (who has become quite an entertaining companion and thoughtful host), and Babajan the cook who appointed himself to guard over our lives and the even more precious vegetables.

We drove first to Utrot through exquisite scenery, keeping close to the river as it turned and tossed down the valley. Much of the wood along the way has been felled, and it was sad to contemplate what the scene would be like say twenty-five years from now. The rest-house at Utrot had its own graveyard quite literally in its backyard. Our lunch was cooked fortunately in one of the village kitchens while we drove further to Ghabral along the pot-holed mud road to the final appendix of a bridge. We stopped there and for a while played near the river – N attempting to fish, Fidge wading in the icy waters.

Lunch at the rest house – spinach, cheese and *teenda* (gourds) – after which we returned to Kalam and then onto the other branch of the forked road that took us to Usho and on to Matiltan. Beyond Matiltan, the road was blocked by a glacier. We left the car there, crossed over it and meandered towards the river. A real, rustic delight – sitting on the boulders, watching the rippling emerald green water cascade past, looking up at the snow-capped mountains, inhaling the fragrance from the generous pine trees, and listening to the clamour of one's own thoughts.

Scraped ice from the glacier and gave Fidge her first ice lolly.

We returned to Kalam for tea, prepared the fire in our room and ate walnuts while we waited for dinner. After dinner so spartan that even Gandhi-ji would have approved, we sat inside and listened to the servants as they entertained us with local songs, accompanying themselves with a long-stemmed sitar and an earthenware pitcher. The repertoire was in Pushto, slipping back periodically into an imaginative but inaccurate rendition of *'sajan teri qasam'*. JS got up to dance, as did two of the singing quartet. While they were doing so, there as a tap at the door. Within a split second, the instruments were down and the merry minstrels had their pistols at the ready.

21 April:

Spent the night buried under four blankets, and even then N and I had to cling to each other for warmth.

After a leisurely breakfast, we left Kalam with our virtue and our money intact, and a degree of regret. Our stay brief though it was could not have been more pleasant or relaxing.

Streaked through (for our intentions were quite naked) almost every wayside curio-shop but failed to convince any of the shopkeepers that our appreciation was more valuable than our money.

The afternoon we spent ensconced in the colonial comforts of the Swat hotel. It is provincial in all respects except for its rates which are competitive with any of the Intercontinental hotels. The hotel leaflet announced that the rate would be Rs 10, excluding food.

"How much for the drivers?"

"Rs 15 with food."

22 April:

A *hartal* today, this time by students. The day we arrived in Saidu there had been a congregation of the Wali's army – a motley lot of soldiers dressed alike in black militia shalwar and shirt with a black beret – milling outside the Mingora Public Library like a disturbed nest of black ants.

They were agitating that as the Government had taken over Swat state, they should not be disbanded but absorbed as regulars in the Pakistan Army but with the proviso that they should be posted in their home state. No doubt they shall want better remuneration than the pittance doled out by the Wali – a maund of wheat per year for each soldier – and at the end of a lifetime of service a parting handshake of Rs 500 paid lump-sum to see him through his old age and to defray the costs of his funeral.

We were cautioned on the road to Malakand would be blocked by this raggle-taggle rump of an army, determined to march to Islamabad on foot to present their case to ZAB. The town was closed because of the students, the way out by the ex-army. The only course open to us when the future and the present were blocked was to go into the past.

Armed with my copy of Stein, we motored to Udegram. To have gone up to the battlements along the upper ridges would have taken too long and in the blazing sun unfair to Fidge. We took our bearings from the map in Stein. The road from Saidu is more of a broad path, along one side of which are houses built up to the ruins excavated by Dr. Tucci. The road ended at a graveyard opposite Pir Khushal Baba's ziarat. Above us, visible from the road, loomed the north-western tip of the fortifications. Other ruins merged into the rocky hillside.

Young urchins – the amateur archaeologists of our day – besieged our car. One, appropriately named Sikander[9], produced a coin and a broken metal bangle. Another produced from the folds of his ragged tunic a rusted arrow-head. Some more coins appeared and a double-pointed needle. We bought all of them for Rs 20.

Taking Sikander and Daulatmand (another amateur Tucci) we moved towards Ghalegai and Shankardar. Just before the stupa of King Uttarasena, we stopped near some concrete steps that had been built leading up to the grotto containing the images reproduced by Stein (Fig.23) and identified by him as being of King Uttarasena himself. The images have been smoothened away through continuous fawning by curious careless hands. The large Buddha image carved at the base of this grotto, almost on the road-side, escaped our attention until we looked for it.

Stein's recognition of the rock face resembling an elephant's head as described by Hsuan-tsang (Stein's 'Chinese patron saint') intrigued me. I walked down the road hoping to recognize it from the photograph Stein's book (Fig, 22). I located it but it seemed hardly the prominent landmark that had impressed Hsuan-tsang and Stein. It was only on the return journey later in the day, when approaching it from the Ghalegai side, the road curved to the left and again to the

---

[9] According to Stein, Raja Gira's castle at Udegram was in fact the citadel of Ora that fell to Alexander during his invasion of Swat.

right, the elephant's head became instantly recognisable. Stein's photograph had misled me. The proper approach had not been from the Malakand side but from the village. I realised then what an impact this natural anthropomorphic feature must have had on weary travellers who, on seeing it, knew that around the corner lay the Uttarasena stupa and a night of welcome rest.

From the elephant's head, we drove to Barikot - the old fort of Bazira mentioned by Arrian. The drive to the hill is along the southern face and after a turn to the right along the canal, one comes to a bridge. We left our car at the bridge and continued along the rough foot-path that skirted the northern hem of the hill. N and I climbed almost two-thirds of the way up, sufficiently high to see the fractured remains of battlements and stone walls. The path along the riverside was a short cut for pedestrians and from our height we could see a number moving to and from their afternoon meal. A shepherd boy reclining on the rocks shared our admiration for the dramatic view across the Swat river.

A nap after lunch at the hotel and after having a puncture fixed – the first since the car left Karachi – we moved off in the direction of Abbottabad via Swabi. It had been our intention to go straight to Peshawar and then continue to Abbottabad for the Kaghan Valley. Jehanzeb persuaded us to alter our programme as he wanted to take us around Peshawar.

We took the chance and left for Abbottabad. As we neared the foothills of Malakand, we noticed a group here and there of stragglers from the Wali's ex-army, making their individual way back to Swat. They were sprawled all the way up the mountainside, along both sides of the road, some walking, others sitting, the more determined of them digging in for the night. Joined by Chitrali dissidents, they were at their thickest at the turning before the residence of the Political Agent Malakand. Suddenly their group came to an abrupt end. The road ahead for twenty yards or so was clear. On the far side were ranged the Pakistan Frontier Service Corps, assisted by the Pakistan police, determined not to let the Swatis and the Chitralis pass.

Had I known the condition of the road ahead of us, I would have been less inclined to take our hitchhiking maulvi seriously. In fact, I would not have taken him at all. He seemed innocent enough as he stood on a street corner at Mardan. We asked him the way to Swabi, and before we knew it, he was on his way to Swabi in our car. It did not take him long to squeeze our driver Sharif off the back seat so that he could say his prayers full length. A couple of sharp jolts almost terminated his state of grace. I could hear him telling Sharif how close he felt to death at all times, pointing for emphasis to the wayside graveyards we passed. His crooning a *qirat* did not disturb me as much as his belated warning that the road from Swabi upon which we were travelling was dangerous. Robberies had recently been committed there. After the rape and thefts at Kalam, that is all the assurance I needed.

I dropped our crooning maulvi despite his entreaties that he would like to accompany us 'as our body-guard' as far as Abbottabad. I drove like a demon through Topi to Tarbela. The guards there, not expecting any visitors at that time of night, let us through unchecked and so we were able to drive along the dam itself, illuminated dramatically by strong arc-lights. A stray thought went through my mind that it was really to Ayub Khan that we owe the concept and the initiation of monumental projects such as the dams at Mangla and Tarbela.

We arrived at Abbottabad at about 10.00 p.m. First to the Palace Hotel, which was quite deserted. It would not have been rejected as an admirable setting for a Hitchcock thriller – all corridors with confusing turnings. We chose the Springfield Hotel. Room 5 – the Princess Suite – was opened up for us. The beds looked used and grubby, the sink had no water, the lavatory was eastern-style and out of order. The manager surveyed the situation and took control immediately.

"Bring a bucket of fresh water here," he ordered.

I opened the hotel's copy of *The Pakistan Times* and read its shameful, shameless obituary of Ayub Khan. It began:

Death has laid its icy hand on F.M. Ayub Khan and in the face of death all controversy is hushed. There is an old Lain maxim: Nil nisi bonum –

say nothing but good of the dead – and some might like to strike it as the right chord on the last dirge on the passing of a former President. But no beating of muffled drums can alter the verdict of history. Of course, one must be objective in taking a last look as the career of a fallen colossus, who strutted on international stage for a whole decade and then dropped like a winter leaf – an object of pity in the sunset of his life. It is an irony of fate that the people who applauded Ayub as an elder-statesman and acclaimed him as an Asian de Gaulle finally cast him away as a cardboard Caesar. How the future historians would adjudge his rise and fall is difficult to say, but he deserves a fair epitaph.'

And the PT's epitaph contained this ungenerous assessment of Ayub:

'The man who rose to power by stealth, retained it by design, and made and marred the fortunes of millions, ultimately beat a retreat and sank into oblivion: 'Like an Arab, old and blind; Some caravan had left behind.'

Mian Iftikharuddin from whom General Ayub Khan had wrested control of *The Pakistan Times* newspaper in 1959 has had his revenge.

Shahnaz and I returned from our holiday in Swat via Nowshera to spend a few days with her maternal uncle Col. Raza Khan. He had been a prisoner of war held by the Indians and the effects of his incarceration were still apparent from the measured, guarded way he spoke and moved. For the first time, relaxed in the company of his family, he spoke of the hardships of camp life, sharpened by the fact that as the senior-most military officer and therefore held responsible by the Indians for any infraction by his fellow prisoners.

I recorded in my diary one telling exposé of the mentality of some of our soldiers. According to him, 'it was the procedure that upon admission in the camp, all valuables such as watches and transistors were declared and retained by the Indian authorities in safe custody. On transfer of a POW from one camp to another, the valuables of the transferees were also forwarded. One particular officer was due to be repatriated and went to collect his transistor.'

Being the POW Camp Commandant, Uncle Raza accompanied him. 'The transistor brought out was different and better than the one that the officer had surrendered earlier. The details of the original confiscation were on record, a fact not known to the officer concerned.

"Is this yours?" the Indian officer asked the Pakistani.

"Yes!" the claimant replied emphatically.

"Would you like to make sure it is in working order? Just in case. How many batteries does it need?"

The Pakistani officer looked perplexed. He stammered. The Indian officer came to his victim's rescue. He ordered his subordinate to get eight batteries from the Mess. They were brought and given to the Pakistani.

"See if they are the ones you require," the Indian said politely. "We can have them exchanged if they are not the right ones."

The Pakistan officer looked at the batteries, tried to determine how to open the transistor. Eventually the Indian showed him the way. The batteries were fitted, the transistor found to be in working order, and the Pakistani officer exposed without effort.

Shahnaz had been born in Peshawar and so it seemed appropriate to spend a few days there. We made side trips to Landikotal to obtain a juicer/blender (cheaper here for being smuggled from Afghanistan) and to the Khyber Rifles Mess. The Mess struck me as a shabby ruin, the pretentiousness of its slogan notwithstanding: 'Anybody who was anybody has been here.' Less volubly advertised was the reality that nobody became anybody by coming here.

Returning to Karachi and to the Pakistan Tractors Corporation office put me back into the thick of the muddied relationship between PTCL and BIM / Millat Tractors. I continued to make official trips, oscillating between Lahore to meet the Millat people and to Islamabad for meetings with the Government on tractor pricing and imports. Meetings would be convened and then cancelled without notice.

One meeting that I assumed would be definitive was the PTCL Board meeting, convened on 15 May. Javed Talat (still a Deputy Secretary in the Ministry of Production but boxed in by the new Secretary S.B. Awan) behaved with flamboyant almost reckless panache, a daring he could afford because he was leaving the Ministry for the newly formed Fertiliser Corporation to work with Syed Babar Ali at Lahore. He put up a formidable barrage of hot air balloons intended to distract Mufti who presented with a faltering conviction his plan for the merger of PTCL and Millat.

A few days later another meeting was convened, this time in the Prime Minister's Secretariat in Islamabad. As usual, no one in the BIM knew exactly what to do or to say at a meeting the agenda for which no one was aware. Some thought it related to tractor availability, others on tractor pricing. To be on the safe side, I prepared a brief on both.

The meeting began at 12.30, an hour and a half late. Feroze Qaiser (still dependent on crutches) took the chair. Malik Khuda Bukhsh Bucha and Yaqub (Secretary Agriculture) sat like Gog and Magog on either side of him.

"The agenda for the meeting," FQ began in his usual mellifluous tone which by its sweet reasonableness precluded any argument or debate, "is the question of mark-up on tractors."

Mufti lit his pipe and taking a deep draught exhaled the first innocuous puff. It lingered above the table, a signal for battle to commence.

"What are you proposing?" MKB enquired, enticing Mufti within range.

"Well, sir. In my humble opinion, the present mark-up is too low. It should be at least 15%."

"15%," thundered Yaqub. "That's extortion. We were thinking of reducing, not increasing it."

"Mufti-sahib," Malik Khuda Bukhsh hooted. "You made Rs 45 lakhs profit on motor cars last years on a turnover of Rs 1 crore. Please do not apply those profiteering tactics on our poor farmers, of whom I am one. We cannot afford to support these claims."

Mufti faltered under the sudden unexpectedly forceful attack and lost the initiative. After that onslaught, he smiled weakly, defensively, and grinned ingratiatingly in agreement. The voluminous papers I had prepared were all but ignored.

The meeting dragged on, some discussing particular cases while others wanted a definition of principles. At some point, my papers suddenly reappeared for discussion. In one part of the papers, I had demonstrated that it paid an importer to bring a tractor completely built up (CBU) than in completely knocked down condition (CKD) because the mark-up was calculated on imported C&F values.

During the debate, Feroze Qaiser left the meeting to receive a delegation from the World Bank. He returned to the deliberations but was too tired to listen to details.

"Let's fix the Massey Ferguson tractor price at Rs37,500. Is that all right, Malik sahib? OK, Mufti? Fine. No more arguments, please."

Malik sahib – a tall imposing figure, dressed always in a dust-coloured sherwani – epitomised the Punjabi landlord. His priorities were to see what he could get out of his lands and what he could get out of the Government. The latter yielded more and therefore had priority. Mr. Bhutto depended upon his advice for all matters relating to agriculture, just as he relied upon Feroze Qaiser to unravel knots in the economic and financial sectors.

Malik sahib had an earthy, rustic way of expressing his ideas and framing his questions, and pretended to be just a country yokel awed by the verbal dexterity of the urbanized bureaucrats. Malik sahib's mandate covered water allocation between provinces, seed distribution, fertilizer management, and ensuring tractor availability. The situation regarding supply of MF tractors from Massey Ferguson had not improved. It remained below the Government's expectations and the public's demand. It had also thrown the whole progressive manufacturing programme in jeopardy. Mr. Bhutto wanted to appease the farmer's lobby and Malik sahib wanted to please Mr. Bhutto. To the prime minister and at every forum below, Malik sahib exhorted the import of Russian tractors. He recited his mantra so often that he began to believe it. 'The Belarus tractor is ideal for Sindh. It is perfect for the hard soil conditions there.' Mr. Hashmi, I recall, told me that it was not the traction power of the tractor that mattered in such conditions. It was the strength of the plough.

Malik sahib was not one to be thwarted by such accuracies. At his suggestion, a delegation needed to be sent to Russia to negotiate the earliest supply of Belarus tractors. I was deputed to travel to Moscow, and if necessary to Minsk (where the Belarus factory was located) to conduct the negotiations. My companion would be Mr. Ghulam Mohammed Adamjee, known also because of his company's name as Fecto. He had the exclusive agency for importing Russian tractors, and it was the only agency that had not been transferred to the Pakistan Tractor Corporation. All the others – such as IMT, Ford, and Fiat - had been brought into the public sector. Ironically, the socialist Russians refused to allow the transfer of their franchise to a Pakistani public sector enterprise.

Once I reached Moscow I realised why.

CHAPTER 5

MOSCOW & MINSK

I had never been to Moscow before. I would have found it difficult to cope with its brittle novelty had it not been for the wily intrepidness of my travelling companion G.M. Adamjee 'Fecto'[1].

I knew of him but had never met him. Initially he treated me with caution, unsure what to make of me. I was educated, qualified, and nominally a government servant. He was a Memon businessman (I was about to say hustler), self-made, savvy. One day he explained to me how he had made his money.

"I used to sell small transistor radios. As I had no marketing outlet I had to travel to each city by train, often sleeping on platforms. One day, I wrote to Toshiba and asked them whether I could assemble and manufacture their transistors in Pakistan. They sent me an agreement which I signed. The Toshiba people asked me to meet them in Japan. So I flew to Tokyo and there at the airport was this team from Toshiba waiting to welcome Mr. Adamjee. After all the passengers had disembarked, they assumed that Mr. Adamjee had not been on the plane. I then introduced myself as Mr. Adamjee. They looked shocked. You see, they were expecting Mr. G. M. Adamjee of the Adamjee group[2]. From their looks, Aijaz-sahib, I could tell that they realised that they had signed a contract with the wrong Adamjee. But it was too late. They had

---

[1] 'Fecto' was an acronym for Far East Commercial and Trading Company which handed electrical and home appliances. GH Adamjee 'Fecto' died in April 2007, at the age of 81.
[2] The Adamjee group owned the largest jute mill in East Pakistan, and after Mr. Bhutto's nationalization lost ownership of Muslim Commercial Bank and their interest in Mohammadi Steamship Company. Despite this they had owned Adamjee Sugar Mills and Adamjee Cotton Mills, Karachi.

me as their partner."

'Fecto' Adamjee [GMA] used this seminal and for him lucrative misunderstanding to diversify into tractor imports and later into cement, sugar and paper packaging.

We travelled together to Moscow on 26 May, leaving Karachi on an Ilyushin 62 aircraft. Everyone sat wherever they fancied, and because Adamjee knew the drill, he quickly commandeered a row of three seats, put me in one, sat in another and placed his briefcase and basket of fresh vegetables for the Pakistani Ambassador on the one in the centre. The rest of the passengers stormed in with an almost unbelievable burden of obviously un-weighed hand luggage. The heavy-limbed Russian stewardesses ignored them.

The interior of the aircraft imitated a Boeing, except that although it seemed to contain everything a plane needed except for some reason oxygen masks. The inside had a rough utilitarian finish.

The plane stooped at Tehran to pick up passengers. We lost the centre seat to a heavy compact Azerbaijani woman. She put some of her hand luggage in the racks above us, and what was too large to fit there, she placed under her seat and then sat upon it. She spent most the journey to Moscow rummaging in her commodious handbag from which she would extract wrist-watches, cigarettes, lighters, notebooks, candied fruits – everything that she knew would fetch a good price on the black market in Russia. To sustain herself, she took swigs from a large bottle of Johnny Walker whiskey.

The meal served on the aircraft consisted of a salad followed by tea. I took the small slab of sugar and immersed it in the tea cup. Speaking to me in Russian, she indicated that the sugar had to be retained in one's mouth and allowed to sweeten each sip of tea.

Gradually, as we neared Moscow, I noticed that the jollity of the passengers began to wane. By the time we landed, it had evaporated. From my window, I could see the deep red setting sun reflected in the large pools of water spattered across the flat countryside. We landed at about 9.00 p.m. The passengers alighted in submissive order, supervised by a uniformed Russian guard who stood with his arms and legs akimbo, blocking the aircraft's doorway. He ensured that only one busload could leave the aircraft at a time.

I had expected the weather to have a chill about it but it turned out to be surprisingly mild. Immigration and custom formalities were minimal. Our hosts Messrs Tractoroexport had sent two young officers (they must have been in their late twenties) to receive us. They introduced themselves as Alexander Afanasev and Mikhail Brusentsov. They were to remain with us throughout our stay.

They put us in a taxi. We asked the driver whether he could take us to the Pakistan Embassy so that we could deliver the perishables Adamjee had brought for the Ambassador. This released a loquacious response from the taxi driver. He told us that his duty finished at 10 p.m., and therefore he was not prepared to takes us anywhere other than straight to the hotel.

My notes read: 'Most of the building en route appeared new, very few pre-1918. The buses and the trolleys were full but not to the point of discomfort. Few shops. A large supermarket located strategically close to the housing colonies; a kiosk or two in street corners but otherwise little sign of the crass ubiquitous commercialism one encounters in western capitals. Slogans on large billboards containing the most enduring of the massages from the most durable of their leaders. Oddly enough, Brezhnev took precedence over Lenin. Nowhere have I seen any sign of Lenin, except on the small badge on the immigration officer's tunic and later on the flag at the Ostankino hotel where we were to be lodged.

The hotel is located on the outskirts of Moscow. It appears to cater for a provincial clientele. There was an initial tussle over rooms between the young female receptionist and her elder dour superior – a matron with a severe scallop hairstyle and bright lipstick applied liberally on lips beyond kissing.

"Do you mind sharing a room?" Alexander asked me.

"No," I replied, but I hope we will have separate beds."

Room 123 was allocated to us. Passing the three policemen observing us from the only sofas in the lobby, we entered an ancient lift and emerged on the first floor. A matron sat at a strategically placed table on the landing. She booked us in and told us that she would cater for our needs.

The double glazed windows, installed to keep out the Muscovite winter cold, must have come in handy as late as a week ago. It had snowed last Sunday. Our room contained everything we needed but not a convenience more -

narrow beds, a sliver of soap, and a small towel the size of a bath-mat for each of us.

On 27th, my first morning in Moscow, the sun having set late last night was up and shining at 4.00 a.m. Reminded me of the old Aga Khan who claimed that he needed only 4 hours of sleep a night.

GM with a foresight born of previous deprivations had brought with him a month's ration of Lipton's tea-bags, sugar and a tin of powdered milk. His mother had added for good measure a liberal load of home-made halva.

Some miscommunication made us expect Brusentsov at 9.00. We therefore skipped breakfast and strolled outside the hotel. Opposite the hotel, in the Botanical Gardens, some young men stood behind the railings and gesticulated with their fingers – 3 or 4. That signified the rate they were offering for the US 1. (The official conversion rate was $1=0.74 rouble. We had been warned against changing our money through these unorthodox brokers. Such ploys were standard tactics used to trap inexperienced foreigners.

Mikhail Brusentsov arrived at 9.30, stammering apologies. The taxi took us past the 300 m high Ostankino tower (it had a television station on the ground floor), and as neared the centre of Moscow proper, one recognized sights familiar through tourist brochures. At one stage, our driver almost had an accident with an oncoming bus.

"What would have happened if there had been an accident?" I asked Mikhail.

"To us, nothing, "he replied. "If the cars are damaged perhaps, the taxi driver would have been fined."

"How much?"

"If the damage was costing 200 roubles, then 20 roubles would be recovered from the driver – if it was his fault. If the other driver was to blame, he too would have had to pay. The State would bear the rest."

Before going to the Tractoroexport office, we stopped at the Pakistan Embassy on 17-Sadova Kudrinskaya. The chancery lay closer to the road, hiding the residence of the ambassador behind. We were told that Ambassador Dehlavi was in hospital, his wife was still in the bathroom, but the cook was available to receive the haunch of meat (which had 'gone off' by then), and the softening vegetables GMA had carried with such diligence from Karachi.

While we waited in case Mrs. Dehlavi has a message for us, a Pakistani – tieless and wearing a grubby raincoat – attempted to engage us in a conversation on the current political scene in Pakistan. I am not sure what it was about him that put me on my guard: was it the absence of a tie, or the way he kept his hands thrust deep in the pockets of his raincoat, or was it the hard determination detectable from his unblinking eyes? Whatever it was, it made me suspicious.

"What is really happening in the country?" he asked.

"You read the papers, don't you?" I countered.

"Yes, but they give only the Government line!"

"It is your government as much as it is mine."

He looked directly at me and seemed to be using his gaze to winkle out of the recesses of my mind a shred of dissatisfaction with Bhutto's government, so that he could report that to his superiors. I stared back, until he yielded and left us, mumbling to himself.

From the Embassy, our taxi took us past the Bolshoi Theatre building, along the Kremlin walls, the Lenin mausoleum built of stone the colour of coagulated blood, and deposited us at the Tractoroexport offices located in an old, weather-beaten building that had once housed the Ministry of Foreign Affairs. Now the Ministry had joined the Ministry of Foreign Trade in a tower constructed close to the Kremlin.

Heavy wooden double-doors opened into narrow lobby. The lift was equally cramped, accommodating five slim foreigners on the way up and a well-fed Russian couple on the way down. The door of the Tractoroexport office was closed against us. Mikhail hammered on it loudly.

"I told the man downstairs to phone our office to tell them that we were coming up."

Once inside, GMA and I were ushered into a bland room with simple grey chairs and a table. At the far end of the room lay the office table of the occupant. The only decorations were a small bust of Karl Marx and a large portrait of President Podgorny.

Some minutes later we were joined by Dr. S. Sukhikh, the Deputy Director and the man who would be my negotiating counterpart. He must have been in his early forties, slim and polite until thwarted.

I explained the purpose of my visit, which was to:

1. Assess the status of the current contacts concluded by Messrs Fecto for supply of Russian tractors;

2. Investigate the reasons for the sudden stoppage of production of their Model MTZ 50 and Super that had hitherto been imported into Pakistan;

3. Consideration of the proposal by Messrs Tractoroexport to supply Model UMZ 6 (60 HP) in 1974 and 1975.

4. Discussion on the possibility of progressive manufacture of Russian tractors.

Essentially, Tractoroexport had decided (without assigning any reasons) to stop supply of the popular MTZ 50 to Pakistan and to replace it with an unknown UMZ 6 model. My mission was to find out why.

The discussions on that first day were laboured. Dr. Sukhikh rotated like a tethered goat around his demand that I place an order for the unknown UMZ 6 and that I should inform him of my requirements for the year 1975. As a sweetener (aware that Pakistan needed tractors in a hurry), he offered 500 UMZ 6 tractors that could be supplied within nine months.

In my reply to Dr. Sukhikh, I made clear that we needed to know why supplies of the MTZ 50 had been stopped before we could consider any other model. I emphasised that it would not be worth our while to introduce 500 units *de novo* into Pakistan.

At times Sukhikh's lips would purse and he would bare his teeth at me with undisguised impatience. Undaunted by his tactics, I insisted that no decision could be made without my visiting the tractor plant located at Minsk where the UMZ 6 was being manufactured.

The meeting could have been completed within half the time, had Sukhikh not attempted to wear me down with repetitive proposals. This initial meeting ended with my asking them to furnish certain information (e.g. the commonality of parts between the MTZ 50 and the UMZ 6) and to arrange a visit to the Minsk plant.

Sukhikh warned me that it might take a week or so for permission to be issued– if it came at all – but he would try. I replied that I understood his imperatives if he would understand mine. I could not sign any contract without seeing the UMZ 6 or visiting the plant where it was being made.

My meetings with Sukhikh and his colleagues took place in the mornings. They would end by lunchtime. The afternoons were free. I suspect Sukhikh thought this was some subtle form of punishment, to leave us – GMA and a novice – alone and unattended in Moscow. For me, nothing could have been better. GMA and I had all the time and opportunity to explore the sights of Moscow.

On that first day, GMA introduced me to the protocol and rituals of eating in public restaurants. He chose my initiation with the Uzbekistan restaurant – the only one he said he could trust not to slip ham or pork into his food. It was drizzling when we arrived at the restaurant. Outside, a queue of sodden Uzbeks waited, dressed in the main shabbily, with uniform square black caps embroidered in white balanced on their shaven stubbly heads. GMA, taking advantage of the departure of some lunchers, barged beneath the outstretched arm of the doorman, muttering: "Delegation, Delegation!" Mikhail and I, being inexperienced, were too slow and so found ourselves locked out. One of the Uzbeks in the queue noticed GMA and jerking his head towards his companion laughed knowingly: "Ah, Delegation! Delegation!"

Inside the restaurant was crowded, its customers primarily Uzbeks of all classes – rich suited types and poor sun-burnt ones. The ceiling of this regional restaurant had an appropriately ethnic touch – floriated Persian designs touched up heavily with gold. The food would not have been out of place in any *kabab* or *tikka* joint in Karachi. Mixed grill and a greasy rice *pulao*. The only novelty for me was the appetizer – a bun filled with a minced meat savoury. After each bite, I could feel it expand in my stomach until I feared I would not be able to face the main course.

Opposite us at the same table sat two men and a woman. GMA with characteristic bonhomie offered them some of our lunch. They refused with such firmness that it seemed as if they had been monitoring our conversation, which I discovered later they had. The meal cost us all of ten roubles.

After our first lunch in Moscow, GAM took me to see the Exhibition of Achievements. To reach it we had to pass a spectacular soaring homage to Russian rocketry. The centre-piece was the tapering trail of a silver star shooting towards the sky.

To describe the Exhibition of Achievements as awe-inspiring would be to belittle the impact of its monumental pavilions. One entered through a long series of arches, dominated the hammer and sickle that led into a broad avenue, at the far end of which was a large pillared central pavilion, its golden spire surmounted by a large star. Within it was an extensive map of the USSR, lit up to show the rate of development since the days of the Revolution. The greatest development occurred during the period 1964-1970 – the period of Nikita Khrushchev's rule – but nowhere was there any mention of his stewardship.[3]

Nearby under construction, I noticed the USSR pavilion that had been designed and set up for the Expo '70 exhibition in Canada and brought back to Moscow for re-assembly as it was considered too expensive to leave behind in Montreal.

The central fountain had a circle of gilded statues of buxom women representing each of the states in the USSR – symbolic daughters of a Mother Russia.

For me the most interesting contained an exhibition called Astronaut's Hall, housed in hangar large enough I suspect to accommodate an Ilyushin aircraft. Hovering above dangled a rocket. Each stage of Russian development in space technology and its pioneering achievements – the Sputniks, the Vostoks, etc. - had a place among the exhibits. A bust in the central Rotunda honoured Yuri Gagarin, the first man to orbit the earth in 1961. Valentina Tereshkova – his compatriot and the first woman astronaut – was similarly but less prominently honoured. I looked around for any mention of Laika the first dog (also Russian) which had been propelled into space in 1957. I recalled the anguished protests registered by the RSPCA[4] in London at the time, condemning the inhumanity of Soviet scientists for such a barbaric experiment. Had they but known, the Soviets cocked a snook at the RSPCA

---

[3] Nikita Khrushchev had been removed ten years earlier (in October 1964) from his position as First Secretary of the Central Committee of the Soviet Communist Party. He died in 1971.
[4] Royal Society for the Prevention of Cruelty to Animals.

by stuffing another dog (Laika had died during the flight and never returned to earth) and then – dare one make the analogy? – like the embalmed Lenin put it on display.

By the time we had finished touring the exhibition (it would have taken even longer had all the pavilions been open to the public), we left through the arched entrance in continuous rain. Mikhail waited there to give us the tickets to a performance of *Swan Lake* by the Bolshoi Ballet company. I had hoped, like every tourist to Moscow, to see it in the original Bolshoi Theatre - a gracious old rose and white building with Palladian columns, its facade not unlike that of the Royal Opera House in Covent Garden. The Bolshoi Theatre was undergoing extensive remodelling and refurbishment. The performances that would have been held there were relocated to the newly constructed Palace of Congress, situated within the Kremlin itself. We joined the hordes of ballet devotees, tourists, diplomats and official delegations and passed through a cordon of security personnel. I noticed there was a man at the bottom of each escalator and another at the top, observing every person travelling up or down.

Inside the hall, every class found its own level: delegates in the front (I had seat 54 in Row 3), diplomats in the middle rows, tourists at the back, and above in the balcony seats local Russians.

The stage was enormous – half as large again I was told as that of the Bolshoi Theatre. I did not know enough about ballet to make an informed judgment except that I did note in my diary that I thought that the Bolshoi dancers danced with a greater sense of drama than their English counterparts whom I had seen at Covent Garden in 1965.

I still have that evening's programme with me. It is in Russian. Mikhail translated the names of the principals for me: Tatiana Golikova[5] danced Odette/Odile; Medvedev the lead role of Prince Siegfried; and the conductor was A.A. Kopylov.

During the interval, rank, status and the origins of one's currency were forgotten in the mêlee as the audience stampeded up the escalators to the buffet on the third floor. Although everyone had to queue for everything purchasable, no one went back without. At the third warning bell, the mad scramble reversed its flow as the audience made its way back to the hall.

---

[5] Golikova danced with the Bolshoi from 1965 to 1988. She died in 2012.

Once the performance was over, Mikhail took us back to the hotel by Metro. We entered at Lenin Library Station. No words can describe the impact one's first sight has of the Moscow Metro. The Tsars would have felt quite at home in its extravagant splendour. Considering the volume of passenger traffic it handles, I could not see a shred of paper, a speck of dust nor a blemish on the trains and the stations. Chandeliers, grandiose mosaics extolling the achievements of Leninist Socialism, bookshops at every junction with 'official literature, miles of marble-lined corridors. In the Moscow Metro, cleanliness is next to anti-Godlessness.[6]

It was with regret that I quit the Metro and caught a taxi with GMA to our suddenly very provincial hotel.

The next day (28th), we made our own way to the Tractoroexport offices. En route we thought we might as well meet the officials in our Embassy. We stood outside the hotel and waited and waited. Taxis in Moscow, GMA had warned me, were as rare as foreign currency. Something else GMA told me was that hitching a lift from private cars was allowed. He had a sixth sense which enabled him to spot vehicles likely to give us a lift. Suddenly, GMA like an eagle spotted his prey. He flagged down a passing car, and without waiting for a response from the 'hijacked' driver, he settled down beside him on the front seat and began a conversation.

"Boris. Yes, Boris.."

"Nyet," the driver replied. "Ivan ..."

"Ivan. My friend Ivan," beamed GMA, exuding goodwill which he underlined with a bear-hug while Ivan was driving.

Ivan dropped us as close to the Embassy as he could manage without a detour. GMA tipped him in roubles. We walked the rest of the distance. The buildings in that area consisted primarily of offices, most of them with a flower or two in a vase placed in the window.

At the Pakistan Embassy the guard gave us a friendly smile and a nod of recognition. Not many Pakistanis travelled in and out of Moscow. Remembering the faces of those that did could not have been difficult for him.

The Embassy offices lay behind the main building. They must have been

---

[6] I visited Moscow for the second time, in 2010. The Metro looked a little worn in places but still commanded one's respect for dramatic grandeur.

servants' quarters and stables during pre-revolution times. The Russian secretary ushered us into the office of Fatmi, the Second Secretary – a youngish, energetic chap who spoke Russian fluently. The only name I had been given before I left Karachi had been of Hadi Ali – the son-in-law of the neuro-surgeon Dr. O.V. Jooma. I asked to see him. Fatmi led me to Hadi's room. Before we could enter, Hadi waved Fatmi out. We waited and a little while later, Hadi emerged to speak to me. I introduced myself, and added that I was Ayaz's younger brother, after which Hadi's tone changed to one of unctuous cordiality.

I asked him who the inquisitive chap we had encountered on our first visit to the Embassy.

"Oh, he's the security chap. Very efficient, I'm told."

"But one whose side is he – ours or the Russians?"

"I've often wondered about that myself."

Fearing we might be late, we caught a taxi to the Tractoroexport offices. We need not have bothered. The meeting amounted to nothing more than net practice. Sukhikh had no intention of discussing anything substantive. He introduced Mr. Ivan Dvujilov (Director, Implements) who tried to persuade me to buy Russian made agricultural implements. When I failed to bite, Sukhikh summoned Mr. Chuprygin (Director Transport). He spent what remained of the morning's session coaxing me into importing Sukhikh's UMZ tractors by road from Minsk, through Kushka, across Afghanistan, and into Pakistan via Chaman. An added advantage, he assured me, was that the tractors would reach the Pakistani famer sooner if they were shipped by road than if they were shipped by sea.

I replied as calmly as I could that, thanks to the common thinking of the Soviet government and that of the United States, the Suez Canal would most probably be opened shortly. Therefore, Soviet ships would be able to ply as before without incurring the penal surcharge of going around the Cape. Anyway, I pointed out to Chuprygin, so far we have been offered 500 units and those too spread until April 1975. Eighty tractors a month did not justify a change to the traditional and more efficient methods of transportation between our two countries. Chuprygin's small mouth pursed even further.

Despite the sterility of the meeting, Mikhail remained cheerful, accompanying us to the Hotel Rossiya that overlooked Red Square. Something that startled me was that the restaurant menus throughout Intourist hotels such as the Rossiya were uniform. It varied from day to day but never from restaurant to restaurant on the same day.

I suggested to Mikhail that we could visit the Armoury Exhibition in the Kremlin after lunch. That was not possible. The tickets had to be paid for in hard currency. Instead we took a walk around Red Square and the outer walls of the Kremlin. Mikhail then drove us to Moscow University – one of Stalin's famous wedding-cake monuments. Set on the hills overlooking Moscow, it had been built on the site from which Napoleon had his first glimpse of the city during his ill-fated invasion of Russia in 1812.

The following day (29ᵗʰ), on my way to the Tractoroexport offices, I asked Mikhail where we could stop at the office of our Commercial Secretary's office. The Secretary Mr. A.A. Qazi had given me instructions how to find his place. Mikhail took us to the right complex – a taciturn compound reserved for diplomats - but to the wrong building within it. I knocked on the door. It was opened by an English lady from the British High Commission. She invited me in and took me to her larder window from where she pointed out the block I was looking for. I could not help noticing the almost industrial quantities of provisions she had stored in her larder – tins of soup, vegetables, tomato puree. It was enough to withstand the siege of a Moscow winter.

I briefed Mr. Qazi on the status of my discussions with Tractoroexport. That did not take long as there was little progress to report. My third meeting with Sukhikh was more or less a reprise of our earlier meetings. He wanted me to commit to a purchase of UMZ 6 tractors; I wanted to see it first and the plant where it was being manufactured.

GMA took me to the Ukraine Hotel for lunch. A large building near the Kutozovsky bridge, it had a splendid dining hall done up in deep red and white. The waitresses were uniformly large and ungainly.

As we had the afternoon free, GMA and I strolled through Dom Igrushki (the Moscow equivalent of Hamleys' toyshop). I had my eye on a tractor (the size of a tricycle) for Fidge. Its price (ten roubles) was not the deterrent; its bulk was. From there, we caught a taxi to Gorki Park, where we strolled, watching Muscovites uncurl like crocuses in the sunshine after their winter hibernation.

Naturally, everyone had an ice cream cone in their hands – except us. Both GMA and I were gasping for a cup of tea. We joined the end of a queue and when after a longish wait we reached the head of it, we were told that we needed to pay in advance at another counter. We decided to indulge ourselves and have a slice of a tempting cheesecake. Much got lost in the translation between us and the sales assistant. We discovered that we had paid for a cream pastry. The Russians I noticed gorged themselves on brown bread and stewed sausages.

Finding a taxi outside a popular resort like Gorki Park would have been impossible. We had no choice but to walk a fair distance across the Crimean bridge to Crimean Square where we managed to stop a private car. The Russian owner-driver charged us three roubles for taking us to Ostankino hotel, twice the taxi fare (GMA complained) for the same distance.

Having reached the hotel, I was loath to go back into main Moscow for dinner. We decided to try out the Ostankino hotel's own restaurant, located in another block. It became obvious that few of the residents and certainly no outsiders used the place. One would have thought that there being so few diners, the staff would have been more attentive. Instead, it took them two hours to serve us three courses. We entered at 9.00 p.m. and left at 11.00 p.m.

Looking around the dining room, I realised that food was the curse of the Russian drinking classes. They drank continuously, stopping only for a morsel of whatever happens to be on the plate in front of them.

Ever since we had landed in Moscow, neither GMA nor I felt an appetite for breakfast. On 30th, we went to the Ostankino dining room where a breakfast buffet had been paid out. We ate as sparingly as we would have at home. The Russian guests – especially those who had come to Moscow from the provinces – piled their plates vertically with sausages, bacon, mashed potatoes, gravy, beans, ending with a fried egg instead of a gold star at its apex.

At Tractoroexport, Sukhikh, realising that he was not making any headway with me, pulled out his superior, the Director Mr. Alexej Shibanov. The Director smoothed Sukhikh's feathers and was altogether more conciliatory. That afternoon, acting on the advice of our Commercial Secretary, I paid a visit to his counterpart in the Commercial Section of the Canadian Embassy. I took an appointment from Mr. G.M. Deyell, First Secretary, who received me with his assistant Richard Groundwater. I had been told by Sukhikh that many of their tractors were being exported to Canada, but he was cagey about specifics.

By contrast, Deyell could not have been more forthcoming. He gave me statistics about Canadian imports of Russian tractors (1971: 25; 1972: 95; 1973: 675) and something more valuable – a special report by Dr. C.L. Barber on Canadian Farm Machinery. The report bore out Deyell's information that the Russians had begun targeting Western markets for their heavier horse-powered tractors. They devised an arrangement by which Tractoroexport entered into agreements with joint ventures or local companies based in Canada, France and the United Kingdom. Tractors were then sold to these at a transfer price roughly equivalent to the prices charged by Tractoroexport to barter customers. The ultimate selling price would be linked to local conditions which were invariably higher, with the added advantage of being in 'hard' foreign currency. Tractoroexport's share of the net profits after deduction of local expenses would be repatriated to Moscow. Effectively, Tractoroexport received the transfer price plus profits/dividends, all in valuable hard currency.

Deyell's specimen calculation made it very clear.

(Canadian $ per unit)

1.	Transfer price from Tractoroexport to JV		$3,000
2.	Selling Prince in Canada		$7,300
	Less: Transfer Price	$3,000	
	Local Exps.	$1,300	$4,300
3.	NET PROFIT		$3,000
4.	Share of Tractoroexport @51% $1,530		$1,530
5.	Effective return to Tractoroexport		$4,530

Now I could see why Tractoroexport wanted to stop supplying MTZ 50 tractors to Pakistan. They would have been subject to barter provisions. By diverting these tractors to western countries they would earn hard currency. To meet their barter obligations, they wanted to fob us with the UMZ 6 which we would have been obliged to take to square up the barter imbalance.

I needed some facts and statistics beyond the report Deyell had provided. Quite fortuitously, I found a bookshop that specialised in Soviet government publications. I asked them whether they had any material on Russian imports and exports. The salesperson produced one bound in red that contained tables of all Russian trade up to 1973. I memorised the Russian word for tractors and then having found the relevant table, I had someone at the hotel (I did not want Mikhail to know what I was up to) identify the countries for me.

A summation of the figures revealed that taking the three years – 1971, 1972 and 1973 – 75% or so of all Russian tractors went to the Socialist Bloc of countries. These included Bulgaria, Cuba and East Germany. Interestingly, China stopped importing in 1971. Almost half of tractors exported to Europe went to France. Out of Asian countries, Pakistan took more than half of the 3,073 exported in 1973. It surprised me to see that India has stopped importing in 1971. Perhaps because India had a very active domestic progressive manufacturing programme.

For the next few days, Sukhikh tried to wear me down by bringing in the Director in charge of pricing and two representatives from Zapchastaexport - the organisation responsible for export of spare parts. I asked them to give me a comparison of the commonality of components between the MTZ 50 and UMZ 6.

"Substantial," I was told.

"Yes, but exactly how much?"

"We will let you have a list shortly." When it did come, it was apparent there was no critical functioning part in the UMZ 6 that was common to the MTZ range. It was a completely different model, manufactured in a separate factory at the UZNY Machinotroiteleny plant 'somewhere in the south of Russia'.

I pressed the Zapchastaexport representatives for an undertaking that, should we import the UMZ 6, supplies of spare parts would be assured as long as the tractor was in use in Pakistan.

"Of course," came the pat answer.

"How long have you been making the UMZ 6?"

"Oh, ten years."

"Then why don't you supply them to us in CKD condition?"

To this they refused to give an answer, as it was beyond their remit.

Although I knew that I could not return to Pakistan without some sort of agreement with Tractoroexport - even if was for the UMZ 6 – I wanted

Sukhikh to know that I was not fooled by his glib and oily assurances.

The showdown occurred on 6 June. Sukhikh maintained the pressure and heightened it by bringing into the meeting his Vice President Mr. Monaenkov. I knew that Mr. Monaenkov spoke English. He chose not to.[7]

I decided to call Sukhikh's bluff. The meeting began with a reiteration by me of all the data Sukhikh had provided me in our previous meetings. I focussed on the figures of the MTZ 50 and UMZ 6 tractors. I asked Sukhikh whether I was correct in my understanding that manufacture of the MTZ 50 had ceased.

"Yes," he said, raising his eyebrows in exasperation.

At this I leaned down and removed from my briefcase the red book of Russia's export statistics.

I did not need to know any Russian to comprehend Mr. Monaenkov's aside to Sukhikh.

"Where did he get that from?"

"I don't know." Sukhikh replied.

I then began quoting the figures I had extracted from the book.

"Oh, those are incorrect," Sukhikh stammered.

I knew he was cornered but I was in no mood to let him escape.

"Are you telling me that these statistics published by the Soviet Government are incorrect?"

Sukhikh blanched and looked helplessly at the air-grille in the ceiling above where he and I knew the microphones monitoring our conversations were hidden.

"No," he said very softly.

Then turning to Mr. Monaenkov, I said: "Sir, I know that you speak English. Let's conduct the rest of the meeting in English. It would save time."

I would like to believe that I got the better of Sukhikh on that crucial occasion. But he had his revenge in a more subtle way.

---

[7] In fact, Tractoroexport being an institution with an international clientele, ensured through training that all its employees were fluent in at least two if not three foreign languages. Alexander Afanasev, for example, spoke French and Spanish; Mikhail Brusentsov Italian and German.

During our earlier discussions, I tried to show off by placing the small Boucheron alarm clock that Massey Ferguson had given to Javed Talat and me during our visit to Luzern. It was compact and fitted into a smart black crocodile skin case. I placed it on the table between Sukhikh and myself.

"There," I said, "I have set the alarm for half an hour. I expect your reply before the alarm rings."

Sukhikh reached out, took the alarm clock in his hands, examined it carefully, admired it, and then asked me: "Is it made in Pakistan?"

Throughout our discussions, Sukhikh deflected my proposal that the franchise for Belarus tractors should be transferred from Fecto to the Pakistan Tractors Corporation. My argument that the PTCL being a state organisation stood more eligible than a private sector one cut no ice with him. The most he would concede was an arrangement by which PTCL could be the franchise holder but with Fecto as its sole distributor.

"That would depend on what arrangement you have in place with Fecto?" I told Sukhikh.

Reluctantly, very reluctantly, and then only with GMA's grudging permission, the agency agreement between Tractoroexport and Fecto was produced and handed to me. It specified the commission (5% on FOB prices, payable abroad) Fecto received on all exports by Tractoroexport to Pakistan.

"Dikra [son]," GMA whispered to me in Gujrati. "I have to share the commission that with you know who in Islamabad." I understood why there had been such a powerful lobby in Islamabad pressing for the import of Russian tractors - of any model.

Towards the end of my second week in Moscow – the original plan had been to stay only one week - the permission to visit the tractor plan at Minsk came through, as I had suspected it would. Sukhikh knew he would not have a deal without that visit. Until we left for Minsk, GMA and I occupied ourselves with visiting as many tourist spots as we could.

We managed after a false start to go the top of the Ostankino tower. We arrived a minute after it closed at 8.00 p.m. and were refused entry. The Tretyakov Gallery was another must-see. The entrance lobby with its magnificent staircase and different kinds and colours of marble reminded one how inevitable the Russian Revolution had been. The Museum of the

Revolution extolled the sacrifices of those who had suffered or died during that bitter period of Russia's history. On display I noticed the first Russian tractor made in 1924, and a portrait of the Grand Duchess Sofia in her cloistered cell in the Novodevichy Convent after she had been defeated in a power struggle by Tsar Peter I.

"Why is she here?" I asked the guide. "She was a Romanov."

"Ah, yes. But she was against the Czar. Therefore, she is a revolutionary."

For me the most telling display was a small (it was short as Stalin himself was) containing memorabilia of the man who had done more to delineate the identity of modern Russia. Prominently on display were not his medals or his photographs, but just his sten gun. That said it all.

The guide book on Moscow that I found indispensable cost me no more than one rouble. I bought it from some street vendor outside the Kremlin walls. I still have it. When I opened it a few days ago, I found in it the ticket to the Diamond Fund. I had forgotten that the Russian Crown Jewels collected over three centuries by the Romanovs were, like the Iranian Crown Jewels in the Bank Melli in Tehran, collateral underpinning the national currency. The ticket for the Diamond Fund was issued by the Ministry of Finance.

Over the years I had seen photographs of the various members of the Imperial Royal family wearing these treasures. Lord Twining in his book on the crown jewels of Europe, had included details of diamond tiaras, necklaces, the fabled Orloff diamond set in a sceptre, and of course the two Imperial crowns used during the coronation of the Czar and his Czarina.[8] I knew that Agathon Fabergé, the son of Carl Fabergé (famous for making the famous bejewelled Easter Eggs for Czar Nicholas II to give to his wife Alexandra and his mother Marie Feodrovna on occasion of Easter every year), had been ordered by the Soviets to make an inventory of the State jewels. He spent almost two years dismantling all the pieces and weighing each stone. The diamonds alone weighed an aggregate of over 25,000 metric carats.

As the exhibition space was limited (probably for security reasons), the time of admittance was specified. My ticket read '14.20'. The first case contained a sapphire aigrette and diamond corsages. The second, more corsages and diamond brooches. The third had the crowns, the famous tiaras,

---

[8] Lord Twining, *A History of the Crown Jewels of Europe* (London, 1960).

and the Orloff diamond. The fourth and last case had various diamond studded chains and badges of the Order of Saint Nicholas. I went as close to the glass as the guards would allow and imagined the scene in the Kremlin when these jewels would have been worn on royal functions. They must have been an awesome sight.

The Armoury within the Kremlin required a separate ticket and could be seen without pressure. We climbed up the staircase to the First Armoury Hall. The display was breathtaking. Each item deserved time to be appreciated on its own and for itself. Each was a work of art that honoured the craftsmen – whether Russian, Chinese or Indian - who had dedicated their working hours to creating objects of such ineffable beauty.

I made a brief note in my diary of the pieces that impressed me most. In the First Hall, Boris Godunov's 10,000 rings, horse trappings with bejewelled anklets, a gun beautifully inlaid with ivory, a Mughal jade dagger inset with uncut rubies. The Second Hall (painted green and white) displayed swords and more jade-handled daggers (obviously Mughal in origin), valuable religious icons (some had had their paintings removed and probably sold), and the Czars' personal reliquaries, all gold encrusted.

The Third Hall (this one blue) had a solid gold cup, Potemkin's platter, and nuptial crowns. One exhibit I can never forget. A large four panel screen of Chinese embroidery made in Suzhou caught my eye. One side of the single ply cloth had been embroidered in a sylvan scene with a profusion of colourful flowers. As one walked around to the other side, the picture was of a seascape with foamy waves splashing against rocks. I must have taken the Chinese embroideries years to make and was quite literally fit for a king, in this case a Czar to whom this superb piece had been sent as a gift by the then Emperor of China.

The Fourth Hall (all red and white) housed the gifts of silver proffered to the Czars as tribute, mother of pearl flagons, Sevres china sets, and for me the most interesting of all – the Tercentenary Easter Egg that had been made by Fabergé in 1913 to commemorate the 300th anniversary of the founding of the Romanov dynasty. The outside of the enamelled egg was set with miniature portraits of the various Romanoff Czars and Czarinas, and within the surprise was a globe showing the territories under Czar Michael in 1613 and those under Czar Nicholas II in 1913. Within a year of that egg's presentation to

Czarina Alexandra Feodrovna (Nicholas II's wife), the First World War had begun. Within another four years, the Czar would abdicate and the Romanov dynasty would come to an untimely, bloody end.

The Throne Room contained Ivan the Terrible's ivory throne, the diamond throne with distinctively Indian motifs, the double throne of Czars Ivan and Peter, imperial coronation robes hanging off unworthy mannequins, and a royal mews of imperial coaches – some with wheels and others with sledges for travel across the snow steppes.

Even in a country as rich and as huge as Russia, nothing can compare with the opulence of the Imperial treasures in the Kremlin. One of the saner acts the Bolsheviks did on assuming power in 1917 was to have all these treasures sealed. Some items did disappear – some smuggled out by the fleeing White Russians, others stolen, and a few like the Imperial nuptial crown auctioned in London during the 1920s by a cash-strapped Soviet government to raise hard currency.

After the Kremlin exhibition, every other tourist sight would be a let-down. As GMA and I had time (our afternoons and evenings were free), we caught a performance of the noted Moscow State Circus. It meant a metro ride. During it, I noticed a young boy – not more than twelve years old – standing alone with his face towards the doors. At first I thought he must be inordinately shy. Mikhail explained that the boy was Jewish and therefore none of the passengers would mix with him. It made me realise that anti-Semitism had not died out in Russia. There was still a price to be paid for being Jewish.

The last time I had seen the Moscow State Circus had been in London in 1956, when it had been brought to perform during a Christmas season. Its star was a clown named Oleg Popov, known also as the Sunshine Clown. The acts at this latest performance were breath-taking. I asked how performers were selected.

"We have a Moscow Circus school, where talented children are sent for training. From there they are selected and employed according to their ability. For example, dancers are trained in our academies. The best enter the Bolshoi, the second best go our Provincial ballet companies, others to the state circuses, and the remainder finds jobs as cabaret dancers in theatres or restaurants.

Once or twice, we made a trip to GUM – the huge department store that occupied one length of Red Square. After a few futile enquires, it became obvious that whatever was on display was not available. I noted down the prices of menswear: 95 roubles for a suit, a pair of shoes 13 roubles, and a blouse 24 roubles. The cheapest goods available were Russian perfumes. Their prices ranged from 5 roubles up to 10 roubles. Even these were not exempt from the need to advertise Russian technology. The perfume bottles had been blown in the shape of Vostok rockets. Patriotic, but decidedly unfeminine.

One of the sights on my list of 'must-see' was the Novodevichy Convent, a monastery turned necropolis, located in the south-western corner of Moscow. The grounds contained the graves of prominent Russians – poets, musicians, composers, and politicians. The monument I wanted to see commemorated the burial spot of Nadezhda Sergevna Alliluyeva, Stalin's second wife who committed suicide in November 1932 after a public argument with her husband. Even if she had died of old age, the blame would have fallen on Stalin. For years, the suspicion lingered that he had either shot her himself or had someone else eliminate her.[9] The monument to her showed a head with the hair in a chignon and a hand emerging through a white granite obelisk. She looked almost ethereal.

The other grave I wanted to see was that of Nikita Khrushchev. I had read his denunciation of Josef Stalin (his mentor) before a stunned 20th Party Congress in 1956. Khrushchev remained in power until 1964 when his colleague Brezhnev removed him in a Kremlin coup. After his death in September 1971, Khrushchev's body was refused permission to be buried along with other Soviet leaders of his rank in the walls of the Kremlin. The reason given was 'lack of space'. It was interred instead in the garden of the Novodevichy Convent. When I visited it in 1974, the grave was marked by a granite slab. His memoirs which had been smuggled out of Russian had not been published then[10], neither had those of Andre Malraux, French President de Gaulle's Minister of Culture. I believe it was in Malraux's memoirs that I read the famous exchange between them regarding the Khrushchevs and the Kennedys.

"Monsieur le President," Malraux is supposed to have asked de Gaulle, "what do you think would have been the consequences, had Premier

---

[9] Her daughter Svetlana Iosifovna Alliluyeva caused an incident when she defected to the West in 1967. She lived in the US for many years.
[10] *Memoirs of Nikita Khrushchev*, edited by Sergei Khrushchev (University of Pennsylvania, USA, 2005-7).

Khrushchev been shot and not President Kennedy?"

"Well, I can tell you one thing for sure," de Gaulle replied. "Onassis would not have married Mrs. Khrushchev!"

When I think of it, GMA must have been quite bored by my cultural forays. If he was, he never complained. He came into his own at mealtimes when he would take control, finding us seats in crowded restaurants, hustling the waitresses to expedite service, or just chatting to whoever shared our table with us. In those days, one never knew who one would sit at the same table. On one occasion, our companions were a well-to-do American couple. That they had never been to Moscow became obvious from the way they ordered their meal. Having placed an order for soup, they sat sipping their wine.

"Have you ordered anything else?" GMA asked them

"No," the wife replied, "We thought we would order that after we had our soup."

GMA looked at them pityingly. "Order everything you want at the same time. Otherwise you will be here for hours."

The longest time it took us to be served occurred in the plush Ukraine Hotel. I recorded in my diary that it took an hour per course, and the menu consisted of a standard three courses.

Rummaging through my papers of this visit, I came across a bill of our meal at Hotel Rossiya. Borsch soup cost us 1 rouble 4 kopecks, roast turkey 3 roubles 2 kopecks, bread 10 kopecks, fizzy water 36 kopecks, cucumber salad 36 kopeks. The total bill for both us, including taxes, amounted to 5 roubles 51 kopecks.

From my notes, it was during this meal at the Rossiya that we encountered a garrulous Russian who decided that he should while away his time by baiting us.

He spoke a few words of English, enough to be obnoxious.

When one the rather buxom waitresses served us a course, he asked me whether I fancied her. "Nyet," I replied, pointing to the gold ring on my finger.

Then he offered me some wine from his carafe.

"Nyet," I said again.

"Why?"

"Allah nyet!"

"Allah, where?" he persisted.

I waved my hand in a circular motion skywards: "Allah, everywhere."

"Ah!" he exclaimed. Then, pointing to a waitress serving on the first floor balcony, he asked me: "Allah?"

"Nyet, for me Allah, everywhere," I replied. Then, looking directly at the man standing between the serving doors who pretended to read a newspaper while he observed all the diners, "For you, though, your Allah is that man there." Suddenly my companion turned pale as he realised that I had identified the KGB man in the restaurant.

As permission to visit the tractor plant at Minsk had become available, on the evening of 6 June, GMA, Mikhail and I caught an overnight sleeper for Minsk from Moscow's railway station. Our compartment had four berths – three for us and the fourth soon to be occupied by a stranger whom GMA named Boris. Mikhail and Boris drank beer continuously for as long as they could, so that by the time we reached Minsk next morning, the atmosphere in the cabin was foetid to the point of suffocation.

GMA were received at the Minsk plant by its management and escorted around. I noticed two streams of production – one red and one blue. I asked the Production Manager why. "Red - export. Blue – local."

The model being made in red was the MTZ 50 and the one in blue the UMZ 6. As we passed through the factories, I stopped to examine a chart on a wall. It showed the daily and cumulative production (differentiated by colour) of both types of tractors. It was not difficult to glean that Dr. Sukhikh had lied. The MTZ 50 tractors which Sukhikh had insisted could not be exported to us because production of that model had ceased, were still being made. Except that they were destined for hard currency markets, like Canada, the United Kingdom and the United States.

We were driven out into the countryside for lunch and then taken to the memorial at Khatyn, 50 kilometres from the city. We alighted in what looked like a building site in the early days of construction. All I could discern were the foundations of buildings – no walls, no windows, no doors, no roofs. The green countryside rolled away from us as far as the eye could see, The only sound that could be heard was the slow toll of a bell, one ring to recall each of the 147 Belarussian men, women and children (including 75 under the age of 18) that had been killed by the Nazis.

Having learned about the Second World War from western history books, I had never appreciated the sacrifices the Russian people had made during that conflict. Just the province of Belarus lost 2 million of its inhabitants (a quarter of its population) during the three years of Nazi occupation between 1941 and 1943.

That visit to Khatyn with its haunting single sound repeated at intervals and carried across the empty countryside is something I cannot forget.

We caught the night train back to Moscow. I had got the information I needed, and I suppose equally importantly for Mikhail he managed to get two cans of grease for himself from the Minsk plant which was unobtainable in Moscow.

We reached Moscow station at 8.00 a.m. Waiting at the platform, holding a black bag, stood Mr. Chuprygin, Director Transport. As soon as we alighted, he took a document out of the bag and handed it to me. It was a protocol that he wanted me to sign agreeing that all our future imports of tractors from Russia to Pakistan would be by road through Afghanistan. He must have known that I could not sign such a document and that too under a state of quasi-duress. I read it quickly and then put it away in my black bag.

GMA and I caught the Aeroflot flight for Karachi in the evening. The Tractoroexport were quite obviously disappointed that I had not agreed to anything they wanted. Sukhikh I was told was at his dacha and Mikhail pleaded that he could not accompany us to the airport.

On entering the aircraft – another Ilyushin - I discovered my cousin Abida Hussain inside. She was returning to Pakistan after attending from some conference or the other. I put the toy tractor I had bought earlier for Fidge at our feet. I knew no one would stop it being exported. It was red in colour and had been paid for in hard currency.

CHAPTER 6

IN THE UREA

The report on my trip to Moscow extended over 18 pages of text, with annexures. In its summary, I emphasised that Tractoroexport had been misleading us by contending that production of their popular MTZ 50 had been discontinued. I had seen it myself coming off the assembly lines at Minsk. The Russians were committed (on paper at least) to supply Fecto 744 units under their existing contract with him, an obligation they had no intention of fulfilling.

The barter arrangements between our two governments contained a firm allocation of $3 million for tractors for 1974, and a provisional allocation for 1975. If someone in the government did decide to import the UMZ 6 tractors, I had negotiated 1,000 tractors at a price of $3,000 per unit for delivery July 1974 through June 1975, and an additional 1,500 units at $3,100 per unit for delivery July 1975-June 1976.

I knew that no one in the government would read my report or use it to base a decision whether or not to import the UMZ 6 or not.

Soon after my return, a decision was taken to appoint Frank Alfrey the Managing Director of PTCL. He was already the CEO of Millat Tractors. His formal induction took place on 19 June. It so happened that a team from Massey Ferguson had come to Karachi to discuss the MF progressive manufacturing programme.

Alfrey's induction did not take long. The acting General Manager – Mr. N.N.A. Qureishy who was also a Board member and had been asked to handle PTCL's affairs after Hashmi's resignation – made clear what he thought of

Frank. He addressed barely two words of welcome before leaving the PTCL office. I noted in my diary:

> 'While FA was still trying to convince himself that he stood at the pinnacle of his ambitions, I had his briefcase and glasses moved unobtrusively into the GM's office and handed him the keys to Hashmi's desk. I hope one does not appear morbid or sentimental in referring to it as Hashmi's desk still, rather like Mrs. De Winter's persistent possessiveness in Daphne Du Maurier's thriller *Rebecca*. But the truth is that SAH was such a forceful part of PTCL's creation that for us pioneers who shared the excitement of those seminal months, the room would be SAH's room, *his* room, *his* desk.

In truth, I felt sorry for Frank. He pleaded for time to study the manufacturing programme before meeting the MF team.

He accompanied Humayun Mufti and myself on a quick visit to Abbottabad where a meeting had been scheduled with Capt. Gohar Ayub Khan (the son of former President Ayub Khan). We had gone to discuss the modalities for the transfer of the FIAT tractor franchise to PTCL.

Mufti and Gohar Ayub were not strangers to each other. They had worked together during the Ghandhara Industries days before nationalization and earlier still, before Gohar Ayub and General Habibullah (his father-in-law) parted company and Mufti joined the General. Gohar Ayub received us in his house that reminded me of Hitler's mountain retreat of Berchtesgaden in the Bavarian Alps. Not quite as dramatic but good enough for a Pakistani facsimile. The Capt.'s house was situated arrogantly on the highest point of the hill – "At least five feet higher than the Governor's House", he boasted.

Sitting with him and Mufti on the verandah, I noticed a building on the opposite side of the shallow valley.

"Is that building higher than yours?" I asked the Capt. mischievously.

"Well, yes," he conceded. "It's foundations are five feet higher than mine. But my roof is higher."

Mementos of his illustrious father populated the interior of the house. Photos of the Field Marshal addressing the nation at the outbreak of the 1965 war (his Bay of Pigs, I thought to myself), at state functions, and some Technicolor portraits of the old man by Gulgee.'

In all this rather sterile activity in PTCL, a brief shining moment occurred in an unexpected way. In my absence, Shahnaz had been approached by one of our friends in the advertising business and asked whether she could spare Momina to appear in TV commercial for the milk product Similac, and whether she herself would do the voice over.

I returned from the airport on 26 June evening and caught the advertisement being aired on PTV. Momina (then all of seventeen months old) melted my heart as she – with great concentration – lifted a small globe, placed it on a tin of Similac, and then sat back to gaze at her achievement. N's mellifluous voice assured the viewers: "The whole world loves Similac."

On 2 July, I received a call that would determine our lives for the next five years. Javed Talat rang me.

"Come over," he said.

"Where are you speaking from?"

"Lahore."

"But ..."

"It's decided. We want you to join us at the Fertiliser Corporation. I'll see you in Lahore, if you like when we can discuss it further. Alternatively, I'll be in Islamabad on the 4th."

Having recovered from the surprise, I mentioned that I too would be in Islamabad on 4th for a meeting with Feroze Qaiser at 11.00 a.m.

"Good," he said. "I am due to met him at 12.00 p.m., so I will see you there."

'Can this be true?' I asked my diary. 'It's one of the largest corporations – with the lucrative link to the Arabs.'

The following day, I left for Islamabad where at Rawalpindi airport I encountered Frank Alfrey. He announced: "I hear J. Rahim is out!" The news was confirmed at the Secretariat. Rahim had been fired for insubordination.

Uncle Jehangir Khan (at the time Joint Secretary in the Ministry of Provincial Coordination under Hafeez Pirzada) had the low-down on the showdown. According to Uncle JK, Bhutto and J. Rahim after a lengthy party meeting had a critical confrontation over dinner.

"I dismiss you," Bhutto shouted at his senior minister.

"Who are you to dismiss me?" Rahim retorted."*I* dismiss *you!*"

When J. Rahim returned home, the police came to him and served him with a dismissal notice. Rahim pulled a gun and in the fray shot 4 bullets, one hitting a policeman. At this, he was assaulted and physically beaten up.

When the doctor summoned by Rafi Raza arrived, all Rahim could mutter through swollen bleeding lips was: "They beat me up. They beat me up..."

I noted in my diary: 'JR is now in the CMH[1]; Rafi Raza has taken up Rahim's ministerial portfolios, and the PM is bent on destroying both JR and himself.' One was reminded of the famous cartoon by Sir John Tenniel, published in *Punch* in 1890. Captioned 'Dropping the Pilot', it depicted Kaiser Wilhelm II looking smugly over the railing of his ship while his humiliated Chancellor Otto von Bismarck descended the gangplank.

For the meeting with Feroze Qaiser on 4th, I had to brief Humayun Mufti at breakneck speed in the time between his leisurely breakfast and his meeting with the Secretary. Sensing that he would arrive late for the meeting, I hitched a lift with an official going for the same meeting.

"What's the *gup?*" he asked me.

"I wanted to ask you the same question. Where is Rahim?"

"I don't know. I tried to contact his son who works in the Planning Commission, but he is not in his office. Do you know where the minister is?"

"Why don't you try at the CMH?"

By this time, he was backing his car out of the driveway. "Tell me quickly! I have to pick up Masud Zaman[2] as well, and as soon he is in the car, we will not be able to talk."

When Masud did enter the car, although the topic of conversation did not change, the method of discussing it did. Suddenly, everyone was using the

---

[1] Combined Military Hospital.
[2] Joint Secretary Commerce.

language of the impersonal bureaucracy, the dialect of the survivors. "He was a good man, but ...", and "His contribution to the public sector was immense, but if only he had..."

The meeting on tractor availability and pricing was attended by more people than I had expected and of a higher level of seniority than usual: Feroze Qaiser and Malik Khuda Bukhsh Bucha (both Special Assistants to the PM), three Secretaries (Production, Agriculture, Industries), JS Commerce, Abid Hussain (Chairman SHEMTC[3]); Humayun Mufti, the Controller General of Prices and Supplies, a representative from the ADBP[4]. Among the observers sat Durrani (the rather superfluous Member Finance in BIM), Shahid Ahmed (equally superfluous as Chief Economist BIM), Lari (an Agricultural engineer), and myself.

Feroze Qaiser opened the meeting by rummaging through the working papers. He turned to Mufti for guidance. Mufti turned to me.

"Aijaz, would you mind explaining the position to us?"

I was asked to move my chair close to the head of the table and found myself seated between Malik Khuda Bukhsh Bucha and S.B. Awan (Secretary Production). Discussion started and whenever it began to stall, I would refer the participants to the relevant annexure. At one stage, I found myself conscious of a disembodied voice (mine) intoning: "Now, gentlemen if you will turn to Annexure IV, you shall see..." And they all dutifully turned their pages in unison.

The meeting lasted two and half hours. Outside the committee room of the PM's secretariat, the Chairmen of different corporations including Syed Babar Ali waited for their meeting with FQ. I was expecting Javed Talat to be there but after the traumatic events of the day before, I was not surprised at not finding him in Prime Minister's House. Javed as the only Deputy Secretary with only an Additional Secretary Allauddin Ahmed between him and the Minister had been suspected of being too close to J. Rahim. I avoided meeting Babar Ali and went instead with Bajwa (the CGP&S) who appeared quite impressed that I had been able to handle such senior people with anything like a passable competence.

---

[3] State Heavy Engineering & Mechanical Corporation of Pakistan
[4] Agricultural Development Bank of Pakistan, responsible for providing loans for tractors.

"Jaleel," Bajwa told his ACGP&S as we drove back to the Secretariat," this chap (pointing at me) will become a Special Assistant to the Prime Minister one day – provided he has the necessary backing!"

On the return journey to Karachi that night, I found that my seat was next to that occupied by Mr. A.R. Faridi.

"It's rather upsetting, isn't it, sir?"

"Well, I suppose it will be alright in the end."

I mentioned that I had seen the publicity film he had had prepared on the Pakistan Steel Mills project at Port Bin Qasim. I waited for his reaction.

"Yes. We shall have to alter that a little," he replied, and catching my eye, realised that we were both thinking of the all-too-conspicuous inclusion of J. Rahim in it.

On Sunday morning (7th), I answered to telephone and heard Syed Babar Ali's voice.

"Aijaz," he said, "We're looking for someone who is hard-working, honest, and efficient." He paused for a moment, as if he did not share the endorsement of my sponsor Javed Talat, "...and we think you are the right man for the job."

"I am very flattered," I replied, "but I hope my being your nephew is not going to be a hindrance."

He laughed. "I've told them that when he could not belong to his father, he could hardly belong to me."

I was not amused. "I thought I had outgrown that," I retorted.

At first events moved quickly. The very next day, I flew to Lahore where I had a meeting with Frank Alfrey to tell him that I would be leaving PTCL. Leaving him on a deflated state, I drove to meet Javed at the NFC offices in the Tail Wing of Al Falah Building. He wanted me to join NFC but underlinedly.

In the evening I called on Chandi and her husband Fakhr Imam. Chandi was making her own career move; she had decided to quit the PPP. As they had been invited to SBA's to hear Farida Khanum sing, I decided to tag along. The performance took place in his drawing room from which sofas had been removed. Farida Khanum sang with sensuousness, although most of this as lost on Soofi Tabassum, planted by SBA like some venerable but impotent presiding deity in front of her.

The rest of the family sang their own refrain: "So, when are you joining SBA?"

Bunny Said had a variant: "He asked me whether he should take you!"

As I was alone in Lahore, I made use of my time, after a gruelling day with Frank Alfrey at Millat, by visiting Shakir Ali in the house Nayyar Ali Dada had designed for him using brunt bricks. Khalid Iqbal also there, keeping Shakir's company.

Later I stopped at 3 Habibullah to meet Mummy and Waqar. There, Sister (our nanny) as vague and adorable as always.

"Mummy, do you know Aijaz has just come back from Morocco?"

"From Moscow, dear," I corrected her, as gently as I could.

"Now why did I say Morocco?"

Javed Talat called me the next day and asked me to drop in at the NFC office. Confident and ebullient as always, Javed told me: "SBA is here. Come over immediately."

I did. A short chat and then he picked up the phone.

"I've got Aijaz with me. Shall I bring him in now?"

From the reply he received, I could tell that Javed's enthusiasm was not mirrored by SBA. JT left me, returning a few minutes later and accompanied me into SBA's office. SBA sat behind a large desk opposite the door. He noticed me slip on my jacket.

"No need for a jacket. No such formalities here!"

He spoke briefly about the changes that had taken place in Islamabad, repeating mainly what JT had disclosed earlier – the new Minister's castigation of the Chairmen for inefficiency and extravagance, his referral of all the corporations to the Secretary Production. The only exceptions, SBA said with a hint of upmanship, would be the NFC and also the Steel Mills.

He then mentioned a conversation he had had with my elder brother Aizaz. SBA's PA Sahil, like trillions before him, had mistaken our names and connected SBA to Aizaz instead of to me.

"I asked Aizaz why you had left them. He replied that in our way of doing business, one and one make eleven. To Aijaz, they total two."

I thought to myself: 'So, my credentials have been reaffirmed by my previous employers.'

Coming closer to the reason why he had found it necessary to speak to JT alone before calling me in, SBA narrated a remark that the new minister Rafi Raza had made to him when he sought his approval for another senior appointment.

"That's alright by me," RR had replied, "but I hope he is not a relative of yours."

Having heard this caveat, SBA did not want to proceed with my appointment without a formal approval from the minister. I felt crushed and humiliated that SBA should have discussed my case with everyone except the person who would have the final say. To ease his predicament, I drafted a letter about myself from SBA addressed to the minister.

Now that it had become clear that the clearance of my appointment would take time, I left Lahore by the afternoon flight, only to find SBA on the same aircraft.

We sat together as he cross-examined me further about my professional experience. His own professional knowledge I discovered was limited (understandably) to the private sector. It did not surprise me therefore to hear him lapsing into gossip and petty enquiries into my fractured relationship with my brothers.

I heard nothing from either Javed or from SBA for the next few weeks. At the Pakistan Automobile Corporation (the BIM Member Automobiles' organization under a different banner), Mufti and his acolytes had begun to feel the pressure exerted by a revived Ministry of Production. The days of *laisser faire* when MDs would travel abroad (foreign trips were still a perk) for the flimsiet of reasons or someone like Jalil Alam could circumnavigate the world faster than Phileas Fogg, just to familiarise himself with auto manufacturing facilities in other countries, had been brought to an end by the new minister.

I described a meeting convened by Mufti at his office. I could find no better purpose for it than to administer 'colonic irrigation' to his errant MDs. Not that it had much effect. By the end of the session, they felt that they had been victimised by government functionaries, jealous of their independence. To pay lip service to the ministry's instructions to curtail unnecessary expenditure, they undertook not to stay at the Intercontinental Hotel in future and to abjure what Mufti described as 'conspicuous consumption.' They were firm about one thing: they would not entertain any government official with drinks and dames. "Ungrateful sods!" muttered Jalil Alam.

The NFC matter dragged on unconscionably. I found myself a pawn between the Ministry of Production, Babar and Javed at the NFC, and Mufti supported by Alfrey in PTCL. On 16th Mufti asked me to stay after our meeting with the IMT representatives. He mentioned that he wanted to make me a MD and move Frank Alfrey to a desk job, but he could not tell me when. The latest orders from the Ministry reconstituting the PTCL Board of Directors could not have been less encouraging. Frank Alfrey and I both stood excluded from the PTCL Board. Mufti confessed that he felt insecure about his own position as Chairman PACO.

Inevitably, rumours began to oscillate about my appointment in NFC. Noor (a senior engineer in PTCL) heard from a relation of his in the government that my appointment had in fact been approved.

I did what any sensible, rational man would have done in the circumstances. I had my horoscope done. Normally, I would have gone to Mureed Hussain, who sat in the Bombay Hotel on I.I. Chundrigar Road. This was too serious a matter to be left to a palmist. I needed a seer. I asked my father-in-law Agha sahib to accompany me to see Agha Hafizian, the Shia scholar who had conducted my nikah in 1971. He sat as was his wont on a white sheet spread on the floor. Before him he had a small scribe's desk.

Agha Hafizian consulted some books and then with quiet deliberation, he wrote on a piece of paper in Persian: *Kar–e-Lahore behtar ast* - A move to Lahore would be beneficial.

All I needed was for the Ministry of Production to see my future as clearly as he could.

I did consult the astrologer Mureed Hussain later. The moment I stepped into his first floor office, separated from his bedroom by a shabby curtain, he asked me: "How long have you been in this job?"

He calculated my horoscope. His reading forecast:

1. A new job, a new car and a house on the ground floor in Lahore.

2. The approval for this shall come from Islamabad, probably after an interview with the minister. (MH had no idea of the reference SBA had made to Rafi Raza on my case.)

3. The news shall come between 2nd and 9th August this year.

4. By or after 9th November, a considerable change in fortunes – more money, etc.

5. Travel abroad again this year.

6. Something is blocking my progress - either a spell or just some well-aimed shaft of jealousy.

Almost as he had overheard Mureed Hussain's predictions, Humayun Mufti asked for my personal file. Some days later, he called me and asked me whether I had spoken to SBA recently.

"I have just had a word with the Secretary Production. He has asked for your bio-data. It seems that the Ministry has questioned Javed's nomination as General Manager Finance & Planning in NFC because he does not possess the qualifications for the post. SBA may bifurcate the post and make you GM Finance. If he does, it is for you to decide whether you would like to go on to the NFC or stay in PTCL. I have told you I cannot guarantee you the GM-ship or MD-ship of PTCL. I can try but in the prevailing circumstances, it may not be worth a try. If you wish to go to the NFC, I have told the Secretary and SBA that I cannot release you before 3 months. Fair enough?"

On my way home, I regretted allowing myself to be vulnerable to SBA and particularly to JT's machinations. Javed planned on leaving for Harvard to attend its Advanced Management Program. He told me later that when he told SBA on their first meeting that he was going to Harvard, SBA could not wait to have him in the NFC. For SBA, as I would discover, the Harvard AMP was akin to performing corporate Haj.

Javed kept me informed of the progress (or the lack of it) of my case. One night, after a dinner at which Ayaz was present, Javed thought he would demonstrate that he knew the ropes in Karachi. "I met your brother Ayaz at Mumtaz Bhutto's last night. He told me that Rafi Raza is Mumtaz's man. So I asked him to get Mumtaz to tell Rafi to expedite your appointment."

I recall a conversation between Javed Talat and the other Javed (Javed Hamid) whom SBA courted assiduously for the post of Manager Planning in NFC. Javed Hamid was serving as the Director in the Planning Commission and clearly unhappy with the diminution of the role of the Planning Commission under Bhutto's socialist government. Javed Talat had his own grievances.

"They [i.e. the government] must realise." Javed Talat remonstrated, "that in order to get the best talent, they should be prepared to pay for it."

Javed Hamid reminded him that one the less palatable but extant effects of nationalisation was the standardisation of pay-scales in public sector organizations. Javed Talat refused to be deflected by such technicalities: "No! No! It's a question of priorities. If the Government wants to see the NFC succeed, it must permit us an open hand."

"Would you concede, "I asked JT gently, "the same priority to NFC were you to be, for example, in the State Heavy Engineering Corporation?"

"I would not have joined the State Heavy Engineering Corporation," he replied airily.

After sitting on some interviews, I dropped Javed Talat at the Palace Hotel. "The problem is," he said, "I am used to working fast. It irritates me to have to work with people who are slower than I am."

"But isn't that what management is all about…"

He wasn't listening.

One evening I invited him for dinner at our flat. The other guests Shahnaz and I had called were my cousin Niloufer and two friends - Naushaba and I. H. Burney who published the outspoken and therefore controversial magazine *Outlook*. Just the mention of Burney's name put Javed on his guard. He need not have been apprehensive. The Burneys forgot our invitation. That gave him the liberty to be more open and candid than he might have been otherwise: the take-over of industries - 'a political rather than a socialism driven act'; J. Rahim? - 'a scatter-brain'; and the BIM - 'corrupt'.

The NFC appointment dragged into the first week of September. Quite suddenly, I received a telephone call from JT's personal assistant. Could I fly down to Lahore for an interview with the Minister on 2 September? This was followed by a confirmatory telegram inviting me for an interview to appear for an interview for the post of 'Chartered Accountant.'

The interview with Rafi Raza, J. Rahim's successor as the Minister of Production, took place on a Sunday, 1 September. Waiting in the antechamber at NFC, I encountered Saiduddin, the rags-to-riches success symbol who had moved from being the Regional Representative for PIDC in Lahore to being the MD-designate of Pak-Arab Fertilisers Limited at Multan, and whom success could not spoil – he still wore shoes without socks; also Jaffery, a fellow CA and FM of the Kohinoor Group, nervous at being casually dressed and ill-prepared to appear before the minister; and Pervaize, a pupil of Dr. Shahnawaz whom the good Doctor was loath to see develop. F. Alam – the Chairman of the Cement Corporation - had somehow got mixed up with us interviewees and could not understand why. Saiduddin added to Alam's discomfort by needling him on the current export price of cement.

I was summoned at 1.00 p.m. The minister whom I had never met before was young looking and courteous. He smiled to put me at ease. To his right sat Mr. S.B. Awan, Secretary Production, and to his left SBA, Dr. Ahmed Shahnawaz[5] and Javed Talat.

As an opener, Rafi Raza asked me: "What's wrong with the PTCL?"

"Nothing," I replied. "Nothing at all. What you want to know is why I want to leave PTCL. The answer is that I have been asked to join NFC." I waited a few moments for this to sink in, before continuing: "There is of course another, equally important reason. The PTCL is basically a technically oriented organisation. Although I am the Acting GM there, my qualification is in Finance. On comparing the responsibilities of my present position and those attached to the NFC post, it is obvious that I could gain more experience professionally in the NFC."

Rafi Raza asked me about Maurice Apple & Co. ('a small firm of accountants, with clients who were in the main sole proprietorships or partnerships'), the ICP and Bela Engineers. Then S. B. Awan took over: "What is the money market situation nowadays?"

I replied: "Our foreign exchange reserves have fallen by 200 crores, and the rupees in circulation have gone up." ·

---

[5] Dr. Ahmed Shahnawaz, because of his considerable expertise in consultancy, had been appointed Chairman of NDISC – National Design and Industrial Services Corporation. It was expected to provide consultancy and advisory services to the public sector.

"Well, what I meant to ask you was, how would you set about raising finance for projects?"

I explained the role of PICIC and IDBP, the expectations of the newly formed NDFC[6], the withering fertility of the insurance sector and banks as sources of long-term financing, and the use the Government had made of government guaranteed debentures, and the reason why they could not rely upon this channel anymore.

Suddenly, the minister leaned forward: "What would you do," he asked me, "if you were in my position?" As he was saying it, I knew I had him. I waited a few seconds before replying: "You have asked a very pertinent question. But you should have asked me this question two years ago." I elaborated by describing the types of controls one could institute, etc., but my retort seemed to have impressed him. It was too close to the reality of his predicament not to have made him realize that I knew exactly what he was tacitly admitting.

Some two hours later, I was called back into the conference room. Everyone else had left except for SBA and JT. They were all smiles now. Javed beamed: "Next time, don't open your mouth. Don't put up such a good performance. Instead of approving your appointment in NFC, the minister wants you in his ministry in Islamabad. We had a devil of a job getting him to agree that you work with us."

SBA's relief was genuine. He knew as I did that the interview was not as much of me as of him. My credentials could not be questioned; at stake was SBA's judgment in proffering me as a candidate.

Was it Agha Hafizian's *istikhara* or Mureed Hussain's astrological forecast, Shahnaz's prayers or the amulet G M 'Fecto' Adamjee gave me the morning of my interview that swung the decision in my favour? Perhaps, a little something from each.

---

[6] National Development Finance Corporation had been established to arrange project and working capital financing for all the companies and projects in the public sector.

CHAPTER 7

LAHORE BEHTAR AST

Could it really be almost two months since I last made entries in this diary?' I asked myself on 29 October 1974.

Once the permission for my appointment in NFC had come through, I made plans to move our luggage to Lahore. The first imperative was obviously to find accommodation there.

Agha Ikram Khan (the Administration Manager of NFC) identified a number of options. The one I settled on consisted of a compact, self-contained half-portion of a larger house in Ghalib Road, Gulberg. It had two-and-a-half bedrooms with attached bathrooms, an open drawing-cum-dining area, two commodious verandahs overlooking two gardens, one in front and the other behind the house. The garage and servants' quarters lay beyond the back lawn.

When I moved into our Karachi flat in 1971, my belongings consisted primarily of an antique four poster bed, books on art, Shakir Ali's paintings and some second-hand sofas. Over the first three years of our married life, we managed to collect enough to fill two truck loads. I could see how much from my flat window when it was placed on the driveway, waiting to be loaded on to the trucks.

I thought Fidge might be disturbed at seeing her home being dismantled, but she regarded packing as a game. Once, I heard a mewing sound come from one of the cartons. I opened it and found that Fidge had packed our Siamese cat in it.

I preceded Shahnaz and Fidge to Lahore. I wanted the house to be functional before they came. Shakir's paintings with their dark reds and sombre Prussian blues of course limited the colour scheme. I had one wall in the drawing room painted dark blue. It proved to be a perfect backdrop for some of our smaller paintings. Paradoxically, the cheapest furnishing materials I could find were not cotton but velvet (at Rs 26 per yard), and the cheapest marble green onyx.

I reported for duty at NFC on 1 October. Javed Talat and I overlapped briefly, long enough for him to give me specific instructions on how and where he wanted his allowances remitted. His room was allotted to me.

The NFC in those early days occupied an entire first floor of what was known as the Tail Wing of Al Falah Building, an office block that occupied one corner of Charing Cross, later renamed Faisal Square after King Faisal of Saud Arabia. Below us Citibank had a branch, the manager of which Shaukat Aziz moved up the corporate ladder within Citibank and ultimately returned to Pakistan to become prime minister under General Pervez Musharraf.[1]

The NFC staff had been transferred from PIDC's Lahore office, following the promulgation of the WPIDC Transfer of Projects & Companies Ordinance 1974. Rather like nationalisation under the Economic Reforms Order in 1972, at a stroke, ownership of units (whether taken over or units within PIDC) stood vested in the new Corporations. To NFC's share fell four operating fertiliser plants – the Natural Gas Fertiliser Factory at Multan, the Pak-American Fertilisers plant at Daudkhel, and two smaller units at Lyallpur (now Faisalabad) and Jaranwala. In addition, the NFC had been given responsibility for executing three major projects – the expansion of the Multan factory and the establishment of two grass-root facilities in Sindh and in N.W.F.P. (now Khyber Pakhtunkhwa).

The NFC plants produced both nitrogenous and phosphatic fertilisers. Its share of the domestic production of nitrogenous fertilisers represented 23% of the total. The larger factories in the private sector like Dawood Hercules at Sheikhupura and Exxon Fertilisers at Dharki in Sindh accounted for the remaining 77%. Phosphatic fertilisers such as Single Super-Phosphate needed to be used as a concomitant with nitrogenous fertilizers but were less popular both with manufacturers (costs too high) and consumers (benefits questionable). NFC had a 100% monopoly of them. The marketing and

---

[1] Prime Minister of Pakistan from 20 August 2004 to 15 November 2007, and in parallel Finance Minister from 6 November 1999 to 15 November 2007.

distribution of NFC produced fertilisers lay in the sluggish hands of the Punjab Agricultural Development and Supplies Corporation (PADSC). Pricing of fertilisers had to be determined annually by the Controller General Prices & Supplies. The CGPS operated at its own sloth-like pace. For example, the prices of fertilisers had not been finalised nor notified since 1969-70. This delay I discovered had been deliberate. The Government was duty bound to pay the producer as a subsidy the difference between the higher cost of production and the lower controlled selling price to the farmer.

The NFC and its units employed 3,200 executives and workers. As no-one in NFC head office had been given the responsibility for personnel matters, I took over. I discovered that unionized workers were employees of the respective companies, where there were companies. In the case of ex-PIDC units (e.g. NGFF at Multan), which were not corporate bodies, technically they remained employees of PIDC until their employment could be regularised with NFC. So, in effect, the employees in the NFC group fell into three categories: unionized staff, executives employed in NFC subsidiaries, and those who did not know who their employer was. A further complication awaiting me was that the agreements with the various collective bargaining agents (CBAs) expired on different dates. This encouraged a CBA to negotiate terms better than the ones the last CBA had obtained. Another challenge that required resolution was to develop such pay scales that would be incentive enough to attract persons from the private sector but not a disheartening disincentive for those already on lower public sector scales.

Bhutto had expressed his determination to make Pakistan self-sufficient in its agricultural inputs – hence the emphasis on progressive manufacture of tractors, farm implements, and fertilisers. The precipitous increase he demanded in fertiliser availability meant that NFC had to increase its production from 306,400 metric tons to over 1.5 million tons. Out of all the nine other corporations (except for the Pakistan Steel Mills which was a behemoth on its own) NFC could demand and did receive priority when it came to allocation of funding out of a limited pool of fiscal resources. Ironically, foreign exchange – whether through loans, grants, or aid – proved to be more readily available than rupee financing.

In order to understand exactly what the NFC was engaged in, I took custody of all the files that had been brought from the PIDC branch office and over a weekend, I cannibalised them. I sorted all the papers according to subjects and projects. Gradually, the pattern I sought began to emerge. Not only did I know which documents and correspondence existed but I knew where to find them.

With Babar Ali away on one of his all too frequent trips abroad and Javed in Harvard, it was left to me to represent NFC at the Fertiliser Coordination Committee, convened at the NFC Board Room on 12 October. I had been in the job for less than a fortnight, and I suspect my ignorance about the fertilizer industry showed. Secretary Production S.B. Awan asked me a few questions about the output of each factory and then with ineffable courtesy, he said: "I know that you are new to this sector. The information I need is this, this and this. Could you ensure that it is available for us in time for the next Coordination meeting?"

Malik Khuda Bukhsh Bucha chided me with the gentle reproof: "Mufti tells me you slipped through his fingers." Yaqub (Secretary Agriculture) asked: "You are working here as well?" Rafi Raza had the last word. I saw him into his ministerial flagged car, and as I stood waiting for him to drive away, he looked at my dark suit, silk shirt, gold cufflinks and the Rolex watch (a wedding gift from the Aghas), and said with a sigh : "Oh, to be a Chartered Accountant!"

I could not resist replying: "We have been known to envy lawyers sometimes." As one of the all too many lawyers[2] in Bhutto's Cabinet, he got the joke, smiled and waved a friendly goodbye.

Working closely with SBA exposed me to the darker side of his moon. His reputation as an astute, successful businessman had been based on choosing competent partners such as the Swedish Rausings and then leaving the day-to-day management to their expatriates. It took Packages Limited more than twenty years to wean itself away from such an expensive dependence. Coming from such a protected environment into the brittle public sector, he assumed that a frontal, no-nonsense, confrontational posture would work with the Government. It took him time to learn that governments do not humour prima donnas, especially when they come from the private sector.

My irritation after the first three months of trying to adapt to his highly centrifugal style of management must have been acute. My diary entry reveals

---

[2] 'For my part I must own that I wish the country to be governed by law, not by lawyers.' Edmund Burke, quoted in Sampson, A., *Anatomy of Britain Today* (London, 1965), p.162.

my irritation:

'The past few months have been a continuous effort in preventing SBA from causing himself and the NFC permanent damage. I don't think I am being either unfair or unkind to him by saying that whenever he opens his mouth, it is to put his other foot in it. Whether it is in the office, dealing with subordinates; or whether it is to the Ministry whom he regards as a cumbersome crown – heavy on his brow but the unavoidable symbol of his status; or even when handling international companies and bidders such as Snamprogetti, Heurtey and Kellogg (all bidders for the Mirpur Mathelo Fertiliser project). To all he demonstrates an unbelievable irresponsibility and immaturity.

Sometimes I have been frightened by the naiveté with which he has been handling the projects entrusted to NFC. The Mirpur Mathelo project alone is likely to cost $138 million in foreign exchange with another Rs 40 crores in Pak. Rupees, the Pakistan Fertiliser[3] and the Chinese Urea plant[4] in Hazara approximately another Rs 40 crores – and he has made no plans idea of their financing. To talk to him about the practicalities of life – about finance, or about people, organizational structures, etc. – is to cause him to stop talking, and that for him is an unnatural condition.'

During this time, Awan sahib caught up with the Pakistan Automobile Corporation. In a night of the 'long knives', Mufti's acolytes – Salar, Jaleel Alam, Ashfaque Ahmed, Z.U. Khan, Karanja of Naya Daur Motors, and a number of others - were asked to resign.

"If they did this to me, I would resign," SBA spluttered.

"But then you are not Humayun Mufti. There are two ways one can bring down a tree – by hacking at its roots or by cutting its branches."

Mufti did not seem noticeably disturbed at the change in the ministry's attitude towards him. I met him some days later in the ministry itself. I waited outside the office of the Secretary. Mufti walked in and sat next to me, so placing himself that he should see (and be seen) by the minister, when he

---

[3] Owned by the Jaffer group in Karachi, the company was nationalized in 1972 and its urea project relocated at Haripur Hazara.
[4] A 600 MTD Urea plant donated by the People's Republic of China.

walked past to his office. Sure enough, Rafi Raza walked past and noticed Mufti.

A few minutes later, the turbanned *daftari* came and saluted us.

"Sahib is remembering you."

Mufti responded with speed. Turning to me, he said:" If the Secretary asks for me, tell him that I am sitting with the minister."

He returned less than a minute later. "He wants *you!*"

The year 1974 ended on a sour note. Javed Talat returned from Harvard to find me well ensconced in NFC. An added abrasion for him came from the Government's intention to designate all those in the pay scale of Rs 2,700 – 200 - Rs 4,500 as General Managers. This would have meant that I would be General Manager Finance and therefore at par with him. Javed refused to accept such a situation, even though no formal orders had been issued by the ministry.

Aftab Ahmed, who had left Dawood Hercules to join the NFC as General Manager Technical, was sent by SBA to mollify Javed. This delegation of any unpleasant task I noticed remained a feature of SBA's management style. He had used me as an intermediary between Aftab and Pervaize, both of whom handled the technical aspects of NFC's projects. "They are a classic example of one plus one equalling zero," SBA told me. "You sort it out." I did. Pervaize resigned and returned to Dr. Ahmed Shahnawaz's consultancy firm. Aftab become the General Manager Technical.

Aftab's mission proved to be more painful. He received an earful of recriminations against me, most of them fed to Javed while he was at Harvard by his wife Farida Talat from Lahore. Her source from within NFC was Agha Ikram, the Manager Administration. Javed accused me of manoeuvring to supplant him from the GM-ship. Aftab's intercession with Javed ended on a note of conciliation. Javed agreed that I could be designated GM Finance provided he became the General Manager Planning. (Javed Hamid had decided against joining NFC.) The next morning, Javed changed his mind. He met SBA and told him that he would prefer not to remain in the NFC. "The atmosphere here has changed."

Even after all these years I can see how manipulative I must have been to secure a position for which I felt professionally and administratively qualified.

For Javed, the raison d'être of leaving Islamabad and the Ministry of Production had been to move to Lahore and to be part of the management team that would set up three large fertiliser plants in as many years. But Awan sahib did not like Javed. He held him responsible for the flaccid supervision of the Board of Industrial Management after nationalisation. It did not help Javed's case when he tried to undermine Awan sahib soon after he took over as Secretary. He had assumed that Awan sahib would have been so distracted by the tragedy of his daughter's death[5] that he would not have had time to attend to the minutiae of the ministry's day-to-day affairs, and refused to share control. SBA told me afterwards that this trauma had caused Awan sahib to lose his short-term memory. That explained the diligent, almost obsessive note taking by Awan sahib during meetings. I assumed it must be a bureaucratic idiosyncrasy until I learned of its real cause.

During that winter of 1974 into the spring of 1975, all of us at the NFC were embroiled in negotiations to select the engineering contractors for the Mirpur Mathelo project. At 1,700 MTD of Urea, it would be on the largest such plant in Asia. International firms were desperate to secure it, not simply for its own sake but because they had an eye on the Indian market. The Indians, we were told, were waiting to see who we would select so that they could follow our choice.

The Indians were not the only ones with an interest in our decision. The Fauji Foundation – with a surplus of Rs 10 crores burning a hole in its pocket – declared its intention to enter the fertilizer industry. It had grown from managing the pensions of army servicemen into becoming one of the largest business conglomerates. General Rao Farman Ali (who made an undignified escape from Dacca in December 1971) had been 'rewarded' with its chairmanship. Yusuf Pasha (a fellow chartered accountant and husband of Rashida Khuhro[6]) was my counterpart in Fauji. I had met him first in 1967 during my brief posting to Rawalpindi where I had gone to assist in the establishment of the ICP branch office there.

Fauji Foundation expressed a desire also to establish a large fertiliser plant based on the same source of feedstock gas from the Marri gas field in

---

[5] His daughter, married at the time to Talal Bugti (Nawab Akbar Bugti's son), died under suspicious circumstances while she and Talal were staying in Faletti's Hotel, Lahore.
[6] Rashida was the elder daughter of M.A. Khuhro, once Chief Minister of Sindh before his ouster by General Ayub Khan in 1958.

Dharki. Within a radius of twenty-five miles, three plants would be operational – those of NFC, Esso and Fauji. The railways would be required to transport about four thousand metric tons of fertiliser every day. "It will make the station master at Dharki the richest man in the railways," SBA commented laconically.

In NFC, discussions with the various bidders enabled us to sophisticate the cost estimates of the Mirpur Mathelo project. Our estimate hovered close to Rs 180 crores. The Fauji proposal to the government spoke of Rs 240 crores. As both plants would be based on similar technologies and had the same designed capacity, the presumption within government circles was that either the NFC had under-estimated its project cost or the Faujis had inflated theirs. The additional cost of transporting the gas from the Marri gas field twenty-five miles away to the Fauji plant alone could not explain the eye-popping difference.

A meeting of the Fertiliser Coordination Committee was called by the Government to make a comparison of the two cost estimates. SBA made his position clear at the outset. "I will not discuss Fauji's figures. I am here only to defend ours."

The members of the FCC probed and questioned, and in the end explained the discrepancy away as being due to interest and other costs. During that meeting, our NFC team and the Faujis sat on the same side of the table, with the Government representatives led by Rafi Raza opposite. Sitting uncomfortably between the NFC and the Faujis was Dr. Ahmed Shahnawaz, the technical consultant to both. He had the invidious responsibility of justifying two differing cost estimates for almost identical projects. Being the consummate consultant, he managed to satisfy both his clients and the government. A few months later, SBA narrated the course of a meeting the chairmen of the public sector corporations had with the prime minister. Discussion focused on the location of a paper mill. Zulfikar Ali Bhutto looked down the table at SBA and said: "You are supposed to know something about the paper industry. Where do you think it should be set up?" After SBA gave his opinion, Bhutto looked further down the table at Dr. Ahmed Shahnawaz: "Aren't you a consultant? Where do you think it should be located?"

Dr. Shahnawaz moved his chair closer to the table so that he could be seen by Mr. Bhutto, and replied: "Wherever you like, prime minister!"

SBA had an ambivalent attitude towards consultants. For years he had relied upon advice from Mr. Yusuf Bhaimia, one of the senior partners in A.F. Ferguson & Co. – the auditors of Packages Limited and other group companies. Yet, he kept on the wall of his office at NFC, a cartoon that showed two executives in conversation. One says to the other: "Should we call in the consultants – or should we make a mess of it ourselves?"

My diary of these days reminds me that after our meeting on comparative pricing of our projects, I thought it appropriate to call on Yusuf Pasha at his house. I entered and was ushered into a modest drawing room dotted with lacquered wooden furniture from Hala in Sindh.

"Rashida, Aijaz is here," he shouted from where we were standing. Rashida entered. "Aijaz is with the NFC nowadays."

"Aren't those the people who are setting up *cheap* fertilizer plants?"

I felt as if we were procuring our equipment from Woolworths.[7]

In a way she was right, but for the wrong reason. We were not buying cheap equipment. We just did not have all the money needed to implement such an ambitious project. Commitments had been made by King Faisal of Saudi Arabia, of which $50 million had been earmarked by the Economic Affairs Division for NFC's Mirpur Mathelo project, but no one knew when the Saudis would release the money.

Rafi Raza as the minister responsible advised us to go ahead with the selection of the engineering contractor on Dr. Shahnawaz's assurance that as long as $10 million would be available in a few months, that would cover the Engineering Consultant's fees and expenses. The remaining $40 million would be required once design had been completed and procurement of equipment begun. I felt it was like entering Maxim's for a meal with only enough money in one's pocket to pay for the first course.

Rupee financing remained a constraint. The story doing the rounds in Islamabad, I wrote in my diary, was that when the Secretary General Finance Mr. A.G.N. Kazi was asked to identify the constraint on money in circulation, he replied: "Only the printing capacity of the Security Printing Corporation."

Discouraged by such hurdles, Fauji Foundation withdrew from the race,

---

[7] A low price supermarket chain popular in post-war Britain.

That left NFC alone in the field. A debate started on the viability of setting up one large ammonia plant with a capacity of 1,000 MTD feeding two streams of urea, or an ammonia plant of 1,200 MTD feeding two streams of 1,000 MTD of urea. Had it been restricted to in-house deliberations, we would have looked less foolish. Instead, as discussions on the draft continued with the three firms bidding for the engineering contract, it became clear to everyone around the table that we had yet to decide the plant's capacity, even its location.[8]

The three firms – the Italian Snamprogetti, the French Heurtey, and the British-American Kellogg International – was then invited to make a sales pitch. Snamprogetti offered the 1,000 MTD ammonia/1740 MTD urea combination. They did so with confidence because they owned Nuovo Pignone – the only company in the business which could make compressor that could feed a single train of 1,740 MTD Urea. Heurtey proposed a different, weaker combination of a Kellogg ammonia plant with two trains of urea. Kellogg wanted the NFC to replicate the 800 MTD ammonia /1,500 urea combination being used already in Pakistan by Dawood Hercules in Sheikhupura and by Esso at Dharki.

Each of the three bidders emphasised its uniqueness. The Kellogg representative – a rather haughty Englishman with a double-barrelled name – told us with a whiff of condescension: "I will not make a sales pitch to you gentlemen. You know us. We are Kellogg. We are a known name. And with us," he added, as if it was the clincher, "you will have no language problem."

"Ah!" I replied. "That means you will be learning Urdu."

Once the technical options had been identified, narrowed and then finalised, the commercial negotiations commenced. We submitted a draft contract to Snam and to Heurtey. Discussions on that took almost a fortnight. Despite our efforts to have the two competitors come on different dates, or if that was not possible, then at different times, and when even that failed, in different rooms. I am sure they both knew that the other was in Lahore or in the NFC office. SBA rather gave the game away by calling the leader of the French Heurtey delegation Degois by the name of Snam's team Debard!

To receive their final bids, a team was constituted, comprising Dr. Imtiaz

---

[8] Mr. Bhutto had promised his Punjabi constituency that the first fertiliser plant would be set up by his government in the Punjab.

A. Khan, (Joint Secretary, Ministry of Production), Mr. M. Shafi (Financial Advisor to the Ministry of Production), and Syed Babar Ali. Each bidder submitted a sealed envelope. Dr. Flenkenthaller (who led the Snamprogetti team), before giving his, asked bluntly whether anything was to be paid 'outside the contract'. Mr. Babar Ali shook his head. Flenkenthaller then inked in a figure, sealed the envelope and pushed it across the table towards the committee members.

With the technical and commercial bids in, we clubbed together at NFC to prepare the minutes of the Negotiating Committee's meetings and its recommendations for a decision by the minister. A special meeting of all the concerned ministries was summoned by Rafi Raza to discuss the recommendations.

SBA, Aftab, Dr. Shahnawaz and myself attended. Opposite us was a phalanx of Federal Secretaries, the noisiest of whom was Aftab Ahmed Khan (Secretary EAD) whose forte consisted of recalling and reciting a couplet suitable to the occasion. I remember A.G.N Kazi (Secretary General Finance), Allauddin Ahmed (Additional Secretary Production) and I.A. Imtiazi (Secretary Agriculture) noticeable amongst them. The Secretaries sat on either side of Rafi Raza and Shaukat Awan.

Babar Ali was invited to present his recommendation. He described the stages of the negotiations and the technical implications of each proposal. He concluded by saying with a force that he hoped would extinguish any opinions to the contrary: "I want Snamprogettti."

"What you think, gentlemen?" Rafi Raza asked the Secretaries. Each in turn voted for Kellogg: "It is a tried and tested technology"; "Let us stick to someone we know and trust."; "Old is gold."

"Well, you've heard what the Government's view is," Rafi Raza told SBA.

"I don't care. I want Snamprogetti."

"And what happens if they fail?"

"You can have my head."

I whispered something to SBA. He looked at the minister. "You know what my finance man has just said to me?" He then repeated my remark: "He says that I may think my head is worth $180 million, but the Pakistan

Government does not."

"We are inclined to agree with your finance man," Rafi Raza replied.

The impasse had hardened into a stalemate. Snamprogettti vs. Kellogg. Suddenly, Awan sahib intervened: "But one should not exclude Heurtey altogether. I can see some merits in their proposal. Dr. Shahnawaz, could you refresh our minds about the salient features of Heurtey's bid?"

Brilliant, I thought to myself. Awan sahib, the quintessential bureaucrat, had avoided a showdown by throwing a distraction into the ring.

In the end, on 27 January 1975, the Government gave the go-ahead to award the engineering contract to Snamprogetti. No sooner had this news become public than SBA received a legal notice from Messrs. Creusot Loire, a French firm, reminding him that PIDC had committed to award the contract for this fertiliser plant to them. The basis of Creusot Loire's claim lay in a letter that had been issued some years earlier (on Bhutto's orders) by the then General Manager PIDC. It promised in effect that the contract for this fertiliser plant would be awarded on a turnkey basis to them. (All our negotiations with the three bidders had envisaged a cost-plus procurement strategy.) The Minister instructed SBA to invite Creusot Loire for a meeting.

The French team came to Lahore while we were in the throes of negotiating the fine print of a contract with Snamprogetti. Just as we entered the NFC Board room (we being SBA, Dr. Shahnawaz, Aftab, Pervaize, and myself), SBA turned to me and whispered: "You do the talking."

As I began my pre-oration, thanking them for travelling to Lahore at such short notice, etc., the leader of the French side Mr. Perrier asked why Creusot Loire had not been invited to bid.

Before I could reply, SBA blurted out: "Because we don't trust you. You are crooks, and we don't want to do business with you." (He had been told by Aftab and Pervaize that Creusot Loire had provided the equipment – some of it defective - for the PIDC/NGFF plant in Multan.)

"Oh, I see," Perrier replied.

SBA would have continued had I not squeezed his kneecap under the table.

"What the Chairman meant to say," I began, "is that while we are aware of the commitments made by PIDC to you, we are not in a position to execute that obligation."

"And why not?"

"We have referred the matter to our Government and we have been instructed to inform you that the Government concurs with our position."

"Who in the Government, may I ask?"

"For obvious reasons I cannot disclose that. But I assure you that it has been decided at the highest level."

The French took turns to get me to swerve, to make a mistake, but I stuck to the mantra that the government had instructed us to make our position known to Creusot Loire. Eventually, after a veiled threat that they might contemplate legal recourse against NFC, the team gave up.

As they filed past us on their way out of the Board room, they shook hands with each of us. When the leader Perrier reached me, he stopped and whispered: "Monsieur, my compliments. That was truly a *tour de force*."

We heard nothing from Creusot Loire after that, or should I say NFC heard nothing from them. On 31 January I answered the phone. It was Anderson, the local representative of Creusot Loire in Pakistan.

"Will you be available in Lahore on 8th?"

"Certainly. Why?"

"I have just received a cable message from Creusot Loire asking you to join them. One of their representatives will be flying to Lahore on 8th by the morning flight and he wants to meet you before returning to Karachi the same evening. I need not emphasise that the matter is confidential. It is between Creusot Loire and you. It has nothing to do with the NFC."

The Creusot Loire man came on 8th. "You will recognise me," he told me when he phoned to confirm his arrival. "I am six and a half feet tall." And so he was. He loped out of the lift in the hotel and then gamely folded himself to fit into my Volkswagen. (Every officer entitled to a car in NFC had been given, on SBA's orders, a Volkswagen. To set an example, he drove one himself. I twigged him: "You can afford to live beneath your means. You have a BMW at home.")

The Creusot Loire interviewer explained the role CL was playing in the spectacular commercial bonanza in the Middle East and their need to recruit acceptable representatives. "An Arab would not be acceptable to another Arab. A Lebanese would be suspected by every Arab. The Indians are regarded as Hindus and the Bengalis no one wants to know. That leaves you Pakistanis, who for some reason enjoy acceptability in every Gulf state. Mr. Perrier felt that with your background and education, you would be most suitable."

He asked me whether I was mobile enough to live in Paris for a year and then be posted to the Middle East. I replied I was, and to reinforce my commitment I took him home to meet Shahnaz before dropping him at the airport.

Flattering though that offer was, it proved sterile. I heard nothing from Creusot Loire ever again.

Seductive as such offers were, I knew that my responsibility lay with NFC. The negotiations with Snamprogetti proceeded day by tiring day. Aftab, Pervaize and I assisted by our legal advisor Dr. Parvez Hassan represented NFC; Dr. Flenkenthaller and his two aides – Stacul for technical details and Geniale for commercial terms – represented Snam.

It took over a month to complete an agreed draft. That was sent to the Government for approval, and such was Rafi Raza's keenness to have the project started that Awan sahib and his team at the ministry gave their clearance without reading its fine print. They did not have the time.

Some-one who had all the time in the world was a lowly Section Officer in the Ministry of Finance. He sent me a query which read: 'We have examined the contract proposed to be executed between the NFC and Snamprogetti. We note that NFC has undertaken to return to Italy the body of any Snam employee who dies in Pakistan. You will recall that in the earlier contract between Pak-Arab Fertilisers Ltd and M/s Kellogg International and Messrs Uhde, no such undertaking had been given. Please explain the reason for such a deviation, and why there is a potential loss to the government.'

I wrote back: 'You will observe that NFC has undertaken to provide return air tickets to every Snam employee from Milan to Pakistan and back. We have checked with PIA staff. They have informed us that it would be cheaper for NFC to ship a dead expatriate in a recumbent posture than send him alive in an upright condition. There is therefore a potential *saving* to the public exchequer.' I heard nothing more from the Section Officer.

The date of signature of the Snam contract was fixed for 21 February. Even until the afternoon of that day, I had no idea where the plant would be located. It had yet to be decided by Mr. Bhutto whether the plant would be at Mirpur Mathelo in Sindh or at Machi Goth in the Punjab. I went to the airport to receive Rafi Raza who happened to be flying into Lahore. In those days one could go up to the steps of the aircraft. Rafi Raza emerged, saw me and said: "Put down Mirpur Mathelo in the contract. We can always change it."

Then suddenly he noticed Mani Rahman - the PR officer at PECO – and the blue Mercedes that once belonged to PECO's pre-nationalisation owner Mr. Latif.

"What are you doing here?" Rafi asked Mani tersely. "Go back to your office, and take that damned car with you. I don't need it, and neither do you."

I returned to Al Falah building where I had left Dr. Flenkenthaller standing literally in the same clothes he had flown in that morning. His luggage had been lost somewhere between Milan and Lahore. It would have been impossible to have had a suit made for Dr. Flenkenthaller in three hours. Lahore was not Hong Kong or Bangkok. The best I could do was to offer him one of mine. The jacket fitted but the trousers needed slight alteration. A tailor in Al Falah building was put to work on that. Another made a shirt and I brought some of my ties for Dr. Flenkenthaller to choose from.

Just before the press could be allowed in to cover the event, Dr. Flenkenthaller stood in front of a mirror in SBA's office, admiring his borrowed plumage. To complete his ensemble, he took first one red tie, then another of a different colour, then a third.

"Which one should I wear?" he asked me.

Geniale, who had a comic streak in him, wordlessly banged his head against the wall in exasperation.

Once the agreement had been executed, we exchanged gifts. I organised onyx plates heavily inlaid with coloured semi-precious stones like agate and cornelian for them. They gave Babar a small tape recorder, and to Aftab and myself some books on Italy. As required under the Government rules, we notified the Ministry of these unsolicited gifts. In time we received official approval to keep them.

The one gift I did not declare was the beautiful doll called *Ciccio Bella* which Stacul and Geniale had brought for Momina. It remained her companion for years.

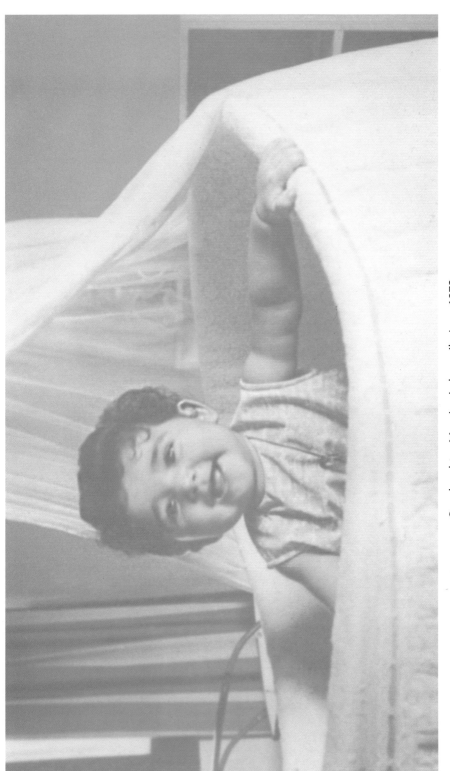

Our daughter Momina in her crib, June 1973.

Breakfast at Miandam (Swat), 18 April 1974.

Shahnaz and Momina, dressed for their first Eid in Lahore, October 1974.

FSA with Dr M S Randhawa and Dr W.G. 'Bill' Archer, Wagah border, Lahore, 1 March 1976.

FSA, Dr MSR, Bill Archer and Mildred 'Tim' Archer, 1 March 1976.

FSA, Bill and Tim Archer examining the Manaku colophon on the Basohli
Gita Govinda in the Lahore Museum, 1 March 1976.

Tim bibi, FSA, WGA and Robert Skelton, after my lecture at the
Los Angeles Colloqium on Pahari Painting, Los Angeles, 10 September 1977.

WGA and FSA, beside the grave of Maharaja Duleep Singh, Elveden, 16 October 1977.

Mubarika sharing her cot with her elder sister Momina, Lahore, May 1976.

An addition to the family. The first copy of my *Pahari Paintings & Sikh Portraits in the Lahore Museum*. Photograph taken by the late Ajmal Hussain, 31 May 1977.

FSA, Auntie Nayyar Agha, Shahnaz and Ved Mehta on his arrival at Lahore airport,
27 September 1979.

CHAPTER 8

DEATHS & DEPARTURES

While the negotiations on the Mirpur Mathelo project were in swing, I learned on 22 January 1975 that Shakir Ali has suffered a stroke and had been hospitalised. Shahnaz and I drove to the United Christian Hospital. We found him in the general ward, one patient in a row of anonymous beds. He lay immobile, frail with his eyes closed, his face dark and taut. For a moment, I thought he was dead. He remained asleep all the time we stood by his bedside. To let him or his attendant know that we had been, I scribbled our names on the carton of Complan and the biscuits we had brought.

I went back to the UCH the next day. Shakir was awake. He looked livelier, recognizing me at once. He raised his left hand in greeting. I held his hand and stroked his temples. He couldn't speak but moved his expressive eyes freely.

"Don't worry," I tried to console him. "You'll be alright soon." He looked at me directly and gently shook his head.

His irascible brother-in-law informed me that the Government was having Shakir shifted from the UCH to Mayo Hospital.

I visited Shakir the next time on 25th, at Mayo Hospital. He had been put in the Albert Victor ward. Shakir looked wan and restless. He raised his head occasionally to look around him. His sister and niece who sat by his bedside thought he was trying to recognise those in the room. To me, his condition appeared worse than in it had been when he was in UCH. There, he had been able to move his right leg during exercises and even his limp right hand opened and shut perceptibly.

The following day, Shahnaz and I went to see Shakir at the AV Ward. His condition was manifestly serious. No-one seemed to know what was going on and I couldn't help feeling that he was unlikely to get better. I doubted whether I would see him alive again and so said a silent private farewell.

On 27th I phoned the National College of Arts in the afternoon and was informed by some clerk that Shakir had died a short while earlier and everyone at the NCA had left for the hospital. When I reached there, I discovered that the hospital authorities had been more efficient transporting him out of the hospital than they had been when admitting him.

I drove to Shakir's house. Khalid Iqbal was standing near the gate. "Well, that's the end of another chapter!"

We entered the house together. Shakir lay on a cot placed in the bay of his drawing room, just beside his bedroom door. On the wall, framed, hung his Pride of Performance medal. His face had been bound by a bandage holding his chin in place. How odd, I thought, to do that to someone who had been so reticent during his lifetime.

I scribbled in my diary afterwards:

'Shakir has gone – his baser elements he has left behind him. Khalid, dear Khalid, lost himself in considerate industriousness making arrangements for the transportation of the body to Karachi and the possibility of a burial in Lahore in the Model Town graveyard. Ijaz ul Hassan, upset but voluble, sat beside Shakir's body and wailed at Nasir Shamsie's shameless plagiarism of his article on Shakir. Others came and went, one muttering to the television reporter about how silent Shakir had been, how introverted, but *so* important, *so* indispensable to the art scene in Pakistan.'

The tragedy of Shakir's death hard on the heels as it were of Chughtai's was accentuated by Shakir's now prescient jest when he attended the memorial service for Chughtai.[1] "Karamat Ali[2] may be right," Shakir had quipped. "If anything happened to me, Chughtai would chide me for not leaving him in peace even in the hereafter.'

---

[1] Abdur Rahman Chughtai had died on 17th January 1975, some days before Shakir.
[2] Shakir's cousin.

That evening B.A. Kureishi came to our house. He was in a mood to reminisce: "When I got Shakir fixed up at the NCA, there were complaints against him – that he used to frequent coffee bars, that he wore his hair long. I taxed him with these criticisms. To which he replied that as far as coffee bars were concerned, he had to frequent them because he could not afford anything better. And his hair? Well, cutting them shorter would not improve his looks."

Shakir's funeral took place on 28 January. It should have started at 10.00 a.m. At 9.30 a.m., it was discovered by the wooden coffin assembled by the NCA carpentry workshop was 7 feet long, half a foot longer than the size ordered.

"But why such a long coffin?" I asked someone from the NCA.

"Just in case. The body stretches a little afterwards."

"Look, if the poor chap couldn't make it to 6 feet during the 60 odd years of his lifetime, he is unlikely to catch up once he is in his grave."

I discovered others were also questioning the length of the coffin. The reply of the Carpentry Head at the NCA deserved to be recorded for posterity: "Because we made the same size of coffin for Chughtai sahib. We could not do anything less for Shakir sahib!"

There was a long delay at each stage of the 'public ceremony', as Khalid described it. He knew that Shakir would have preferred a simpler ceremony. Some staff at the NCA clamoured for a 'temporary or *amanat*' burial or until ground for an Arlington-style cemetery worthy of our national artists could be allocated by the Government. I silenced the more vociferous with the retort: "But that's what I thought the National College of Arts was."[3]

"*Amanat?*" B.A. Kureishi questioned. "There is no such thing. People believe in this sort of business, but I have seen what happens to a body in such cases. I can assure you there is nothing left. All that is said about the body of an '*amanat* burial' being preserved is poppycock. In any case," he added with a

---

[3] It became something worse. In August 1976, a criminal assault case (plainly fabricated by a disgruntled female student) was registered by the police against Shakir's successor and four of his fellow teachers. According to *The Pakistan Times* newspaper report: 'She alleged that the five accused took Ghazala to a posh house in Gulberg, which also had a swimming pool. She was stripped naked, and they had a swim for four hours. During this period all the five accused made love to her by the side of the swimming pool. Ghazala maintained that she had tried her best to stop their "advances" but failed as they had started to threaten her." Shades of Christine Keeler and the pool at Cliveden.

sobering realism, "that whole area is waterlogged."

In the end all the bickering made no difference. Taken to the New Garden Town graveyard, Shakir was laid to rest in his over-sized coffin, next to a boundary wall on the other side of which was a public urinal.

I wrote in my dairy: 'Shakir deserved better from all of us. There is talk of converting his house into a museum[4], even of having him transferred to be re-buried in the garden of the house itself. Shakir would not have minded my borrowing these words of T.S. Eliot's as an epitaph for him:

Ash on an old man's sleeve

Is all the ash the burnt roses leave.

Dust in the air suspended

Marks the place where the story ended.'[5]

Another death that had much more significance for us at a national level, and certainly within the NFC, occurred on 25 March 1975, when King Faisal of Saudi Arabia was shot by his own nephew Prince Faisal bin Musaid publicly in a *majlis*. Conspiracy theorists argued over whether the assassin who had returned from the U.S. might have been 'indoctrinated' to do it by powers within and outside Saudi Arabia, opposed to King Faisal's reforms.

The news of the murder was broadcast throughout Pakistan on the 5.00 p.m. news. Almost within the hour, posters of the late king began to appear on the back of auto-rickshaws, buses, even private cars. Much later, I learned from a printer in the Urdu bazaar that he had printed 200,000 of these posters as fast as his machines could operate. He sold them at Rs 1 per poster. "I have never made so much money so quickly in my life." Within days, a morbid interest fermented in the minds of the public, and in response large lurid posters in technicolour appeared, depicting images of the late King Faisal as ruler, being assassinated, and then in the top right corner seated on a prayer mat telling his beads in a cloudy heaven while in the bottom left corner his murderous nephew suffered in agony, roasted by the fires of hell.

---

[4] The Government of Pakistan, through the active intervention of Abdul Hafeez Pirzada (then Minister of Education), purchased the house at Rs 2.25 lakhs.
[5] From T.S. Eliot's poem *Little Gidding*, the last of his *Four Quartets*.

My immediate concern had less to do with the fate of the Saudis but with the $100 million of their money that had been promised us. Half of it had been earmarked for the Mirpur Mathelo project and it was my job to ensure that it could be obtained as quickly as possible. The loan had yet to be ratified by the Saudi Council of Ministers. Aftab Ahmed Khan (Secretary EAD) during our meeting on 11 March in Islamabad had assured me and the visiting Asian Development Bank team reviewing the project that the ratification was 'a mere formality'. He waved his lit cigar airily in their faces to signify his lack of concern over such minor technicalities.

Gradually, as the Ministry of Production fleshed out with more Joint and Deputy Secretaries, it began to exercise greater control over the corporations and their subsidiaries. Mr. Awan instituted a regimen of quarterly review meetings with each corporation at which the operational performance of their companies and implementation of their projects were reviewed against targets. Not surprisingly, most of these companies did not have any budgets or cash flows to speak of, nor did they use any project scheduling techniques like CPM or PERT[6].

SBA had insisted that we at the NFC should be as progressive as possible in our reporting and control procedures. For example, he introduced us to the manner in which, within Packages, he had the preceding month's production figures available on his table in the morning of the first day of the succeeding month. It was not difficult to implement. The producing units sent us their daily production figures by telex. These were accumulated, so that all it required was for the final day's production to be added. That gave us their monthly production.

Similarly, as the bulk of the cost of fertilisers – i.e. raw material and gas consumption, labour costs and overheads – were known and invariably close to budgeted figures. We knew what the notified selling prices were. We could calculate therefore the profit or loss of each company by the 3rd of each month. It took a little practice to improve our guess-estimates, but at least this technique was better than waiting for figures that would arrive a month late and be useless for timely decision-making.

Aftab Ahmed on technical matters and I on financial matters shared responsibility as General Managers at the corporate level. SBA left it to us to

---

[6] CPM= Critical Path Method; PERT= Project Evaluation and Review Technique.

hire suitable people to man our departments. I had four departments reporting to me - Planning, Finance, Commercial and Personnel. I know on paper it sounds suspiciously like empire-building. My justification for such an accumulation of authority was that the Corporation needed to put its stamp on each of the subsidiary companies to ensure coordination and reporting uniformity. On Planning, for example, allocation of funds – whether in local currency or in foreign exchange – had to be presented in a consolidated form through the Ministry to the Ministry of Finance for inclusion in the Annual Development Plan. Individual or arbitrary submissions were rejected, as PACO discovered to its cost. The Ministry of Finance held the purse strings – for project financing, for working capital allocations through the newly formed National Credit Consultative Committee (NCCC), and for subsidies to meet the differential between the higher cost of production and the lower Government-notified selling price. NFC's Commercial Department had regular but not full-time responsibilities. While each of the units did their own procurement of spare parts, for bulk imports such as sulphur (Morocco remained a preferred source because of its dependable quality) and rock phosphate (from Jordan), there was an advantage in placing a bulk order through a centrally coordinated, competitive bidding.

Management of the personnel proved a headache. It need not have been. Experience in the BIM and later PACO though had taught me that this would always evoke strong passions and degenerate into a turf war. NFC proved to be no exception.

The NFC had inherited executives from PIDC. They had all been on PIDC's strength and governed by PIDC's scales and service regulations. This had been done to allow mobility within the PIDC units without the loss of seniority. Under the new Ordinance they stood transferred to NFC. Within the NFC we could see the sense of continuing with this system, especially when new professionals had to be recruited from the market. A further, important consideration came in the form of the young trainee engineers whom we employed. Almost 500 of them were inducted, put though a year's training programme at PAFL Daudkhel (we assumed, mistakenly, that there was nothing to distract them in the wilds of Mianwali), and then seconded to the various operating units. More experienced hands could then be freed to meet the requirements of the projects in anticipation of their commissioning.

The plan to have a common cadre of executives found favour with every subsidiary company – except Pak-Arab Fertilisers Ltd, the Multan factory/project in which NFC owned 70% and Abu Dhabi National Oil Company (ADNOC) owned 30%. This investment by Shaikh Zayed bin Sultan Al-Nahyan had been made, both as a token of his generosity, and as a far-sighted measure to allow Abu Dhabi nationals to obtain training in the fertiliser industry before ADNOC set up its own fertiliser plant at Ruwais.

The downside came from the insistence of Saiduddin (its Managing Director), encouraged by his GM (F) Jaffery, to have separate pay-scales for Pak-Arab employees linked to these given by ADNOC to its own employees in Abu Dhabi. To advocate his case, Saiduddin would ensure that he would pick up the ADNOC Director on PFL Board – an Abu Dhabi *watani* called Nasser Abdullah – from the airport whenever Nasser flew into Lahore to attend a Board meeting. On the way to the NFC office, he would indoctrinate Nasser, who would then present Said's views in the course of the meeting as his own.

I could not let the avariciousness of two or three senior executives upset or retard the implementation of NFC's strategy especially when everyone else in the group agreed with it. I ensured their views were heard by organising periodic meetings of the CEOs/General Managers of all the NFC subsidiaries and allowed each to have an equal vote. That took the wind out of Saiduddin – for a while. He played ADNOC as an ace; for trumps he relied upon SBA who admired Said for being 'self-winding.'

Within the Government, a power-play of a different sort was under way. Sensing that with the increased control of the Ministry of Production over the Corporations, he would lose his relevance to them, Feroze Qaiser while still PM's Special Assistant on Economic Affairs pulled rank as the Vice Chairman of the BIM. He convened a meeting in Karachi of all the corporation chairmen to coordinate their budgets for the fiscal year 1975-76. My diary entry caught the absurdity of the proceedings:

> '4 July. A farcical meeting with FQ to discuss the NFC Budgets. His approach was so completely juvenile and 'unprofessional' (the latter defect I pointed out to him politely) that by the time the review ended at 11.00 p.m., attendees were either asleep or wished they had been.'

The following day, prime minister Bhutto convened a conclave of all the MoP chairmen. SBA had wanted his presentation to be brief, succinct and memorable. Aftab and I worked for days leading up to it, synthesising all the information we thought the prime minister should know about the fertiliser industry – demand, production, imports, pricing and subsidies, project schedules and expected availability by 1980 (i.e. during his second tenure as Prime Minister).

With the help of Roomi of the Art Department at Packages, we refined the display cards (remember, it was an age before Powerpoint) and finally reduced them to ten large cards. I had a second set of smaller cards that SBA could hold in his hands as notes. We did rehearsals, timed him, and ensured a smooth flow. The whole presentation lasted just under ten minutes.

On his return from PM House after the meeting, SBA could not contain his euphoria. His presentation had been by far the best. He had little or no competition. His colleagues made garbed presentations and became confused when they realised that they had lost the interest of the PM. The only chairman who remained resolutely boring was Mr. A.H.A. Qazi, Chairman of the rump PIDC after all its major companies had been amputated from it. He should have the least to say but he spent a precious hour saying it. Because he was a senior Sindhi, Bhutto humoured him, pretending to listen with bi-polar interest.

A few weeks later, on 24 July, an undaunted Feroze Qaiser convened yet another meeting, again at Karachi. I described the proceedings to my diary:

'The topic today was supposed to be *Capital Re-structuring of the BIM companies*. I had warned Jawaid Mirza (Secretary BIM) against requiring the presence of the various chairmen. As representatives of the collective control of the public sector organisations would be there – e.g. the State Bank of Pakistan, the Executive Banking Council (EBC), the Ministry of Finance, etc. – he needed only one person from the BIM to prepare a consolidated statement of financial requirements. In any case, the financial requirements of the various corporations and their units had already been reviewed by the Ministry of Production.

Jawaid Mirza and Feroze Qaiser, intoxicated by the idea of being able to summon such a high-powered meeting of chairmen at the slip of a pen, shredded our advice. The result was an unforgettable debacle.

The meeting had been called at 10.00 a.m. All the bigwigs arrived on time – the Governor State Bank, the Chairman EBC, the Chairmen and/or MDs of NIT and ICP, NDFC, and of the corporations. Feroze Qaiser reached the NSC building on time, but instead of joining the meeting, he went into a huddle in the room of the Member Finance[7] to chalk out a strategy. He merged 40 minutes later, took the chair and began with an exaggerated emphasis on the obvious:

"You gentlemen were kind enough to give the BIM companies credit support of Rs 40 crores last year. By the Grace of God, we in the BIM have not only remained within those limits, but if I am not mistaken we have even repaid some substantial part of it." He beamed benignly and benevolently at the participants. Looking at one of them, he asked: "You, sir, are from the State Bank. You control the purse strings of the country. What is your view on the financial performance of the BIM?"

The Deputy Director of the State Bank looked up from an emptying table (his Governor had quit while he was still ahead), and said: "The SBP is a banker to the Government, not the BIM. We implement government policies through the banking sector. Specifically, we do not comment on meetings for which no agenda has been issued and for which no working papers have been circulated. I have nothing further to add."

"You are quite right," Feroze Qaiser murmured. Then turning to the bearded Financial Advisor to the Ministry of Production, he asked encouragingly: "Shafi sahib, you are from the Ministry of Finance. What is your view?"

"If the State Bank has nothing directly to do with the BIM, the Ministry has even less so. In any case, I do not have a brief to make any comments."

Feroze Qaiser then turned his gaze at Khawaja Ziauddin (from the PBC) who happened to be sitting in front of me. Ziauddin glanced over his shoulder, winked at me and then attacked: "The total amount borrowed by the BIM as a group from the commercial banks is …Rs 185 crores."

---

[7] Amanullah Durrani, an ex-banker. He was abroad on sick leave.

"Eh?" spluttered Feroze Qaiser.

"PERAC 84 crores," Ziauddin intoned, "PACO 34 crores, NFC 3 crores, ...'

Feroze rounded on Allahwalla, Chairman, State Petroleum Refining and Petrochemical Corporation. "But, Allahwalla sahib, why have you borrowed 84 crores?"

Allahwalla answered with devastating simplicity: "Sir, because the price of crude oil has gone up."

At this, SBA whispered to me: "I am going to beat all records by not saying a word."

I whispered back: "I will do one better. I won't remain in the meeting."

By the time the meeting ended four and a half sterile hours later, everyone I was told was queuing up to jump from the fifteenth floor in exasperation.'

Our financial position at NFC eased when on 6 August 1975 we received a formal commitment of $30 million through the EAD for the Mirpur Mathelo project. Once the Saudi money came though, the Asian Development Bank also confirmed its commitment. The Scandinavian team leader Gruppe tried to pressurise me during the loan negotiations at Lahore to including an undertaking that PSFL would build a railway track from the project to India's Rajasthan border. The more I resisted the harder he pressed, so much so that he threatened to recommend to his Board that it withdraw from the Mirpur Mathelo project.

I took him to Islamabad for a final round of meetings with the EAD. I made Gruppe wait outside the office of I.A. Khalil (then JS, EAD) while I briefed him on Gruppe's unwarranted request.

As soon as we entered Khalil's room, even before Gruppe could sit down, Khalil shot off a salvo. "You have asked for a railway line from Mirpur Mathelo to the Indian border. Out of the question. Now, are there any other matters requiring EAD's attention?"

The 9th and the 10th of August required me to stay in Islamabad as the Ministry and the EAD celebrated these precious commitments by the Saudis and the EAD. At one dinner, I recall, Khalil become entangled in a discussion with the Saudi Ambassador Riyadh al Khatib. They were talking about the Suez crisis in 1956 when General Nasser closed the Suez Canal.

"You see, your Excellency, the British behaved very badly towards Nasser. When Anthony Eden visited Cairo, he more or less ignored Nasser. And that, as the British say, was the last straw on the camel's back."

"No," the Saudi ambassador replied. "I think that is an old Arabic saying."

"Oh no, your Excellency, I assure you," Khalil continued haughtily, "it is quite definitely a British saying."

"It cannot be a British one," the Saudi diplomat countered softly, without looking up from his plate, "because, you see, the British do not have any camels."

I wished the increasing solvency of the NFC had infected my personal finances. At the time that PSFL had almost $50 million worth of commitments, I had Rs 200 in my personal bank account. Even a year later, on my birthday in 1976, I confided to my diary:

> 'We creep into gilded poverty. I bring home Rs 3,600. Telephone, gas
> and electricity bills and motor car expenses are paid for. Yet we do not
> have a paisa left by the end of the month. We have Ayub the cook at
> Rs 300, Zulaikha the maid at Rs 200, a gardener at Rs 60, and a
> sweepress at another Rs 60. Their salaries take up 20% of my salary.
> Milk costs another Rs 150 for 2 seers a day. By the 5th of the month,
> I have disbursed Rs 2,000 with nothing to show for it.'

Another person living at his own level of penury in Harley Street (a suburb of Rawalpindi) was former president Yahya Khan. He had been shifted there from the secure house in Abbottabad. As I had to spend a few days in Islamabad attending a two day course on CPM organized by the Planning Commission, I called his son and arranged to meet him on the evening of 2nd August. My notes remind me:

> 'Yahya looked trim and fit, despite the rigours of being incarcerated at
> home with his family for company. He was considerably more outspoken
> about contemporary political events than I expected – the PM, for example, he
> described as "a buffoon". I thought it best to ignore the temptation to discuss

events across the border[8]. Taking a cue from his complaint that no-one appreciated how long and how much he had laboured to bring China and the US together, I began by asking him about Mao, Nixon, etc.. His comments were:

MAO: "Is he deep?" YK's reply: "Like an ocean!"

NIXON: 'A true friend of Pakistan,' with an emphasis on the word 'true'. "He came to Lahore and wanted to talk after lunch. I told him: "Look here, Mr. President. In this country, we have a custom. We sleep after lunch. I'm off for my siesta and I suggest you do the same!"

KISSINGER: 'A Jew, and very capable. He was frightened about going to China. He even had the audacity to ask me to accompany him. I told him that I'd give him a tin helmet and send one of my generals along with him, if he insisted. Zhou Enlai had given me his word that he would look after him. When Kissinger returned, he looked extremely relieved and grateful."

ZHOU ENLAI: 'Courteous, far-sighted, but like a mouse in front of Chairman Mao. I spoke to him about establishing contact with USA while I was still the C-in-C. He wouldn't give a proper reply. He'd say "You'll hear from me." And no sooner than I had reached Pindi, than I received a message from Zhou that it was alright to go ahead and open negotiations on his behalf. He trusted me and always had confidence in me.'

On the far wall I noticed a small 2' x 3' carpet, adorned with a portrait of the General at its centre.

"Is that a painting, or what?" stammered Ali Yahya.

"It's the carpet presented to the General at Persepolis in 1970.[9] A similar one was presented to each Head of State."

"How did you guess?" a disappointed Ali asked me.

"I read the newspapers," I replied patiently.

"He's quite right," the General remarked. "I remember it was given quite

---

[8] Prime Minister Mrs. Indira Gandhi had declared an Emergency in India on 25 June 1975.
[9] During the celebrations marking the 2,500[th] anniversary of the founding of the Persian monarchy.

a lot of publicity."

In the corner of the drawing room lay encased in plastic the small fragment of the moon rock and the Pakistan flag bought back by the Apollo XI astronauts and presented by President Nixon to the people of Pakistan. Yahya Khan had taken it away with him when he left President's House. He obviously regarded this (and Mme. Nur Jahan's favours) as one of the perks of the presidency.[10] He knew which one to take home.

October 1975 brought with it an opportunity to visit Milan. I had arranged to meet the Snamprogetti people in Milan and spend about ten days with them organising the procurement procedures on behalf of PSFL. The procurement in the Pak-Arab Multan project had alerted us at the NFC about the dangers of procuring on a cost-plus basis. While no-one could have seen the impact the dramatic increase in oil prices would have on international commodities, Pak-Arab's vulnerability was inordinately acute, and costly. Almost all its major equipment had been ordered on a cost-plus formula, linked to raw material prices of steel, etc. As those increased, so did the cost of Pak-Arab's equipment. It had become a nightmare. No-one in Pak-Arab knew (or wanted to know) how much the equipment component of its project would cost.

We did not want to repeat that mistake in PSFL. I was keen that we should install a mechanism within PSFL by which as soon as bids were in and the order placed, the project cost of equipment would be updated. Like that, there would be no surprises.

My intention had been to stay for ten days – from 15 to 25 October – and to return before the Asian Development Bank team arrived in Lahore in the first week of November. Permission was sought in the usual way, and much to my surprise granted within days.

SBA called me into his office. "Awan sahib has approved your trip."

I asked him for how long. "Oh, the ten days you asked for."

We had a private joke between us that Awan sahib would try to pare every proposal. If you asked for ten days, he would counter with five; if you proposed two cities, he would approve one.

---

[10] This unique memento remained with General Yahya Khan, and later his son Ali Yahya. It is understood that is now in the possession of Yahya's grandson.

"I cannot believe Awan sahib has approved the whole ten days," I told SBA. "In which case, which half of me is going?"

Once I happened to mention to SBA that Awan sahib was in the wrong ministry. He should have been in the Pakistan Atomic Energy Commission. He was the only Pakistani I knew who could have split the atom. SBA being SBA could not keep a good joke down. He immediately told Awan sahib. It was to Awan sahib's credit that he saw the funny side of it, rather than taking offence.

I left for Milan on 15th, a Sunday. No sooner than I had entered the Snam offices on the Monday than I was handed a telex from SBA instructing me to return to Lahore, as the ADB team would be there on 22 October. My ticket had been a discounted one, and so it took a couple of days to have it changed. For me, more critically, that meant surrendering some of the precious foreign exchange I had been hoarding to do some shopping for Shahnaz and Fidge.

It seemed a shame to waste a weekend in Italy. Dr. Flenkenthaller arranged for me to be driven to Florence and to Portofino. Even though it could have become the archetypal trip busy American tourists are mocked for – 'Say, bud. Where is the Mona Lisa? I have double-parked!' - I managed to see the sights of Florence, such as the Uffizi, the San Marco monastery and the Bargello. The one place I insisted on visiting was Villa I Tatti – the house where the art-connoisseur Bernard Berenson[11] had lived for almost sixty years, and died at the age of 94, in October 1959. I had read many of Berenson's studies – in particular Seeing and Knowing (1956), and his The Sense of Quality: Study and Criticism of Italian Art (1962 edition). In this latter work, he included his brilliant identification through deductive comparison of a little known artist whom he christened Amico di Sandro (a Friend of the better known artist Sandro).

At Berkhamsted School, one of the books I had borrowed from the Public Library and then bought for myself had been Charles Cammell's slim volume Memoirs of Annigoni (1956). It contained a very sensitively drawn pen and ink sketch by Annigoni of a bed-ridden Berenson, a few years before the

---

[11] Born Bernhard Valvrojenski in Lithuania in 1865, Bernard Berenson became famous after the publication of his monumental and authoritative works on Venetian, Florentine, Central and North Italian painting. He lived in I Tatti for almost sixty years, dying there in 1959.

scholar's death.

Mrs. Barbeschi from Snamprogetti who took me to around Florence had no idea where *I Tatti* was located. Asking passers-by, we managed to learn that it was somewhere in Fiesole, just outside Florence. We found it, and parked in the gravel courtyard. The cream-coloured villa had been bequeathed by Berenson to his alma mater Harvard University as a centre for Renaissance studies. Scholars in paintings, literature, poetry, ceramics, in fact anything to do with the Renaissance (but it had to do with the Renaissance) could stay at *I Tatti* and conduct research, drawing upon Berenson's magnificent library.

It broke my heart not be able to go inside. I had to make do with a stroll in the gardens and enjoy the view (as BB did every evening) through a descending avenue of poplars towards the city of Florence in the distance. White doves pecked in the gravel at my feet. I picked up a single feather and brought it back to paste into my diary. I still have it.

Mrs. Barbeschi took me to Portofino. I am not sure whether it was that particular time of an evening when the sun sets and makes Portofino glow with a special incandescence. It was unforgettable.

Just before my departure from Milan, Dr. Flenkenthaller invited me to have a meal in his spacious flat located in the centre of the city. Now that the contract was behind us, he spoke openly about the leverage our agreement would have for them in India and the effectiveness of Ottavio Quattrochi (their representative in New Delhi). I asked Dr. Flenkenthaller at what level could Quattrochi penetrate into the echelons of power there.

"Oh, directly into Prime Minister's house!" he replied, with a trace of smugness.[12]

The return flight to Pakistan could not have been more of anti-climax. I wrote of it: 'Guns at Milan airport, guns at Rome airport, more at Athens, and yet more at Karachi. Oh, the monotony of modern air travel!'

I flew directly from Karachi to Islamabad, arriving there a few minutes before the ADB meeting started.

---

[12] Some time Dr. Flenkenthaller also revealed that when Mrs. Indira Gandhi was arrested by the Janata government, she sent Sonia and her children Priyanka and Rahul for safety to Quattrochi's house.

"How was your trip?" Mr. Allauddin Ahmed, the Additional Secretary asked me.

"In five words, sir: 'Slam bam; thank you, Snam'." He could not see the joke.

Gruppe, the jowly ADB team leader, asked whether I could take him to Mirpur Mathelo on a site visit. As he could spare only a day, it meant a three and a half hour charter flight from Lahore and the same amount of time back. We made an early 6.00 a.m. start from Walton airport. The aircraft was a single propeller, three-seater Cessna with a canvas body. I sat in front with the pilot. Gruppe preferred the marginally roomier third seat behind.

The pilot performed his checks and then taxied along the runaway. He had just taken the plane into the air above a sleeping Gulberg when he suddenly banked and descended slowly, landing at Walton airport. As we neared the hangar, he motioned to the attendant. "The communications system!" he mouthed. He had forgotten to check whether he had it. The attendant ran into the hangar to retrieve it. The pilot plugged it in and then, turning to the negligent but unrepentant attendant, he asked him: "Did you remember to wash your face this morning?"

We took off again, and after a long and boring flight we landed at the air strip maintained by the Esso Fertiliser plant at Dharki. Mr. Gruppe and I were shown the PSFL site by one the engineers posted there. Gruppe asked to see the Marri gas field from which gas would be supplied. We were driven there over shrub land in a four-wheeler. The driver stopped and asked us to alight. There, in front of us, was a gas manifold. The engineer pointed to it and said: "Marri gas!"

"You mean, that is where the gas will come from?" Gruppe asked me in a tone that betrayed his incredulity.

"Yes," I replied.

"For all three plants – Esso, Pak-Saudi *and* the Fauji one?"

It seemed unbelievable but under that modest manifold, beneath where we were standing was an invisible reservoir of natural gas upon which three large fertilizer complexes would depend.

Esso staff gave us a quick lunch at their Americanised mess and then escorted us to our Cessna. The return journey took longer than the outward one. Perhaps it just seemed longer. In any case, at some stage, the pilot began to look apprehensive. I asked him if everything was alright. He confessed that as it was almost twilight, he was flying 'blind'. He knew he could not land at Walton airport in the dark, and therefore had notified the Lahore airport control tower that he had already landed, even though we were still almost an hour away.

"I will keep a look out on the left. Would you mind keeping a look-out on the right?"

"What should I look out for?"

"Oh, Indian planes," he said. He was taking the plane in a narrow flight corridor between the Risalpur Air Force base and the Indian border. Too close to one side and the Pakistanis would intercept us; too close to the other and the Indian planes would shoot us down.

Finally, our fragile, vulnerable plane landed in the dark at Walton airport.

Gruppe asked me as we alighted: "Was everything alright?"

You will never know, I thought to myself.

Of all the specialists sent by international financial institutions for our projects, the person I found hardest to warm to was the Norwegian Gruppe. And yet I suppose he did find someone to warm to. One night, I received a telephone call very late at night from the Intercontinental Hotel where he was staying.

"Is Mr. Gruppe known to you?"

"Yes," I replied.

"He and his Filipino companion have had a fight. She is standing half-naked in the corridor and he won't let her back into the room. Could you please arrange for them to stay at another hotel?"

Gruppe was recalled to the ADB headquarters at Manila. It would be some time before we saw him again in Pakistan.

CHAPTER 9

BOOKS, BILL-BABA, & A BABY

If SBA behaved like a demanding mistress, the NFC acted like an insatiable concubine. Often I had little time in the evenings for our daughter Momina. She made me aware of it one day when she noticed I was absorbed in reading some papers. 'Ganda Babi,' she said, petulantly, 'Bad Babi'. She came to me later, rested her head on my hand and kissed it very deliberately. If I happened to be typing, she would sit on the typewriter keyboard and look at me accusingly. And she was all of two and half years old.

One of the victims of my neglect became the catalogue of the Pahari paintings and Sikh portraits in the Lahore Museum. I needed at least a month – or its equivalent in undisturbed evenings to complete the text, but without a publisher in hand, it did not seem worth the effort. Meanwhile, Taufiq Rafat, the Resident Director of the newly-established National Book Foundation – Bhutto's attempt to 'nationalise' the publishing business – contacted me. We had met through an introduction by Khalid Iqbal on a number of occasions in Lahore. Taufiq was an accomplished poet in English and ran a moderately busy furnishing business. His Managing Director Yunis Said I had met on and off at Farrukh N. Aziz's over dinner. Yunis expressed an interest in publishing the Persian and the Mughal miniatures section of my catalogue. I had hoped that my catalogue would cover the LM collection of paintings in its entirety – from the earliest Jaina *Kalpa Sutra* manuscript and the Sultanate *Lor and Chanda* folios, the Persian, the Mughal, the Rajasthani, the Pahari, and the Sikh, ending with the rather wishy-washy paintings of the Bengal School. That would have meant including over 750 miniatures. It was ambitious but do-able. I knew I was no Ananda Coomaraswamy and could not match the meticulousness of his catalogues of the Indian collections in the Museum of Fine Arts Boston, USA.[1]

The ground realities, as they say, were that no publisher wanted to undertake such a gargantuan task. Over 750 catalogue entries with supporting illustrations, some of them in colour? Too expensive. One or two would have done it – probably shoddily – provided I underwrote the cost. So when Yunis at the NBF suggested that he could publish the first part – the Persian, pre-Mughal, Mughal and at a push the Rajasthani sections – on the grounds that they were 'Muslim' in subject, I jumped at the offer. He had Mehr Nigar Hussain (Farrukh-apa's sister) and Nahid Jafri[2] working with him as his Advisors. I sent them the manuscript and gradually it took shape in their hands, reaching the page proof stage. They compromised on the illustrations by including small inserts of each painting against the catalogue entry. We settled on the title *Mughal and Related Miniatures*.

Being a government body, and a newly established one at that, it was long on programmes and short of funds. In my files I have come across a note from Taufiq dated 2 April 1975, in response to a bill from the Lahore Museum for photographs taken for the book: 'For God's sake, have a heart. I'm sure you'll feel very guilty if I'm dismissed from NBF for submitting such bills. Am returning them for suitable correction.'

The National Book Foundation took almost three years to vacillate. Meanwhile, Yunis and Taufiq had left the NBF. My last communication with NBF on file was a letter I addressed the new Managing Director Dr. A.R Malik on 29 June 1978. He had come to see me at the NFC office a week earlier, not to discuss the book but an application for a job by a young nominee of his Abdul Aziz Jatoi. Jatoi did not get the job, and I never saw my book. The Foreword that Stuart Cary Welch of the Fogg Art Museum at Harvard had generously written languishes unpublished in my files.

In parallel to the NBF book, a casual conversation with Dr. Ahmad Nabi Khan (then Director of Archaeology at the Lahore Fort) opened up the opportunity of writing on the Princess Bamba collection of paintings, on display in the Sikh Gallery. This superb collection had not been properly

---

[1] A. Coomaraswamy published three such catalogues on the MFA collection: *Part 4 Jaina Paintings & Manuscripts* (1924); *Part 5 Rajput Painting* (1927); and *Mughal Painting* (1930).

[2] Wife of Kamal Azfar, then an upwardly mobile protégé of Mr. Z.A.Bhutto.

examined by any scholar. When it was acquired by the Pakistan Government, Dr. F.A. Khan had compiled and published a slim monograph on the collection in 1961. It had the deficiency of being more a list than a descriptive catalogue. Bill Archer had used some of the Princess Bamba pictures in his catalogue of the V & A Museum collection of Sikh paintings.[3] Bill had had to rely upon monochrome illustrations which did not do justice to the colours of the paintings. More importantly, neither Bill nor anyone else had analysed the centre-piece of the collection – Schoefft's magnificent panorama of the Sikh Court of Lahore. It contained almost 100 figures, many of whom had played a significant role in Sikh politics of the time.

Ahmad Nabi Khan had been approached by Jamil Mirza of Elite Publishers in Karachi to write a monograph, if not a book, on the Princess Bamba collection. Mirza's objective had less to do with Sikh history than with advertising the quality of colour reproduction that his printing firm could now produce. He had imported some modern colour separation machines and expensive four colour printers. He wanted something more durable than calendars to showcase his facilities. Ahmad Nabi sahib suggested my name to Jamil Mirza.

I wrote in my diary on 24 May 1975:

'I decided to make the monograph in the form of a series of mini-biographies, using the paintings as pylons to support the historical narrative. The paintings do lend themselves to such a presentation. There is the large Darbar painting containing almost the entire Sikh court. There are the Amritsar painting with the Honigberger connection, Sher Singh's superb portrait, Rani Jindan's picture, and the ones of Duleep Singh at various ages.

To see where Maharaja Sher Singh was murdered on 15 September 1843, Shahnaz and began our quest to trace the garden of Shah Bilawal. No one at the Lahore Fort knew where it could be found. Eventually, a clue was given that it was somewhere behind the Engineering University, near Kot Khwaja Saeed, off the Grand Trunk Road. We searched for it, were directed first to the *mazar* to which the remains of Shah Bilawal had been removed on Ranjit Singh's orders by Fakir Azizuddin. We then asked where the *baradari* could

---

[3] W.G. Archer, *Paintings of the Sikhs* (H.M.S.O., London, 1966).

be found. That was about half a mile away, the squatting villagers told us.

We motored over a dirt road and turning left spotted it on the fringe of habitation. The *baradari* is still intact. It is looked after by a chowkidar from the Department of Archaeology. The Department at Lahore Fort had no idea of his existence! The room in which the man insisted Sher Singh had been shot had a marble screen with a perforation through which the fatal bullet was fired. The main hall consists of a long room decorated with uninspiring murals similar to the ones in the chambers of the Rani Mahal at Sheikhupura Fort.

Behind the *baradari*, not four hundred yards away, is Sher Singh's *samadhi* – a simple white structure containing the commemorative lotus buds marking the cremation spot of the maharaja and his two *satis*. What tragic ends both father and son had!'

Another monument we sourced out was the tomb of the French General Allard. It lay hidden behind an office bock in upper Anarkali. Precariously raised, it retained most of its original features. Within it were the graves of Allard and of his young daughter Charlotte who had predeceased him.

My interest in this period of Sikh history overflowed into the present. At the end of June 1975, Shahnaz and I attended the commemoration service held at the *samadhi* of Maharaja Ranjit Singh opposite the Lahore Fort. This had been the first delegation of Indian *yatrees* allowed into Pakistan post 1971. The Pakistani authorities made sure that they remained within the compound of the *samadhi*. Security was not difficult. The *samadhi* had only one gate.

On 29th morning, the anniversary of Ranjit Singh's death in 1839, Shahnaz and I went early. We walked up the steps into the raised *samadhi*. About three hundred Sikh pilgrims sat around the marble cupola. By 9.00 a.m. when we arrived, the Granth Sahib had already been recited. Speeches were under way, each extolling in different words a common theme: the virtues and the capabilities of the old maharaja, especially his cyclopean magnanimity towards other religions. Periodically, there would be shouts of 'Sat Sri Akal!' at which some of the younger Sikhs would look furtively at Shahnaz to gauge her reaction. She had learned how to contain her reactions and would have continued doing so, had one of the Sikh ladies not taxed her with a snide remark about Yahya Khan and Nur Jahan.

"He happens to be an uncle of mine," Shahnaz told her.

Unabashed the lady persisted: "Wasn't he a lecher?"

Shahnaz's reply could not have been more remedial: "No more so than Ranjit Singh, really."

There was some confusion whether the Sikh *yatrees* would be allowed out. Permission was doled out to one family – Professor Pritam Singh of the Guru Nanak Dev University. We escorted him around the Fort and the Badshahi Mosque. Looking at it, Dr. Pritam Singh asked me: "Fakir sahib, has there been any change in its features since the Sikhs left?"

"No," I responded, "only in its usage." [We both knew that the mosque had been converted into an ammunition store by Ranjit Singh.]

"You have given a very pertinent reply," he admitted ruefully.

It took me almost three months to come to grips with the Pahari catalogue. I knew that once I started, I would have to maintain my speed. On 29 November, I made this triumphant entry in my diary:

> 'I can hardly believe it. *Pahari Paintings & Sikh Portraits* is finally complete. What a disproportionately massive significance it had assumed in my life. Sarwar, my PA, performed absolute wonders by typing it at such speed that he finished typing pages before I had time to write them. The Ms runs into 480 pages, although not all the entries take up a whole page. There are 288 illustrations. Baig sahib[4] performed another minor miracle by having the Royal Academy pictures photographed and printed over a week-end. I didn't think he would be able to manage it, but he did, and I will always be grateful to him for it. By a stroke of luck, Mr. Smith of Simon Carves[5] came to Lahore, en route to the U.K. I entrusted him with the Ms. I learned from him by telex today that that he has contacted Dr. WGA and that he would be sending the Ms to him by registered post. Now it is in the hands of the gods!'

Fortuitously, in February 1976, an opportunity came to visit London. Actually, my destination was Manchester where the Simon Carves offices were

---

[4] M Baig, Librarian at the Department of Archaeology & Museums in Karachi.
[5] Engineering Contractors to the Pakistan Fertiliser plant at Haripur, formerly owned by Jaffer Bros,

located. SBA considerately gave me permission to leave a few days earlier so that I could meet Bill over the weekend. I caught a taxi (madness at £8!) from the airport to his house in North London's Chalk Farm. He opened the door for me and after a slight Anglo-Saxon hesitation he responded warmly to my embrace. He took me upstairs to the attic – the guest suite, complete with a bed, a table and a chamber pot. We collected Tim Archer from the India Office Library (now in Blackfriars Road), returned home to 18 Provost Road for dinner and to the welcome news that Philip Wilson (publisher of Bill's *Indian Paintings from the Punjab Hills*) had agreed to publish my *PP & SP*.

Philip Wilson, the son of Peter Wilson (Chairman of Sotheby's) came around the following day to discuss terms. He had been allowed to publish art books under the name of Sotheby Parke Bernet. SBP agreed to publish *PP&SP* provided they could get a bulk order for 500 copies from India and Pakistan. On those sales I would get 5% of the actual receipts (i.e. £287.50, as he would be selling at 55 % discount). On the next 250 copies, nothing. On any sales above 750 copies, I would receive £2.50 per copy, i.e. 10% of the selling price. Philip expressed his keenness to have Oxford University Press Karachi and New Delhi on board as co-publishers. After some discussion we agreed that it might be more prudent to have separate publishing by-lines for the supplies to OUP New Delhi and to OUP Karachi.

For the next four days, Bill and I ploughed through the manuscript, making changes, corrections, adding the chapter introductions he had asked me to include after his initial reading of the manuscript some time ago. It was tiring and I must admit trying, but in the circumstances, unavoidable if wanted Bill's imprimatur on the book. Bill curbed my tendency to be too meticulous with the caveat: "Aijaz, remember, compiling such a catalogue is the art of the possible. You have to draw the line somewhere and ignore any research that may have come afterwards." By Saturday evening, the manuscript – grubby but complete – was ready. "Dear Aijaz," Bill said, "your original manuscript was perfect, a little *too* perfect." Bill expurgated a number of illustrations (the ones showing Radha and Krishna in coitus were the first casualties) and cleared the colour illustrations. Philip had decided to include sixteen colour plates.

I left for Manchester the next morning. I could not have cared less about Simon Carves and their claims for compensation. I returned to London on Wednesday night. On Friday, Philip's editor Anne Jackson (an attractive, painfully thin red-head, in her late twenties) read the foreword Bill had prepared for inclusion in *PP&SP*. Even on re-reading so many years later, it exudes a generous appreciation of my work. Bill contrasted my book with his. His, he said, had dealt with style, mine with subject matter. He described my *PP&SP* as the indispensable sequel and complement to his *IPPH*. One phrase in Bill's Foreword however rankled. He referred to my 'unimpeachable English'.

"Bill, is 'unimpeachable' a fair word to use?" Tim-Fibi asked him.

The ICS in Bill emerged. "Tim darling, anyone picking up a book written by a Mr. F.S. Aijazuddin is bound to think that it is full of *babu* English. So I have to tell them straightaway in my Foreword that it is *not*."

Anne Jackson's editorship could not have been more precise or surgical. She put me in my place by asking me why in the very first sentence of my Introduction I had written: *The Lahore Museum had ursine inclinations*. I thought it rather clever. Anne did not.

"What do mean by *ursine*?" she questioned.

"Well, bear-like," I replied.

"Then, why don't you say so?"

After that, I christened Anne *La belle dame sans merci*. She caught out many more mistakes and removed them, improving the text immeasurably. By late Friday evening, everything was tied up. I had signed the contract with PWP, the manuscript as complete and ready for composing by the printers, and the additional pictures listed. I stood one step closer to realising an ambition that had rankled within me for a decade.

Dr. M.S. Randhawa's Foreword to *Sikh Portraits by European Artists* reached me in while I was still in London. Bill read it and then with the confidence that only friends can exercise, he 'improved' MSR's foreword.

I had decided to call that book 'Borrowed Majesty'. It was a phrase borrowed itself from the account of the Russian Prince Alexis Saltykov, who on meeting Sher Singh in 1842, described him as having 'a sort of borrowed majesty' about him. Both Bill and Dr. Randhawa felt that the title needed to be more connected with the subject. I changed the title from Borrowed Majesty to the descriptive but to me prosaic Sikh Portraiture by European Artists. The title changed again to Sikh Portraits by European Artists when Bill told me it would clash with that of his wife Mildred 'Tim' Archer's book *British Portraiture in India.*

When I think about it, I can hardly believe that it took me only six weeks to write 'Borrowed Majesty'. Once I had the structure in my mind, the rest fell into place. I remember using every spare moment to ferret in my books on Sikh history, even on one occasion making the five hour journey to Daudkhel with my books and research material in a carton beside me on the rear seat. By end of June 1975 copies of the manuscript were with Jamil Mirza's people who wanted to check its originality, with Ahmad Nabi Khan to verify its historical accuracy, and with Bill Archer in London. Jamil Mirza wanted Zafar Ahmed to take the colour transparencies of the paintings. Zafar managed to photograph all of them, except for the huge Darbar scene. That could not be removed and therefore had to photographed in situ. The dim lighting in the under-funded Sikh gallery did not help. Zafar made a number of attempts. Finally he achieved the result he wanted.

As soon as Jamil Mirza returned from his trip abroad, he issued Elite's agreement in principle to publish Borrowed Majesty. His man Iftikhar told me that if done on art paper, the book would cost Rs 40 per copy, and Rs 30 on craft paper with the illustrations being printed on art paper.

Bill knew of my discussions with Pakistani publishers. He advised that I should wait until *PP & SP* came out, and then cash in on it with *SP by EA*.

In March 1976, Bill and Tim Archer made a programme to spend a few days with us at Lahore in the first week. He and Tim were due to stay as guests of Dr. M.S. Randhawa in Chandigarh. Bill was also being awarded an honorary doctorate by the University of Punjab, Chandigarh, for his studies in Sikh art-history. Before the Archers came, I spent two days cleaning the spare bedroom, scouring the bathroom, ironing their sheets before making their beds, framing pictures for their room, doing everything that neurotic hosts do.

Shahnaz and I had imagined that we would have to spend a lot of money re-doing the room but we were able to re-decorate it for a fraction of the estimate. Instead of dyeing the carpet, we washed it; for curtains we borrowed a tip from Auntie Kalyani, bought blue bedspreads from Gultex and converted them into thick, impressive curtains. I brought some drawings of Zulqarnain Haider that were hanging in Mummy's house and had them framed. The room with its blue colour-scheme looked cool and welcoming.

Before we went to bed Shahnaz asked me: "At what time do you want to be woken up in the morning? I know you won't be sleeping at all tonight."

I recorded details of their visit in my diary:

'We were all up at 7.00 a.m., even Momina who was excited to see the real Dr. Archer. She had heard so much about him that she assumed the first foreigner she would meet – it happened to be Husin Alsegaf - would be Dr. Archer.

Almost immediately after we reached the Wagah/Atari border, Agha Ikram caught up with us and accompanied us to the border crossing. A moment later, Tim-bibi and Dr. MSR appeared in view on the Indian side. We met through the gates, I invited Dr. MSR to step into Pakistan, which he did. (In those days, the border guards on both sides were more accommodating.) Dr. MSR looked quite young for his age (he was nearing 67), with bronzed, luminous skin that glowed in the morning sunshine. I escorted Dr. MSR and the Archers into the garden of the Rangers' Guest House, where Agha had arranged chairs, coffee and cake. While we sat talking, the photographer[6] Dr. MSR had brought with him to record our meeting took pictures.

Dr. MSR spoke in rapid Punjabi, asking about everyone and everything. We shared a laugh over his collaboration[7] with J. Kenneth Galbraith ('He's basically a cynic'), talked about the fertilizer industry and about art. Suddenly, Dr.MSR turned to Bill and said: "We have always regarded Goswamy as our successor. Our real successor is Aijaz!" Shahnaz told me afterwards that I looked at this point as if I would burst into tears.

As a gift I had taken a copy of *Legacy of the Indus*[8] inscribed for him. He flicked through its pages, gratified to see his beloved Punjab so vividly represented. After about three quarters of an hour, during which the Customs and Immigration formalities were done and we had been photographed in every permutation of grouping, we escorted Dr. MSR to the Indian side of the border. He embraced me very warmly, and then walked across the white line into his Punjab.

---

[6] The photographer's name was Rode, whose father had a shop before 1947 in Lahore.
[7] Published under the title *Indian Painting: Scenes, Myths and Legends* (New Delhi, 1961).
[8] By Samina Quraeshi.

We drove in one car to our house in Ghalib Road. Agha followed with their luggage in a second car. I showed them to their room. A little later, Tim emerged to note with relief that our lavatory was an upright one. "You have no idea," she told us. "At Jagdish Mittal's in Hyderabad we had to squat 'Eastern' style. I could manage it – just. But, poor Bill....'

Iqqy and Shahida Saigol[9] arrived to meet the Archers. They had missed them in London, as they themselves were travelling to Karachi later that afternoon, they were keen on seeing them.

A quick lunch and then we went straight to the Punjab Records Office stored in Anarkali's tomb within the Punjab Government Secretariat. The Director Archives Ch. Nazir Ahmad showed us around, especially the receipt issued to Maharaja Gulab Singh's Vakil for the purchase of Kashmir, and also Sher Singh's signature in English which I intended to include in my *SP by EA* book. A sterile visit to the National College where Khalid Iqbal could not be found, Khalid Anis who had done his thesis on Sikh murals had not been informed, and the new Principal was absent. I should not have been surprised. When I called a few days earlier to tell him the Dr. Archer would be visiting Lahore, he asked me: "Dr. Archer? Dr. Archer, who?"

From the NCA we walked across to the Lahore Museum. Bill in casual trousers and in comfortable but inelegant sandals. I asked the attendant on duty whether Mr. B.A. Kureishi was in. Suddenly from behind a pillar BAK emerged, resplendent in a dark suit with a gold chain dangling from his waistcoat pockets. BAK had expected that Dr. WGA – a fellow ICS officer – would drive up to a roll of drums and a blast of trumpets. Instead we sauntered in like dusty tourists. Dr. WGA's failure to remember that BAK had been in the ICS – despite BAK's Masonic reminders "And which batch were you?" etc. – did little to assuage BAK's disappointment.

The miniature paintings that Bill had come to see lay in complete confusion. I put them into some order and then more or less stage-managed the show. WGA was photographed with the Manaku description, old Balwant Singh of Jammu/Jasrota, and against the fine

---

[9] Close friends and collectors of Indian miniatures.

portrait I identified as being of his son Mian Ram Singh painted I believed by Nainsukh. Examining it closely, Bill concurred with my assessment. Halfway through our examination for the collection, the lights failed. The rest of the study had to take place by candlelight.

Dinner we had at home, after which I took out some of our Sindhi embroideries to share with Archers. It was a gesture of reciprocation for all the occasions they had taken the trouble to take out items from their vast collection to show me in London.

On 2 March, we made an early start for the old city, caused some disruption among the classes being held in the *haveli* of Raja Dhian Singh, slid across the Badshahi masjid floor in over-sized over-shoes, and were received in princely state by the Sikhs (complete with ceremonial-blue turbans) at Ranjit Singh's *samadhi*. Bill examined the wall frescoes carefully, and fortunately did not notice that many of them had been retouched by students at the Department of Fine Arts of Punjab University, under the supervision of Khalid Iqbal. Khalid would not have done so, had it not been ordered by the Punjab Government. It wanted to demonstrate to the Sikh *yatrees* that their monuments were being properly looked after.

We had tea on the lawn at the base of the *samadhi*, and then moved to the Fort. We had what I can only describe as a hilarious time at the Princess Bamba Gallery, our every move being photographed by the diligent photographer from the Department of Archaeology. The only hiccup occurred when the photographer asked Tim to stand in front of the portrait sketch of the louche Rani Jindan. She remonstrated: "I refuse to be photographed next to *that* woman!"

Dr. Ahmed Nabi Khan obliged us with a lunch *al fresco* on the verandah adjacent to the marble Diwan-e-Khas. Our next stop was Jahangir's tomb in Shahdara.

We compressed so many sights into one day that by the time we returned home, Bill needed a rest. SBA invited the Archers for dinner that night and thoughtfully called Sardar Karim Nawaz (Director Archives), and Roomi from Packages. It turned into a relaxed evening with the conversation gently lapping across the dining table.

On the morning of 3rd, I let the Archers sleep late. I had forgotten that both of them were in the 60s, almost twice my age. After a leisurely breakfast, we drove to Sher Singh's *samadhi* at Shah Bilawal. No sign of a chowkidar, which was a blessing for we were free to explore it.

On the way to Shalimar Gardens, Tim told us how disappointed she had been to see at the Srinagar Shalimar Gardens. All the pools had been painted an electric blue and the lawns dotted with mushroom lights. No sooner had we entered our own Shalimar Gardens than she was confronted by the sight of bright blue pools and mushroom lights!

We picked up Shahnaz on the way back for a quick lunch at Salloo's restaurant, located in the basement of WAPDA House. The place overflowed with Ismailis. Obviously the Aga Khan was in town.

Bill had been very keen to see Abdur Rahman Chughtai's collection of miniatures. He knew that during the 1940s, whenever any large batch of Pahari paintings were offered to the Lahore Museum, the then Curator Samarendranath Gupta would distribute them among colleagues at other museums and among friends, one of them being A.R. Chughtai.[10] Chughtai was very secretive about his collection. He would not permit anyone to see it. I had to arrange our visit through B.A. Kureishi. He accompanied us to Chughtai's studio – a custard-cream three storey building on Ravi Road, close to the Christian graveyard opposite Taxali Gate. Chughtai himself never appeared. We were received by his brother Abdur Rahim Chughtai who looked at each of us separately, frisking us with his eyes. He led us into a dining room on the first floor, left us to retrieve the pictures and then returned with them, placing them on the bare dining table.

Examining each painting in Bill's company was an education in itself. Chughtai had some interesting Mankots, exciting Kulu ones, a few from Mandi, and some folios from the famous *Bhagavata Purana* series painted in the 1780s for Raja Sansar Chand of Kangra. For me, the cruellest cut was to discover that his collection contained not one, not two, but five illustrations from the 1730 *Gita Govinda* series by Manaku. I died of envy five separate times.

---

[10] In those days, A. R. Chughtai taught painting at the Mayo School of Arts (now the National College of Arts). He was deeply immersed in the revivalist Bengal School of enlarged miniatures that E.B. Havell had encouraged.

Mercifully, throughout what for me was a transcendental experience, Abdur Rahim Chughtai kept his mouth shut. After the last painting had been put away, Bill and I were still savouring the delicious after-taste of seeing such superb miniatures. Suddenly, Abdur Rahim interrupted our reverie with: "Mandi, shandi! All these so-called Pahari paintings were done in *Lahore*."

Bill shook his head. "No, I assure you they *were* painted in the Punjab Hills."

"I tell you they were painted in Lahore," Abdur Rahim insisted, and then, as if he had not done enough damage, he persisted with the assertion: "All done by *Muslim* artists."

"But how do you account for the overt Hindu subject matter?"

ARC would not be so easily deflected. He insisted blithely: "Muslim artists working for Hindu rajas."

B.A. Kureishi stepped in with a question: "Do you have any Mughal paintings?"

"Oh, lots of them," ARC contended. "But they are somewhere else at the moment," without specifying where.

We took our leave, heartbroken that such a fine cache of paintings should be left in his grubby hands. On the way back, BAK mentioned a story about the Chughtais and Mr. Bhutto. He narrated how during the state visit of the Shah and his empress Farah in 1966, Bhutto wanted to present her with a painting by Chughtai. The family was contacted by the Foreign Office. Abdur Rahim laid down three conditions: firstly, that the empress herself should ask to see them, the second that she should see them in their Ravi Road house, and the third that only he and his nephew Arif would be present in the room with the empress. Bhutto was so incensed that he threatened to have the whole collection nationalised!

B.A. Kureishi invited us for drinks at his house in Gulberg in the evening. His acquisitions dotted on his walls of Gandharan sculpture, Gardner ceramics, fake miniatures revealed him to be more a collector than a connoisseur. He plied Bill with drinks. Bill, I knew, could not take more than couple without becoming merry. By his third Bill could not have been more convivial. Our cook Ayub did us proud with a superb meal that more than compensated for his *faux pas* when on the day of their arrival, he had cooked only half the chops Shahnaz had given him.

Before they went to bed, I had the Archers sign all their books for us. I have them still. The one I treasure most is Bill's brilliant, seminal essay *Indian Paintings of the Punjab Hills.*[11] He inscribed it: 'For Aijaz. This is where it all began…W.G. Archer, 3 March 1976'. That was the very book that had inspired me to study the subject seriously.

Bill spoke about his own books and what had prompted him to write them. While he became famous for his numerous works on Indian miniatures, his persistent passion was poetry, especially folk poems. It was this urge that made him record the poetry of the Uraons, a tribe in Ranchi (Nagpur).[12] And it was this feel for poetry that encouraged him to edit Sir Richard Burton's translation of *The Kama Sutra* by Vatsyayana.[13] "You know, Aijaz," he mentioned to me once. "Although I have written so many books, the only one from which I made any money was my edition of Burton's *Kama Sutra.* You see, its publication came in the wake of the court case over D. H. Lawrence's *Lady Chatterley's Lover.*[14] Suddenly, pornography became the rage. After my book came out, I found myself receiving all sorts of quasi-pornographic books to be reviewed. I had to tell them that I was *not* a dirty old man!"

I had planned this visit of the Archers to Lahore so many times in the mind and it had gone so smoothly and so perfectly that I did not want it to end. But I knew it had to. Bill and Tim had to return to Chandigarh to meet Dr. Randhawa. We drove to the Wagah border. Waiting for us stood Rode, the photographer whom Dr. Randhawa

---

[11] Published by HMSO, London, 1952.

[12] *The Blue Grove: The Poetry of the Uraons* (London, 1940), and later *The Dove and the Leopard: More Uraon Poetry* (London 1948).

[13] *The Kama Sutra of Vatsyayana.* Translated by Sir Richard Burton and F.F. Artbuthnot. Edited with a Preface by W.G. Archer (London, 1963).

[14] In November 1960, the British Government prosecuted Penguins Books under the Obscene Publications Act 1959 for publishing Lawrence's novel, that contained explicit descriptions of sexual intercourse. Penguin Books won the case. This landmark decision foreshadowed 'the permissive society' in the UK.

had brought with him to the border when the Archers crossed on 1 March. He handed me a red album inscribed by Dr. MSR. It showed on the cover a bridal couple hugging shyly, and beside it a metal plaque that read 'Lovely Memories'. I opened it. It contained photographs of the Archers' arrival.

The Archers left, and I am not embarrassed even after forty years to admit that I wept when we said goodbye to each other at the border. I am not sure how much I meant to them. They certainly meant more to me than they may have known.[15] Once Bill returned to London, he moved our relationship one notch higher. While Tim Archer had been 'Tim-bibi' to us, he had remained 'Bill'. In one letter, however, he ended with: 'Wait for it. Yours ever, BILL-BABA!'

The next entry in my diary after the departure of the Archers on 4 March bears the note: "No sign of our little one!"

'The little one' referred to our second child who was due by the end of March. On 12 August, Shahnaz told me that her gynaecologist had confirmed her pregnancy. I remembered the admonition of my uncle Lalla Amjad (SBA's eldest brother) after an Eid family lunch in December 1974. Noticing a number of his nieces in varying stages of pregnancy, he stopped me on my way out with the remark: "Now, don't you go and have any more babies!"

My response had been too quick: "Lalla, you make it sound as though we are going home expressly for this purpose!"

With our second child, Shahnaz and I wanted to avoid the last-minute complications that had disrupted Momina's birth. But as the adage goes, man proposes; a doctor disposes. The gynaecologist who had been attending Shahnaz throughout her pregnancy suddenly decamped for Peshawar and apologised that he would not be back in time for the delivery. Some friends directed us to a Dr. Yusuf, a robust, rotund man with fair pudgy fingers. We checked his clinic off Zafar Ali Road. He showed us the rooms where the delivery would take place, and by way of reassurance also took us into his small operating theatre. "In case, God forbid, it should require a C section, I have all

---

[15] Dr. MSR had made his feelings plain to me. In my diary I noted that in a letter he sent to me after our meeting, he said: 'As I told you, you are my true successor in art studies. With your brilliant prose and keen sense of observation, I have every reason to expect that you will have a great opportunity for productive research ahead of you.'

the facilities here."

Shahnaz's labour pains began on 31st evening. Dr. Yusuf assured us that she would not have to stay overnight at the clinic. "See you at breakfast, then!" he said chirpily.

I described the subsequent trauma in my diary:

'1 April: Up most of the night massaging N's back. At 7.30 am we took her packed bags and went to the clinic. I settled her first in one room, discovered the light bulb was missing, and moved her to the other. Prolonged, slow labour. At 12.00 p.m., Dr. Y indicated that he was concerned about the reliability of the scar tissue resulting from N's first C-section. He said he hoped he would not have to perform a C-section. He ordered lunch for N – roast chicken and salad. This seemed to confirm his expectation that N would have a normal delivery, or at least one that did not involve chloroform. After a glucose drip had been administered, the frequency of N's contractions increased. They were now three minutes or so apart, lasting a minute or so.

I returned home to be with Momina and had been there long enough to finish a cup of tea when Nazir the driver came in the second car: "Doctor wants you, now."

I did not dare say goodbye to Momina, sneaking out as silently as I could. I sped to the clinic. Dr. Y stood waiting for at the door. "You naughty boy," he scolded me with a wave of his podgy fingers. "You have been driving too fast! I have decided to operate. I cannot do it here as I do not have an anaesthetist. I have made arrangements at Lady Willingdon Hospital. The anaesthetist will join me there. We operate at 7.00 p.m."

We bundled N and her belongings into a car and rushed across the city to the hospital on the corner of Ravi Road/Fort Road.

My first impression was indelible. An incredibly filthy stretcher trolley was wheeled outside to receive N.

"Don't you have a wheelchair?"

"No. That's broken."

The Emergency Room was no more encouraging. Three young lady doctors sat occupied with comparing the tones of their nail polish. One of them handed me a list of medicines I needed to buy.

"Where do I get these from?"

She pointed in the direction of the pharmacies on the opposite side of Ravi Road. Dodging the tongas, buses and cars, I criss-crossed the busy road, and having procured the supplies, I handed them to the robed attendant in the delivery room. He accepted the bag of medicines and exchanged them for another paper.

"A pint of blood, please."

"Where do I get that?" I was directed towards the hospital's blood bank. Even Dracula would have been ultra-cautious taking a sip from its stock. The man in charge sat at his table smoking. Its top was littered with dirty used phials. I volunteered my own blood.

"Have you got a slide?" he asked his assistant.

"No, I don't have any spirit either."

I yielded a pint of my blood, overruling their protestation that a wife should not be given blood provided by her husband. Without waiting for the mandatory rest, I rushed upstairs to the operating theatre with the blood.

At 8.05 p.m., Auntie Nayyar and I heard an infant scream. A few minutes later, a nurse sauntered out.

"Born at 8.05 p.m.," he told Auntie.

"And the sex?" she asked.

"A girl.'"

Ten minutes went by before a nurse brought our daughter Mubarika out. She looked small, her features evenly proportioned, with a fair skin, a decent head of black hair, and noticeable brown mole on her forehead. 'Should note that,' I thought to myself, 'in case someone tries to switch babies.'

I waited until she opened her mouth to bellow her remonstrance, and then quickly touched her lips with some honey and recited the *azan* in her tiny ears.

Auntie Nayyar and I waited impatiently for N to be wheeled out of the operating theatre. Sometime later, another robed figure emerged.

"Are you the patient's husband?" he asked me.

I feared the worst. "The anaesthetist is asking for his money. He is demanding Rs 400 but we have beaten him down to Rs 300." I was too stunned to refuse. Auntie N pressed me to ask him whether Shahnaz had not come around yet. She hadn't, and didn't for a full hour after that. When they did bring Shahnaz out, she was still dazed and incoherent.

"What have you done to her, you wretched man?" I shouted.

Shahnaz recovered in the special labour ward. As soon as she regained full consciousness, she clamoured for some pethadine. I had sent three phials into the operating theatre amongst the batch of supplies for the operation. Being expensive, not surprisingly, the phials had 'disappeared'.

I sent Nazir the driver to get some. When he did not return for some time, I chased after him and found him waiting outside a nearby pharmacy. He told me that the only shop in the locality licensed to sell pethadine closed at 10.00 p.m. On learning about Shahnaz's condition, the shop's neighbours sent someone on a scooter to bring the owner and have him open his shop. I raced back with three more phials and handed them to Auntie N for safe keeping.

The conditions in the hospital could not have been more chaotic. The labour ward was crowded with heaving, moaning women. They put Shahnaz into a small room, which she had to share with another hidden behind a screen but quite audibly in the throes of a painful labour.

The effect of running about so vigorously after having donated blood caught up with me. All of a sudden, I felt very faint and broke out into a cold sweat. I lay down on the unhygienic stone floor and prayed that I did not lose consciousness. Auntie N found me supine behind a screen. She gave me some water and told me to go home. It was by then 2.00 a.m.

Sleep came fitfully that night. At 7.00 a.m. I returned to the hospital to relieve Auntie N and Agha Ikram whom I had called during the night to be available at the hospital in case Shahnaz needed anything. The hospital looked less forbidding in daylight, or had I just become more familiar with it and inured to its crass inefficiency?

I found Shahnaz still in the special labour room. On the far side of the brick wall I could hear a mother-to-be expelling her load. Auntie N, apprehensive about the lack of hygiene and the very real danger of infections, wanted to bring Mubarika into Shahnaz's room. I searched for her and discovered her in a cot, under a pile of towels in the delivery room.

The hospital bassinet looked like the original iron cage, suspended from hooks at such a dangerous tilt that even the baby's featherweight of 7 lbs. caused it to list. I opened Mubarika's nappy to change it and noticed that she had not been bathed. Her meconium stuck to her reddened backside. I asked the young male doctor on duty where I could wash my hands, his reply was curt: "Attendants are not supposed to use the washing facilities in the labour ward."

"It is not a question of rules," I countered. "It's a question of simple hygiene. I want to feed my daughter and I cannot do that without first washing my hands." That did not move him. I decided to find a sink myself, and eventually did trace one in the doctors' common room.

It worried me that Mubarika had not been examined any paediatrician to test her reflexes. My colleague at NFC the DGM Technical Mahmood Bhutta had introduced me to his brother Dr. Tariq Bhutta who happened to be a paediatrician. He came as some sort of timely angel. He examined her thoroughly, declared her fit and normal, and in reply to my direct question whether it would be safe to take a day-old infant back home with me, he replied without a second's hesitation that I should.

At 4.00 p.m. in the afternoon, a patient in Room 12 was discharged by Dr. Yusuf, much to her surprise and that of her husband who arrived in the evening to take her home and discovered Shahnaz lying in her place. Room no. 12 was a microcosm of the hospital itself – dirty, full of sluggish mosquitoes. Its attached bathroom needed a fortnight of diligent scouring. One sight of it made me decide to follow Tariq Bhutta's advice. I put Mubarika in the car and with her now elder sister Momina drove them home.

Momina's reaction to her younger sibling could not have been more welcoming. She was fascinated by the petiteness of her latest and live *Ciccio Bella*. On the way home, she introduced Mubarika to everything we passed – "That's a tonga, that's a horse, that's a rickshaw, that's a bus..."

Reaching home I broke down, crushed at the absurdity of having to bring home an infant less than 24 hours old, and with not one family member other than Auntie N to help. Momina gave Mubarika her first feed, cradling her and occasionally stroking her forehead and kissing her hands. It required enormous courage on Shahnaz's part to agree to be parted from her new-born.

For the next few days, until Shahnaz was discharged from the hospital, I had to alternate between doing duty attending to her by day and at night attending to the baby at home. Whenever Mubarika would wake up crying for her feed, Momina would wake as well, and I would find myself having to cope with both simultaneously. There would be times when Momina, seeking reassurance, would insist upon sleeping in the bassinet next to the baby.

It took Shahnaz a few more days to recuperate. By the 4th she could walk. We brought her home on 5th. My three Graces were together at last.

CHAPTER 10

BLOOD-LETTING AT NFC

By June 1976, I had been in NFC almost a year and a half. Gradually the reporting relationship between the NFC and its subsidiary companies/projects evolved into one the Ministry of Production wanted. The Ministry relied upon the NFC to coordinate all technical, financial, commercial, administrative and personnel matters and to institute a reporting mechanism that would allow the Ministry to remain informed about key developments. I organised quarterly meetings of the MDs/GMs at which we reviewed their performance. Each CEO was given as much time as he needed. More importantly, these reviews took place in the open, so that every GM knew how other units were performing.

Some of the subsidiary companies (especially the larger ones like Pak-Arab Fertilisers and Pak-Saudi) chafed at this imposition. They regarded their reporting responsibility as being to their Board, not to the NFC. That did not take much time to resolve. NFC happened to be the major shareholder in all of them.

I confided to my diary on 2 June 1976 (my 34th birthday):

'In the NFC I sit like Cassandra. For more than a year, Saiduddin (MD Pak- Arab, Multan) has been skilfully evading all my attempts to obtain an accurate estimate or reliable projections of Pak-Arab's capital cost. After considerable coercion, and only after I told him that if he did not submit a PC-1, he would not be eligible for any ADP allocations for 1975-76 or 1976-77, did Saiduddin relent. He had one prepared that indicated a total cost of Rs 1,250 million. Even while it was being finalized for presentation to the Ministry, it became obvious to everyone except SBA (who remained for some inexplicable reason *sous le charme* of Said) that the actual cost was likely to exceed this figure substantially. I tried to warn Pak-Arab but Said remained obdurate. He was determined to camouflage the final bill. In the last review meeting with the Minister [Rafi Raza] on 14 April, Saiduddin suddenly confronted the Minister and the Secretary [S.B. Awan] with a demand for foreign exchange of $6 million – '$3 million to meet the cost of erection and the remaining $3 million towards escalation.'

"You have put a gun to my head," the minister complained. "If I agree, I have to beg for the money from the Ministry of Finance, and as I know they do not have that kind of money, I shall have to go directly to the PM himself and explain why this could have been foreseen earlier. If I don't agree, you'll accuse me of holding up the project."

After a while, the minister looked at me: "In my opinion, it is absolutely necessary to find out how much is required in all – both in foreign exchange and in local rupees." Awan sahib agreed. The meeting ended on a sour note with the constitution of two sub-committees, one comprising Jawaid Mirza and myself to assess Pak-Arab's foreign exchange needs, and the second under another Joint Secretary Ehsan ul Haque to compute the civil works costs as these made up the bulk of the rupee costs.

On the way out, Saiduddin said to me reassuringly: "Don't worry! I told the minister that you learned of these figures only yesterday." The gall of the man was incredible. Didn't he realise that I was not under a cloud? He was.'

The Ministry officials lived in an empyrean of their own. Their disconnection with reality became apparent when they were confronted with problems. For example, when Jawaid and I were evaluating Pak-Arab's financial requirements, he questioned why Pak-Arab needed additional ammonia storage tanks.

"Why can't they store ammonia in a warehouse?" he asked me.

With an absolutely straight face, I explained that I was sure that Pak-Arab would have no problem storing liquid ammonia in a warehouse - provided someone from the ministry undertook to do the stock-taking.

The foreign exchange projections, once we had built up the figures under each heading of outflow - equipment, erection, etc. – shot up further to $ 103.99 m., against Pak-Arab's estimate of $ 99m. It took almost five weeks and countless meetings to recalculate the rupee requirements. When at last they emerged, the project cost hit Rs 183 crores. It had begun with Rs 88 crores (1972), Rs 102 crores (1974), Rs 126 crores (1975), and reached Rs 150 crores (early 1976).

SBA who had been blissfully under the impression that Saiduddin was 'self-winding' and dynamic, has now been confronted by the error of his own wilfulness. The World Bank, the Asian Development Bank, the Government – all had objected to Said's appointment as MD Pak-Arab. It has cost us almost Rs 183 crores to find out how valid their objections were. Aftab Ahmed (my counterpart in NFC as GM Technical) conceded that I was right in pressurising Pak-Arab, and wished that he had supported me at the time.

Much to Said's discomfort, I have suggested to Awan sahib that the revised costs should be presented to the Pak-Arab Board before being forwarded to the Government. Said wanted to lob this time-bomb thrown directly into the lap of the Government. I sent off a telex to the ADNOC directors asking for a meeting.

On 12 June, the meeting was held in the minister's room in Islamabad. I described it in my diary as a 'massacre'. I flew into Islamabad directly from Karachi where I had gone to arrange Rs 5 crores from the local banks for Pak-Arab. The minister, I noticed, had lost weight since I last saw him. I wrote:

'He's likely to lose more after he had heard Pak-Arab's explanations. A charitable way of describing the performances by Saiduddin and Jaffery is that they were ludicrous and shameful. They tried bravado, cheated, and misrepresented until it was clear that the minister was not prepared to tolerate their flaccid answers. Of course, the NFC had its nose rubbed in Said's mess. Repeatedly, the minister asked me whether I knew about this. It became so humiliating and galling to be associated with these wretched people, and sickening to have to defend them. After the debacle was over, SBA, Saiduddin, Aftab and I drove to the airport to drop Said and Aftab who were returning to Lahore. I told them exactly what I felt. What the hell, I thought to myself? I have had enough of SBA's weak attitude towards Said whom I regard as not much obstructive and evil as down-right stupid.'

On 21 June, I travelled to Karachi, accompanied by SBA, for a meeting with Mr. Pirbhai, Chairman of the Pakistan Banking Council. I knew that no bank either alone or in consortium would be in a position to make a commitment without the PBC's approval, despite Pak-Arab's conviction that the banks were just *waiting* to hand them Rs 24 crores. The situation there became comic. Saiduddin did not appear. His GM (F) Jaffery slunk in side rooms. When I did manage to trace him, he asked me: "Am I needed?"

SBA and I spent a pulpy 40 minutes with Mr. Pirbhai. He explained that the credit allocations to the public sector were governed by the National Credit Consultative Committee. During the year 1976-77, the BIM had already burst through the ceiling of its allocations, and it planned to borrow at least another Rs 90 crores the following year. This did not include the Rs 24 crores Pak-Arab needed. 'Where is all this money to come from?' I moaned to my diary. 'The Government doesn't know; the IMF does not want to know; and Pak-Arab couldn't care.'

Once Pak-Arab's financial shortfall had been brought to the notice of the Abu Dhabi National Oil Company (the NFC's partners in the project), its nominee on the Board Nasser Al Suweidi came to Lahore, accompanied by two consultants from Booz, Allen & Hamilton.

My diary entry for 18 July bristled:

'It is said that the fate of a premature prophet and that of a timely fool is the same. In the NFC, having been dismissed by SBA as the latter, I am being given the sterile, belated status of the former. All my earlier efforts to get Pak-Arab to divulge information about the project costs were blocked by Saiduddin, supported invariably by SBA. Since the last meeting with the minister, and more particularly the more recent one by ADNOC's Woodward and Bernstein team, SBA has been slowly re-assessing his hitherto unequivocal commitment to Said. The final straw occurred when preparing the Brief for the Ministerial Review scheduled for 16 July. PFL predicted September 1977 as the Ready for Commissioning date, and November/December 1977 as the commencement of commercial operations. While we were discussing these dates, I asked whether they had been arrived at taking into account the current delivery schedule of equipment and a realistic erection programme. "Oh, no," I was told. "Include the dates we have given you in the Brief. During the meeting with the minister, we will tell him that June 1978 is the likely date of commercial production." For the first time I heard Khalid Saeed (Saiduddin's GM Technical) express his disagreement: "That won't wash anymore."

PFL was required to prepare its part of the minister's brief and to send it with Aftab the following day. Imagine our surprise when we read the 'corrected' date of commercial production had been advanced during the night to November 1978! I thought it was a typing mistake. Unfortunately, it was uncomfortably deliberate. When I asked for the PC-1 to be revised, Saiduddin addressed a note to SBA as Chairman explaining that the revised dates had been prepared by 'experts' and had already been discussed with him. Without actually admitting explicitly, his note implied that the responsibility for the revised dates devolved equally on SBA. For once, this was too much – even for SBA.

Yesterday (17 July) SBA met the other SBA (Secretary Shaukat B. Awan) and Rafi Raza in Islamabad and told him that he wanted to remove Saiduddin. To judge from the alacrity with which both of them accepted SBA's proposal, it was too apparent that they had been waiting for SBA to admit his mistake in selecting and then supporting Saiduddin.'

It did not take many days for Said to be removed. On 20 July, SBA called him into his office at NFC and asked him to resign. Saiduddin did so, adding the ineffective sting – 'as desired by you.' A few hours later, Jaffery also threw in the towel.

While Pak-Arab occupied an inordinate amount of our time at NFC, its significance stood dwarfed by Mr. Bhutto's sudden 'nationalisation' of cotton ginning, flour milling and rice husking units. Bhutto tried to defend his action by clarifying that it was not nationalisation of an *industry*, as such. What had been taken into public ownership had been 'speculative seasonal ventures'.

Bhutto's action had an effect beyond what he could have imagined. He had been led to believe that there would be 2,300 units in all. The Government discovered that there were 2,100 rice husking units alone. Within days, the Government began to doubt its ability to control and manage so many processing units, located in every constituency throughout the country. A new Secretariat had to be established to manage them. Mr. Allauddin Ahmed (our Additional Secretary) was appointed Secretary. He had two Additional Secretaries to assist him, and six Joint Secretaries to help them. And interestingly, Bhutto made Syed Shahid Husain (his Special Assistant on Economic Affairs) announce and justify the take-overs on national television. There could have been an un-kinder cut. Shahid Husain (then an EVP at the World Bank) had been sent by its president Robert McNamara to act as a curb on Bhutto's impetuous forays into whole-scale nationalization / Islamic Socialism. Bhutto had turned the tables on them.

On 9 Sept, sitting outside Mr. Pirbhai's office at the PBC, I encountered the General Manager Finance of the instantly established Rice Milling Corporation.

"How much are you asking for?"

"Rs 20 crores," I told him. "And you?"

"We need Rs 500 crores," he replied, airily.

The following day, I had to escort Mr. Segawa the Japanese Executive Director in the Asian Development Bank, Manila. As long as he was in our control at NFC, the arrangements were faultless. At WAPDA, they descended into a fiasco. First port of call was Mr. N. C. Syed, Member (Water), who after deploring the dangerous level of the water table, ran out of steam. He passed us on to Mr. Cheema, Member (Power). Cheema, being a CSP officer on deputation from the Economic Affairs Division to WAPDA, proved to be insufferably condescending.

"How long have you been in Manila?" he asked Segawa.

"Since November 1975. But I have been in Manila before as a Commercial Attaché."

"Oh, you must have been there before the war. Didn't Japan invade the Philippines?"

I squirmed with embarrassment. Segawa did not move a muscle.

During this period I received a request from Rafi Raza's office if I could look after Priscilla Baines, an English house guest of his and his wife Rosemary. He called himself personally to thank me for agreeing to escort Pricilla around

Lahore. He hoped it would not be too much trouble, etc. He called again the following day and repeated his gratitude.

"I am not asking you as the Minister of Production," he emphasised.

"Look, you are not likely to remain a minister all your life, and I certainly do not intend to spend the rest of my working life in the NFC."

We accommodated Priscilla at the Pak-Arab Dak house in Gulberg. (Bhutto had ordered that the word 'Guest' should be replaced by 'Dak'.) Rafi Raza picked her for dinner from our house. Both Shahnaz and I were impressed that he should have visited the house of one of his 'subordinates' without any formality. No other minister in the People's Government would have bothered.

One of the places Shahnaz and I took Priscilla sightseeing was the Fakirkhana museum in the old city. Our guide – Mrs. Mughisuddin – pointed to a miniature of a European woman.

"Akbar's Portuguese wife!"

"Oh, how interesting!" Priscilla replied. "And which wife was she?"

"One of Akbar's many, many wives," Mrs. Mughisuddin repeated in rehearsed, remembered English.

Later I told Priscilla: "She says that with feeling, for she herself was the last of many, many wives of her late husband."

At the NFC, in parallel to making arrangements for Pak-Arab's financing, I had to ensure that Pak-Saudi (the project at Mirpur Mathelo) had timely funding. The loan of $22 million from the Asian Development Bank came through on 22 August. Not a moment too soon. Everyone – Snamprogetti, the equipment vendors, our team at Basingstoke, the Government and everyone within the NFC – had reached breaking point in anticipation. I conveyed the good news to Awan sahib.

"Congratulations, sir."

"Congratulations are due to you, Aijaz. You have seen this through personally."

The loan from the Asian Development Bank eased the commitment by the Saudi Fund for Development. Its Vice Chairman Dr. Mahsoun Jalal[1], accompanied by Osama Faquih[2], his Director of Capital and Credit, came to Lahore on 10th October to discuss the project. The Saudis had already committed $50 million to it. The SFD relied upon ADB's due diligence before approving their loan.

Dr. Jalal and Osama Faquih had flown in from the Far East and spent most of their first day sleeping off their jet lag. We arranged the best suite at the Intercontinental hotel for them and borrowed Abida Hussain's blue Mercedes for transport.

They had assumed that the PSFL plant was somewhere in the vicinity of Lahore. Our first formal meeting took place at the NFC offices. Sherwani the GM of the PSFL project came woefully unprepared, and for some inexplicable reason most of his senior staff was absent. I had to make the presentation on the project to the Saudis.

After a lunch at Salloo's, I took them shopping for green onyx. Osama intrigued me. He was such a stickler for detail that he examined the veins in each marble vase he handled before he chose one to buy.

SBA monopolised the two Saudis – one night inviting them to meet his elder brother Lalla Amjad who spent most of the evening recounting his friendship with King Faisal when they were together in the United Nations. On the way home after another 'dry' dinner, Dr. Jalal leaned over to me in the car and said: "I hear Karachi has some *lively* entertainment."

Osama was keen of visiting the site at Mirpur Mathelo. We hired the same Cessna aircraft that I had used for Gruppe's flying visit. The trip was uneventful. When we alighted at the plant site, the PSFL staff had arranged for a band of local musicians to play for us. The instruments were not in tune, and neither were the performers. Half-way through, Osama asked me politely: "And what is the tune they are playing?"

---

[1] Dr. Mahsoun Jalal, born in 1936, had begun his career as Professor of Economics at the University of Riyadh from 1967-1975. He served as Vice Chairman and Managing Director of the SFD (1975-1979), before becoming the Chairman of the OPEC Fund for International Development (1979-1982). He died in 2002.

[2] When I checked Osama's career on the internet I discovered that he had changed the spelling of his name to Usama Jafaar Al Fakih. I discovered that he was a year younger than I was. He served later as President Arab Monetary Fund in Abu Dhabi (1989-1994), and later as Saudi Arabia's Minister of Commerce (1995-2003).

"I am not sure," I replied. "But I think it is a Sindhi folk song."

Once we were on our rounds, I asked the administration head: "What were they playing?"

"Our national anthem," he replied.

On 12 October, I accompanied Dr. Jalal and Osama to Karachi. Dr. Jalal and I sat in the First Class bulkhead seats. Osama insisted that I sit with Dr. Jalal, while he occupied the seat behind. Across the aisle another Arab sat with a wicker basket with compartments, each occupied by a hooded falcon encased in a cloth sheath. No sooner had the aircraft begun its take-off than the birds began to agitate. The Arab leaned down to pacify them. This was too much for Osama. He unbuckled his belt even as we were in an ascent, pushed his face between our seats, and said to me earnestly, repeating himself in case I misunderstood: "He is from *Abu Dhabi*. He is from *Abu Dhabi*. He is *not* a Saudi. He is *not* a Saudi."

The stop-over in Karachi meant for Osama another round of shopping for his family. For Dr. Jalal, my brother Ayaz through his better contacts had organised an evening at the rooftop nightclub of the Excelsior Hotel. The seediness of the surroundings did not deter Dr. Jalal, nor did the presence of some raucous Abu Dhabian habitués who cat-called encouraging obscenities at the scantily clad dancers. He managed to maintain a cogent conversation despite the distracting performance by one of them – a nubile English girl – who did everything but smoke an outsize unlit cigar.

The Saudis left next morning. I was in a hurry to see them off as I had to return to Lahore to prepare for my trip to London. Mr. Awan had approved that I could visit London for meetings with the procurement team at Snam's offices at Basingstoke. To ensure that Pak-Saudi's procurement was monitored and controlled better than Pak-Arab's had been, we had posted a team of three NFC managers at the Snam offices - Anees Ahmed to handle the financial side, Aezaz Hussain to look after the IT side, and an engineer Zahid Aziz for technical matters. In those pre-internet days, one had to rely upon telegrams or telex. Bids would be evaluated and assessed by Snam and our team, and then telexed to us at Lahore for approval. Once the order had been placed, its details would be telexed to Lahore where we updated the quantum of commitments. Occasionally, private messages would get included by mistake. I remember asking Aezaz to buy some baby's clothes for Momina from Mothercare. A telex from him arrived, listing PSFL's orders during the week, and added to it a postscript: "Which size of frilly panties do you want?"

I caught the flight for London from Islamabad on 17th. The plane stopped at Tehran but we passengers had to remain on board as the Shah was also landing at approximately the same time. Flying over Tehran I noticed spectacular development – houses, parks with shimmering pools, and on the tarmac, a traffic jam of military aircraft. I remember thinking: 'What will he do with all this hardware?'

My companions on this trip were Habeeb Husain (Additional Secretary, Ministry of Production, and an elder brother of Syed Shahid Husain) and I.A.K. Sherwani, the MD designate of Pak-Saudi Fertilisers. When we reached London, to my surprise we were paged on the loudspeaker and then whisked through the Immigration and Customs by PIA staff. Aezaz Hussain drove me to Bill's house in Chalk Farm. I walked up the familiar stone steps and when he opened the red door, I bent and touched Bill's feet.

The next morning, Bill dropped me at Gloucester Road Tube Station where Sherwani and Aizaz were waiting to drive me to Basingstoke. At the Snam offices, we had an internal meeting to update HH and then broke for lunch. HH expressed a preference for every dish except his own. He coveted my soup and someone else's trout.

For the duration of our stay in London and at Basingstoke, each one of us had a story to tell about HH and his idiosyncrasies. Aezaz complained about how HH suddenly, while they were on a motorway, would ask him to make a stop so that he could urinate. Apparently, HH had a problem with his bladder. I explained to Aezaz that HH being an obedient bureaucrat responded to instructions. So, whenever he spied the road sign 'P', he felt bound to respond.

I had my own brush with him when we visited the Kellogg International office, ostensibly to review the Pak-Arab project. We were received by a Mr. Grimmond. I briefed HH on the project and then in Urdu I enumerated the reasons why we had not awarded the PSFL contract to Kellogg. No sooner I finished than HH repeated to Grimmond in English everything I had just said in Urdu.

At Basingstoke, HH and I were introduced to Mr. Merco, Snam's MD. Guardedly, he hinted at the likelihood of a delay in the PSFL project. "A realistic projection would be advisable, rather than an unrealistic miracle."

I couldn't resist the retort: "Mr. Merco, had we expected miracles, we would not have come to Snam. We would have gone to the Vatican!"

The meetings with the NFC projects ran parallel to my sessions with Philip Wilson and his team over my book *Pahari Paintings & Sikh Portraits in the Lahore Museum*. Its galley proofs had been brought to me in Lahore by Anees on 19 June. Philip had sent me also Xerox copies of the monochrome illustrations. It gave me such a thrill to see the book taking shape finally. I corrected them and again relying upon a courier rather than the post I returned them to Philip. My carrier pigeon stayed in Karachi for a week longer than I had anticipated, and it was only when I received a telegram from Philip on 22 July that the proofs had had arrived in their offices that I could breathe again.

During my stay in London, they showed me the design of the cover. I had no problem with their choice of the Guler miniature showing Krishna and some gopis, or with the Basohli picture of Devi to be carried on the reverse. What disturbed me was the oval cartouche in which the title, my name and Bill's were compressed. It looked as if Krishna Goverdhanhari would be holding the two of us aloft. The final version had the title set prominently against some green foliage.

I spent a weekend checking the final text proofs and those of the illustrations. Inevitably there were slight glitches - a full page illustration of Guru Nanak had been composed back to front, with, as a result, a left-handed Mardana. I stayed up half a night preparing the Index, typed up its fifteen pages, and some last minute instructions for Anne.

Most of the evenings Bill, Tim and I spent together. Bill's obsession at the time was to trace Guru Govind Singh's *kalgee*. It had been listed by Sir John Login in his inventory of the Lahore Darbar *toshakhana* following the annexation of the Punjab in 1849. Bill's son Michael (a specialist in ceramics at the V & A Museum) came for dinner once. Witty and precise, he caught me out when I mentioned that the tomb of the Holy Prophet (PBUH) in Medina had hereditary eunuchs in attendance: "How can eunuchs be hereditary?"

One of the treats of such excursions to London was to visit bookshops. I gratified my interest in miniature painting, and as Shahnaz's proxy her fascination with palmistry and the occult. I discovered many of the books Shahnaz had asked for (and some she did not know about) at a fascinating shop called *Atlantis*, off Museum Street. It specialised in everything supernatural and sciences such as palmistry, astrology and numerology, even the self-style reincarnation of Satan – the infamous Aleister Crowley. Where else but in a London bookshop would one hear a shop assistant say: "Could you wait a minute? I have to find this gentleman a copy of *Occult occurrences behind the Iron Curtain*."

I learned that Shakirullah Durrani, my former boss at Investment Corporation of Pakistan, had moved to London. He was heading a bank owned by some Saudis. He lived close to Ashwin Malde in Arkley. I noticed his corporate affluence - two cars, a chauffeur driven Mercedes (black car, white driver), two brown servants, a large sumptuous house over-decorated with mementos from his foreign tours, and a lingering smell of curry. Especially prominent were objects Samina had collected when he was MD of PIA and still *persona grata* in China. It was rumoured that on his watch, he had allowed the CIA to install cameras on the underside of the wings of PIA aircraft flying across China.

He received me with great warmth, blowing away the residue of our previous altercation. Over dinner we discussed the impact of nationalisation. I knew he enjoyed a good story, especially when it might be at the expense of others. The one I narrated to him happened to be about Brig * Mehdi Ali Shah, the Finance Director of PIDC and A.H.A. Kazi his Chairman. "Brigadier," Kazi shouted to him during a stormy confrontation between them, "if we had been in the Army, I would have had you court-martialled for mutiny!"

"What does a brigadier know about finance?" Durrani commented.

"About as much as a captain, I reckon", his brother-in-law Asad Hayat responded.[3]

Before I left the Archers, I took them out for a meal at the Green Garden – a Chinese restaurant in Swiss Cottage. Both Bill-baba and Tim-bibi enjoyed the relaxed pleasure of eating out without having to worry about 'afters' or washing up.

When the car came to collect me for the airport next morning, Bill

---

[3] Shakirullah Durrani had begun his career as a captain in the Pakistan Army, took early retirement, and followed an upward trajectory in the financial sector as DMD of PICIC, MD of ICP and then Governor of the State Bank of Pakistan.

playfully collected everything he could lay his hands on, including Tim-bibi's handbag.

"A *handbag?*" I asked in a mock Edith Evans / Lady Bracknell voice. That relieved the tension of what might otherwise have been a tearful farewell.

At the airport, I bought a copy of *Playboy* and its new counterpart *Playgirl* for Shahnaz. On the plane I wondered whether in Saudi Arabia, where the punishment for murder is beheading, for theft amputation, importing liquor imprisonment, would the smuggling of these magazines be punishable by penilectomy?

The plane was crammed with a horde of carpet-bagging Westerners of every European nationality. A clutch of Swedes swigged feverishly from bottles of whiskey as if it would be the last drink in their lives.

The plane landed at Riyadh airport at 3.00 a.m. Waiting on the tarmac, resplendent in his white *dish-dash* and patterned *burnoose* stood Osama bin Faquih. He greeted me with a kiss on each cheek. He took Habeeb Husain and myself into the VIP lounge. Prominent I noticed were portraits of King Khaled <u>and</u> Crown Prince Abdullah (recently designated Crown Prince). This tacit acknowledgment of the political realities of power in the kingdom following the assassination of King Faisal was necessary. I recalled the torpid attitude of King Khaled during his visit to Pakistan. He brightened up only when he saw a procession of camels, buffaloes and a pair of nilgai.

We suggested to Osama that as we were to meet him at 8.00 a.m., we did not need a hotel just for a few hours. We could freshen up at the airport. He looked mortified. "Please," he pleaded, "you have to stay at the hotel, even if it is only for a few hours. You have no idea how difficult it is to get rooms in Riyadh nowadays. If you do not show up, we will never be given accommodation there again."

The hotel could not have been more Spartan. Fragile prefab beds assembled from left-over crates, an over-perfumed sliver of soap imported from South India, and a breakfast that consisted of an untoasted slice of bread and tea with powdered milk. For these comforts, we were charged Riyals 345 per person (approx $100 in those days). Habeeb Husain thought we should make the Saudis pay for our rooms. I countered by saying that they were giving us a loan of $25 million. It would be meanness on our part to ask them to pay also our hotel bill.

I paid and kept the receipt.

"What do you want to keep that for?"

"I want to show my children a bill when a hotel room in Riyadh cost only Riyals 345!"

SFD's offices in those early days were located in a block of adapted flats. The discussions with the new staff members of SFD were brief and cordial. Later, I met Dr. Jalal and Osama alone. They gave me a set of gold cufflinks made from Saudi coins. When Osama left us, I asked Dr. Jalal whether there was any possibility of my being accommodated in the SFD.

"Aijaz," he said, "Can I speak to you frankly? I understand why you should want to leave the NFC. But I have seen you in Pakistan. In your own country, you are a prince. Here you would be no better than a 'kalb' – you know, a dog. No Saudi will tell you that. But that is how we Saudis view you expatriates. My advice is look outside Saudi Arabia."

We left Riyadh later in the afternoon. At Jeddah, HH misplaced his luggage tag, and while trying to find it opened his briefcase, spilling its contents and his precious pills on the pavement. When I returned to Lahore and NFC, SBA did not improve my mood by telling me that his successor as Chairman NFC[4] would be ... Habeeb Husain!

I became victim or rather Shahnaz and I both became victims of a hoax of a different sort. On the night of 10 July 1976, Shahnaz answered a late night telephone call, to be asked by an anonymous voice whether I lived in this house, gave my full name, and then asked for a message to be conveyed to me that my mother-in-law had passed away in Karachi. We rang Auntie Nayyar immediately in Karachi. She answered sleepily and then the line disconnected. We could not get through again.

Next morning, a Sunday, SBA had convened a meeting on Pak-Arab. He was irate at the hoax calls he had received during the night. The first informed him that his brother Syed Wajid Ali had died in Montreal; the second that his brother-in-law Akhtar Ahsan had died in Lahore. Akhtar being in Rawalpindi at the time could verify his existence; it took almost half

---

[4] SBA had taken the NFC assignment for three years. The tenure was due to expire in 1977. He reminded Rafi Raza and Awan sahib of this perhaps once too often. They suspected him of flaunting his indispensability.

the night for the family to contact Lalla Wajid in Canada.

At NFC, the Pak-Arab and the Pak-Saudi projects continued apace. The attention paid to safety on such complex sites paid off. Safety hours without an accident were notified daily on a notice board. The only two fatalities occurred at Pak-Arab Multan. An engineer entered a laboratory and turned on the light switch. A spark from it ignited the gas that had leaked during the night and filled the laboratory. He died in the resultant explosion. The other accident was all the more tragic for being avoidable. A photographer commissioned to take photographs of the project site was hoisted in a cradle high above. When he reached the maximum height, he signalled to the crane operator. The operator misread the signal to mean that the photographer wanted to go even higher, instead of being lowered. The crane hit the tip of the boom, tipping the photographer out. He fell over 200 feet to his death.

At Pak-Saudi, SBA grew increasingly disenchanted with Sherwani. He complained that Sherwani was managing the project with only three engineers. 'Everything is contained in Sherwani's black diary. No one is taken into confidence and therefore no subordinate accepts responsibility.' At one time, SBA wanted me to replace Sherwani. I warned him not to, but I could not prevent him from proposing this to Rafi Raza. He turned SBA down for the very reasons I had given: 'Too young, not Sindhi, and your relation.' Habeeb Husain told me afterwards that had SBA not been so hasty, I stood a real chance of being appointed as MD PSFL. Unfazed by the rejection, SBA put forward another name - Javed Hamid.

In mid-November that year (1976), while in the Secretariat at Islamabad, I intercepted Hafeez Pirzada (then Minister of Education). When he realised that I did not want (a) admission to a university, and (b) that I was not importuning for a scholarship, he relaxed. He took me into his office for a cup of tea. I noticed that while every other office in the Secretariat sported a portrait of Quaid-e-Azam, his had a huge portrait of Quaid-e-Awam Zulfikar Ali Bhutto. I told him about the publication of *PP & SP* and showed him Philip Wilson's catalogue. He promised to write to ZAB to accept a copy from me when it was released.

Bhutto happened to be the last foreign dignitary to meet Chairman Mao Zedong. Six months later, Chairman Mao died. I wrote about the event in my dairy:

> 'The Karachi evening papers carried carbon-copy headlines *Mao is dead*. Expected though it was I for one took the portents of the recent earthquake in China seriously, it came as a shock to see the news in cold print. All the western newspapers immediately set off as if at the sound of starter's pistol on a marathon of speculation as to who would succeed Mao. Bhutto made a lengthy and at times moving statement eulogizing Chairman Mao, ending with the quote from Allama Iqbal *Bang-i-Darya*: "*Hazaron saal nargis apni benoori par roti hai/ Bari mushkil say hota hay chaman mein deedawar paida!*"

> Alas, the effect was mitigated when two days later the Indians showed Amrohi's film *Pakeeza*, the final scene of which shows the bier of a courtesan (Meena Kumari) being carried while a voice-over intones: '*Hazaron saal nargis apni benoori …*'

> The scenes of Mao's lying in state were very moving. Rows and rows of weeping citizens, workers, students all filed past with tremendous dignity and demonstrative grief. An embalmed Mao on display, first open and then under a glass case, his face gradually sagging with terminal tiredness.'

On the other side of the world, in November 1976, a peanut farmer from Plains (Georgia) Jimmy Carter was elected 39th president of the United States. I counted the number of times he mentioned the name of Pakistan during the presidential debates. Thrice – and all of them with faint damns. He certainly did not lust after Pakistan in his heart.[5]

Against this backdrop of national and international changes, the spotlights in my life came from Shahnaz and Momina, now a talkative three year old. I recorded some of her remarks, priceless to me as a parent.

---

[5] The reference is to Jimmy Carter's admission- "I've committed adultery in my heart many times" – that appeared in his interview with Playboy magazine, in November 1976.

On 25 December she asked me: "Babi, aren't you going to the office today?"

"No, darling. Today is a holiday. It is Quaid-e-Azam's birthday."

"Will he be having a birthday party?"

"No, sweetie. He is dead."

Momina (perplexed): "Why did he die before his birthday party?"

And another, when she picked up the phone. SBA came on the line and recognizing her voice, said: "This is Momina speaking."

"No, it is not," she replied. "You are NFC speaking."

CHAPTER 11

THE 1977 ELECTION & ITS AFTERMATH

The 1970s began with Z. A. Bhutto's victory in the general elections held in December 1970; they ended with his hanging in Rawalpindi jail in 1979.

In that tumultuous decade, perhaps the most turbulent in Pakistan's history, the year that stood out was 1977. I must have been extremely busy over the winter of 1976/7, because the earliest entry I made in my diary is dated 11 February 1977.

> 'Since November, much has happened, and is still happening. The main event of course is the general election called by ZAB. His action in calling for elections now had more to do with the situation across the border.[1] It had the desired purgative effect. Mrs. Indira Gandhi was forced to accelerate her own election plans and consequently to push her son Sanjay closer centre-stage before he has had time to learn the part. Jagjivan Ram by changing sides has left the players and joined the audience hurling rotting epithets at Mrs. IG and her heirless Youth Congress. The latest news is that Sanjay has been summarily withdrawn from the race.
>
> ZAB, having pulled the stopper out of his own bottle of politics, is strangely undisturbed by the grimaces and bad breath of the genies he has released. Air Marshal (retd.) Asghar Khan has accused him in

---

[1] Mrs. Indira Gandhi's unpopular Emergency was still in force.

public (and received a show of hands from 3 lakh supporters in rallies at Lahore and Rawalpindi) of being a non-Muslim, a traitor and a cheat. Many regard ZAB as being surprised, even intimidated at the vituperative attacks by Asghar Khan and other members of the Opposition. Others suspect ZAB of exhibiting a dangerous over-confidence.

It is possibly too early to determine the margin of the winner. That ZAB will win (and presumably also his PPP) is accepted by all – what remains in doubt is the extent of that margin. One (the most attractive of the fleeing PPP rodents) is wagging her tongue furiously in an effort to swim as far away as possible before her Titanic goes under. More loyal rats – enough to sink the PPP ship anyway – still crowd around and cower between their Captain's feet. The mood is one of naked and shameless opportunism.

Rafi Raza has been given the responsibility of allocating precious life-belts to persons clamouring for selection by the PPP high command. He called at SBA's and unburdened himself about the trying role he is made to perform. According to him, the PPP is totally unprepared for this election. Each man wants a ticket and each ticket holder wants ZAB to *fix* the results in his favour. Dr. Mubashir Hasan (Secretary-General, PPP) has advised all those who have benefited *materially* (the word is as Dr. MH used it) from the present Government's policies to take their hands out of their pockets and to assist their benefactors – otherwise they would be skinned alive!! A serious threat to those who have fattened themselves by skinning others.

SBA, flattered that RR should have called, nevertheless is very upset on hearing that RR has recently purchased a house in London worth £50,000. RR admitted that he wanted to get off the tiger's back but did not know how, or when. One of his final pronouncements was that ZAB was a *wadera*.'

A fortnight later, at Islamabad, I was startled to see a large poster of General 'Tiger' Niazi electioneering. Instantly I could think of at least 93,000 reasons for him not to emerge from his rat-hole. That he should choose the Pakistan National Alliance (PNA) as his launching pad is as unbelievable as

Ford's *faux pas* about Eastern Europe.[2]

'What mal-odours this election campaign has released! Asghar Khan abuses ZAB in the most provocative way. Begum Wali Khan advocates restraint but she is a female feline in a pack of hyenas. They are prepared to use her to attract votes and will afterwards relegate her to the subordinate position her gender and their religious beliefs dictate.

ZAB has begun to rail, flail, and in private wail at the sheer incompetence of his electioneering team. Dr. MH had been given the responsibility of mobilizing the PPP and had apart from a limitless supply of funds and official resources, that most precious element – TIME. Instead of constructing a sturdy, manageable framework of party offices and party workers, he has lost forever the advantage ZAB thought he had when he decided to call for elections.

"Where is the support you all assured?" he is said to have shouted at Sadiq Hussein Qureshi. A question to which not surprisingly SHQ had no plausible reply as SHQ's 'uncontested' victory in Multan has just recently been questioned, and objections to it upheld by the Election Commission.

ZAB is making desperate, dramatic moves in widely advertised public meetings to rekindle the rapport between the mob and himself. He has spoken everywhere, taken his audiences into confidence on questionable political decisions and less justifiable personal habits. He moves the juggernaut of his political machinery into motion through sheer personal effort. Not all those efforts have been successful. His admission that as he works 18 hours a day, he is entitled to drink a little[3] did not endear him to the general public. In fact, quite the reverse. Many asked: "Why did he have to say that at all?"

ZAB has not just one but an aviary of albatrosses around his neck. One special emissary of his – Khan Habibullah – winged his way across the borders where he made the most incredible speech before

---

[2] As incredible as President Gerald Ford's assertion during the 1976 US presidential debates: '*There is no Soviet domination of Eastern Europe and there never will be under a Ford Administration*'.

[3] Bhutto contended that while he drank alcohol, he did not drink the blood of the poor.

an Indian audience. He began in English, switched halfway to Urdu. "I know that you know our language.' When I told Hayat Mehdi (then D-G, India in the Foreign Office), he moaned: "At least you were watching it on television. I was *there*!"[4]

Prize rumour making the rounds: John Gibney, US Vice Consul, Lahore, tells me "I hear that if Asghar Khan wins, he will make Syed Babar Ali the Foreign Minister."

'6 March. Election Eve. The tide appears to have turned in favour of ZAB and thereof he has not yet disassociated himself from the PPP. The PNA by taunting the lion has succeeded in arousing him. The past three and a half weeks have seen him springing on the flanks of the electorate and clinging until he brings it down. His proverbial stamina has reasserted itself, undiminished and without any visible effects of drink, etc., belying the opposition's coarser accusations.

It is not an election, but a referendum as Salim Raza described it the other night. The electorate is being asked to vote for Mr. Bhutto or against him. The issue is as simple as that. Apart from the illusory unity of the PNA, their persistent personal attacks against ZAB have begun to pall disagreeably. Tiger Niazi's support has had a retrogressive effect and Asghar Khan's 'informed' pronouncements have been off the mark. He has claimed for example that Mrs. Nusrat Bhutto has fled the country when in fact she was addressing the Red Cross in the same city where he was. There is a credibility gap between the PNA leaders and the electorate Mr. Bhutto intends to step in between. We will know tomorrow.'

That night, Mubarika took her first steps. By the time we returned from dinner, she was able to walk unaided half way across the room. She made more progress walking upright in two hours than democracy in the country has over 30 years.

'7 March. General Election for the National Assembly, and therefore a public holiday. Streets deserted, particularly the Mall. I went to the NFC office to prepare for the ADP meeting with Awan-sahib

---

[4] I had gone to see Hayat Mehdi in connection with the visa application of Mulk Raj Anand who wanted to visit Pakistan with his wife. Later, he added the name of his assistant Dolly Sahiar. Mehdi asked me: 'How many women does he need to bring with him?"

scheduled for tomorrow.

After lunch N & I walked to the roundabout at the end of Ghalib Road to check whether we would be eligible to vote. The system in force was that four hundred yards from each polling booth, each party had set up an office to confirm the voters' lists. The office at the roundabout belonged to the PNA. It had a large picture of Khurshid Kasuri hung from a temporary awning. Even at 3.00 p.m., with another two hours to go before the polls closed, there was no visible rush. Except for a few persons who stood around for want of anything better to do, there appeared to be no-one at the party's office or at the polling booth.

The PNA official made a cursory search for our names.

"I have 12-C on my list, and 14-C, but no 13-C."

"But you must have 13-C. Our landlady Mrs. Butt must have been registered. She has lived in that house for years."

"No. No 13-C. But you can have 8-C if you like. They have not shown up."

We cast our vote. The PNA turned to weightier considerations. He complained to his companion: "Shabnam has not turned up..." [Shabnam was a popular film actress.]

His disappointment was short-lived. A few minutes later, Mehdi Hassan the singer arrived to cast his vote and was welcomed like visiting royalty.'

Despite the distraction of the elections, Awan sahib held his meeting on the ADP. NFC's requirements of Rs 134 crores was disposed of quickly. A truism in Government known as the bicycle-shed syndrome is that the higher the request, the less time is spent discussing it.

When the results - a landslide victory for the Bhutto's PPP - of the elections to the National and to the Provincial Assemblies were announced, the opposition parties refused to accept their validity. The landslide was followed by an earthquake. On 17 March, Asghar Khan, dining in Mei Kong restaurant in Lahore, was arrested mid-meal.

On the Indian side, the after-shock occurred in Amethi (the Nehru family's home constituency) where Mrs. Gandhi lost. Her son Sanjay was also defeated. By the evening of 21 March, the results were overwhelmingly in favour of the Janata party and unmistakably against Congress.

That day, I wrote in my dairy:

'The CREEP[5] precedent has an added relevance for us. ZAB like Nixon was assured before his re-election of a substantial majority, but like Nixon he was not content with a comfortable, fairly acquired majority. He wanted a large mandate that in its surfeit would sicken the appetite. The appetite that sickened was of the electorate: students, labour and then the general public revolted. Schools have closed down, the Karachi Pathan labour has burnt over 1,400 trucks at Republic Motors, and a curfew has been imposed in Karachi.

Lahore is comparatively quiet. Karachi-ites, it is said, have sent Lahoris bangles to wear.'

By 25 March, the movement against Mr. Bhutto had hardened. The PNA refused to accept the validity of the elections, and therefore the PPP majority. They demanded three things of Mr. Bhutto:

1.   His resignation a prime minister;
2.   A new Election Commission which enjoys the confidence of the people;
3.   Fresh elections to be supervised by the Judiciary and the Armed Forces.

It seems simple on the face of it, yet how does one implement such demands. If ZAB should resign as PM, he will still be a member of the National Assembly. If re-elections take place he can still be elected. Should he not be elected, ZAB would be more dangerous out of power than in power.

The Election Commission already comprises three Supreme Court judges. Not that I have any truck with Justice Sajjad Ahmad Jan and his penchant for film actresses. (He recently crowned Nur Jahan *Malika-e-Tarranum*.) But assuming that these three judges could not be relied upon, which others does one choose from, and how does one

---

[5] Richard Nixon's Campaign for the Re-election of the President.

obtain confirmation from the people of their acceptability?

And how does one ensure impartiality in elections managed by the Army and other organs of the present government? After all, didn't the Army 'manage' the Provincial Elections for the PPP?[6]

Each person had his own reaction to the elections. SBA declared one morning: 'It's a matter of days. Sunday, at the latest. He has to go by then, or he will be thrown out! I can't work for a Government I do not believe in. I am sick, emotionally sick by all this.' His niece Chandi remonstrated in the evening: "Mrs. Bhutto is being given a seat in the National Assembly! Martial law is being declared tonight."

The next morning (26 March) I checked the papers at 8.15 a.m. No Martial Law. No Mrs. Bhutto in the NA. A *hartal* was declared by PNA, even though its leaders were in jail. At 8.30 a.m.,when I ventured out to go to the office, there was less traffic on the roads but by no means a *hartal*. A latent hostility existed towards the government. ZAB remained undecided whether he should award the NA seat to Mrs. Ashraf Abbasi or to Mrs. Bhutto. By the evening he had opted to preserve peace at home – Mrs. B got the ticket.

The situation did not improve. On 30 March, I noted in my diary:

'ZAB has been sworn in at Islamabad, and sworn at in every city in the country. Karachi is still under partial curfew. Multan has seen serious action by the police against demonstrators, Lahore bubbles over the brim with occasional processions organised by the High Court Bar Associations and by women's action groups. Nawab Akbar Bugti has been 'associated' with the women's procession today in a vain attempt to be arrested.

ZAB has announced his new cabinet. Ignoring Burke's advice about preferring to be ruled by law, not lawyers, 14 out of the 22 new ministers are lawyers. Rafi Raza is relieved that he has been relieved. He goes abroad for a year for medical reasons [his wife Rosemary suffered from a surfeit of politics]. In his place, Farooq Leghari has been made Minister of Production. Farooq had been a classmate of mine at Aitchison College in the 1950s and later a CSP officer (1967

---

[6] I was referring to a report published in the *Morning News* on 10 March that the elections for the Provincial Assembly had been held 'peacefully', because the Army had been deployed at polling booths.

vintage). His appointment gives SBA a golden opportunity of accelerate his departure from the NFC. I pity Mr. Awan and other CSP officers in the Ministry of Production. They will have to work under a minister who was their junior in the service by decades. Awan sahib will opt out. It will be interesting to see whether JT will hitch a lift upwards with the new minister.

In the afternoon, I spoke to RR. He thanked me for calling and for remembering him at all. "People don't normally on these occasions." I told him how grateful I was for everything he had done for me and his numerous personal kindnesses. He responded warmly but with a palpable poignancy in his voice. "You have a good minister," he said.'

Farooq held his first meeting with his ministry officials, appropriately on 1 April. He spoke to them of the significant contribution made by BIM companies in the past to the national economy, and the pivotal role they would play in providing a solid economic base to the country. The press release ended with the ambiguous phrase: 'The Minister urged the officers to work with utmost dedication and a sense of urgency as they were dealing with throbbing organisations which brooked no delay.' Reading that news item, I recalled a meeting on 24 March between Habeeb Husain and Feroze Qaiser, in which HH told FQ bluntly: 'The operating results published by the Finance Group of the BIM for November are very depressing, and therefore politically dangerous. I do not know why the Opposition did not use them during the Elections. Anyway, we should not print the consolidated results any more or even circulate them. This information should be sent to the Minister the Secretary, yourself and me.'

Farooq Leghari came to the NFC offices on 2 April. He addressed all the General Managers whom I had assembled in the NFC Board Room. I paraphrased his remarks: 'NFC has done well. Needs to do more. I'm a former bureaucrat but I understand both their uses and their limitations. I'm accessible to all – management, labour, everybody.' All this was said with calm, from the waist upwards. Below the table, I noticed his feet nervously scraping the carpet into furrows.

After Farooq had finished, I spoke on behalf of my colleagues. I reassured him of our commitment and told him we were conscious that we could enjoy any praise only after we had delivered the three fertilizer complexes. I spoke about SBA's contribution as Chairman and stressed that NFC's relation with the Ministry was extremely cordial and productive, lest he walk away with smears of vomit against the ministry. After listening to FAL[7], I adapted Shakespeare's aphorism to him: 'Some are born great, some have greatness thrust upon them, and the rest are just voluble.'

My assessment of him at the time read:

> 'He struck me as inexperienced and indiscreet. An unfired clay pot. Taken up by his position (he has already reprimanded his ministry's peons and requisitioned the BIM Guest House for his own personal use), he emphasized repeatedly that he was a *politician* and that he was in Lahore for *political* work, and was going to Karachi for more *political* work. He is in for a very rough time both at the hands of his own ministry and of outsiders. The CSPs are unlikely to forgive his defection and will not relish the prospect of working under him. Mr. Awan, I foresee, will take him around, introduce him to everyone in the BIM and then unobtrusively arrange his own departure. At the Government level, FAL will have little influence over his cabinet colleagues. He lacks RR's experience and winsome ability to get his own way with the ministries. A more dangerous possibility is that his inexperience will allow the economic hawks – Secretary General Finance A.G.N. Qazi, Secretary Planning, Secretary EAD – led by the new Minister of Finance Abdul Hafeez Pirzada to badger him into submission.

Farooq's indecisions had all of us at the NFC in a whirl. On 7 April, FAL informed us that he wanted to visit Mirpur Mathelo from Karachi, spend an hour touring the site, then continue to Pak-Arab at Multan where he would spend the afternoon, and then travel to his constituency in DG Khan. Awan sahib wanted a full review of the NFC companies made to the minister at Multan. The Brief was prepared at speed. Arrangements made to transport all the GMs from Daudkhel, Faisalabad and Jaranwala to Multan.

The next morning, we learned that FAL had flown into Lahore directly as ZAB had come to cobble together a provincial cabinet from the scrap heap of Punjabi politicians. FAL decided that he would fly to DG Khan instead. The review programme of NFC companies had to be scrapped. Salahuddin

---

[7] SBA and I decided we could hardly refer to him as 'FL'.

Chaudhry (GM Pak-American Fertilisers, Daudkhel, arrived at the NFC office to be told that he should turn around and make the five hour journey back to Daudkhel.

On 9th, Mr. Bhutto's presence in Lahore triggered off violent demonstrations outside the NFC offices, which stood opposite the Punjab Assembly building where the swearing-in ceremony of the MPs was to take place. Another locus of the demonstrations was the Pak-Arab office in Dyal Singh Mansions, where the police had set up a barrier to prevent demonstrators proceeding down the Mall towards the Assembly building. Many were shot, more hurt by *lathis*. The unofficial count was 3 dead and over 40 wounded.

That evening Rafi Raza came to our house for a drink. We had met a few days earlier at SBA's. There he had tried to console me by saying that FAL would be 'alright'. "After all, you could have had Malik Nur Hayat Noon." Alone in our home, he talked more openly. I asked him whether ZAB had any plans for his second term: "In his first term, he nationalised industries, the banks, life insurance companies. He emasculated the bureaucracy. Now that he has dismantled the grandfather clock of our governance, how does he propose to reassemble its parts?"

"He has no such plans."

"Then, we are truly sunk," I told him.

Rafi asked me to meet him again at the Pak-Arab Guest House in Gulberg. He put the air conditioner on 'to dull any bugging devices'. We discussed everything. I recorded some of his comments in my dairy:

'RR: "Has anyone commented on my departure?"

FSA: "You were there yesterday. You are not there today. To the public, that is all that matters."

RR: "What should I do?"

I told him that he had got out with tremendous grace and goodwill. He should not hang about, waiting for someone from the conflagration to call out to him. Like Lot, he should not look back. Use your family, I stressed, use your health, anything, but go. ZAB will not let you go of his own accord. He does not want you, yet is loath to release you.

I gave him my opinion of ZAB – vain, heartless (look at the way he treated Hafeez Pirzada over the Qaddafi letter episode), vindictive, contemptuous of *all* human beings, jealous of Indira Gandhi because she represents everything he would like to have been, and couldn't. To have achieved so much by dint of his own efforts is not enough; Bhutto wants to exorcise his past. His love-hate relationship with Ayub Khan, and how he was not man enough to attend AK's last rites.

RR agreed quietly and with a trace of distress said: "Someone asked me whether I had been given a letter of thanks, and I had to say "No"!"

"Why should you expect one?" I replied. "Begum Liaquat never got one, and it would not have cost ZAB the postage..."

RR spoke of writing two books. I twitted him: "One for the auditors and the other for yourself?" He laughed. The first book, he explained, would be on Pakistan's genesis and the relentless tragedies – Quaid-e-Azam's death, Liaquat Ali Khan's assassination, the two Martial Laws, and then the East Pakistan debacle. The second would be more in the nature of a personal memoir, on the emergence of the PPP – in his words, 'a wonderful opportunity gone to shambles'. He knew that it would be too potent to be published just yet.[8]

On Mrs. ZAB? 'Worse than he is.'

The bill for the Pay Commission's recommendations: 'Rs 177 crores.'

Before our reverie was interrupted by his sister and her friend, I thanked Rafi for his support: "People like me are Himalayan sherpas. We carry your baggage on your way up, and we offer you a drink on the way down. But we never make it to the top with you."

Rafi Raza, like us, could do no more than watch the collapse of ZAB's government. As ZAB became increasingly desperate to retrieve the situation, he became more indiscriminating in his alliances. He called on the Jamaat leader Maulana Maudoodi at his house. He called on Pir Pagaro in his suite at the Intercontinental Hotel, Lahore. But he could not stem the tide of defections – Aitzaz Ahsan and A.H. Kardar, Dr. Mubashir Hasan (his

---

[8] Twenty years after Mr. Bhutto's death, Rafi Raza published a sanitized quasi-memoir under the title *Zulfikar Ali Bhutto 1967-1977* (OUP, 1997). He later edited *Pakistan in Perspective 1947-1997* (the Jubilee Series), published by OUP in 2003.

Secretary-General PPP)[9] from the party, and General Gul Hassan and Air Marshal Rahim from their ambassadorships which were tantamount to exile .[10]

Clashes continued between the PPP and PNA gangs. A PNA procession passed the Rattan cinema owned by a PPP die-hard Din Mohammed. Open firing by PPP, retaliation by PNA on the PPP offices, stabbing and conflagration – leaving 3 dead and 89 injured.

Bhutto appeared on television on 17 April. He appeared confident and bristling to confront the Press. I described it as 'Fireworks meets the Networks'. He explained the Constitutional reasons why he could not resign and should not resign, among them the errancy of the PNA, etc. He stole the thunder of the right-wing maulana parties by banning liquor and nightclubs. 'Cigars are still permissible", he said, with a conspiratorial smile, and then brandished a huge, *lathi*-sized one at the camera.

Bhutto then ignored another piece of advice from Edmund Burke, just as he had disregarded the first about having too many lawyers: 'The use of force is but *temporary*. It may subdue for a moment; but it does not remove the necessity of subduing again: and a nation is not governed, which is perpetually to be conquered.'

After Bhutto's broadcast, I wrote:

> 'He has no intention of going anywhere. It was obvious that he spoke from a position of tactical strength, reassured of support from the Army and Russians. It seems both the Russians and the Americans want to spend enough to shake him but not to topple him.'

The next day, there was another milder demonstration, this time by PIA pilots agitating for higher salaries. In Islamabad, Hafeez Pirzada announced that the Government had not only accepted the recommendations of the Pay Commission (which verged on the over-generous) but improved upon them.

---

[9] 'Cassio, I love thee; But never more be an officer of mine.' Shakespeare's *Othello*.
[10] Another Pakistani ambassador fell victim to an order, this one from Cupid. A report on *The Pakistan Times* (28 April 1977) read that a Pakistani Ambassador in Europe, in love with a married woman in Austria and settled with her husband for her release. The husband asked for £40,000. Unable to pay the amount, the lovelorn ambassador approached the Government of Pakistan, asking to be appointed as a middleman for international contracts. He ought to have been aware that the GoP was itself clutching a begging bowl. Eventually he married her, without the aid of the GoP.

Over the next few days, disturbances continued at Karachi. A curfew was imposed there, after a train was burned when its hapless train-driver ran over some equally hapless demonstrators who decided to lie across the tracks in its path. A PPP mob had a bloody fight with a PNA mob. In Lahore, PIA went on a sympathetic strike for more wages, as did the Railways. Demonstrations became a frightening show of arms.

'21 April (10.30 p.m.): 'Here we go again! Martial Law for the third time. Selectively at Karachi, Hyderabad and Lahore. A curfew at Lahore from 12.00 p.m. We of course were blithely ignorant as we were out for dinner with the Inventa team (here for the PSFL erection negotiations). On the way back we wondered why there was frenzied buying in the Gulberg area.

The pride of each of the combatants prevents them from yielding, and yet neither of them is strong enough to succeed with unilateral action. They have to sit together and talk. Maudoodi has been shifted from Haripur Jail to Sihala outside Rawalpindi. Wali Khan has also been brought to join the PNA leaders 'for discussions'.

April 22: 'The streets are quiet. Our road, normally busy, has not felt the tread of any private car all day. We stood at the gate for over an hour and saw one rickshaw, one scooter, an Army truck with about 12 soldiers parked some doors away. The soldiers checked a passer-by's credentials, and then moved on.

Banks have declared a separate 'concurrent' strike against being neglected in the Pay Commission awards. No one is likely to need banks in the next few days anyway, except my PA Sarwar. He has to arrange a bank guarantee to have his brother released from police custody for smuggling foodstuff into his ration-shop.

The curfew was lifted between 1 p.m. and 3 p.m. We drove past the armoured trucks with their mounted guns parked on the Main Boulevard. Single troopers were deployed along the Canal and the Mall, and also at each major junction. The PNA/PML office in Davies Road was strangely quiet.

April 23: The curfew has been lifted between 8 a.m. and 12 p.m. The usual mad rush for provisions by nervous consumers. We were trying to buy bread from on Jail Road (our usual bakery in Gulberg was under siege) when we learned that the curfew was being imposed again after 10.30 a.m. We rushed to see Granny [Mrs. Tajuddin Pir], delivered some bread and butter to her and then rushed home to be with the children. The cause had been the shooting of two persons at Masjid e Shuhada on the Mall.

The television and radio carried repeated announcements that the Army would shoot on sight and deal with obstructionists under the powers of the Army Act 1952. "The maximum penalty is DEATH", we were told.

Those who get married in the war, I said to myself, must learn to live in a curfew.

24 April. The curfew had been lifted from 4.00a.m. to 10.30 a.m., to allow cows to be milked, fruit to be picked, bread to be baked, and fishes caught to feed the incarcerated multitude. I went out at 6.00 am and noticed early birds scavenging for over-priced worms. Vegetable and fruit (bananas now Rs 10 per dozen) were in greater supply than yesterday but supplies were not enough to bring down the prices.

Nawa-e-Waqt newspaper has been silenced. It refused to publish its edition today. The newspaper vendor offered me a choice of *Mashriq* ('it has four pages') and *Imroze* ('it has six pages'). He would not answer when I asked him which contained the most lies.

The Government has banned all news about the PNA. Nawabzada Nasrullah is behind bars. Begum Wali Khan also. The National Assembly is being called, as is the Senate. General Tikka Khan, who lost us half the country through his heavy-handed actions, is being elevated to become the Interior Minister. The Information minister insists on the front page of *The Pakistan Times* that except for the expulsion of Sardar Shaukat Hayat, 'no other resignation has been received.' Yet on page 5, the same paper carried Mian Salahuddin's decision to resign his seat on Thursday. The National Assembly resembles now 'a rotten carcass of a boat not rigged, nor tackle, sail or mast; the very rats instinctively have quit it.'[11]

April 25: Situation quieter now that the PNA front-benchers are

---

[11] William Shakespeare, *The Tempest*, Book I, ii, p. 146.

behind bars. Rafi Raza phoned to say goodbye. My words in hindsight seem prophetic. He has received a telegram telling him that Rosemary has had a nervous breakdown.[12]

April 28 (evening): ZAB made his historic broadside. The American elephant was baited mercilessly by the Bhutto gnat. The real issue, Bhutto asserts, is not political at all. "It is to get me out. And why do they want me out? Because I have not yielded on the nuclear plant issue." Bhutto's timing is as always good. He spoke with the confidence and assurance of a victor.

29 April: The impact of his speech is already apparent. Most people are publicly decrying the intervention of the CIA. They assume it is because it did not succeed in toppling him, it has been totally unsuccessful. I cannot help feeling that at this early stage, the Carter administration would not want to have ZAB's blood on its hands. They wanted to 'hustle' him, to shake him, but not to go so far as to remove him. Their confidence in the PNA despite its nine-star spangled banner is less than their desire to see ZAB in power, but with restraints and suitable controls. The misbehaviour of the Americans has brought the Russians out strongly in his favour. The Bear unlike the Elephant is not expected to remember. Therefore the Bear has forgotten the 1965 war and Tashkent. It has given us $330 m. as conscience money. The change in government in India became for a moment a cause of concern for the Bear, particularly after Morarji Desai's impetuous outburst against the Indo-Soviet agreement of 1971.

Interestingly, the most silent of our neighbours – the Saudis – have intervened. Representing an Islamic government, which is more than aware of powerful force of economic realities, the Saudis would be on the best position to act as the catalyst between the PPP and the Islam-pasand parties. After all, the Saudis are financing our nuclear plant, as much for their own needs as for ours. Removal of ZAB, who still has many years of fire left in him, would not be in their interest at all. But they do recognize that he is too volatile. The special envoy sent by the Saudis was asked how he could ensure that any agreement between

---

[12] This proved later to be a ruse by Rosemary to prise Rafi out of Islamabad.

the two parties would be implemented by either side. He replied that the Saudis would stand guarantor to ensure implementation by *both* sides.

The Long March that started from the BBC and should have ended in Islamabad was a 'paper' exercise. Over 2 million people were to traverse over 190 miles, and now suddenly everyone is denying that there was ever such a plan. When I heard that it was in the offing, the only parallel I could find between Mao's troops and the PNA Long Marchers was that Mao's troops had to boil and eat their own shoes. The PNA marchers *'jootyain khain gay'* (i.e. would eat someone else's shoes.)

1 May: 'What a difference in the man! ZAB, instead of the PNA, drove around Rawalpindi making impromptu speeches. He held in his hand a letter from US Secretary of State Cyrus Vance[13] issued on Friday 4th after his speech to the National Assembly. The letter has asked Bhutto to discuss the PNA's 'grievances quietly.' ZAB took full advantage of Carter's belated recognition of his electoral victory to make side-swipes at India's electoral maturity, the PNA-CIA conspiracy. He imitated Carter's 'meet the people' techniques. Addressing a crowd, he held the Vance letter aloft and asked the crowd to tell him *quietly* whether he had its permission to respond to the Secretary of State's letter.

Anyone who is still a Pakistani cannot but help feeling proud of ZAB's skill and tenacity. The one word that all the western papers (*Washington Post*, *The Manchester Guardian*, to name just two) is 'brilliant'. He is a first class Foreign Minister. He needs to be an equally effective Prime Minister.'

5 May: Much politicking at Sihala. Asghar Khan being excluded, also Pir Pagaro. *The Pakistan Times* reported: "It is by now clear that the leaders busy in discussions at Sihala are scrupulously keeping Pir Pagaro out of their counsels. They do not appear to trust his discretion, if not his judgment. Possible trouble tomorrow. Agitation is threatened after Friday prayers.

---

[13] Cyrus Vance was Secretary of State under President Jimmy Carter, 1977-1980.

6 May: Strict curfew. Even bona fide pass holders found it a trial to get to their offices. It was lifted between 4.00 a.m. and 9.00 a.m. Heard in the afternoon of the shooting of 2 persons and injuries to 10 others. A bad sign. Curfew with an increasing intensity tomorrow.

7 May: Went to the NFC office. No one else there. The MLA people wanted the public to exhibit special stickers on their cars before allowing them through. A policeman posted every 30 yards along the Mall. The PM must be coming to Lahore.

The milkman delivered milk during curfew hours in the afternoon. "How did you get past the barriers?" I asked him.

"The individual constable is doesn't bother me. It's the group at main junctions. They keep me standing for hours."

"But doesn't the milk go bad?"

"They don't give it a chance. They drink it. You see, they have to. They have had nothing else to eat or drink all day."

9 May: The PM proposes to send his ministers to negotiate with the Sihala strikers. Pir Pagaro is elucidating as only he can the importance of the 32 points put forward by the PNA. *ThePakistan Times* quotes him as saying: "Now, No 2 point is No 1, No 3 is No 2, and No 5 is No 3..."

The Chief Election Commissioner Justice Sajjad Ahmad Jan (I christened him *Spotty* after ZAB called him a dog) has gone abroad, 'on health grounds'.'

SBA returned from a visit to the United States burdened with gossip. He unpacked the following tidbits:
1. The Shah has reneged on his commitment to guarantee a Citibank loan of $300m. It was supposed to be a 'person to person' undertaking by the Shah to ZAB.
2. The actual bill for the pay increases awarded by ZAB will be Rs 400 crores.
3. The Consortium Aid to Pakistan meeting was postponed by us at the behest of the Americans but held informally with a thumbs-down conclusion.

4.   SBA has been offered a job by Snam (which he refused) and an advisorship by IFC (which he has accepted gratefully).

5.   Dr. Mubashir Hasan told all to ZAB before quitting.

6.   Nur Hayat Noon and another minister have resigned. Farooq Leghari is in hot water with ZAB. Three independent sources have repeated the popular rumour that 2 brigadiers have resigned and are under house arrest. One brigade refused to obey orders to fire on civilian demonstrators and has therefore been transferred to Gujranwala.

13 May (Friday): 'ZAB had an important announcement to make; the PNA an important demonstration to hold after Friday's prayers. Restrictions were at their maximum. No-one, not even the curfew pass holders, was allowed to travel by car, rickshaw, or scooter. An official *paya-jam* (or wheel jam) this time. Despite the stringent precautions, demonstrations were held. All India Radio announced more resignations from the Martial Law Authority.

ZAB appeared on television at 5.30 p.m. Halting, a little over-tired and tense. Kept repeating 'The point is ...'. He produced a white rabbit of PNA's reply to his proposals of 11 April, and then proceeded to dissect it, oblivious of the mess it made. Eventually he reached the climax of his speech. Almost everyone I know expected him at this stage of his speech to announce his resignation. Instead, he put his hand back into the hat and pulled out - a dodo. He announced a referendum, on the presumption that as his power comes from the people, he is entitled to go back to the people.

Even this concession was too much for ZAB. Having swallowed the unpalatable, he followed it with a tracer, a warning to his detractors that there would be changes after the referendum, some basic changes as it was clear that this type of democracy had limitations and couldn't work.

14 May: Curfew lifted for a long time by a depressed Army. They regretted it by 11.00 a.m., when fighting broke out in the old city. Common apprehension regarding the referendum and its inherent sterility.

16 May: Curfew lifted during working hours. SBA reluctant to get back to work lest his commitment to the NFC crystallises again.

He lent me a book of poems *Tao te Ching* by Lao Tzu. I found the following poem apposite to our present condition.

> *Whenever you advise a ruler in the way of Tao,*
>
> *Counsel him not to use force to conquer the universe.*
>
> *For this would only cause resistance.*
>
> *Thorn bushes spring up wherever the army has passed.*
>
> *Lean years follow in the wake of a great war.*
>
> *Just do what needs to be done.*
>
> *Never take advantage of power.*

25 May: While I was sitting with SBA, his 'special' friend put his head around the door, saw me and left. A little later, SBA came to my room: "He is from the Intelligence. He says the Amy has given ZAB an ultimatum. Solve it by 3 June, or we take over.

28 May: The pressure is beginning to tell on ZAB physically. According to *The Pakistan Times*[14], Bhutto said during an interview that he respects Mairaj Mohammed Khan 'who left us in a moment of emotion.' He regrets that J. Rahim 'should have been with us at these trying times.' 'Dr. Mubashir Hasan also deserted us at a crucial time.' Everyone around him has been hasty. He has become Othello: 'Reputation, reputation, reputation! O! I have lost my reputation, I have lost the immortal part of myself, and what remains is bestial.'

29 May: 'The Government is totally bankrupt. It has overspent, extravagantly and recklessly. Allocations made with deliberation by the Ministry of Finance, have been flippantly and secretively flouted by the same ministry, without the knowledge of the State Bank or the Pakistan Banking Council. At present there is a serious impasse between the three to determine who will face the IMF and with what explanation.

Hafeez Pirzada as Minister of Finance has brought out an Ordinance

---

[14] Dated 28 May 1977.

to permit demonetisation of notes which have been 'defaced' by PNA supporters. There are few such notes. Everyone knows that. What they also know is that this is yet another desperate ruse by the Government to cheat its own public. They will try by this latest manoeuvre to staunch the flow of fiscal blood but do nothing to apply the tourniquet where it is most needed.

The PNA and the Prime Minister are crawling closer. ZAB has conceded 'quietly' each of the PNA's demands. He has agreed that all the PNA leaders will be freed before negotiations commence. They have a lot of venom accumulated against him and edge closer to him to be within striking distance. The atrocities perpetrated against them are unspeakable: Mrs. Asghar Khan put into a lonely sanatorium which houses only males; Asghar Khan himself in a cage, watched 24 hours; Sherbaz Khan Mazari in a Class C cell; Maulana Noorani, even worse. ZAB will have a lot to answer for. The Saudis are trying to bring the two parties together. It is a shame that we should need them at all. It is an added humiliation that the PLO[15] which has no nationality of its own, should be offering us a charity fund to subsidies our self-inflicted losses. The gall of it! And the shamelessness of the government in advertising it.

14 June: Talks continue between the Government and the Opposition. ZAB, Hafeez Pirzada and Maulana Kausar Niazi for the PPP; Maulana Mufti Mahmood, Professor Ghafoor Ahmad and Nawabzada Nasrullah for the PNA. Asghar Khan shouts 'foul' occasionally from the sidelines. Pir Pagaro is no doubt placing his bets on both.

ZAB is caught in a tight vice. He has nowhere to go and no-one wants him to stay. The Army, the Saudis, and his own follies are forcing him to swallow the bitter pill of compromise, coated as it is with distasteful realisation that the PNA can never be a viable government, nor a particularly beneficent and merciful one to him and his party stalwarts. His main strength has become his principal weakness. Foreign policy (his forte) has fractured around him. He has alienated the Americans, the Chinese by espousing the Russians, and the Arabs.

---

[15] Palestine Liberation Organisation, led by Yasser Arafat.

The Indians do not want to know him and are talking over his bowed head to the Iranians. The Shah having withdrawn his guarantee for the $300 m. loan from Citibank is blasé to the point of hostility. Bhutto has reduced the country to such a shambles that no-one in any party wants to rush in and set it right.

21 June: The PPP government and the Opposition have come to an agreement. It covers the appointment of Governors, bureaucrats, and a second general election later this year. From the PNA's point of view, they have got ZAB to admit that the March elections were null and void. They have made him agree upon a joint approval before any senior appointments are made, yet could not prevent him from appointing Ghulam Mustafa Khar as his Special Assistant on Political Affairs. Before the Saudis could, he claimed singular credit for the Accord.

5 July 1977: Heard on All India Radio that the Armed Forces had taken over the administration in Pakistan and had taken the PPP leaders including the *former* Prime Minister Zulfikar Ali Bhutto and PNA leaders into protective custody. No further news until mid-morning when it was announced that General Ziaul Haq had called upon the President[16] and upon the Chief Justice of the Supreme Court[17]. He is to address the nation on television this evening.

Based on the limited information available, political pundits opined that:
1. Armed Forces are united, at least to begin with;
2. Administration has been taken over but no Martial Law – yet;
3. ZAB is being forced to resign;
4. Will the 'protective custody' be permanent or temporary?

Speculations / news from different quarters:

From Ayaz in Karachi: Six PPP arrested (ZAB, now in Murree; Mumtaz Bhutto, Hafeez Pirzada, Maulana Kausar Niazi, General Tikka Khan and Mustafa Khar in Chaklala) plus 9 from the PNA. ZAB woken up at 3.00 a.m. and taken into custody.

From Aezaz Hussain: Coup by brigadiers, with shooting before Ziaul

---

[16] Fazal Elahi Chaudhry, fifth President of Pakistan (1973-78).
[17] Justice Anwar-ul-Haq, 9th Chief Justice of the Supreme Court of Pakistan (1972-1981)

Haq came on the scene.

From Anees Ahmed: Shooing in PM's house in Rawalpindi, sounds heard by neighbours.

From Karachi papers: Assemblies dissolved. Fresh elections on 8 October.

From SBA: Hafeez Pirzada beaten up for resisting. ZAB and others at Chaklala.

If there was one person who had no idea what was afoot in Islamabad, it must have been Minister of Production Farooq Leghari. The very day the Army took over, he issued through the press 'a categorical assurance that the government had no intention to nationalise more industries.'

CHAPTER 12

THE NEW GREEN IS KHAKI

That first day - 5 July 1977 - of the new military rule after five years of civilian government was spent by us in anxious anticipation. At 7.00 p.m., the television announcer introduced Ziaul Haq as 'the Chief of General Staff and Chief Martial Law Administrator'. That set the tone for the speech. I noted:

> 'Martial Law for the 4th time; National/Provincial Assemblies dissolved; Ghulam Ishaq Khan *de facto* PM; ZAB's puppet to continue as president; ZUH to be CMLA; Federal Secretaries are to be heads of their respective ministries. ZUH spoke 'without ambition' of his resolve to hold elections later this year, in October. Meanwhile, no electioneering until he says so, and then elections, when he says so. Will the electorate be expected to vote the way he proposes? ZUH has set a time limit on his ambition, which I suppose is an improvement on Yahya Khan's open-ended mandate.
>
> Questions that prick uncomfortably:
> 1. How will he ensure fair electioneering if he includes or excludes ZAB?
> 2. Even if he hands over power to a duly elected government, does he not foresee his successors emasculating the Army as ZAB had almost succeeded in doing?
> 3. What does he propose if the electioneering gets out of hand?
> 4. Isn't this the Army chief chosen by ZAB?
> 5. What are the solutions to our recurring economic problems? Will GIK be strong enough to steer this leaking ship?'

The next morning, SBA confirmed that the first move had been made by ZAB. He ordered the arrest of the PNA leaders and sent the Frontier Security Force (FSF) to do it. The Army followed, and caught the FSF in the act. FSF thought that the Army had come to assist them. Immediately afterwards, the Army moved against the PPP leaders. Hafeez Pirzada shouted at and abused the arresting officers and was given the 'J. Rahim special'. Khar also protested but was silenced with a threat of violence. ZAB was supposed to be in PM's House and would be kept there until he discloses his assets and disgorges his wealth. The Army is trying to get hold of his tapes.

Later in the day, at lunchtime, the news came that Vaqar Ahmed (Cabinet Secretary), Rao Rashid (DIB), Masood Mahmood (FSF) and others had been arrested.

Within the NFC, these changes made for titillating conversation over cups of tea. Our main concern was what would happen after SBA's departure as Chairman, and more immediately how could we salvage the delay in the award of the erection contract by PSFL?

By the beginning of 1977 almost all the machinery needed by PSFL had been ordered. There would be sometime between the arrival dates of the equipment and erection on site. Prudence (and common sense) demanded that parallel to procurement the selection of the contractor for the erection works had to be made. Sherwani had kept the plans in his black book, sharing them with no one, not the ADB nor the SFD. For reasons that I suspected, I too was not included in PSFL's belated invitations to bidders. I noted the sense of desperation within the NFC and soon enough within the ministry at the impact of a delay:

> 'On 2 February I found myself sucked into the whirlpool of SBA's excited presentation to Mr. Awan. After listening to SBA's and Aftab's review of the bids from CIMI/SAIPEM and INVENTA/MAN/MANNESMAN, Mr. Awan turned to me:
>
> "Have you anything to say on these discussions?"
>
> I tried to hedge, without success.
>
> Mr. Awan read the signal and continued: "I want you to prepare a report on the negotiations."

Returning to Lahore, I tried but whichever what I examined the sequence of the negotiations, a flaw was detectable.'

We returned to Mr. Awan on 24 March. 'The meeting with Mr. Awan was very dignified considering he had Sherwani to take to the water. SBA disowned Sherwani early in the meeting and increased the distance between them by muttering 'Gadha, gadha' while Sherwani tried to justify his inaction to Mr. Awan. Aftab bravely sided with Sherwani.[1] The final decision after considerable 'oratory' on my part was in favour of the INVENTA-MAN-MANNESMAN consortium on a cost-plus basis.

For me, professionally, becoming familiar with these international funding institutions – the World Bank, the Asian Development Bank, Saudi Fund for Development – was rewarding enough. The added bonus came from meeting officers sent by their respective headquarters to monitor our projects. Of the many I had responsibility for, two were special. The first was Husin Alsegaf, an Indonesian whom I had first met through the Shis in London in the 1960s, while I was studying accountancy at Maurice Apple & Company. After qualifying, Husin returned with his wife Idjah to Indonesia where he served with the government before joining the World Bank in Washington, DC. By that time they had two children – Hadi and Latifah. Ever thoughtful, Husin would bring with him from the States gifts and toys for the girls and toiletries for Shahnaz. Through him we became acquainted with a colleague of his – Mario Artaza, a Chilean. Meeting Mario made me realise what a haven the World Bank could be for politicians from unstable third world countries. Mario had been closely associated with the Chilean leader Salvador Allende, a Marxist who like Bhutto embarked upon a programme of nationalisation within his country. Allende too was ousted by his military junta. In 1973, Mario who had been the Chilean Chargé d'Affaires in Washington got a job at the World Bank. It was certainly junior to anything he had done in Chile but he never alluded to his altered, reduced status.

I had not met any Latin Americans nor (when I think of it) many since. Mario though stands out as someone unique. He had the most responsive social antennae and with it an instinctive understanding of sub-continental social behaviour. I witnessed a demonstration of it when on 11 April Shahnaz

---

[1] Aftab and Sherwani had started their careers as junior engineers at the PIDC's NGFF factory at Multan. It explained the strong bond between them. As I told SBA later, liquid ammonia is thicker than blood.

and I invited him and some Pakistani friends for dinner at our home. Among our local guests were Mushahid Hussain, Salim and his wife Paro Raza.[2] While Salim updated us on the looting of banks by organised political gangs, Mario remained reticent, watching Mushahid with an almost feline suspicion. At another such evening, after the meal, Mario noticed that none of the guests chose to leave. Mario leaned towards me and whispered: "I think no one wants to go because they know they will be the next to be talked about."

Mario took the on-going turmoil in his stride. One evening, we were in the drawing room of our home in Gulberg. While he was talking, there was a loud explosion. "A bomb?" he asked.

"No. A hand grenade," he replied, nodding his head in a gesture of understanding, and continued with his story where he had left off.

Like most expatriates, Mario succumbed to gastric infections whenever he came to Lahore. He tried all sorts of allopathic medicines and then asked whether he could meet a *hakim*. I took him to one known to us. The *hakim* held open court. His patients sat in a circle around him, each being summoned to the table for a one-to-one. Mario looked first for any cubicle where he could describe his condition in more privacy. The *hakim* beckoned to him encouragingly. Mario sat on the chair closest to the *hakim*. Undaunted by the inquisitive stares of the other patients, Mario (who knew not a word of Urdu) did the most perfect mime, moving his hands upwards from his stomach to signify flatulence, rotating his hands over his stomach to explain the churning he felt within, and then with a powerful downward accompanied by grunts he conveyed to the *hakim* the end result. It was a performance of which Marcel Marceau[3] would have been proud.

The political disruptions and my professional work at the NFC did not distract me from pursuing the publications of my books. By this stage I had three in progress. The first *Mughal & Related Miniatures* proved elusive. After the departure of Yunis Said and Taufiq Rafat, the National Book Foundation lost interest in it. The publication by the Lahore Museum of my text in a shoddy, badly printed booklet without my name did not help. I remember weeping when I saw it. I felt as if I was looking at the mangled corpse of a child of mine, ravaged by strangers.

---

[2] Salim was then in Citibank, Lahore.
[3] The famous French mime artist.

Jamil at Elite Publishers kept playing hide-and-seek with me over *Sikh Portraits by European Artists*. While I knew that they wanted to use this book as a vehicle for promoting their expertise in colour printing, I knew the title would be a drag on their enthusiasm. And so it proved to be. Their interest shrivelled and then died.

That left me with Philip Wilson Publishers and *Pahari Paintings & Sikh Portraits in the Lahore Museum*. I described it as accident-prone. Despite my meticulous proofreading, Bill discovered a mistake that proved costly for me - £200 to be precise. Returning from a visit to the movies in London, Bill felt an apprehension that I had spelt the name Garhwal incorrectly. Sure enough, he checked my manuscript and found that I had spelt the name of the state as Garwhal, not Garhwal. He told Sotheby's immediately. The composition in those days was done by hand, and therefore those offending pages had to be corrected also by hand. Such post-proof mistakes were at the cost of the author. They were deducted in due course from my royalties.

I had just recovered from this lapse when Bill wrote in March 1977 to tell me that the paper PWP had chosen for the book would not take the printing ink. A new consignment of a different paper had to be ordered. The book would not be ready until May, 'perhaps even later'. I vented my disappointment in my diary:

> 'All these disappointing setbacks. I swallow hard every time my bile of resentment rises within me at being the victim of these repeated disappointments. Having advertised the book to everyone in Lahore and Islamabad, this delay makes me ashamed to mention it. "When is your book coming out then?" is the refrain. I hate the tune already.'

The final proofs of the dust jacket arrived on 4 April. I longed to see the book in its final state.

> 'Tim Benbow of OUP is due to return on 31st morning. No news from him or from WGA about their dinner together. I am a bundle of disorganised nerves over the book. I know what it will look like. I have seen the art pulls, the colour plates and the text layout. The only thing I have not seen is the type of paper they will use and the binding. Yet, the prospect of seeing it put together excites me more than I can describe here. God willing, it should be here before my birthday on 2 June. Truly a grand birthday present – if it gets here, that is.'

On 31 May, I exploded with pride.

'It's here! *Pahari Paintings & Sikh Portraits* is here at last! And it is beautiful. Tim brought a copy back from London. He arrived at Karachi this morning. It was detached from him by Khaliq from our NFC Karachi office, shown to Auntie Nayyar who wept on seeing the dedication to Shahnaz, taken to Nassé at PTCL offices (he had typed the first draft), and then carried by a PIA Captain Dodhy to Lahore. While waiting in the operations room for his plane to land, I had to endure the carping of one Amin Chaudhry (the Flight Operations Officer) who harangued me on the deficiencies of the English language, the exorbitant price of fertilisers, the qualitative difference between NFC urea and DHL urea, his family's sacrifices for Pakistan, etc., etc.

Suddenly an attendant brought a brown paper parcel. It weighed 3 lbs. It was my baby!!! "I have also written a book..," I heard Chaudhry say but his voice sounded far away. My attention was concentrated on my child. I took it home, like Mubarika, less than 24 hours old. Shahnaz opened the door. I gave her the book.

"For you," I whispered to her. She knew that its dedication read simply: *For Shahnaz.*

"I am *so* proud of you."

The production of the book is superb. The colour plates are magnificent, the monochrome ones superlative, but most of all, the printing is an absolute joy. PWP has used a delicately slightly off-white ribbed paper, which gives it a rich texture. One can feel its elegance as one turns its pages. The whole production is most appealing. In fact, it is the best book I have ever seen. But then I boast like a parent. "I have done it!!" as Farah once exclaimed famously after she produced an heir to the Pahlavi throne.

We took the book to Ajmal Hussain's where we had a hilarious photography session *en famille* with the book as the centre piece. From there, I took the book to 3, Habibullah Road to show Sister (Miss Carroll). I owed so much to her for instilling a love of language, poetry and personal discipline in me.'

In those days, one had to book an international call. I booked one and spoke to Bill-baba.

"Did I wake you up?"

"No, I was having my morning tea," he mumbled. I could picture him propped up in his bed and having his tea without his dentures in place.

Later, when their offices opened, I spoke to Philip and repeated my refrain of thanks to him and his team.

My euphoria at seeing the first copy of PP & SP lasted less than a week. It evaporated when the first ten copies (my entitlement as an author) were delivered in London to a PSFL staff member visiting Snam. For some reason, he chose not to bring them himself to Pakistan but consigned them instead to an unknown passenger. The man left them at the Lost & Found section of Lahore airport, where they were impounded by the Customs for 'illegal entry'. My bitterness seeped through my diary entry for 4 June:

> 'I wish I had taken to growing hashish instead of writing books. At least my efforts would have passed through the Pakistan Customs with impunity.'[4] I succeeded in having my books released through the intervention of Z. A. Shah (Member Customs) whose son works at NFC.'

Now that I had copies to present, I gave one to SBA. I sent it to him in his office with a note: 'Modesty forbids me from presenting this to you myself'. Another I gave to Awan sahib. He was extremely pleased and complimentary. "Over the past three years," I told him, "I have been observing you as carefully as you may have been observing me." He wilted and then began talking candidly about himself.

Other copies went to Mr. Mushtaq Yusufi[5] at the Pakistan Banking Council in Karachi. He positively choked with appreciation and generously agreed that the banks to order some copies. He spoke of our 'family traditions of authorship'. Tim Benbow at OUP confirmed that OUP would pay for 200 copies, and I would be expected the finance the rest. He would sell to bookshops, I to institutional buyers.

---

[4] The same courier on a previous visit had carried my corrected proofs to London. He delivered them 10 days later. According to him, he had been off-loaded at Amman airport and slept in the lounge using the packet containing my precious proofs as a pillow.
[5] A leading writer and humorous Urdu columnist.

I showed my mother a copy of *PP&SP*. She stroked its cover, read the dedication to Shahnaz, looked inside the book, and then closing it, she asked me: "Why don't you write something on Islam?"

Ayaz wanted me to present a copy to Mumtaz Bhutto.[6] He and a number of his cronies – I christened them 'his drinking cabinet' – were in Islamabad, recovering from a binge the night before. Ashiq Bhutto appeared, groggy. Dressed in an embroidered organdie white shirt, a blue linen safari suit, diamonds set in a square gold ring, a gold bracelet, and the latest Christian Dior sunglasses. ("He brought back *six* pairs from Hong Kong," his wife Nafisa Bhutto told me.)

I had been waiting for over an hour when Mumtaz emerged at 1.00 p.m. I gave him the book. He avoided the text, flipped through the illustrations quickly, and then stopped when he noticed the miniature of Vishnu's incarnation as Varaha the boar. Mumtaz grunted in recognition.

After my meeting with Mumtaz, I had hoped to catch the afternoon flight back to Lahore. Ayaz insisted that I should accompany all of them to Murree. We arrived at Cecil Hotel at 4.00 p.m. The hotel managed to produce lunch at short notice for their VIP guest. The table talk ranged from the price of whiskey (Rs 440 per bottle) to an imitation of Khar eating snails. On the political situation, Mumtaz did no more than splutter: "PNA? If the PPP does not come to power, the PNA certainly won't. The Army will take over."

On a personal level, my case for promotion from Grade M1 to the higher M2 loitered somewhere within the Ministry. I chafed in my diary:

> 'It had been proposed at RR's specific request in February 1976 – over a year ago. It seems curious how when every other case has been pursued by me has been processed by the Ministry, only mine has been dawdling, orphaned by SBA. I have either lacked the courage or been too much of a gentleman to promote myself. With these ministerial changes on the cards, I told SBA to withdraw my case. I also told Habeeb Husain bluntly that it was humiliating for any person to have his case which had been asked for by the Minister to be held up for a year. I had not lobbied for it. Either I was competent to be promoted or not. HH looked half his size with embarrassment

---

[6] Zulfikar Ali Bhutto's talented cousin. He was then Minister of Communications.

and asked me to 'wait another month'. I agreed because I could not see any purpose either way. There could be no further humiliation were I not to be promoted and even if I was, there would be no satisfaction to be gained in receiving such a belated autumnal laurel.'

Awan sahib finally cleared my case on 17 May – 15 months after Rafi Raza had recommended it.

At home, the girls grew fast by the day. On 29 January, we celebrated Momina's fourth birthday by throwing her first birthday party.

'She was all jitters and then burst into tears when Ayesha from next door peeped through the hedge to see whether there were any guests, and on seeing none, disappeared. I feared the worst, especially as it had turned cloudy. Before we could weep *en famille*, children began pouring in. Parents drove up to the gate to and with obvious relief dropped their progeny on our doorstep. Others sent ayahs with their children. Within no time, we had over 40 children (couldn't count exactly because they just would not sit still). Fossard[7] saved the afternoon by showing two delightful French cartoons, after which we served tea and M's ship-shaped cake. I had littered the space between the plates of food with toffees. Within 15 minutes, forty children and almost as many ayahs had cleared the table.'

Now that Momina had turned four, it was necessary to have her admitted into a formal school. We had placed her the previous September in Les Anges Montessori, established by Nasreen 'Mona' Kasuri in her grandmother's house in Gulberg.[8] Mona had intended it as a feeder system, a preparation for admission to Jesus & Mary Convent. Shahnaz and I followed a well-trodden path used by other parents and applied for admission to the Convent. Shahnaz was interviewed, I was, and then Momina. When she had been given admission, I went to the Accounts office to deposit the first term's fees. Pencilled on our form were the remarks: 'Nice parents; lovely child.' I felt quite gratified until I glanced at another application, this one from a man who was employed in ICI Pakistan Ltd. 'Lovely child; very cultivated gentleman.' Suddenly I felt very uncouth.

---

[7] Dominique Fossard, Director of the Alliance Francaise, Lahore.
[8] This was the crucible for Mona's expansion into the now world-wide Beaconhouse School System network.

Momina's first day[9] at the J & M could not have been more promising. She got up at six, excited and talkative. Her books had been covered with brown paper and fitted into her satchel.

"Why have the schools not opened until now?" she asked me as we drove through a mad skelter of cars on Davies Road.

"Because of political disturbances," I explained.

"Does Mr. Bhutto know that I am going to school?" she questioned.

When we picked her up at the end of her first day, she babbled with relief. The next morning I detected a marked reluctance. Over the next few days, I saw her enthusiasm diminish and then evaporate. I would leave her in her classroom and then watch her surreptitiously from the window. She had been at school less than a week when I noted that 'she looked visibly upset. She would walk towards the door to leave and would be ushered back into her chair. It broke my heart to see her small body racked with sobs.'[10]

On my 35th birthday, I felt I had reason to be satisfied. I had *PP & SP* in my hands, my *Sikh Portraits by European Artists* had been accepted by PWP as a follow-on, I had been promoted to M2 Grade in NFC – all these were achievements, attainments but without any life-altering monetary advantage.

No introspection on my part or description of how I viewed myself could have been more applicable to me than a paragraph I read in V.S. Naipaul's *An Area of Darkness*: 'It is easy for Indians to make fun of Bunty for being called 'Daddy' by his English-speaking children; for his imitated manners; he rises when ladies come into the room; for his foreign interest in interior decoration; for the spotless bathroom and adequate towels he provides for his guests (such attentions in India being beneath the notice of all but the latrine cleaner: the Indian lavatory and the Indian kitchen are the visitor's nightmare). But Bunty is no fool. He had withdrawn from India, but he does not wish to be a European. He sees the glamour of Europe; but, being in almost daily contact with Europeans, he is compelled by his pride to be Indian. He strives too hard perhaps to blend East with West; his patronage of Indian arts and crafts is a little like that of a visitor. In his drawing room, hung with contemporary Indian fabrics, the odd sketch from Kangra, Basohli or Rajasthan or a piece of bright

---

[9] Diary entry, 25 May1977.
[10] Diary entry, 1 June 1977.

bazaar art of Jamini Roy stands beside the Picasso lithograph or the Sisley reproduction. His food is a mixture of Indian and European; his drink is wholly European.'

Except the last sentence about drink, everything else might have been a stencil of my character and personality.

With the publication of my *PP&SP*, I found myself propelled into an echelon of scholars in miniature painting, being taken seriously rather than as a 'gifted amateur.' One manifestation came with the visit to Lahore by Richard Lanier of the JDR 3rd Fund in New York.[11] The Fund had been established by J.D. Rockefeller to promote amongst other things research visits by scholars to the United States. He had been told of my work by Bill Archer who suggested that I should be invited to participate in the Colloquium on Pahari Painting, being organised by Pratapaditya Pal at the Los Angeles County Museum of Art. It was scheduled to be held in September 1977. Lanier had lunch with me, during which he confirmed that I fulfilled the three criteria the Fund required: I was a Pakistani; a 'fresh face' in the field, and I had not visited the US before.

It took another three months for the JDR Fund to process my case. On 23 June, I received a telegram: *Travel Grant to Archer Symposium approved. Letter follows. Lanier.* The letter when it came confirmed that the JDR 3rd Fund would pay for my return ticket (LHR/LA/LHR), an allowance of $45 per day for 30 days, plus $100 extra for incidental expenses.

Almost as an omen, on 10 July, an invitation came from the Fertiliser Institute of America inviting the NFC to send a delegate to a two-day seminar in New York between 18 - 20 September.

A week after the military coup, the situation in the country remained unclear and opaque. Conflicting reports oscillated in drawing rooms about the take-over. Ayaz claimed that ZAB knew nothing at all until he was woken up and taken into custody. SBA interpreted Bhutto's request to have his coffee outside on the lawns of PM House as an act of pre-emption, to prevent the military usurpers from shooting him indoors.

Feroze Qaiser had convened a Budget meeting of the corporations on 7 July. That whole morning no one knew where he was. News circulated that he

---

[11] Richard Lanier came to Lahore on 2 March.

had been called to the Defence Ministry. "Should we read *fateha* over him?" SBA teased Habeeb Husain. Much to everyone's surprise, Feroze appeared, beaming with relief, a surprised Lazarus. He shared his resurrection with me: "Aijaz mian. We are professionals aren't we? Professionals, not politicians. They asked me what I did as Special Assistant to the Prime Minister on Economic Affairs for five years. I told them that I did nothing more than determine the price of onions and rice."

Ziaul Haq had not been in the seat more than a week than he issued a diktat that amputation would be part of our law. The MLA (aka the Muslim Law Authority) took us back 1,200 years with one stroke of a rightist dictator's pen and the police surgeon's scalpel. The mood of the time was:

> 'Everyone expects a coup – either for ZAB or against General Zia. Some interpret this present state as an interlude. If God forbid, ZAB should return, there will be mass murders. If God forbid, ZAB should not return, it will be as bad - for different reasons. Bhutto is a wounded tiger. The prevailing rumour is that ZAB is having a nervous breakdown. Two psychiatrists have been called to see him in Murree.[12] Another source reports that he has suffered a mild heart attack.'

No voice from within the PPP spoke out in support of ZAB. None, I doubted, would ever have the courage to admit Albert Speer's remonstrance against himself for supporting Hitler with such blind obedience: 'For had I only wanted to, I could have found out then that Hitler was proclaiming expansion of the Reich to the east, that he was a rank anti-Semite, that he was committed to a system of authoritarian rule, that after attaining power he intended to eliminate democratic procedures and would thereafter yield only to force. Not to have worked that out for myself; not, given my education, to have read books, magazines, and newspapers of various viewpoints; not to have tried to see through the whole apparatus of mystification – was already criminal. At this initial stage my guilt was as grave as, at the end, my work for Hitler. For being in a position to know and nevertheless shunning knowledge creates direct responsibility for the consequence - from the very beginning.'[13]

---

[12] Bhutto had been removed but was still in the Army's custody to the State Guest House in Murree.

[13] Albert Speer, *Inside the Third Reich* (New York, 1970). Albert Speer served as Hitler's Chief Architect before becoming his Minister of Armaments and War Production.

On the 15th I made a flying visit to Islamabad on behalf of SBA to meet the Swedish Ambassador. I was sent to caution him against accepting the appointment of Brigadier Malik (former Chief Secretary Punjab) as the Pakistani ambassador-designate to Sweden. SBA's terse message to the Swede was: 'Hot potato; cold storage.'

Zia's increasingly frequent pronouncements indicated a latent affliction of 'foot and mouth disease.' He told American correspondents that he intended to hold elections within 90 days, yet commented disparagingly about the PPP and the PNA Opposition. He accused ZAB of fiddling the elections on a large scale (especially in the Punjab), yet expected ZAB to abide by the Legal Framework Order. In his press conference, he appeared candid, sincere and disarming.

A quick trip to Islamabad and a brief meeting with Awan sahib resulted in an approval for my trip to attend the Fertiliser Institute conference in the US. To my surprise (and delight) the ministry issued the permission within a day.

While I was in Islamabad, I called on Colonel Siddiq Salik, Zia's Public Relations Officer. Tim Benbow had given me to check the page proofs of his book *Witness to Surrender*.[14] Siddiq Salik and I had lunch together and later sitting in his office in the ISPR at Rawalpindi (Zia was still operating from GHQ), we exchanged notes on his book. It was a well-written, occasionally moving account of his service in East Pakistan in 1971 as PRO to General 'Tiger' Niazi, his capture and his incarceration as a POW in Agra jail. I teased him a little by telling him that I suspected he had been more of a soft corner for Yahya Khan than even Nur Jahan.

"Twice," I told him, "you have mentioned Yahya Khan's long and languid eye-lashes!" He quickly saw the need to change that. I found Siddiq to be a naturally quiet, sensitive man and obviously concerned over his first book. I felt very 'old' guiding him about authorship. At times, I could see mirrored in his eyes my own anxieties over *PP & SP*.

Occasionally, our reverie would be disturbed by intrusive telephone calls from people who wanted to ingratiate themselves with the new leadership. One of his jobs, he told me, was to write Zia's speeches and to vet those prepared

---

[14] It was published later that year.

by institutions for Zia to read at some function or the other. Siddiq's reprimand to one such writer interested me: "Don't you realize that the CMLA does not want to be bothered with local or provincial matters? He thinks at the *national* level." Zia, I thought to myself, has no intention of leaving. Siddiq rose to become a Brigadier-General, working continuously with Zia until they both died in the mysterious C-130 crash after taking off from Bahawalpur on 17 August 1988.

Those who saw a photograph of Ziaul Haq and Bhutto in the Murree Guest House could glean from their body language that neither trusted the other. Bhutto sat grim and determined, clutching the arms of his sofa, almost as if to prevent himself from strangling his captor. Zia sat on the edge of his sofa, suspicious of the man who had once been his superior and his benefactor. Zia had been selected and promoted out of turn by Mr. Bhutto personally. Bhutto felt that as Zia had come from Jalandhar (India) in 1947, being a 'mohajir' he would not have a constituency within the army. Zia proved him wrong by calling upon the support of the largest constituency of all – Islam.

Zia released Bhutto and soon regretted his action. Bhutto converted his train journey from Rawalpindi to Lahore into an overnight political whistle-stop tour. He appeared at the door of his coach, made rousing speeches, challenging Zia to do his worst. Zia had him arrested at Lahore and did just that two years later in April 1979.

To counteract sympathy for Bhutto, Zia (presumably through Siddiq Salik) had an account published in *The Pakistan Times* about the humiliation of J. Rahim and his son. Rahim released a 15 page statement to a group of newsmen at his home in Karachi. It was unsparing in its criticism of Bhutto by his most senior minister and political confidant, the Trotsky to Bhutto's Stalin.

Convinced that the elections would be held, Asghar Khan nominated Khurshid Kasuri as the PNA candidate for NA 111-1, in opposition to Mr. Bhutto. 'The Tehrik chief,' the news item read, 'thought that Mr. Khurshid Ali Kasuri was more educated than Mr. Bhutto. He received his education in four foreign universities, including Oxford and Cambridge. He spoke better English and was as well dressed as the PPP Chairman.'

Zia's policy of desensitizing the public began with floggings conduced in the open. The report of one such flogging left little to the imagination:

'Thousands of people watched in awe as a head constable, convicted for accepting a bribe, was flogged in front of Kot Lakhpat Jail on Wednesday afternoon (10 August).

The crowd had started gathering in front of the Jail from Lahore city and nearby villages before the flogging took place. An estimated 10,000 persons jam-packed the lawn when the jail gate was opened to bring the head constable out. He was fixed to a triangular frame and stripped below the waist.

The jail flogger waving his cane, soaked in oil, ran up to the head constable. He cracked his cane on the back of the victim who shook slightly in pain. And the flogger kept running up to the convicted policeman each time delivering a blow. At one stage a doctor checked the head constable and decided that the flogging should continue.

After 10 flogs the head constable was unscrewed from the frame and taken away by two Army men inside the jail. He is to serve one year's imprisonment for his crime.'

Cartoonists were quick off the mark. One of them showed a bearded lawyer advocating for clemency before a military tribunal. The caption read: 'Before the court awards punishment, may I point out that the defendant is a promising left-hand spin bowler?'

I found a more serious quotation from Horace's *Epistles*: *Quid quid delirant reges plectuntur Achivi.* (For every folly of their princes, the Greeks feel the lash.)[15] The Ancient Greeks and modern Pakistanis would have more than Alexander the Great in common.

---

[15]Quintus Horatius Flaccus (Horace), *Epistles*,I,ii,14.

CHAPTER 13

BELATED HONEYMOON – I

Ever since our marriage during the 1971 war, Shahnaz and I had never had even a belated honeymoon. I had been abroad on a number of occasions but that had always been on official PTCL or NFC business. I suppose Shahnaz could have accompanied me on those, had the per diem allowances in dollars approved by the Government been generous enough to finance the cost of two persons. They were hardly enough for a single person, unless one stayed with friends or relatives. An unspoken disincentive was the attitude of the Ministry of Production under Awan sahib. The Ministry was still smarting from the excesses of the chief executives and senior executives of the automotive companies who thought nothing of going around the world on 'fact-finding' tours. Being Government, it swung fiercely in the opposite direction and discouraged what ministry officials viewed suspiciously as 'foreign junkets'.

Now that I look back on it, I must have been daring to have asked for and then obtain approval from Awan-sahib to attend the Fertiliser Society seminar in New York. I elongated my programme to include a visit to Riyadh to meet the SFD, Jeddah to perform umrah, a stop en route in London, and of course to participate in the Colloquium on Pahari Painting in Los Angeles.

Shahnaz took our two girls to Karachi first to settle them with Auntie Nayyar. I followed on 22 August 1977. Had we but known what Auntie Nayyar had gleaned from her almanac or *jantri*, we would have avoided travelling on what are defined in the *jantri* as qamar-dar-aqrab (or days of the crab). They occur on different times in each month. They share in common a maleficent impact that manifests itself in losses, delays or misfortunes. We were to have our share of these during the two months we planned to be away.

The first disruption to our programme occurred even before we left Karachi. Our British Airways flight for Jeddah got delayed. When we did take off, we treated ourselves to a steak and red wine lunch (the bottle appropriately bore the brand name 'St. Christopher'). At Jeddah, our stars dimmed further. Our luggage could not be traced for about an hour.

We were received by Mr. Inayatullah, a staff member of the Bank AlJazira – a Saudi subsidiary of the National Bank of Pakistan. My maternal uncle Syed Amjad Ali (a SEVP in the National Bank) had alerted him of our programme. Mr. Inayatullah took us to his home to refresh ourselves and to change our clothes into *ahrams* before performing umrah.

I had seen the Ka'aba before and so my reaction was tempered by familiarity. For Shahnaz, her first sight of the epicentre of our faith took her breath away. There is something very compelling in that black cube – the religious equivalent I suppose and as mysterious as the scientists' Black Hole. We walked around it, touching its bare walls (the black covering is usually hitched up like an Edwardian skirt, to avoid being besmirched). We could without jostling kiss the Black Stone (then convex but now after millions of kisses worn away into a concave). I could pray in the Hatim, an area on one side at the Ka'aba protected by a low semi-circular wall. The Hatim is reputedly the place where Hazrat Ali was born and where Hazrat Ismail and his mother Hagar were buried. Their graves lay directly beneath the rain water-spout jutting from the Ka'aba's roof, to catch the outfall of any rare rain.

The Inayatullahs guided us through the rituals of an umrah – the circumambulations of the Ka'aba, the seven trips between the rocky promontories of Safa and Marwah, the snipping of a lock of one's hair, and then a prayer of thanksgiving. I kept up with Inayatullah throughout until I noticed him performing yet more prayers with metronomic perseverance. My knees after repeated contact with the marble floor had begun to feel sore. So I sat back and let him continue alone.

After a while, I overheard Shahnaz ask Mrs. Inayatullah: "How many prayers is one supposed to read during umrah?"

"Well, actually, we have said all those that are required. It is just that we have three daughters and my husband has vowed to read 100 prayers in the Ka'aba for a son."

The next morning, I had to leave Shahnaz at the AlJazira guest house and make a quick trip to Riyadh to meet the Saudi Fund for Development staff regarding the disbursement of the SFD loan to Pak-Saudi Fertilisers Ltd.[1] The jinx continued to haunt me. My flight to Riyadh was delayed. I arrived midday to be met by Tony Hamaguchi (a Japanese SFD employee) and taken directly to Osama Faquih's office. I noticed that the SFD had begun to expand. It now had a Deputy Managing Director located in the SFD hierarchy between Osama and Dr. Jalal. The DMD Masaoud received me with the distant condescension that a lender shows to a borrower, albeit an institutional one.

Dr. Mahsoun Jalal could not have been friendlier. I presented him with a 3' x 5' silk carpet with the insignia of the SFD which we had had woven in Lahore. The Customs at Karachi had tried to prevent me from taking it out of the country. They demanded an export permit for it. I explained to them that it was a gift for the Saudis – a cheap way of saying 'Thank you' for a $50 million loan. They remained obdurate. It was only when I refused to leave without it that the Custom's official relented and waived me through.

Osama referred me to Dr. Ashraf, a Pakistani expatriate, for discussions on the final loan agreement. Dr. Ashraf caught me off guard by being irritatingly conscientious on almost every clause, determined to be more Muslim than the Saudis. We resolved everything but only just before I caught the flight to Jeddah. Dr. Ashraf made me feel as if I should not have been walking away with all my ten fingers.

The jinx continued. My return flight to Jeddah got cancelled. Osama had me put on an earlier flight. Among the other inconvenienced passengers, I noticed a Saudi wearing ... gold-plated shoes!

Mir – the wizened but incredibly efficient attendant at the AlJazira guest house – received me at Jeddah airport, bringing with him the disheartening news that the staff of British Airways had threatened to strike. We were booked to leave for London on 26th. Now, that flight looked in jeopardy.

Our original plan had been to visit Medina for a day. Fretful and apprehensive, we cancelled that programme and went instead to the AlJazira office. The jinx caught up with us there. We had just begun sending off telexes to Karachi and London when a fire broke out in an upstairs apartment, forcing

---

[1] We had changed the name of the company from Mirpur Mathelo Fertilisers Ltd to Pak-Saudi Fertilisers Ltd. to acknowledge the Saudi Government's funding.

us and everyone else in the building to vacate. At the British Airways office, we managed to persuade the BA staff to put us on the special flight they had arranged in lieu of the scheduled one on 26 August. Shahnaz and I spent the evening at the Haram Sharif and on a quick visit to Mount Arafat accompanied by the ever helpful Mir. Where else could have one expected to encounter such a God-send?

We reached Jeddah airport early on the 26th morning and found the jinx had preceded us there. The BA flight had been delayed by three hours, and then by another three. It left at 2.30 p.m.

Because of the BA strike, Heathrow airport looked empty and deserted. The airline bus into town offered us a choice – Victoria or Victoria? What the driver meant was, did we want to be dropped off at the Buckingham Palace Road terminal near Victoria station or at Victoria station itself. It made little difference. He dropped us off on the road between the two. We caught a taxi to 18 Provost Road where Tim-bibi and Bill stood in wait on the doorstep.

Shahnaz had never met Ashwin Malde nor his wife Bena, or their two young children Aadarsh and Angie. We spent the day with them at their house in Barnet, returning in time for dinner at the Archers. Tim and Bill had invited Donald Lightbown[2] (the Librarian at the V & A Museum) and Natwar Singh (the Indian Deputy High Commissioner in London). Natwar Singh belonged to the Bharatpur family of Indian royals and had married Heminder Kaur, the eldest daughter of Maharaja Bhupinder Singh of Patiala.[3] Always conscious of his quasi-royal status, Natwar insinuated himself into London's literary circles by reviewing books for the *Financial Times*. Over a convivial dinner, he expressed a keenness to review my book *PP & SP*. I was delighted and flattered, but also on my guard.

"Please," I pleaded with him, "do not say how wonderful that a Pakistani should be writing about Indian miniature painting."

"Of course not," he retorted. "It is a work of research that stands on its

---

[2] Some years later, Tim-bibi collaborated with Donald Lightbown on a catalogue to mark the VAM exhibition *India Observed: India as viewed by British Artists 1760-1860* (London, 1982), installed for the Festival of India.

[3] Natwar Singh wrote a biography of his father-in-law titled *The Magnificent Maharaja Bhupinder Singh of Patiala (1891–1938)*, Delhi, 1997. More recently, smarting from a rejection by Mrs. Sonia Gandhi and the Congress Party, he published a controversial money-raking memoir *One Life is Not Enough: An Autobiography* (2014).

own merits."

Sure enough, when Natwar's review appeared in the FT in December, it read unrepentantly: 'That a young Pakistani should take time to bring out a volume on Hindu and Sikh paintings is yet another proof of the common history and heritage of the two countries.'

While I had my book and the forthcoming lecture at Los Angeles to keep me distracted, Shahnaz felt the absence of our two girls acutely, so much so that when we spent the Sunday with Ashwin and Bena, Shahnaz found it difficult to be affectionate towards some-one else's progeny.

A few days later, Bill and Tim invite Giles Eyre over for a meal. Giles had made a name for himself as a dealer in British Indian objêt d'art. He began trading under the name Hartnoll & Eyre, and later after Hartnoll dropped out of the partnership, he teamed up with Niall Hobhouse. Giles – a bachelor – had a waspish tongue that forgot nothing and narrated everything. Entertaining to a fault, his conversation covered a gamut of subjects – Victoriana, the British Royal Family, the provenance of royal jewels, Indian colonial history, his memories as ADC to the Punjab Governor Sir Bertrand Glancy, and a salacious reminiscence of his assignations with Begum A---- Q----, whom he would meet in a private box at the Plaza Cinema in Queen's Road, Lahore.

Giles invited us to his shop in Duke Street, off Piccadilly. He kept certain select items on display on the ground floor to attract the walk-in customer. The bulk of his stock he kept in the basement, and it was there that he showed us four lithographs by Charles Hardinge of Lahore and some water-colours by William Simpson. I coveted the Hardinge's particularly as I had used them one year for the annual calendar issued by Packages Limited. Syed Babar Ali had wanted something unusual, different to the stereotypes that his Art Department would manufacture every year. I had been researching in the Punjab Archives stored in Anarkali's Tomb within the Punjab Government Secretariat. There I noticed original lithographs by Emily Eden, Dr. Dunlop and by Charles Hardinge – all faded but interesting nevertheless. I had four of them – of the Badshahi Mosque, the Hazuri Bagh, Ranjit Singh's *baradari* and Jahangir's tomb at Shahdara – reproduced half page, accompanied by a smaller view of the same location taken more recently (Then & Now) and with them an explanatory text. To give it an archaic touch, we used a cream coloured paper that at first glance passed off as vellum. The print run of 15,000 copies yielded next morning only 14,000. The printing staff on the factory floor had secreted 1,000 of them in their baggy shalwars and smuggled them out of the factory. By the next afternoon, these calendars were selling briskly in Anarkali market at Rs 15 a piece.

The one painting I did lust in my heart over (to use Carter's mis-judged phrase) was one of the interior of Jahangir's tomb by William Simpson. It was done during his trip to Lahore in the entourage of Lord and Lady Canning in 1864. Giles' prices were too expensive for us to afford. One was being asked, I knew, to pay less for the pictures than for the prohibitively expensive location of his shop.

I had read in the papers of an exhibition at the V&A Museum of the works of Carl Fabergé, goldsmith and jeweller to Czar Nicholas II of Russia and his family. Many of the choicest pieces had been lent by H.M. the Queen from her collection at Sandringham. These had been inherited by her from her great-grandmother Queen Alexandra whose sister was the Dowager Empress Marie Feodrovna of Russia. Alexandra was an aunt therefore of Nicholas II. She made known to her friends that if she was to be given any gifts, she would prefer bibelots from Fabergé. These consisted invariably of flowers or animals worked in enamelled gold and set with precious stones. Queen Alexandra with the caprice that only princes can show commissioned Fabergé to make a set of the farm animals in Sandringham Farm. He carved a quasi-menagerie of birds and animals using semi-precious stones such as agate, cornelian or jade.

The showpiece for me at the V&AM exhibition was the famous irreplaceable Imperial Coronation Egg, made by Fabergé's team of craftsmen for Nicholas II as a present to his wife Czarina Alexandra to commemorate their coronation in 1897. The surprise within the beautifully enamelled egg (its colour and motifs were echoes of her coronation robes) was a small working model of the coronation coach, complete with articulated wheels and minute folding steps.[4]

Tim-bibi had arranged with one of Bill's colleagues to 'smuggle' Shahnaz and myself into the exhibition by the side door available only to Museum staff.

---

[4] The Imperial Coronation Egg was bought in 1927 from the Russian Government by Snowman of Wartski (Fabergé's London agent) and in 1979 sold to the US millionaire Malcolm Forbes for $2.16 million. In 2004, this unique and eight other Fabergé eggs were sold to the Russian oligarch Viktor Vekselberg for a reputed $100 million.

Otherwise we would have had to join the lengthy queue of thousands that snaked outside the museum along Old Brompton Road.

Before we left London, I had a working lunch with Philip Wilson in his offices overlooking Covent Garden market, during which he confirmed his agreement to publish *Sikh Portraits by European Artists*.

Shahnaz and I flew out of London on 1 September, accompanied by our invisible jinx. The British Airways flight got delayed, leaving eventually at 1.00 p.m. This gave us time to speak to Bill and Tim. They told us they had received letters for us from Auntie Nayyar in Karachi. We were able to have them read to us over the phone before we left for New York.

Inevitably our first sight of New York's skyline made an impact that has never dulled. We caught a taxi to Hotel Taft on 7th Avenue where we had been booked by the JDR 3rd Fund.[5] Richard Lanier – its young director – came at 7.00 and took us home to meet his wife Mary and their young adopted baby daughter Marie. The Laniers lived in an open loft on the first floor of what had once been a factory warehouse near Wall Street. Its high roofs overarched the various cubicles that created separate sitting, dining and sleeping areas. For dinner, they had ordered in a dinner box – a three storey carton containing cold chicken, salads, and fresh fruit. Both Shahnaz and I were struck by its novelty. Used to fast food served on a horizontal tray, it was perhaps appropriate that in New York, our meal should be stacked vertically.

While we were eating, suddenly, the doorbell downstairs rang. I can still recall Richard's expressive response – a mixture of alert apprehension and guarded preparedness.

"Are you expecting someone?" Richard asked Mary.

"No," she replied.

They ignored the bell and continued eating.

The Taft Hotel was within walking distance of Times Square and of the Rockefeller Plaza where the JDR 3rd Fund offices were located. I dropped in there to confirm our programme for Los Angeles. For us, every sight – the

---

[5] The largest hotel in Times Square when it opened in 1926, over the years Hotel Taft had become almost as seedy as its surroundings. A number of porn shops and cinemas showing adult movies surrounded the hotel.   It has been substantially remodeled, converted into a condominium, and its shrunken hotel renamed The Michelangelo.

shops on Fifth Avenue, Tiffanys, Central Park – were familiar yet stimulating. I bought a Michelin guide to New York that proved a boon companion. Using it we could plan our day, taking in for example the Frick Collection[6] (New York's answer to London's Wallace Collection) and the Metropolitan Museum where a Russian costume exhibition was the special attraction.

Despite trekking across New York sights, we had enough energy to see a musical *For Colored Girls Who Have Considered Suicide When the Rainbow is Enuf.* The musical reflected the Afro-American experience and most of its allusions were quasi-masochistic jokes about 'blacks vs. whites', something we understood but which the largely Afro-American audience relished with noisy acclamation.

The next few days were spent doing the New York sights in earnest – a guided tour around the Bowery, Chinatown, St Patrick's Cathedral, the Empire State Building and the Statue of Liberty. The last was less a ritual than a punishment. The weather had turned from comfortably warm to unbearably hot. The temperature peaked at 100° F outside; inside the largely copper casing, one felt like a goose being cooked in an airless oven.

The location of Hotel Taft made it almost impossible to avoid the porn shops[7] and cinemas. We decided to see a film called *Inside Jennifer Welles.* No marks for guessing what the film was all about. Ms. Welles managed to service what seemed like half the population of New York's hotel staff, cab drivers, gym instructors, even Chinese waiters. I read somewhere that after a brief and exhausting career making such movies, Ms. Welles married the first millionaire who proposed to her and then retired into affluent respectability.

I had mentioned to Richard that we would like to see a Kabuki performance. He and Mary accompanied us, after which we had cocktails in Central Park. As there had been much talk on local television channels about a new Japanese film *In the Realm of the Senses.* Even in the permissive 80s, this Japanese film contained too much explicit sex for the censors. Despite their trimming, the impact the explicit relentless sex in the film had on its audience was clear from the contrast between those who had just seen the film and emerged shell-shocked from the expectant innocence of those standing in the

---

[6] A superb collection of art and manuscripts donated by the Pittsburgh industrialist Henry Frick (1849–1919) and now housed in Fifth Avenue residence.

[7] One porn shop had the unambiguous sign: 'Kinks at rear'.

queue to go in. A Roman Catholic Archbishop, after seeing this film, confessed that he 'had learned more in 10 minutes of the film than in his entire life'. Certainly, one of the things he learned during this crash course had been the ingenious ways Japanese courtesans handle boiled eggs.

Perhaps the only antidote to such a surfeit of sex was Rodgers and Hammerstein's classic musical *The King & I*. Shahnaz and I had seen the film, knew its songs by heart. That it was playing on Broadway with Yul Brynner reprising his role as King Mongkut of Siam was an irresistible opportunity, and we took it. The musical and the film derived from it had been banned in Thailand as it ridiculed (albeit tongue in royal cheek) the Thai monarchy. Queen Sirikit, we read later, visited the show in New York, met Yul Brynner backstage and by her presence lifted the royal taboo.

Another more contemporary performance we saw was a musical revue, a collage of compositions by Stephen Sondheim called *Side by Side*. It had opened on Broadway a few months earlier after a successful run in London.

Our travelling companion on the flight to Los Angeles was a fellow participant – Dr. Ashok Kumar Das, then Director of Director, Maharaja Sawai Man Singh II Museum, Jaipur. When we had been introduced to each other a few days earlier by Richard Lanier in his office, Ashok had rather disarmed me with the remark: "I am so jealous of your book!"

At Los Angeles, we were met by Cathy Glynn, the assistant of Dr. Pratapaditya Pal. She managed to fit the three of us and our suitcases in her matchbox of a car (I forget its make) and then drove us to the Farmer's Daughter Motel on Fairfax Avenue. Today it is advertised as a 'kitschy, country-chic boutique hotel…opposite the Original Farmers Market and The Grove shopping mall.' In 1977, it had no such pretensions.

We checked in and soon afterwards encountered in the lobby other participants in the Colloquium. Robert Skelton (Bill's deputy in the Indian Section of the V & A Museum) whom I already knew; Karl Khandalavala, a lawyer by profession and whose monumental work *Pahari Miniature Painting* (1958) had been such an indispensable guide during my researches in the Lahore Museum; and Dr. B. N. Goswamy, the latest entrant into the field of Pahari painting, and his wife Karuna.

Brijen Goswamy's essay *Pahari Painting: The Family as the Basis of Style*[8] had appeared sixteen years after Bill's innovative essays *Indian Painting in the Punjab Hills* (1952) and a full decade after Karl's magnum opus. Brijen had begun his career as a member of the IAS (the successor to the Indian Civil Service). Therefore he belonged to the same lineage of India's civil service as Bill Archer (1931) and Dr. Randhawa (1934). Bill had been Brijen's examiner for the latter's PhD thesis. For this and a number of reasons (seniority in the service, seniority in the field) Bill felt he had a claim over Brijen, a burden Brijen resented. Brijen chafed at this – understandably.[9]

While Bill acknowledged in his magisterial *Indian Paintings from the Punjab Hills* (1973) that Brijen's essay was 'a *tour de force* of some importance', he remained sceptical of Brijen's reliance on a single drawing he discovered in the collection of Chandu Lal, a descendant of a known Guler painter Nainuskh. The drawing showed a semi-naked female figure titled 'Shri Guler' with her fifteen arms outstretched towards the names of fifteen Pahari states, including Chamba, Kangra, Nadaun, Sujanpur, Jammu and Basohli – almost of all of them places or courts where painting was practiced at one time or the other.

Bill's work had been published in 1973. He drew the line of bibliographical references at 1970, including material published before that date but excluding anything after that date.

In 1972, Pratapaditya Pal edited a collection of papers presented at a Symposium on Indian Art.[10] One of them was a paper contributed by Brijen titled 'Of Patronage and Pahari Painting'. In it, he described the many-armed Devi as 'some sort of "magic diagram" recording the tie between the members of the artist family of Pandit Seu and various princely states in the hills.' He went on to argue: 'The whole point of the diagram appears to be to list all the states or persons who provided patronage to members of this family of artists,

---

[8] B.N. Goswamy, 'Pahari Painting: The Family as the Basis of Style', *Marg*, vol. xxi, no. 4, September 1968, pp. 17-62.

[9] This continued even after the deaths of Archer and Randhawa. In an interview with Sunil Sethi, published in *Business Standard* (5 September 2014), quotes a conversation with BNG: 'His mentors, Randhawa and Archer, were remarkable minds but they had their drawbacks. "Dr. Randhawa tended to lump all Pahari paintings broadly under the Kangra school whereas Mr. Archer was unable to read local scripts such as Takri."'

[10] Pratapaditya Pal (ed.), *Aspects of Indian Art: Papers presented in a Symposium at the Los Angeles County Museum of Art*, October 1970.

a statement the greater part of which is verifiable from paintings in the style of the family coming out from many of the states. The document has something of the character of an *aide-memoire* in which the activity of generations of artists is condensed and recorded. Slowly we realize that there is distinct logic in the number of spider-like arms that emanate from this great and awesome tantric deity: it was the patrons who helped her weave her web of painting across the hills.'[11]

Brijen's mellifluousness was not enough to persuade or to convince Bill. His attention was caught by a footnote in Brijen's paper. It read: 'When I first published it, in the Marg article [...], I listed nineteen names in all, including sixteen Rajput states and three Sikh chiefs, as being within circles. I had based my reading of these names then on a relatively poor photograph, which was slightly cut at the top, of this painting. Upon having another occasion to examine the painting, when I was also able to photograph it in great detail, I found that there were in all twenty-three circles on the sheet and not nineteen. In two of these were some names which had been covered with white painting and were illegible: in two other cases, one of which had been left of the earlier photograph and the other partially concealed in a fold in the paper, were the names, "Kulu" and "Jasrota". These names do not occur thus in the list published by me in *Marg*. That is how the list of *states*, as now read, numbers eighteen.'[12]

Bill remained obsessed with this 'new' reading of Brijen's. Bill would maintain to anyone who would listen that the name 'Jasrota' appeared only after he had pointed out its absence to Brijen. The reason why the tiny state of Jasrota became inordinately significant was because there were known, signed and dated pictures by Nainsukh (the son of Pandit Seu) of Raja Balwant Singh of Jasrota. Without the name 'Jasrota', the diagram lost its potency. With it, Bill's life-work of a state-wise classification stood in doubt.

For my paper at the Colloquium I had chosen to talk on a series of paintings in the Lahore Museum of the *Devi Mahatmya*[13] done at Guler in 1781. One of the paintings in the set showed the Devi with her arms outstretched, similar in posture to the Tantric Devi in Brijen's magic diagram, except that in the LM version, the Devi is holding in each of her numerous

---

[11] Ibid, p.131.
[12] Ibid, p.131,fn. 5.
[13] The *Devi Mahatmya* is a part of the longer *Markandeya Purana*.

hands the diverse weapons given to her by the gods and devas.

Bill wanted me to use this similarity between the two pictures to demolish Brijen's argument. I was reluctant to. Even while I was staying with him in London, Bill tried to persuade me to refute Brijen's footnote. The only thing I agreed to do was to show a slide of Brijen's Devi diagram after my *Devi Mahatmya* picture, and let the scholars draw their own conclusions.

The first day of the Colloquium, 8 September, began with a welcome address by Pratap which was supposed to set the tone for the next two days, except that Pratap began by apologising for holding the Colloquium at all. Dick Sherwood, the President of the Los Angeles County Art Museum[14], counteracted Pratap's unexpected negativism by talking warmly and with genuine affection about Bill and Tim Archer. He then invited Bill to make his presentation. All of us were keen on hearing Bill – the acknowledged guru of Pahari painting - talk about the subject that he had quite literally put on the map of India's art-history. He began slowly, illustrating his thematic approach with slides. Bill had us enthralled, so much so that we lost track of time. We had been warned before the Colloquium that we should limit our presentations to 40 minutes, but everyone knew Bill wouldn't. In any case, he deserved all the time he needed. Bill had reached a slide of a Basohli *Rasamanjari*, which depicted a young woman (Radha) remonstrating with a young boy, while Krishna waits in a decorated pavilion on the right of the picture. Between Radha and the boy is a pond into which an axe has been thrown.[15]

"Looking at this picture, one is forced to ask," Bill questioned, "why is Radha angry with the boy? What significance does the *ber* tree in the background have? And why should the axe have been thrown into the pond?"

All of us in the audience sat spell-bound, anxious to hear Bill's erudite analysis of the painting.

Suddenly, from the wings, Pratap rushed on stage and axed Bill mid-thought. "You've overshot your time."

There were murmurs of remonstrance from the audience. Even Dick Sherwood looked discomfited. Bill hesitated, waiting for a reprieve, but Pratap felt that he had to make a point '*pour encourager les autres*'.

---

[14] Richard Sherwood had been its president from 1974-1978.
[15] Reproduced in W.G. Archer, *Indian Paintings from the Punjab Hills* (London, 1973), p.36, Basohli 4(vi).

Pratap did the same thing to Karl Khandalavala. Karl - more used to a courtroom than a lecture hall - made an overlong, rather rambling and unstructured presentation. Robert Skelton elicited a similar intervention by Pratap. The only ones who escaped that afternoon were Brijen Goswamy (practiced and precise) and Tim-bibi whose speech rescued the day.

The Museum had given a dinner for all the participants in one of the galleries. The American hosts came in tuxedos. Those of us on an airline baggage allowance wore what we thought appropriate.

On the second day, Indian scholars like Ashok Das, V.C. Ohri and the famous collector from Hyderabad Jagdish Mittal spoke in the morning. Their presentations were about Mughal painting, as was Milo Beach's. Even Ed Binney's very entertaining lecture appeared to be off the mark. I began to wonder whether I had come to the wrong seminar.

My presentation was scheduled for the last day, 10 September. I had timed it to last precisely 38 minutes, and tested myself with repeated rehearsals in Lahore. However, the jinx managed to find its way to Los Angeles. The system which would allowed me to control the slides from the podium failed. I had to rely upon the Museum attendant to operate it manually.

I had selected the *Devi Mahatmya* for my topic because it was a finite series of paintings. In 1929, the Lahore Museum acquired a complete set of fifty-seven illustrations. The set was divided in 1947, with twenty-two being sent to East Punjab.[16] Five were sent for exhibition to Art of India, Pakistan and Ceylon exhibition in 1947-48 at Burlington House, London. On their return, the newly-established National Museum of Pakistan retained them to form a core of its nascent collection.

The Lahore Museum owned the first and the last folios, and a large number in between. I was therefore able to present the text in its sequence and also illustrate the various dramatic events in Chandiki-devi's battles with the *asuras* in a coherent narrative. An additional point of relevance for the scholars was that the series bore a colophon on the reverse of the last picture. It contained the date: 'Samvat 1838 Phagun', i.e. 1781. This put it a confirmed twenty-five years after Bill's dating of the series as '1755'. The date was important. Dated Pahari paintings were rare. But to me, Bill's ability to ascribe

---

[16] They are now in the collection of the Government Museum & Art Gallery, Chandigarh.

a date to this series to within twenty-five years of its actual date (he had no knowledge of the colophon before I told him of it) was a tribute to his intuitive, inimitable skill as an art-historian.

I adhered to the time allotted to me, and avoided Pratap's merciless guillotine. The opening question came from Cathy Glynn who asked how many times the *Devi Mahatmya* had been illustrated.

"How many times has the Bible been illustrated?" seemed the obvious response.

Karl wanted to know why Pahari artists were more adept at drawing horses then lions. "They had more access to horses than lions."

Brijen asked me an innocuous question about the use of colour by Pahari artists. The sting lay in the supplementary: "Have you ever been to the Hill States?" Both of us knew I hadn't. But his question put me in the category of an arm-chair scholar, and that too from Pakistan.

Pratap did not seem interested enough to have a group photograph of all the participants. It seemed strange to me considering that he had collected all the known names in Pahari painting with the exception of Dr. M.S. Randhawa.

Although I glossed over the Devi drawing slide during my lecture, Brijen and Karuna particularly took its inclusion at all as a personal slight. They taxed me about it afterwards in the hotel lobby.

Dick Sherwood's dinner closed the Colloquium. He gave it in his tastefully decorated home. Shahnaz and I were startled to see the dining room – walls and roof - covered with Sindhi embroideries, cut up to fit. That so reminded me of the Mughal miniatures that had been similarly vandalised to decorate one of the rooms in the Shönbrunn Palace in Vienna, Austria.

Over dinner, Pratap indicated that he was not inclined to have the papers at this Colloquium published. Most of them, he observed, had been repeats or re-hashes of papers these scholars had read at previous seminars. I was disappointed but not surprised. After listening to all the presentations at the Colloquium, I suspected that mine was perhaps the only one that had been prepared afresh for this Colloquium.

The next day (11 September), all of us were herded onto a bus to be taken to San Diego where Edwin Binney 3rd had invited us for lunch and a special viewing of his expanding collection of Indian miniatures. Ed's wealth came from the fortuitous invention by his grandfather of the Crayola crayon. In his youth Ed had been a ballet dancer. He began collecting first ballet prints, then Turkish and Persian miniatures. After he had satiated his interest by buying the best paintings in these fields, he moved into Indian miniatures. Bill (doing for Ed what Berenson had done on a grander scale for Lord Duveen and Isabella Stewart Gardner) acted as his consultant, helping him to select paintings that reinforced his collection, and wrote an exhibition catalogue for Ed when his miniatures were sent on exhibition.

The bus drove us along the San Clemente coast. At one point, the driver identified the residence of former president Richard Nixon. I stood up in the moving bus and bent in the direction of the house.

"I am tilting in favour of Nixon," I explained to my curious fellow passengers, "just as he tilted towards Pakistan in 1971."

We were drive directly to the San Diego Town Hall – a Spanish-style building set in luxurious greenery. We were welcomed with authentic *margaritas* which put everyone in a genial mood. After a lavish lunch (the salads radiated Californian sunshine), Ed took us into a long room where he had laid out his miniatures on trestle tables according to schools.

We were asked to file past, to admire the paintings but not touch them. After each round, Ed changed the pictures from his inexhaustible reservoir. Among them I recognised three folios from the Basohli *Gita Govinda* series of 1730 that I had last seen together with Bill in the Chughtai collection at Lahore.

"You see the problem," Ed asked Brijen. "How does one group them according to families?" And then, when Brijen did not respond, Ed rather unfairly chided Brijen with the taunt: "Well, we all know that Bill dates pictures better than you do!"

During this examination, Brijen announced that one of the paintings contained a date. There was an eruption of excitement amongst us.

"Does anyone have a magnifying glass?" Brijen asked.

"I do," replied Robert Skelton, and he produced from his pocket a small folding magnifier.

Brijen applied it to the picture. It was one of the naming of Krishna in which the infant deity is shown in the lap of his mother while the *purohit* sitting opposite Krishna's parents consults an open book. The inscription appeared on the book and would at first glance have been taken as part of a religious text. A Vikram Samvat date was given equivalent to 1763 AD.

"And what did Bill date this picture?" Robert asked eagerly.

Bill's catalogue of Ed's collection was retrieved. A crest-fallen Robert announced: "Bill has dated it 1760-65."

Later, in London, I narrated the incident to Bill. He had not come with us to San Diego as he was already familiar with the Binney collection.

"And what had I dated it?"

"Between 1760-65," I told him.

"But dear Aijaz, it had to be, didn't it? I mean, it really could not have been of any other period."

I can think of no other incident that demonstrated Bill's uncanny ability to date Pahari paintings with such accuracy. One evening, in the lounge of his Provost Road home, he took out some of the albums he maintained of prints of paintings and sculptures that stimulated him. They were not, as I expected, of Indian miniatures. They consisted primarily of medieval or Renaissance paintings and sculptures juxtaposed with the work of modernists. Bill ran his open palms over each picture, as if he could imbibe its essence or what the Hindus call its *rasa* from such physical contact.

Bill in time would have many detractors — pre-eminent amongst them Brijen — but none could match his unique sensitivity and flair. Sitting in the Indian Section of the V&AM in London in the 1950s, and using a select number of what he believed to be representative paintings (only a few of which were dated), he had been able to deduce that it was Guler, not Kangra, that was a crucible of Pahari painting. Thousands of miles away, in India, Dr. M.S. Randhawa, basing his findings on evidence provided by the families of hill artists, arrived independently at the same conclusion. This simultaneous combustion led to a correspondence and friendship that began in 1953 and ended with Bill's death in 1979.[17]

---

[17] Dr. Randhawa published his correspondence with Bill and other scholars in his *Indian Paintings: Exploration, Research and Publications* (Govt. Museum & Art Gallery, Chandigarh, 1986.)

That visit to San Diego accorded the Colloquium a dignified crescendo. The next day, Shahnaz and I decided to visit Universal Studios on behalf of our children. The jinx on vacation at San Diego returned with a vengeance. On one of the rides, I lost the keys to our suitcase and the precious Boucheron watch that the MF people had given me in Lausanne. That evening my mood was as sullen as Nixon's while he was being interviewed by David Frost.[18]

Shahnaz and I punished ourselves further by going to Disneyland in Anaheim, where, having the rides, and shaken hands with Mickey Mouse and Donald Duck, we selected gifts for the children and wept (literally wept) at standing where our children should have been. We had no right to be there without them.

We returned to the Farmer's Daughter Motel, trussed up our suitcases in plastic twine, and next morning caught a five hour long flight to Cleveland.

The JDR 3rd Fund grant enabled Shahnaz and myself to travel across the United States, to visit museums which had collections of South-Asian art, and to meet scholars whose published works had been such a part of my education.

At the Cleveland Museum of Art, we encountered Dr. Sherman E. Lee[19], surprisingly quiet and shy considering he had been the *prime movere* uplifting the Cleveland Museum from an unfocussed provincial one into one of the most notable collections of South-Asian art, renowned across the world. Its cache of Indian miniatures had yet to be amplified. I was equally interested in the small but select collection of Fabergé objects assembled by someone with the intriguing name of India Early Minshall.

After a day in Cleveland, Shahnaz and I caught the air-shuttle to Washington DC. We flew over the Pentagon.

"Do you recognize it?" a fellow passenger asked me.

"Of course, isn't that we are all ruled from?"

We were collected by Husin and Idjah Alsegaf. Husin we had been meeting on his various IBRD missions to Lahore. The last time I had seen Idjah was when I said goodbye to her at London airport in 1961 or 1962, when she and Husin returned to Indonesia. She had not changed at all – the same

---

[18] The last part - Part 5 - of the interviews had been run on 10 September 1977.
[19] Director of the Cleveland Museum of Art (1958-83), and also advisor on Asian art to John D. Rockefeller III.

warm personality, the same giggly endearing laugh.

On the way to their home in River Road, Bethesda, he drove us past the White House. One moment we were approaching it and the next we had already passed it. I had the same reaction – a feeling of deflation – that most tourists must have felt on seeing it for the first time. It was absurd for me to imagine that the U.S presidents would live in a palace, but even by proletarian standards, the White House could not have been more self-effacing.

At the Alsegaf home, we were introduced to their children Hadi and his sister Latifah, both of whom had been born in Indonesia but were now archetypal US teenagers.

Husin very generously spent the weekend with us, showing us as he must have done countless friends and visitors the sights of Washington D.C. – the interior of the White House, and excursions into the beautiful Virginian landscape to see Harper's Ferry and the underground spectacle of the Luray Caverns, with its unusual stalactite musical organ.

I made a quick overnight trip to New York to attend the two day Fertiliser Conference. Like many such congregations, I found more attendees outside it networking than inside listening to what were quite frankly very boring presentations that absorbed the speakers more than they did the audience.

There I found myself being paged by Dr. Qidwai, an engineer who had begun his career with Aftab Ahmad, Sherwani and Bhutta. Qidwai was employed by SAFCO in Dammam, Saudi Arabia. Keen to impress me with his lodgings (the Waldorf Astoria) and his expense account, he invited me for coffee. We chatted and waited, and waited. After an hour, it was clear that room service had more lucrative business to attend to, and so I left.

I knew no-one would miss me at the conference and so I played hokey, to use an Americanism. I spent the afternoon at the Brooklyn Museum of Art to see the *Gita Govinda* folios the museum had bought from Doris Weiner. It was interesting to trace the movements of these folios, passing from private hands into public collections.

I tried not to waste our time or give up any opportunity to see as many museums as we could. Our next visit was to the Philadelphia Museum of Art, in Philadelphia, a Metro-liner trip away from DC. Its soaring façade made me realize that while the American Founding Fathers had learned revolution and egalitarianism from the French, they looked to the ancient civilizations of Greece, Rome and Egypt for their architecture. Within the museum, replicas had been constructed of a Spanish monastery, an Indian temple, even a Japanese tea house. Shahnaz and I were admiring the exhibits when we heard the sound of padded feet approach us. It was Dr. Stella Kramrisch.[20] She was eighty-one years by then, too old to worry about what people thought of her. Her carpet slippers and hairnet were her dismissal of the world. Her young assistant who followed her suddenly went off on some errand. After about five minutes, she left us to look for him. Ten minutes later he emerged from one of the galleries, looking for her. Finally she returned, relieved that she had not misplaced him.

I was familiar with her through her pioneering book *A Survey of Painting in the Deccan* (1937). The Philadelphia Museum collection had few Pahari miniatures to boast of. But then Dr. Kramrisch did not need any. In her room, she had two Renoirs and an Italian painting from Giorgione's school – all originals. She certainly knew how to live.

The Independence Hall, Benjamin Franklin's house, the site of the Liberty Bell – we soaked in every site. On the way back to DC, we learned of the resignation of Bart Lance, President Jimmy Carter's Director of the Office of Management and the Budget (OMB). *The New York Times* could hardly contain its glee. Carter thought he was doing Bert Lance (his fellow Georgian) a favour by describing him as 'his brother'. The press had a field day. They had another 'Silly Billy' to lampoon.[21]

After Philadelphia, we went to Baltimore to see the collection of the Baltimore Museum of Art. Another neo-classical building though not as impressive as the one in Cleveland. Shahnaz and I were very keen on seeing the Ford collection, belonging to John and Berthe Ford. They had been observers at the Los Angeles Colloquium. Unfortunately they were out of town that day. Our compensation was to see and handle (as the Mughal emperors once did) some fine Mughal paintings of imperial quality, folios from the *Zafarnama*, and

---

[20] Curator of Indian art (1954 - 1972) and later Curator Emeritus until her death in 1993. I did not know at the time that in 1947 her husband Laszlo Nemenyi, an economist, opted to work for the Pakistan government. In 1950, he was discovered shot dead, fully dressed in his evening clothes, on one of Karachi's beaches.

[21] William Carter III was President Crater's younger brother. He made an ill-judged decision to represent General Muammar Qaddafi's Libyan government as its agent in the United States.

the most precious of all – some sketches by the legendary Persian artist Behzad.

Returning to DC, we stopped at the Ford theatre where Booth had shot President Abraham Lincoln. The theatre is an amalgam of a sacred monument, a shrine, a museum and a tourist magnet. One can stand on the spot from which Booth aimed his gun at Lincoln. Downstairs in the basement, every conceivable thing associated with Lincoln's assassination – his clothes, playbills, etc. – were on gruesome display.

We crossed the road to the house opposite where the injured Lincoln was taken after he had been shot. I felt disheartened to see the smallness of the bedroom, the inadequate bed (insufficient for a man of his height), the pillows smudged with blood on shown in a glass case. It reminded me of the squalid condition in which Quaid-e-Azam died in September 1948 – gasping for his last breaths in a hot ambulance that had stalled on Drigh Road, Karachi.

The dinner given that night by Mario Artaza and his lovely wife Gloria surpassed anything we may have done for him in Lahore. The dinner settings were superb - out of a book on high-end entertaining – and the food memorable. Mario was particularly touched that I had selected a book of Pablo Neruda's poems for him.

We spent the next morning at the Freer Gallery soaking in the gamut of its treasures. From there I called in at the World Bank to meet Syed Shahid Husain, then a Director and the highest placed Pakistani in the IBRD.

I asked him how he viewed the situation in Pakistan after Zia's coup.

"Bloodshed."

Yes, I thought to myself, you can well afford to say that from the safety of Pennsylvania Avenue.

John and Berthe called to ask us for dinner at Baltimore. Shahnaz and I caught the train and were taken by them to their three-storey home. We found Robert Skelton there already. After dinner, John took us on a tour of their home – a house, but more a set of interconnected galleries where they could display their art collection. Some of the items such as the Chinese snuff bottles they had inherited from John's father. Every little vessel deserved to be appreciated on its own. Painstakingly hollowed, each was painted with inimitable finesse on the inside, its images radiating through the sides of the bottle. There was nothing that did not reflect the Fords' discerning eye: Chinese bronzes, Tibetan *tankas*, an original Rousseau. They had the near-best, if not the best.

The *pièce de resistance* of their collection was kept in their basement. This was no ordinary basement. John had converted it into a Nepalese Tantric temple, complete with every religious object a votary might need – hollow human skulls, a sacred pipe made out of a human femur, and a drinking vessel that had been the cranium once of a fifteen year old virgin. Shahnaz commented afterwards: "A Tantric temple, in suburban Baltimore?"[22]

Having shown us the White House from the outside, Husin was keen that we should visit its interior. The queues moved faster than I expected. Inside I looked for some of the class that Jacqueline Kennedy was said to have brought to the place. My notes read that rooms appeared small, the furniture mediocre and shabby. The guides disturbed whatever decorum and dignity the house may have had by talking loudly, and periodically challenging the visitors to ask them questions.

After them, the quietude within the National Gallery of Art was like a balm to my ears. The Gallery like most American museums is a microcosm, a tribute to European culture. It had works by Renoir, Rembrandt and Leonardo da Vinci.

Husin took us to Arlington cemetery to see the Kennedy graves. Like performing Haj for someone else, this second pilgrimage to Arlington was for Auntie Nayyar. Kennedy was her hero. We shed a tear on her behalf, and then another for ourselves.

By this time, we were into the last week of our stay in the United States. We said goodbye to friends in the IBRD like Mario, Philippe Lietard and to our uncomplaining hosts - Idgah and Husin. If anyone had a cause for complaint it should have been Husin. We dumped all the toys that we had bought for the girls at Universal Studios and Disneyland on him to transport to Pakistan. I suppose it was a typically Pakistani thing to do. I remember seeing a spoof of a Pakistan in the UK asking his friend if he could carry a small parcel for him to Pakistan for the family. "Certainly," the passenger replied, and then opened a door to show him a room full of such parcels.

---

[22] Shahnaz had written her account of our visit to the Fords' home. It was printed in her book *Lost from View* (Lahore, 1994), pp. 19-23.

In New York, where we arrived on 25th, more visits to museums and libraries. Dr. Lerner at the Metropolitan Museum brought out some exquisite *Gita Govinda* folios from the famous Tehri-Garhwal series painted for Raja Sansar Chand.[23]

Seeing my book on sale was still quite a novelty. I saw copies of it in Paragon Books, whose catalogue I used to receive in Pakistan.

"Is it selling well?"

"Are you its author?" the salesman replied.

"How could you tell?"

"Only authors ask about their books!"

As we had been invited for dinner by the Laniers, we bought some gifts for their daughter Marie from FAO Shwartz toyshop in Fifth Avenue (New York's answer to London's Hamleys in Regent Street). The guests at the Laniers included Robert Skelton, Philippa Vaughan (then with Christies) and Paul Walters (an American collector of Indian miniatures). I recall that the evening bordered on the hilarious. Even the unthawed vegetables and the collapsed soufflé did little to dampen our jollity.

While I was familiar with the Indian miniatures collections in most of the museums, occasionally one would be startled by something unique. That happened at the Pierpont Morgan Library where Shahnaz and I had dropped in on 27th September to meet its Librarian Mr. Virvolke. Perhaps the mood of last night's bonhomie had stayed with us overnight, but we found him hilarious. He was unaffected, witty and disarming. After having been shown some rather lack-lustre paintings, I asked him which of the items in the library interested him the most. That suddenly activated him. He took us into the vault beneath the spectacularly ornate Pierpont Morgan 1906 library and brought out a medieval illuminated *Book of Hours*, a German text of the New Testament inscribed on vellum. For a crescendo he opened the manuscript page of Milton's *Paradise Lost*, and allowed us to read its opening lines, just as Milton had dictated them[24] –

---

[23] Dr. M. S. Randhawa devoted a monograph to this series, published as *Kangra Paintings of the Gita Govinda* (New Delhi, 1963).
[24] John Milton had gone blind by the time he composed *Paradise Lost*. It was dictated by him between 1658 and 1664 to scribes.

Of Man's first disobedience, and the fruit

Of that forbidden tree whose mortal taste

Brought death into the world, and all our woe,

With loss of Eden.

That afternoon, we called on my uncle Syed Amjad Ali in his flat opposite the United Nations. Uncle Amjad had been our Ambassador to the United States and later Permanent Representative to the United Nations. No-one ever retires voluntarily from the United Nations, and neither did he. He obtained a nomination to its Finance Committee (his credentials as our Finance Minister helped) and that enabled him to travel frequently to the U.N. He enjoyed cooking, something he would countenanced in his palatial home in Lahore. His sister Kishwar Abid Hussain called his flat 'Curry Centre' because the smell of spices betrayed the location of his flat to many floors below.

After lunch he walked us through the security cordon and spying Dr. Javid Iqbal[25] who was attending the UN General Assembly that year, he called out to him: "I have brought them thus far. Now, you get them into the Assembly chamber."

Dr. Javid looked miffed, as if he had been asked to walk some-one else's dog.

Inside the cavernous U.N. Assembly, we found some seats in the front and were rewarded when almost panther-like Andy Young[26] loped in to hear the British Foreign Secretary David Owen[27] make his speech. Shahnaz – a fan of Young's - could not have asked for anything more.

Out of loyalty, we sat long enough to hear our own Agha Shahi[28] address the UN GA. I noticed him correcting his speech moments before he was invited to the podium. The speech he delivered had been watered down by him. He omitted a caustic reference to the US Ambassador in India (who had

---

[25] Son of the poet Allama Iqbal. He became later Chief Justice of the Punjab High Court.
[26] U.S. Ambassador to the United Nations, 1977-1979, during the Carter administration.
[27] British Foreign Secretary (1977-1979), appointed by his father-in-law prime minister James Callaghan.
[28] Foreign Secretary under Z.A. Bhutto and then Foreign Minister under General Ziaul Haq

made an anti-Zia statement somewhere), but he did what he had been sent by Zia to do, which was to assure the world body that Zia intended to hold general elections in October, i.e. within ninety days of his take-over. Elections were held eventually, but in November 1988, eleven years later and ninety days after Zia's death.

The following day, we met Karl Khandalavala at the Metropolitan Museum of Art. We were joined by Dr. Richard Ettinghausen, the doyen of American scholars in our field. While Karl and I competed with each other for Dr. Ettinghausen's cerebral attentions, I could not help noticing that the doctor's gaze kept veering towards Shahnaz's cleavage.

The last act of generosity JDR showed us was to invite us for lunch at the restaurant on the 63rd floor of the Rockefeller Plaza. One feels an inkling of divinity looking from that height at ant-like mankind below.

Babar Ali wanted us to have dinner with him at the Harvard Club. He had attended that Advanced Management Program at Harvard and that qualified him to use its facilities. He insisted on walking us back to our hotel, and on the way bought the first edition of *The New York Times.* "Tomorrow's paper today!"he said triumphantly. Once we had reached the proximity of Taft Hotel and Times Square, SBA took one look at the dubious clientele milling around the porn shops and asked us to escort him back to the safety of the Harvard Club on 44th Street.

Our last academic excursion took us to Boston to see the Fogg Art Museum and the Museum of Fine Arts, Boston. The Fogg Art Museum (linked to Harvard University) had been the recipient of Stuart Cary Welch's paintings and also some miniatures of decidedly lesser quality donated by Professor John K. Galbraith. I had hoped to thank Stuart Welch for the lengthy Foreword he had sent to me as a preamble to my abortive *Mughal and Related Miniatures.* He happened to be out of Boston in those days. Professor Galbraith I knew only through news reports of his ambassadorship in India (1961-63) and his collaboration with Dr. M. S. Randhawa in a rather superficial book on Indian miniatures.[29] Years later I asked Dr. Randhawa whether Galbraith knew enough about Indian painting to author a book – albeit jointly - on it.

---

[29] Randhawa, M. S., and John Kenneth Galbraith, *Indian painting: the scene, themes, and legends* (United States, 1968).

"He insisted," was Dr. Randhawa's terse, telling reply.

Shahnaz and I stayed overnight to see two other collections – one that Ananda Coomaraswamy had assembled for the Museum of Fine Arts, Boston, and the second housed in the Isabella Stewart Gardner Museum.

Ananda Coomaraswamy had been one of the earliest scholars in the field of Pahari painting. His *Rajput Painting* (1916) had first drawn a distinction between Rajput painting done in the Rajasthani courts and the styles prevalent in the Rajput hill states of the Punjab. Born of a Ceylonese father and a British mother, Coomaraswamy broadened his expertise from his patrimony Sinhalese art to Indian art and sculpture. His definitive catalogues of the Boston MFA collection, especially *Part V- Rajput Painting* (1926), had been a *vade-me-cum* for me ever since I became interested in the subject. I belonged to those who, like the German scholar Heinrich Zimmer, regarded Coomaraswamy as *'that noble scholar upon whose shoulders we are still standing'*.

Perhaps Coomaraswamy's greatest contribution to the study of Pahari painting had less to do than the geographical bifurcation of styles than to his focus on Pahari drawings. Until then, scholars and collectors had concentrated on finished paintings little realizing that the drawings were in fact the 'stencils' from which families of artists would make copies. He bought a large number of such drawings – particularly of a *Nala-Damayanti* series[30] - which were ultimately donated to the MFA by his friend Dr. D. W. Ross. It amused me to read a request Dr. Coomaraswamy made during his shopping expeditions in the Punjab hills asking for a further Rs 20,000 for paintings, and 39 paisas for postage.

The Isabella Stewart Gardner Museum was within walking distance of the MFA. Italianate in design, Mrs. Gardner's house reflected her love for Italian art, an interest Bernhard Berenson fuelled by acquiring some fine examples of paintings sculptures, and embroideries. She died in 1924. Her will stipulated that the collection should remain as she had left it. The museum remained unchanged, set in amber as it were, a Bostonian equivalent of that other Italianate villa - Osborne House, where the widowed Queen Victoria decreed that everything was to be left exactly as it was when her beloved husband Albert died in 1861.

---

[30] A. C. Eastman, *The Nala-Damayanti Drawings* (Boston, 1959). Eastman understandably dedicated his monograph to Dr. Coomaraswamy.

The museum honoured Mrs. Gardner's wishes but tried to find ingenious ways of 'arranging' objects so that they would not be damaged by continuous exposure to the sun.

To have visited Boston and not had tea near the Tea Museum in Boston harbour would have been almost a sacrilege. Shahnaz indulged herself in some 'open truck shopping' – a novelty we had not seen anywhere else. She bought herself a voluminous grey cape for $50. She was told that it would have cost $400 in any store. This piece of luck attracted the jinx. It made one last effort before we left the States. Shahnaz forgot the box containing the cape at the Tea Museum. Fortunately we had the museum's number. We called and one of the staff told us that it was safe and in their custody. We retrieved it and later that night, we flew back to London. We said goodbye to Boston, to the United States and (I hoped) to our accompanying jinx.

CHAPTER 14

BELATED HONEYMOON – II

Back in London, we stayed again with Tim and Bill Archer. It gave us the opportunity of seeing many of the places that I was familiar with as a student but which Shahnaz had never seen. We began with the National Portrait Gallery and then stopped for lunch with the Sotheby Parke Bernet crowd at the Westbury. They had invited newcomers in the field – Toby Falk[1] and Maggie Erskine[2] - and oldies like Karl Khandalavala. I found myself being grouped with Karl.

I was especially keen for Shahnaz to see the premises of the antiquarian shop Maggs Bros Ltd. in Berkeley Square. That was where I had bought the few miniatures I owned, but more importantly, that was where I had spent time learning about the arcane world of antiquarian books from Mr. Clifford Maggs. Fortunately he was in when we called. He greeted us in the open L-shaped interconnected rooms on the first floor. He had a copy of my *PP & SP* which he asked me to sign for him. Then, he did something quite unexpected. He steered me towards the windows that overlooked Berkeley Square and then, pulling out the chair beside the desk upon which Charles Dickens had written *Pickwick Papers*, he motioned me to sit. He put my book on the desktop and signalled that I should inscribe it for him. I could not have asked for a more affirmative acknowledgement of my catalogue. I know this may sound like a

---

[1] Later Toby Falk collaborated with Tim-bibi on a catalogue of the *Indian Miniatures in the India Office Library* (London, 1981), published by Philip Wilson Publishers under the Sotheby Parke Bernet imprint.
[2] Maggie was being groomed by Clifford Maggs to handle their increasing business in Indian material.

cliché but it made all the effort, the disappointments, the unending wait worth-
while. For that precious moment, Mr. Clifford had made me feel one of the
'greats'.

October 5 represented the anniversary of Bill's first exchange of
correspondence with me when he was Keeper of the Indian Section of the
V&AM. I had written to him at my father's behest to find out whether the
museum had a portrait of our ancestor. In my ignorance I assumed that we
were descended from Fakir Azizuddin, the most famous of the three Fakir
brothers who had served Maharaja Ranjit Singh. He replied that the museum
did not have one of Aziziuddin but it did have an ivory miniature of his
younger brother (and my real ancestor) Fakir Nuruddin. I made a copy of that
first letter and mounted it in card that I had had printed with the heading:
That single rose is now a garden. I gave it to him over breakfast. Bill found it
easier as Englishmen did of his age and background to express his feelings in
writing rather than physically. Bill typed his letters to me himself. They were
replete with mistakes. One of them – when he typed *Juky* instead of *July* -
caused him to christen all such typos 'Juky-isms.' It became a private joke
between us.

Tim-bibi was quite the opposite of Bill's reserve. She loved being hugged.
I noticed the look of unalloyed joy in her eyes when her grandchildren Joshua
and Chloe (Michael's children) visited her. She would secrete small toys in her
handbag or her skirt pockets, and then ask them: "And what do we have here?"

I realised how much she had subordinated her own self to Bill's stringent
demands. While Bill had a study all to himself on the first floor of their Provost
Road home, where he could write his books on Indian art and poetry, Tim-
bibi's own and in its own way equally significant research into British art in
India was stored in a waist-high steel filing cabinet in the dining room. She left
each alternate day for the India Office Library & Records where she worked
in the Prints and Drawings Department, cataloguing its extensive collection.
She was truly a multi-armed devi. She worked silently with her own researches,
she managed a large three-storey house, she entertained a stream of scholarly
guests from India and the United States, she organised Bill's life for him and
then would return in the evening to prepare dinner for them and for whoever
happed to be staying with them. The only exceptions she told me were Gopi

Krishna Kanoria and his wife.[3] Mrs. Kanoria and her husband were devout Hindus. She brought her own cooking utensils and made meals for the two of them herself. The only concession she made was to agree to use Tim-bibi's 'unconsecrated' kitchen.

Necessarily, Tim's own range of meals bordered on the functional. Her specialty consisted of a soup made from left-over chicken. She put everything – chicken meat, skin, bones - into the blender and pulverised the lot. "They are a good source of calcium," she insisted.

Tim's love for Bill had not diminished over the years since their marriage in July 1934. She would pass him while he was sitting at the dining table and affectionately brush the top of his bristled head with her open palm, while he sat like some impassive Buddha, accepting her offering as his due. Many years later, Dr. Randhawa, during our conversations in Chandigarh and in a moment of candour, revealed to me that Bill had fallen in love with someone else and wanted to leave Tim-bibi for the other woman. He sought Dr. Randhawa's advice. Dr. sahib gave it in his usual staccato, pragmatic manner: "This is a just an infatuation. Stay with Tim. She is a good woman. And don't forget. You will need someone to look after you in your old age."

Now that I look on those days, I realise that that Shahnaz and I might have taxed our hosts' hospitality by using their home as a pad from which to make daily forays, returning often late at night only to sleep.

My diary for 8 October, for example, records that we had lunch at the Inn on the Park hotel with Rafi Raza (to whom I gave a copy of my book), Babar Ali and his protégé Bubli Brar. (Her father Harcharan Singh had been at Aitchison College with Babar.) From there, we saw the Graham Sutherland exhibition at the National Portrait Gallery. I had always admired his portraits, in particular those of the author Somerset Maugham and of the equally wealthy cosmetician Helena Rubinstein. Sutherland drew her from an upward angle. She looked like the majestic, over-painted prow of a 19th century schooner.

A visit on another day to Woburn Abbey with Ashwin and Bena allowed me to see in original Pietro Annigoni's fine portrait study of the Dowager

---

[3] Gopi Krishna Kanoria had been an early friend of Tim and Bill during the days of Bill's service in Bihar. Over the years, Kanoria had amassed a superb collection of Indian miniatures. These were published in a catalogue *Indian paintings from Rajasthan* (1958).

Duchess of Devonshire.

One visit that led to another memorable one was arranged by Giles Eyre. He took Bill, Tim and us first to meet the Marchioness of Dufferin & Ava and his wife Lindy. They had through Bill's intermediacy built up a fine collection of Indian and Anglo-Indian material. One entered their elegant house in Knightsbridge and in the room on the left were all British originals and in the one on the right their Indian collection. I noticed a mint six volume set of *Oriental Scenery* [4] featuring aquatints by Thomas Daniell and his nephew William Daniell.

I asked out host whether he had acquired them through Giles.

"No," he replied, tactfully. "The first Marquess was one of the original subscribers."[5]

Giles with his inimitable ingenuity managed to obtain an introduction from the Marchioness to the Guinness family that owned Elveden Hall, once the home of Maharaja Duleep Singh, one of the subjects of my second book *Sikh Portraits by European Artists*.

Mark Zebrowski[6] and his companion Robert 'Bob' Alderman lived close to the Avas. We spent an evening with them. Shahnaz recalled how shocked she was when Bob, clearly the Josephine in the relationship, invited Shahnaz to admire the Punjabi *phulkari* they had bought. It lay spread out on their double bed. Broad-minded though she was, it took her some time to recover her composure.

The morning of 12 October I remember vividly. Bill and I sat opposite each other in their dining room. I had my back to the tall windows that overlooked the basement garden. Tim had gone to the IOL. Shahnaz I think was upstairs having a bath.

Bill again asked me (he has raised the matter a week earlier on 5th) whether I would write an article refuting Brijen Goswamy's treatment and interpretation of the Devi diagram. Bill repeated all his reservations, his suspicion that Brijen had somehow 'doctored' the evidence and slipped in the name of Jasrota as an afterthought. It annoyed Bill that no scholar other than

---

[4] Published in London between 1795 and 1808.
[5] In those days, for such expensive publications, subscriptions were solicited *before* printing could commence.
[6] Mark died of AIDS in August 1999.

Brijen had been allowed access to the actual drawing. Brijen maintained that the Chandu Raina family was extremely secretive and possessive about it. Bill thought this was simply a smoke screen that Brijen had put up to deter scholars (Bill in particular) from examining the drawing closely. I learned from Dr. Randhawa later that he shared all of Bill's reservations.

Gradually, the discussion veered towards the relationship between Bill – the alpha male in the pride – and Brijen, the young virile challenger. Bill recounted how Brijen had let him down on one visit by failing to meet him at the bus stop at Chandigarh after a gruelling journey from New Delhi. This had mattered deeply to Bill, but I did not see how that disappointment should matter to me.

I knew enough about the debilitating impact such scholarly controversies had on both proponents and their adversaries. One continuing confrontation I was familiar with. It was a war fought over the interpretation of a colophon that appeared on the Basohli *Gita Govinda* series of 1730 AD. The controversy was complicated by the appearance of an identical colophon on another series of the *Gita Govinda*, this one painted in Kangra some fifty years later for Raja Sansar Chand of Kangra.

It seems hard to believe that this issue should have absorbed for as long as it did scholars of such eminence as Bill Archer and Dr. Randhawa on one side, and Karl Khandalavala and Basil Gray[7] on the other. The controversy reached its apogee when Bill wrote a brilliant, witty, irreverent Introduction[8] to Dr. Randhawa's *Kangra Paintings of the Gita Govinda* (1963), in which he mocked Karl with the remark that he was 'not over-learned in Sanskrit'. The wounding sentences that Bill crowed over (and Karl silently endured) read: 'For seven years the issue lay dormant [.] Khandalavala, after citing Kane, had been ominously silent. In 1958, however, he roused himself like Siva from his trance. Imbedded in his gigantic *Pahari Miniature Painting* appeared a re-assessment of the inscription.'[9]

Ten years were to pass before Bill healed the breach by dedicating his

---

[7] Keeper of Oriental Antiquities at the British Museum, London. Although Basil Gray's forte was in the field of Persian painting, he had collaborated with his Assistant curator Douglas Barrett in a joint publication: *Painting in India* (London, 1963).

[8] Bill inscribed my copy of this book 'The Introduction that shook the world!'.

[9] W.G. Archer, Introduction to M.S. Randhawa ,*Kangra Paintings of the Gita Govinda* (New Delhi, 1963), pp. 28-29.

definitive *Indian Paintings from the Punjab Hills* to both Mohinder Singh Randhawa <u>and</u> Karl Khandalavala, each of whom had contributed as much as Bill himself had done to the study of Pahari painting.

With this background in mind, I knew that I would be entering a minefield without any detectors. I had too many disabilities already and did not need to battle on Bill's behalf. Very gently but firmly, I declined. Bill persisted over another cup of coffee. I remained adamant. Eventually he gave up: "So, you won't write that article?"

"No." I knew I had disappointed Bill. He wanted me to continue what he believed to be the good fight. It was however not my joust.

On 13th we made a quick day trip to Oxford where Tim Benbow (my OUP Pakistan publisher) hosted us. We did the haunts – the bookshop Blackwell's, Christ College, the Cathedral, a lunch at Westbury Hotel, a stroll through Magdalene College, the Broad Walk, before retruning to London. Philippa Vaughan and her husband (a lawyer who commuted between London and Brussels) had invited a number of guests. The least interesting I noted was Karuna who introduced herself as a Princess of Ceylon. She wore a sari, its *pallu* artfully secured as she wore no *choli*.

Tim and I were keen on seeing again Queen Victoria's retreat Osborne House on the Isle of Wight. Shahnaz had never been there before. We three caught the train to Southampton. I went to cafeteria on the train for some tea for the ladies. The attendant was quite obviously halfway through a sex-change. Even without overhearing his/her discussion with his colleague, I could have detected that here was a woman trapped in the body of a man, and both genders had found a doctor who could resolve the predicament. The attendant would soon be hearing the words April Ashley's surgeon had said to her before her sex-change operation: "Bonne nuit, monsieur", and after it: "Bonjour, madame."[10]

When I last visited the Isle of Wight in the late 1960s, I caught a ferry to Cowes. Now, a decade later, a Hovercraft made the crossing. Osborne House was still recognisably the same. The approaches to the house had been converted into a large parking area for the coaches that brought shoals of tourists each day.

---

[10] April Ashley was one of Britain's first sex-change patients. She later became a famous model.

Tim had arranged for us to be taken around by the Keeper Mr. Sibbick. While the private royal apartments of Osborne House and its gardens had been left intact, the ground floor had been rearranged, or at least its numerous pictures had. Over the years, the British monarchy had collected a number of items with an Indian connection. Except for the Indian jewellery (such as the Timur Ruby and Maharaja Sher Singh's emerald belt) and Edward VII's collection of Indian arms and armour which were stored at Sandringham House in Norfolk, all other Indian objects were on display at Osborne House.

The 'Indian-ness' of Osborne House went beyond its ornate white stucco Darbar Hall, designed and constructed under the supervision of Lockwood Kipling and Bhai Ram Singh. The walls were populated thick with portraits of her Indian subjects and her munshi Abdul Karim, painted by the Hungarian artist Rudolf Swoboda. Prominent and of special interest to me was Franz Winterhalter's dramatic, flattering portrait of Maharaja Duleep Singh and its lesser companion of Princess Victoria Gouramma of Coorg. Despite Queen Victoria's ardent desire to see these two Indian converts to Christianity married to each other, they refused to oblige, much to Queen Victoria's understandable disappointment. Eventually, they both made ill-suited matches.

Mr. Sibbick was very helpful, and even more so after I observed while we stood in the Private Sitting room that had a magnificent view of the Solent, that as Queen Victoria preferred to sit closest to the window, the low footstool under her table could not be hers. It had to be Prince Albert's: he had longer legs than hers.

Back in London, Tim-bibi arranged for us to meet her daughter Margaret – 'Maggie' – and her family. They lived near Bristol where Maggie's husband Richard[11] taught at the University.

Bill dropped us all at Paddington station. He appeared unusually morose, quiet, in fact depressed. On the train, Tim-bibi talked about him and the years they spent in India until 1947. She told us of his deeply evangelical youth and his rejection of his parents' brittle adherence to their faith. She did not go into details but she did let mention that Bill somehow felt responsible for his mother's death.[12] We talked about Bill's passion for poetry. His first

---

[11] Richard died unexpectedly a few years later of a brain haemorrhage.

[12] After their deaths, I found a mention in the memoir Giles Eyre had compiled on the Archers:

books had been about folk poetry[13] and on primitive sculpture.[14]

"Did he ever write any poems for you while you were engaged?" She and Bill had been engaged 'for three long years of separation' before they were married.

"Only short, silly ones," she replied.[15]

She talked about Bill's inclination towards his Labour principles and his sympathy for the Indian agitation for independence, of how on 9 August 1942, he as the District Magistrate in Patna was required to arrest Rajendra Prasad, one of the senior Congress leaders. "Bill had to help push Rajendra's car which wouldn't start, and when they reached the jail, he and Rajendra walked arm in arm through the jail gates together." A few days later, she told us, a crowd of students agitated and it was only when they threatened to attack the Secretariat where all the precious Official and Land records were kept, that Bill ordered the police to fire upon the crowd. Eight students were killed. "This was the saddest day of Bill's whole career in India," Tim-bibi said.

Maggie met us at Bath station with her two adopted children. She and Richard had decided to adopt two Anglo-Jamaican children. They called them Tamsin and Pobbles. We walked around Bath, stopping to admire the Morris dancers performing outside Bath abbey, a former Benedictine monastery. I wheeled Tamsin while Maggie pushed Pobbles in his wheeler. Shahnaz and Tim followed us. I could not help being amused by the reaction of passers-by who would look at me an Asian, then at Maggie a British Anglo-Saxon, and then at the clearly negroid young children. Both these children were remarkably well-adjusted and behaved. While for example we were having lunch, they sat in the wheelies eating marmite sandwiches.

'His [Bill's] mother had just died, and his father followed her shortly afterwards. Bill's last years at Cambridge were clouded by their deaths.' Bill's reaction was typical: "I threw myself into some of the hardest work I have done in my life." See Giles Eyre, Introduction to *India Served and Observed* by William and Mildred Archer (London, 1994), x.

[13] *The Blue Grove: the poetry of the Uraons* (1940) and *The Dove and the Leopard: more Uraon poetry* (1950).

[14] *The Vertical Man: study of primitive Indian sculpture* (1947).

[15] Bill's longer poems he kept and published in his book *The Plains of the Sun* (1948). The opening stanza of one of them gives an insight into Bill's repressed romanticism: 'I request the pleasure of your body/in the pallor of the white light/in the private glove of darkness/in the cold bloom of the night's eye.'

The house that Maggie and Richard lived in had been bought by them out from the sale proceeds of a painting Bill had owned. I saw it hung in the dining room at 18 Provost Road. Bill had sold it at Sotheby's through Peter Wilson. Bill remarked to me once of Peter Wilson's talent as an auctioneer, of how he could use his fingers and his persuasive voice to coax increasingly higher bids out of his audience.[16]

Maggie's house was a twenty-minute drive into the countryside around Bristol. Richard met us barefoot and led us into the house. Looking at the – dare I say it? – condition inside, I was not sure that their 'close to nature' philosophy had any merits to commend it. The final straw for me was when they encouraged their cat to pad across the dining table, sniffing our portions while we ate.

By the next morning, Bill's mood had improved. Giles picked us up in his station-wagon and drove us to Elveden in Suffolk. He drove carefully as the morning mist had not yet lifted. Even when we drove through the entrance gates of Elveden Hall, there were traces of mist lingering still. We alighted and disturbed with our commotion a pair of golden pheasants that were nestling on the stone steps of the house. It seemed a good augury. The Maharaja had been known in his time as one of the top four shots in England.

The house now belonged to the Guinness family. The main house had been bought by the deposed Maharaja Duleep Singh out of a loan of £105,000, borrowed from the India Office.[17]   The purchase almost bankrupted him. After he quit England in the 1880s, it stood empty and unused. The only habitable portion was the extension, a later addition. The caretaker - a Mr. Bailey – lived there. He emerged dressed in tweeds, and received us with a guarded propriety.

He opened up the heavy front door of the main house and escorted us inside. The red brick Georgian exterior gave no clue to the interior in which the main rooms were a pastiche of the Sheesh Mahal of the Lahore Fort. After Duleep Singh had bought the Elveden estate in the 1860s (it covered about 17,000 acres), he had it re-modelled, giving his architect John Norton some paintings and photographs of the Sheesh Mahal from the India Office Library

---

[16] Peter Wilson, the father of my publisher Philip Wilson, began his career as a porter and rose to become the Chairman of Sotheby's, increasing its revenues from $2 m. to $575 m. He died m 1984.

[17] Later the Foreign & Commonwealth Relations Office.

(then the Indian Museum) to draw inspiration from.

Photographs taken of the interior during Duleep Singh's occupancy show a fanciful reconstruction of fluted tapering columns with lotus bases, ornately cusped arches, florid stucco decoration and heavy velvet-padded Victorian furniture. The interiors of the house were bare and resounded to our footsteps as we walked through the rooms. On the back of the cyclostyled note composed by Countess of Iveagh[18] and given to us as a perfunctory guide by Mr. Bailey, I made a sketch of the layout.

The narrow double-doored entrance was flanked by a changing room on the left and a wash room with multiple washing basins on the right, to cater for the shooting parties returning muddied after a day's hunting on the estate. A central corridor had on its left side the dining room with an attached cloakroom, opposite it another smaller dining room, and at the far end the grand ballroom. On the other side of the house, lay the library, a room with an indoor fountain, and at the corner a sitting room with leather walls.

I tried to visualize where Duleep Singh would have hung his collection of paintings of himself, his father Maharaja Ranjit Singh and his relatives by August Schoefft and other artists. These were to be illustrated in my *Sikh Portraits by European Artists*. A recent research has disclosed that Schoefft's large composition *Der Hof von Lahor* (The Court of Lahore) took up the whole wall of the dining room. Smaller paintings including the copy of Winterhalter's portrait of him were distributed in the other rooms.[19]

The main contents of Elveden Hall were auctioned in July 1883, after Duleep Singh took the decision to return to India in an abortive attempt to regain the Punjab. The house, like its hapless owner, had a sorry history after that. In 1893, after Duleep Singh's death, Elveden Hall was sold by his executors to the 1st Lord Iveagh. It remained in the ownership of the Iveaghs, being commandeered for a while during the Second World War by the Royal Air Force.

Auctioneers were called in again in 1984, when Christie's were

---

[18] The Countess in the typewritten note she wrote on dated 23 July 1963 took pains to explain: 'I should very much like to correct the legend that the domed Marble Hall was built by Maharajah Duleep Singh; it was in fact built by the first Lord Iveagh in 1900 and completed in 1903.

[19] Peter Bance, *The Duleep Singhs: The Photograph Album of Queen Victoria's Maharajah* (Stroud, Gloucester, 2004),p.48.

commissioned to sell all the contents belonging mainly to the Iveaghs with a few items left by Duleep Singh.

While the Archers and Giles were being walked about the rooms, I returned to the dining room and from the marble fireplace purloined a small marble lotus bud that had fallen off the foot-rail. I picked up also a pear-shaped fragment of stucco. I handed them to Shahnaz and asked her to hide them in her handbag. We still have them – stolen, and therefore all the more precious.

Mr. Bailey invited us to his part of the house for a coffee and then we walked across the gravel to the nearby Church of St Andrew and St Patrick, where Duleep Singh, his wife Bamba and their young son Edward lie side by side. Giles put some flowers he had plucked from nearby on Duleep Singh's grave. I read a prayer for him.

On the drive back to London, Giles mildly punctured the atmosphere with a question whether we had noticed anything *odd* about the caretaker.

"He is most probably an Iveagh," Giles said, and then explained, "born ... *entre nous*, on the wrong side of the blankets." I recalled that remark when years later I read in Bance's book that 'in the nearby villages, children of Elveden Hall employees were often crudely mocked for their obvious biological link with the Maharajah.'[20]

The next morning, Shahnaz and I caught the 10.30 a.m. train from Victoria for Paris. Those were the pre-Chunnel days. One had to disembark at Folkestone, catch the ferry to Calais, and then board another train for Paris. We had made reservations at the three star Hotel Belmont. For its tariff - FF 123 per night for a double room, with another FF22 for a continental breakfast – and for its location on the Rue de Bassano, it could not have been more convenient for us. We stayed there for six nights. On our first day, we 'did' the Tour Eiffel, and paid at our respects at Napoleon's tomb in Les Invalides. He had been a hero to both my father and to Zulfikar Ali Bhutto. Paris like London and New York are cities to walk in. We therefore walked to the Isle de France hoping to catch the antique bookshops there. I had forgotten the Gallic habit of closing for lunch. We visited the Notre Dame Cathedral and then after they had opened, we rummaged amongst their trestle tables, finding a print of the 'Ruins of Gaur' from Daniells' *Oriental Scenery*. The sides had

---

[20] Bance (2004), p.46.

been trimmed to within a fingernail of the actual picture. That explained why we were able to get it for only FF125. We picked up some maps by French cartographers (a Bonne at FF25, and a Bellin for FF50, a Sanson d'Abbeville for FF200), and the smaller versions of Saltykov's lithographs.

That evening we spent with Patrick Lefebvre (whom we had hosted in Lahore) and his wife Beatrice in their elegant home on the outskirts of Paris.

The following day was devoted to art. We tramped through the Louvre, admiring Old Masters and re-acquainting ourselves with old friends whom we knew through productions. The statues I had wanted to see - Michelangelo's *Slaves* – had been removed and not on public display. Our next stop was at the Musée Guimet to see the General Court collection of paintings. Jean-Marie Lafont had given us an introduction the keeper, a Dr. Jarrige. For some reason which I could not rationalize, he appeared inexplicably shifty. Grudgingly he brought out the pictures that General Claude Court[21] (one of Maharaja Ranjit Singh's more dependable *feranghis*) had collected in the Punjab.

If there is any day that I could pinpoint when I fell in love with Paris, it would be 20 August. It was a Saturday. Shahnaz and I caught the metro to St Germaine-en-Laye in northwest Paris. The magnificent chateaux had known many occupants – King Louis XIV, the British exiled monarch King James II, and the German Army of occupation during the Second World War (it served as its headquarters).

It was a glorious un-crowded autumnal day. The park was strewn with leaves in every shade of rust and gold, waiting to be rustled by any passing breeze. Shahnaz and I did a French version of Omar Khayyam – a baguette of bread, a bottle of chilled white wine, and ourselves for company. Unused to consuming a whole bottle, we lurched and tottered our way back towards the swaying escalator that led into the Metro.

By the time we reached Reuilly Malmaison we had recovered our composure. We owed an ex-emperor at least a degree of sobriety. The Chateau Malmaison had been bought by Napoleon's first wife Josephine at a price Napoleon in his plebeian days could not afford. (It so reminded me of Duleep Singh's improvidence over Elveden). She continued to spend on it, improving the house and its gardens to an enviable level of elegance. The interiors had

---

[21] General Court served the Sikh Darbar between 1827 and 1843. His interest in antiquities made him investigate the Buddhist tope at Mankiyala, near Rawalpindi.

been substantially restored and redecorated. I remember his marble bath lined with velvet; his study with its desk and beside it the small box into which he could slip confidential documents should a visitor enter; Josephine's plush red and gold bedroom with its gilded bed, carved with Egyptian motifs, fit for a French Cleopatra.

After her divorce from Napoleon, Josephine occupied herself with tending a fine rose garden, rearing exotic plants, and by maintaining a menagerie that included kangaroos, emus, antelopes, llamas and black swans. We looked out the chateau's windows and saw a lone white swan trying hard not create any ripples on the placid surface of the lake.

We found a street café where we had a cup of invigorating coffee and then caught a bus to the centre. En route, I noticed a sub-continental face. More importantly, he noticed mine.

He wriggled through the crowd until he reached me.

"Are you from India?"

"No, I am from Pakistan."

"Same to same, *yaar*!"

"Then you must be from Pakistan?"

"No, I am from India."

"Why didn't you say Pakistan, then, if it is same to same, *yaar*?"[22]

He slunk away as quickly as he had come.

"Why did you have to be so rude to him?" Shahnaz asked me.

"I wasn't being rude. I was merely being factual."

We spent a full day at Versailles. What is there to say about a palace that Russian czars once emulated and modern Russian oligarchs envy. After hours of walking through its interminable galleries and enjoying its exquisite gardens, Shahnaz's shoes gave way. She hobbled back to the hotel.

One of the advantages of being taken around by locals – I know because I have done it once too often in Lahore - is one can see places that do not attract the attention of the tourist harried for time. Patrick and Beatrice very

---

[22] This anecdote was included in the 1997 anniversary issue of TIME magazine on the independence of India and Pakistan.

generously took a day off to show us Fontainebleau and then Vaux-le-Vicomte. This had been built for Nicholas Fouquet, the man in charge of Louis XIV's finances. In a sense its English equivalent would have been Hampton Court Palace which Cardinal Wolsey had built for himself. The difference lay in the fact that Vaux-le-Vicomte inspired a germ of an idea in Louis XIV's omnivorous mind (hence Versailles) whereas Henry VIII simply appropriated his subject's pet project.

We returned to London, satiated, on 23 October. We shared the compartment with some Pakistanis (they did not mistake me for an Indian), an ageing Spaniard who announced that his cousins had fought in the war ("Yes, but on which side?" I would have asked, had Shahnaz not been sitting next to me), and a Japanese who had just seen the musical *Bubbling Brown Sugar* (which was about Harlem) and who recounted the plot - scene by scene - to two Afro-Americans sitting opposite him.

We reached the British Customs. I was singled out and asked to open my bag. The officer rummaged among my clothes and then suddenly, triumphantly, he pulled out a packet wrapped in cellophane. He could not have been more exultant, nor I more innocent. The packet contained my wet underpants that I had washed overnight but had not had time to dry.

The last few days in London Shahnaz went with Bena to the Brent Cross Shopping Mall. We made a quick day trip with Ashwin and Bena to see my alma mater Berkhamsted School. The Housemaster of St John's took me around the building. The wooden cubicles in the dormitories had gone, the outside lavatories hadn't.

We were entertained by Tim Benbow's parents whom we had hosted in Lahore. They took us to an obviously expensive basement restaurant in Baker Street. This was 1977 and the Arabs had just discovered London, and the service industry had discovered petro-dollars. We sat down. The maitre d'hôtel handed out the menus. I noticed that mine had prices. Suddenly, Benbow senior took mine away and substituted it with his. I realised why. It had no prices marked. In this subtle way, each guest was encouraged to choose something interesting and expensive without fretting about the cost. By the time we had drunk our coffee, the waiter - assuming that I was an over-rich Arab entertaining poor British clients - brought the bill to me. Mr. Benbow intercepted it again, just in time.

Over breakfast next morning, when I asked Bill if he could keep an eye open for any lithographs by Charles Hardinge or Emily Eden, he and Tim exchanged glances. It was as if they were deciding whether to share their secret with us.

"Phone this number," she said. "Ask to speak to Miss Lynch. Tell them that you are friends of ours and that we have sent you. They might still have some of the things you want. But you must promise not to tell anyone else."

I rang Miss Lynch and made an appointment for later that morning. The address Miss Lynch gave me was of a private house in Upper Berkeley Street. I knew the area because Maurice Apple & Co.'s offices were on the opposite side of Edgware Road. I must have passed that address at least a hundred times before on my way to and from clients. I had no idea that behind the anonymous exterior of a private home hid a treasure trove of 19th century lithographs and prints.

Miss Lynch – a diminutive as Tim-bibi and as energetic – received us and took us into a ground floor room whose tall windows looked out onto the West London Synagogue.

"And what is your name again?"

"Aijazuddin, but you can call me Aijaz."

"Hijaz, she said slowly with exaggerated emphasis. "Hijaz. One has to pronounce it fanatically."

We asked her whether she happened to have any lithographs by Charles Hardinge of Lahore. She opened a drawer and from it extracted some folded brown paper.

"Here," she said, simply, and there were the four views of Lahore that I had been on the lookout for years.

'And might you have any Saltykovs?" I coaxed.

She opened another drawer and from it produced the Saltykov lithographs of the Sikhs.

"Any Edwards of Sindh?" I suggested.

"I have these," she replied, "but only a few of them are coloured. The others are all monochrome, I am afraid."

"Tim-bibi told us you might have some Emily Edens? Would you by any chance have any left?"

Miss Lynch smiled. "Oh, I do like Miss Eden. Don't you?" With that, she removed from another drawer all the Edens I coveted – the famous one of Ranjit Singh, his Anglophile son Sher Singh, the young Kunwar Pratap Singh, and the dandy David Beckham of his day - Raja Hira Singh.

In one afternoon, rather like my acquisition of rare books at Hamid Ali's in 1972, I managed to form an enviable collection of British lithographs. All of them cost exactly £359. To celebrate, Shahnaz and I took Tim-bibi to a performance of Tchaikovsky's *Sleeping Beauty* at Covent Garden.

The next morning, on our final day with the Archers, I thought I would make them fluffed-up omelettes as a treat. I must have made quite a mess in Tim-bibi's kitchen. Normally very calm, she almost broke down she saw that while I was in my ham-handed way washing up her china. I broke first one and then a second saucer. "Aijaz," she remonstrated. "They managed to survive the Second World War and our travels throughout the length and breadth of India, and these thirty years since!" That explained why many of the plates and cups had rivets holding their parts together.

That afternoon – it was a Sunday - Shahnaz and I walked down an empty New Bond Street. We passed the window of Sotheby's. There, in the two showcases flanking the entrance, on display were stacks of my *Pahari Paintings & Sikh Portraits in the Lahore Museum*. And of course that had to be the one day that I had neglected to bring my camera with me. Our jinx had the last laugh.

CHAPTER 15

A CHANGED NFC

Shahnaz and I returned to Karachi early in the morning on 1 October. We entered my in-laws' house and were greeted with gleeful squeals of recognition by Momina. Mubarika we could hardly recognise. Even over a span of two months (we left when she was sixteen months old) she had grown appreciably. Most dramatically, an almost bald head had been replaced by the most luxurious curls. She sat upright on her bed, staring at us quizzically, and then taking her cue from Momina, she relented and came forward to be cuddled.

We asked Auntie Nayyar how she had been to effect this minor miracle. "Nido's milk!" she replied.

I called the NFC office and asked to speak to the new Chairman. Before I had left for the United States, we at NFC had been informed that Syed Babar Ali would be succeeded by Riyaz H. Bokhari, a former Member of the Railway Board and at that time Chairman of Federal Light Engineering Corporation (FLEC). It struck me as politic to call on him before I went away and to introduce myself. Babar's advice (wrong and self-motivated as I discovered most of his advice to be) was that I should not meet Mr. Bokhari. I knew the moment I spoke to Mr. Bokhari that my neglect had been a mistake. It would take me a year or so to expiate my fault.

"I just thought I would let you know that I am back and will be in Lahore shortly," I said by way of opening the conversation.

"Yes," he replied tersely. "Come so that we can discuss business," and then hung up.

Whatever forebodings I had became apparent within moments of my reporting at the NFC Head Office. My diary entries in December 1977 for that period describe more vividly than I am able to recall the tensions of my re-entry into NFC:

'At last, the time to catch up with my diary. And what an incongruous place I have chosen to begin - Ghafoor Mirza's room on the ground floor of Block D in Islamabad Secretariat. I am alone. Today being Thursday, everyone has left early.[1] Awan sahib returned to his office only this morning after a long period of sick leave, and for today at least he has not radiated any ripples by his presence.

This is in fact my first visit to Islamabad in over 4 months. Through September and October I was away, and since my return I just have not had the desire or the heart to see Habeeb Husain or any of his cronies, particularly after what they did during my absence. No sooner had I gone abroad than the new Chairman (SBA's successor R.H. Bokhari) asked for my file in Islamabad at Habeeb Husain's office, and within a day an epistle was dispatched beginning with the words: 'We understand that...' which is officialese for 'We have been informed ..'. All sorts of seamy questions were asked: Why had I gone? With whose permission? How could I as a government employee take earned leave and combine it with an official trip?

The presumption was that I had gone on a junket, and I had been grossly dishonest in my visit arrangements. As soon as I returned, I nailed my detractors by producing letters signed by SBA and the Ministry conveying approval for my visit. The whole business had been so unnecessarily sordid that it left a bad taste in my mouth. It certainly affected RHB's attitude towards me.

The NFC after SBA's departure is not and will not be the same. That does not mean that it will not improve. One certainly hopes so. But the fact is that RHB is an accounts man - 'a dyed—in-the-wool bureaucrat' is how one of the former MDs in FLEC described him. His being also Habeeb Husain's close friend makes the future course of NFC predictably clear. Already, notes are being bandied between offices when earlier, a discussion across a table would have yielded a

---

[1] In those days, Friday being a holiday, Thursdays were deemed half-days.

quick decision. One of the engineers (Tasdeeq Khan) is RHB's son-in-law to be, another is closely related to Mrs. RHB. These connections in themselves are not so disheartening. Hell, I am SBA's nephew, so I can hardly cast pebbles at others. What is depressing is the slack in momentum within the organisation, within its subsidiaries, and within each employee. Everyone seems to be on the look-out for a way out of the NFC. Mahmood Bhutta is waiting for the Fauji's to say "Yes"; his deputy Rathor is looking over his shoulder at the university he left behind (he had brought his unhappy Malay wife with him to Lahore); Asif Mohyuddin (FM Pak-Arab) shuffles impatiently; Zahid Aziz and Khalid Saeed are already abroad, presumed lost. At the BIM, Amanullah Durrani has resigned and left. Feroze Qaiser has been removed from his sinecure. Jawaid Mirza has become the Chairman SHEMTC[2] replacing Abid Hussain. Mazhar Ali has left the State Cement Corporation, and yesterday I learned that dear H.N. Akhtar has been removed from the Finance Directorship of PASMIC.[3]

A most disturbing event which occurred last week was the Ministry's removal of Salahuddin Chaudhry from Pak-American Fertilisers Ltd at Daudkhel. A complaint has been made against him by the Martial Law Authorities that he was being 'a hindrance' in their investigations. He was quite shattered when I had to break the news to him. RHB had refused to tell SC himself. Eventually, when SC did confront RHB to ask what stand he proposed to take on this act of injustice, RHB replied blandly: "The stand I propose to take is ... to do nothing."'

A few days later, I made this entry covering the political situation: 'Ziaul Haq was decidedly in control. He had Bhutto where he wanted him – behind bars. And he had the politicians on their toes, dancing to his tune. On the political level, conditions fester and decompose with seemingly irreversible persistence. Ziaul Haq described by a BBC correspondent as 'naïve'. Like Goldilocks he has been trying out the PM's chair, finds it comfortable and now wants to taste the porridge. He is trapped though by the impetuosity of his actions. The

[2] State Heavy Engineering and Mechanised Tool Corporation Ltd.
[3] Pakistan Steel Mills Corporation at Port Qasim.

Pakistan National Alliance (PNA) is hustling him into handing over power to them and will vilify him if he doesn't; the PPP is playing for time and will crucify him – if and when it returns to power.

Today, by talking about general elections, what everyone means is power, governing power, the clear authority to form an authoritarian government. The PNA[4] having united to topple ZAB from Government has begun to fragment. Asghar Khan and his group of untrained (and some unwilling) party members have broken away from the PNA constellation. His shadow cabinet relies upon their dormant talent of people like Aitzaz Ahsan (ex-PPP provincial minister) to advise on youth matters and Fakhr Imam (ex-PPP ministerial aspirant) on Agriculture. Gohar Ayub rebels and is accordingly expelled. The Shah-in-Shah meets Asghar Khan but remains reticent. Did Asghar Khan fail his *viva voce*?

Asghar Khan's most serious rival Wali Khan has been released by the Martial Law Authorities. Being a wily Pathan he has accepted the favour. The more principled Balochi Marris have refused to accept any favours from this military which according to them have perpetrated 'crimes against humanity' in Balochistan. They remain in jail at the same time as their erstwhile tormentor.

ZAB's predicament is strange and almost unnatural. Who a year ago would have predicted that he would have been incarcerated in Kot Lakhpat jail? Or that he would be brought out at intervals for public exhibition and subjected to humiliation by Justice Mushtaq Hussain? Who would have thought that Mrs. Bhutto would have been injured in Qaddafi stadium, where, during a cricket match, police brickbats would replace cricket bats? She is in UCH with seven stitches to her forehead, lying in the room on the same floor as our friend Neelam Hussein. Who would have foreseen that Mumtaz Bhutto would be hurling defiant, impotent threats at his captors, castigating for keeping him 'not in solitary confinement, but in a torture chamber'? Or that he would spurn eye surgery, preferring to come out of jail 'blind, or as a dead man'?

---

[4] Pakistan National Alliance, a group of nine parties who joined hands against Zulfikar Ali Bhutto in 1977.

The CMLA[5] who began as an Oliver Cromwell has degenerated into a tawdry, opinionated and guile-less imitation of Yahya Khan. I suspect he regards himself as extremely intelligent and perceptive, an opinion that increases as each day passes and he finds himself still in the chair. Zia has just returned from a trip to China, proclaiming that his journey (his 'mission') as 'highly successful in all respects'. I don't think for a moment he realises that the Chinese have treated all our leaders with the same overt warmth and courtesy, honouring less the individual visitor (regardless of his validity) than the country he represents. For some reason, that visit to China is regarded by every fresh Pakistani leader as a sort of 'coronation', anointing them in office.'

The frustration of the PNA leadership could be gauged from an interview Sardar Sherbaz Khan Mazari gave to *The Pakistan Times* on 2 December. He told the newspaper that 'the PNA had welcomed the imposition of Martial Law merely because of past Government's façade of parliamentary democracy had become intolerable, and added that the CMLA had promised elections within 90 days. Now it seems those 90 days are prolonging without any end in sight [.] All I am asking for is that the CMLA should honour the promise he made to us in at our meeting with him in October. He had said that the process of accountability would be completed by March and then it would take about 60 days to complete the electoral process. This means, the polling should be held by May or at the latest by June. That is his own pledge.'

It was almost the end of December that we at the NFC held a review meeting at PAFL Multan to assess its progress. I noted the marked difference between SBA's and RHB's approach:

'Whereas SBA would have toured the plant site and spun the personnel on site into a vortex of activity, RHB chose to retire to his room, reading alone, eating alone, and maintaining a distance from us. Perhaps he is shy as a person. However, it is so marked a difference that everyone feels strange, particularly Aftab who spoke out volubly about the negative effects of the change in Chairmanship. During the review meeting itself (all gas and pious intentions), one of the

---

[5] Chief Martial Law Administrator.

engineers – Masud Anwar –pointedly reminded that Chairman that the Ministry had taken 11 months to process NFC's promotion cases.'

Whenever I visited these plants, especially those I had been involved in from inception, from grass roots, I used to feel quite awe-struck by their huge structures. Back at head office, one could talk blithely about so many crores of rupees or about 10,000 tons of steel, but it was only when one saw on site the amount of cement poured into the foundations or the quantity of steel used to reinforce the structures or the tons of equipment being installed that the physical enormity of these projects hit one. And one felt proud to be associated with such gigantic undertakings – and all in the public sector.

The New Year 1978 began in the NFC with the announcement by Riyaz Bokhari that the Martial Law Authorities would be conducting an investigation into the NFC companies. "To be forewarned is to be unarmed?"I asked him.

Zia's regime, after having ravaged the political sector, now wanted to put its imprint on the public sector. It also began pinching the pockets of the public. A mini-budget raised taxes and reduced duties on bicycles. One NFC driver commented laconically: "I have told everyone to ride cycles and to go hungry."

Zia's press conference on 2 Jan demolished what little credibility he may have had. Malcolm Muggeridge's remark about Great Britain came to mind: 'Any nation that does not know from whence it came, or the direction in which it is headed can hardly be said to have lost its way.'

The reaction by the public was swift. The following day protesting workers at the Colony Textile Mills at Multan were fired upon. Five persons died. Five became fifteen, then seventeen, officially. The informal toll became 69, with 15 missing, some thrust according to one eye-witness down the drains.

A week later I happened to go to Islamabad to give Aftab Ahmad Khan (the voluble Secretary Economic Affairs Division) a copy of PP & SP. Bureaucrats postured about being well-read. He certainly remembered what he read and would spout a quotation at the appropriate moment. As I sat opposite him, I noticed that his desk was as empty as Pakistan's state coffers. He seemed very impressed by the book. He leafed through it and then pushing back his chair, he lit a cigar, waved it in the air, and then asked me expansively:

"And how would you compare these artists with say Raphael or Michelangelo?"

We spoke later about the political scene. He expressed surprise at the pro-ZAB mood in the Punjab: "Despite everything they have heard against Bhutto in the court?"

"When the people have forgiven you seventeen, they are prepared to forgive him one murder."

The current problems, I told him, were not political but economic. "They stop at your desk."

"But how can you get people to tighten their belts?"

"Especially," I replied, "when they do not have trousers on."

I had time that evening to call on Ali Yahya in Harley Street, to enquire after General Yahya who had suffered a stroke a few days earlier. Ali could not have been more vitriolic against ZAB, expressing chagrin that his father's stroke had denied them the opportunity of wreaking revenge just when Bhutto was within reach.[6]

Ali took out from under Yahya Khan's bed the file YK kept on the correspondence that had passed with him as the trusted conduit between Chinese premier Zhou Enlai and Dr. Henry Kissinger. Ali would tease visitors with a peep into the file but never allow a copy to be made of it. He maintained that his father regarded this file as his 'insurance policy', although I could ever understand what protection he thought it could offer him. Before Ali could put it away, I removed a photostat (it was extra) of the 47th document – the handwritten letter of appreciation sent by Richard Nixon to Yahya Khan after Henry Kissinger's safe return from Beijing in July 1971.

Many years later, long after Yahya Khan's death, Ali gave me a photostat set of those papers. By that time, transcripts of the discussions between Zhou Enlai and Henry Kissinger had been released into the public domain by the National Security Archive in Washington. I used both the contents of Yahya's file and the declassified transcripts for my book *From a Head, Through a Head,*

---

[6] Yahya Khan obtained some satisfaction by filing a 57 page affidavit in the Lahore High Court in 1978, during Bhutto's trial. The text of the affidavit was released by the Government of Pakistan some twenty years after Yahya Khan's death. Meanwhile, Ali would give a copy to anyone who asked.

To a Head: The Secret Channel between the US and China through Pakistan, published in 2000.

Ali accompanied me to the CMH hospital nearby. General Yahya lay in bed, pinker than I expected but quite bloated. He had suffered partial paralysis on his left side and could speak haltingly. His hair had turned completely white and fell straight. He recognised me and extended his right hand in greeting. He gave mine a slight squeeze. There was not much to talk about – certainly not Mr. Bhutto – and so after a few minutes I took my leave. I never saw him again.

Appropriately perhaps, I had dinner that evening at the Chinese Embassy, my host being the Chinese Economic Counsellor Mr. Chang Feng-Yang. I had taken some of our NFC personally assigned to the Hazara Urea Project with me.

I ensured that our party arrived exactly on time. We were led into a large reception hall. Mr. Chang sat on side of the sofa, and I on the other. Our staff found chairs set against the walls. Everyone Chinese, including Mr. Chang, wore the same Mao-style uniform. The only distinction between those of the men and the women was that the collars of the ladies' blouses were trimmed with some decorative lace.

The conversation began with pleasantries about Sino-Pakistan friendship, the tangible symbols of co-operation between our two countries, the Urea project, and my health and his.

Meanwhile, an attendant brought a tray of drinks. I being the senior most from our side had first choice. I noticed every drink from whisky at one end to innocuous Fanta orange at the other. Whoever chose first did so from the widest range, and whoever was the lowest in the hierarchy had no choice: he had to take whatever was left.

I had brought with me some crates of mangoes from Multan.

"Ah!" my host said, through his interpreter. "I understand the best mangoes grown in Pakistan come from Multan."

"Your Excellency, I respectfully disagree," I countered. "The best mangoes in Pakistan are grown (pause, for effect) in your consulate in Karachi." I alluded of course to the small significant harvest of mangoes that had been grown in their consulate by the Chinese. Because of their novelty (everyone until then had assumed that mangoes could not be grown in Karachi's sea sandy soil), the first consignment had been sent to Chairman Mao Zedong in Beijing.

"Ah, of course," he agreed, and then after a few moment's concentration, his face lightened. Almost triumphantly, he exclaimed: "But they were grown...by a Pakistani gardener."

At that I gave up. I conceded defeat.

The meal consisted like most authentic Chinese meals of a seemingly inexhaustible series of dishes to excite both the eyes and the palate. It ended with a light soup. The Chinese prefer their soup last. They do not like to build on a lake. Satiated after such an epicurean feast, we staggered to our cars. I discovered later that our two drivers had not been fed. So much for Marxism Leninist socialism, I thought!

I postponed my return to Lahore so that I could meet Lt. Col. Siddiq Salik. We had met by chance outside Flashman's Hotel where I was staying. He asked me to call at PM's house. I did. It was as still as a mortuary. No-one checked my credentials. Everyone on duty including the military police behaved like automatons, saluting everyone who walked past. Now I could understand why Zia's troops could gain such easy access. They must have been like a knife slicing into rancid butter.

Salik appeared out of touch with what was happening in the country. While I sat with him, I heard say to a caller from POF Wah: "For the big man, I want something BIG!" and later, "The CMLA says that his *minimum* level is NATIONAL."

On my way out I noticed that almost seven months after the coup, the nameplate of Bhutto's aide Hamid Jalal still in place in PM's House, just as A.G.N. Kazi's hung untouched in the Ministry of Finance.

Babar Ali had been away for some months doing some consultancy for the International Finance Corporation in Washington D.C. He returned rejuvenated from one trip to West Africa, and of course wanted to relive vicariously the NFC days. He called over to meet him in his office in Packages Ltd. He enjoyed exchanging gossip. His latest morsel concerned General Habibullah Khan. According to him, insiders had told him that the General's name was mud in the IFC. He had set up a spinning unit at the exorbitant cost

of $40 million, out of which $2 million had gone overtly into his pocket for
'consultancy fees.' Babar wanted Aftab and me to leave the NFC and to join
him as members of a team to assist the Omanese in setting up a fertilizer plant
near Muscat. He called both of us together a few days later to repeat his offer.
I know that after SBA had made his pitch, neither Aftab nor I could see this
assignment as a career option.

One evening SBA phoned to say that he wanted to bring a friend over
for dinner. Despite the excellent food that Shahnaz prepared, the friend –
none other than the shipping magnate turned DAWN columnist Ardeshir
Cowasjee - remained silent, almost morose during the meal. After we had
eaten, we moved to the drawing room. SBA suggested that I show Ardeshir
my *PP & SP* book.

"I have already seen it," he said dismissively.

SBA tried to retrieve the evening by asking about our collection of
lithographs and maps.

I put before them a map of India by Sanson d'Abbeville, dated 1654.

"Where did you get this from?" he challenged me.

"I bought it in Paris."

"You couldn't have done! The only other version I have seen of this is
one my grandfather left me."

Once Ardeshir had thawed and reverted to his voluble self, the real
reason why he had come with SBA to see me became apparent. He wanted to
publish the court transcripts of Bhutto's ongoing trial and he wanted me to
edit them. Of course, Ardeshir being Ardeshir did not articulate his request.
He threw enough hints my way for me to glean his true intention.

At the NFC, senior executives began to resign. The first among them –
Asif Mohyuddin (FM at Pak-Arab Multan) – told Mr. Bokhari. He refused
to take notice of it until Asif had given it in writing and it arrived on his desk.

Pak-Arab continued to live hand to throat – its hand fastened on the
Government's throat. They asked for another Rs 12 crores to complete the
project. Awan sahib summoned me to Islamabad to explain its justification.
Funds being scarce, control was enforced NCCC allocations. In theory that

should have worked. However, I noted in my diary my frustration at the situation:

> 'The present position is ludicrous. No NCCC allocations have been made for the current half-year. Against NFC's entitlement of Rs 33 crores for 1977-78, only Rs 14 crores has been disbursed. Almost one-third of the current half-year has passed and there is still no sign of agreement on the NCCC between the Planning Division and the Ministry of Finance.'

After our meeting in his office, Mr. Awan surprised me by asking me to come to his house for a second discussion. With me went Ehsan ul Haq, the Joint Secretary.[7] The location of Awan sahib's house could not have been finer. His house lay on Margalla Road, at the very foothills of Margalla hills. He could have rented the property to an Embassy or NGO for a tidy sum but Government rules stipulated that any government servant with his own accommodation in a city of posting had to occupy it himself. Awan sahib lived in his own home and received 30% of his salary as House Rent Allowance. He felt he had to set an example, even if he suffered a substantial loss.

His single-storeyed house had a side entrance. He received Ehsan and myself and took us into the drawing room that opened into a garden. Beyond that was a view of Margalla hills. When our review of NFC's requirements ended, Awan sahib and I walked towards the door. Ehsan followed us, almost crawling with deference. I noticed a row of walking sticks. There must have been ten, if not a dozen, as many as there were corporations under his control.

"May I ask you a question, sir?"

Awan sahib stopped for a moment putting files into his briefcase.

"Which of these is the one you keep for the NFC?"

I could hear Ehsan gasp with trepidation.

"For that, Aijaz," Awan sahib said with a smile, "your punishment will be to accompany me on my walk."

During these months my literary activities continued in parallel to my official responsibilities at the NFC. My book pushed me one notch higher in

---

[7] It was rumoured within the Ministry that Ehsan, being inordinately suspicious of his wife, was in the habit of locking her up whenever he left for his office.

the estimation of my friends. Sehyr Saigol who had established an Art Centre up the road from us in Ghalib Road, in Gulberg, invited me to give a lecture on miniature painting. Giving any lecture makes me nervous. The one I gave on 4 January 1978 was no exception. I confided to my diary:

> 'The dreaded Art Centre lecture has me wound up in coils of anxiety. I had 80 slides made, put them in order, but continued to be terrified that I might 'dry' up mid-sentence. My first-night nerves kept my adrenalin flowing.
>
> At the Art Centre, people started arrived at 5.30 p.m. By 6.00 p.m., the limited space had been fully occupied. Sehyr and her staff took refuge in her office. Through the open door they asked me who everyone was. My friends proved extremely loyal. By the time I began, the room was packed. There was not a sound from anyone. After it was over, I am told that people had wanted me to continue. The anxiety had been worth it!'

At home, the two Ms were growing apace. More for their future than as an aide memoire for myself, on 23 January I wrote this lengthy assessment of them:

> 'My darlings M^1 and M^2 deserve a paragraph each. M^2 is extremely energetic and voluble, scattering love and Spoonerisms with abandon – 'joorab [sock]' becomes 'dulab', 'balloons' turn into 'laboons'. Her hair has sprung into coils and curls at the nape but lies flat on her forehead. No one is allowed to touch it, leave alone comb it.
>
> M^1 has grown into a lady – confident, opinionated and extremely gentle. She has become increasingly protective towards us, understanding intuitively the nuances of her relationship with us. She is attending the J & M Convent school. I leave her there in a flood of tears, but they last as long a summer shower. Once I hid behind a pillar and observed her: she found her friends and within seconds reverted to her happy self. Her teacher Miss Williams gives her a ridiculous amount of homework each day. It is as much of a strain on Momina as it on us. She bravely ploughs though it, to find the next day that the furrow has been filled again.'
>
> 'On 29 January, we gave a joint birthday for them. I had prepared various games – passing the parcel, musical chairs, and some unusual

ones like magic mats and passing an orange from chin to chin. Shahnaz and I participated in the games which made it all the more fun for the children. Two children at least I learned afterwards complained to their parents: "Why can't you be like Momina's and Mubarika's parents?"'

By 6 March, Bhutto's trial was nearing its conclusion. I recounted in my diary the options confronting General Zia:

'Considerable subterranean tension. The verdict on ZAB is awaited. Everyone believes it will be the death sentence, and many that the judgment has already been recorded exonerating him. Perhaps the popularity of this latter view has been instigated by the Govt./Army to count the flowers that are likely to bloom.

The options open presently are:
1. Sentence ZAB to life imprisonment. That would merely be prolonging their own agony, as such a solution could never be a final one. What the PNA Opposition wants is a permanent, irreversible one, with ZAB's blood on the Army's hands. The Army wants it too, but prefers to see the Judiciary's hands bloodied. The Judiciary may be blind but it is not deaf to persuasion from Zia.
2. Acquit him. Possible but unlikely. This sabre-toothed tiger has been caged too long. His fangs have grown and his claws itch. Releasing ZAB will be like him sending him, a frenzied lion into a den of vulnerable Daniels.
3. Sentence him to death, with the prospect of an appeal to the Supreme Court. ZAB has already ventilated his contempt for the present bench. He will hardly want to exhale any more fiery breath on a higher court. He will refuse to appeal and leave to the Army to carry out the court's orders – if it dares.

The *Financial Times* has already quoted Islamabad's view that CMLA stands for 'Cancel My Last Announcement.'

I feel that a sentence of death will be ZAB's only release order. The outside powers will ensure that. No comment has been made by anyone foreign leader yet. That in itself is ominous. If the Shah would like to see ZAB out of the way, that is reason enough for the Saudis to underwrite his life.

They cannot guarantee his behaviour now, any more than they could a year ago. It must be increasingly clear to them that it would be better for Pakistan to be governed by a Capone they now know that one they have always despised.

The PNA Opposition has displayed its inability to convince the public that it can be a viable government. To many, the spectacle of an Opposition being presented before the public in the daily news 'in batches' (as if they were some sort of vaccine) with which to inoculate any residual ZAB sympathizers.

The situation is like medieval Japan. It is an age of war-lords, each Martial Law Administrator reigning supreme in his province with only a nominal, superficial allegiance to the supreme war-lord who rules the capital Islamabad.

Moving in a separate vortex, the Opposition parties play musical chairs without being aware that the music in the background will never stop. They will be kept in motion. They may eye the chairs they want; they will not be able to occupy them.

Symptomatic outbursts are occurring across the country – a riot in Karachi after the kidnapping of a minor girl, a Shia-Sunni fracas in Hyderabad, labour trouble in Multan, tension in Faisalabad – unconnected incidents perhaps, yet each has in common dissatisfaction with the Army.

It is a year since the general elections that brought Armageddon down on ZAB's head. Have we really regressed that far so soon?'

I noted in my diary for the ensuing days that there had been firing outside the house of three of the judges trying the ZAB case: 'Either some trigger happy PPP party workers or an immature attempt to intimidate those judges.'

On 12 March, a fire broke out at the Karachi Port Trust yard, causing $4 million worth of damage. The fire started simultaneously in three separate places. On 13 March, I was woken by gun fire in Ghalib Road, followed by the sound of cars and jeeps speeding as if on a chase along our road. The next morning, there was no mention of this incident in newspapers, but the public needed to be told that 3 persons were to be shot in public, that Special Inspection Team had been appointed to examine the workings of the Public Sector, and that Messrs Shahid Hosain (MD, NAFDEC) and Aslam Azhar (GM, PTV) had been summarily dismissed.

I drove to the office early that morning and noticed that someone had scribbled on the wall of the Al Falah building facing the Provincial Martial Law Headquarters: "General Zia. Go Back!" The advice was wasted. Zia was in Islamabad, too far away to read such writing on the wall.

CHAPTER 16

DEATH SENTENCES

My diary entry for 18 March 1978 is in red ink – 'to mark a red letter day, and denoting the colour of the week.'

> 'At 1.15 p.m. we were told that the radio had announced the High Court verdict on ZAB's case. The verdict was unanimous. ZAB has been sentenced to death. He has been granted 7 days to appeal.
>
> "How many accused?" I asked Askari Hussain (Director, Public Relations, BIM).
>
> "Five, including Bhutto."
>
> "And how many judges?"
>
> "Five."
>
> "That makes ten in all who have been sentenced to death."

I happened to be in Mirpur Mathelo on that day. A review on Pak-Saudi had been organised on site to be taken by the new Minister of Production General Habibullah (my former employer at Ghandhara Diesels). After I heard that sentence had been passed, I realised that all the senior functionaries in the Ministry – Awan sahib, Habeeb Hussain, Chief Planning, Joint Secretary Operations – were in Mirpur Mathelo, effectively incommunicado. The General kept asking whether anyone had listened to the radio. Obviously he knew. So did the police. They could be seen patrolling the highway outside the factory gate. Possibly Awan sahib also knew. But every one of them continued with their knitting as if they could not hear the sound of the drop on the scaffold.

The review meeting itself had its own oddities. The room was packed with menials, each vying to catch the minister's eye. Bokhari blushing and then stammering before the steady, unconvinced gaze of the General; Habeeb Hussain (seated on the General's left) fawning on him with explanations of how diligent he has been in working on NFC/PSFL's behalf; Dr. Wahab (the new MD PSFL) puffing himself toad-like into an inflated likeness of a Chief Executive; Sherwani seeing through the charade yet enduring it with practiced diffidence; the General criticizing the CMLA by disclosing that conflicting decisions had been landing on his plate every day; and Mr. Awan, not dropping bricks but hurling stones at the Pathan Goliath at his side. Referring to the Hazara Phosphate project, Awan sahib explained: 'The Sarhad Development Authority's efforts in exploiting the rock phosphate reserves have been commendable, but insufficient. The root cause has been the attitude of the NWFP government who behave like a bunch of tribesmen.' I could hardly believe my ears. Awan sahib continued: "They must behave with greater maturity and not squeeze the lemon before it ripens.'

The General remained impassive, unaffected by Awan sahib's remarks. I immediately suspected that this David was provoking Goliath. It seemed inconceivable to me that Awan sahib who is normally so controlled and guarded in his remarks should be so publicly indiscreet, considering that the audience in the room consisted of junior engineers whose ears and tongues had not yet learned to coordinate. I retain a timeless image of the General seated at the head of the table making pithy, terse, witty remarks. One I remember is when he opened the meeting with the observation: "Now, gentlemen, I want you to behave less like bureaucrats and more like public servants. I don't expect you to wake up every morning, stretch three times, and then fart..."

That afternoon was spent in abject apprehension about the situation in Lahore. The radio almost boasted about the reasons why ZAB had been sentenced to death. The BBC changed its tune and became sympathetic towards the condemned underdog.

All of us had to rely upon the radio for our news. And yet, apart from the initial announcements, here was an ominous silence. 'A bad sign', I noted. 'Does the General intend to change his mind? His bark is worse that his bite (prominent teeth had become the butt of current jokes), but will he be bold enough to commit murder?'

Before leaving Mirpur Mathelo, I drove around the plant site, proud at the tremendous progress that had been made since my first visit to a windless desolate site in 1974. Many of the areas were very well-organised, such as the stores. Sad though to see almost the entire plant still lying in CKD condition, a Meccano set costing $ 50 million waiting to be constructed.

On 20th morning, as our train reached Kot Lakhpat station and went slowly past the LEFO factory, one could see all its labour standing upon the boundary walls and upon its roof, waving defiantly. The scene was repeated at nearby factories. The situation within the city was quiet. Police were obtrusively visible everywhere. I heard that three buses had been set ablaze near the old city.

Tension continued the next day as well. Everyone I met horrified at the cold-blooded ruthlessness of Zia and his regime to eliminate Bhutto. "I know he was a rascal," Principal Sister Berchmans admitted during our morning chat after I dropped Momina at J & M. "But he *was* our prime minister."

A young girl passed. She bobbed a 'Good morning' to the Principal.

"I wish they wouldn't send her."

"Why, is she infectious?"

"No. She is Ahmed Raza Kasuri's daughter." Kasuri was the man had lodged the damaging FIR against Mr. Bhutto, accusing him of murdering his father.

Reports reached me that Bhutto, once he had been sentenced, was being treated in every humiliating way as a condemned convict.[1] His clothes had been taken away from him and replaced with seamless garments; his bed replaced by an iron cot. No wonder he complained of insomnia.

The judges became fearful of their own lives. One of them in court dropped the gun he was carrying. He summoned a peon who then picked it up and placed it on the Bench.

---

[1] Some days later, rummaging in the Government Printing Office, I came across a Report of the Punjab Jails Enquiry Committee 1929. Opening it at random, I came across this revealing premonition of ZAB's present predicament: 'If a political worker has neither position nor education nor character and is a poor man he should be classed an ordinary prisoner though he had been convicted under Section 124-A. On the other hand, a rich man having no other disqualification to exclude him from special class should go in the special class in spite of the fact that his is guilty of murder.'

March 22 happened to be Momina's last day at school. We had to see someone in Bahawalpur Road and so we drove down Jail Road. Our driver Rafiq drew our attention to the scaffold being constructed high on the Camp Jail walls. The place was swarming with police and perhaps the most sickening element was the crowd converging on the site. I was haunted all afternoon by the image of that scaffold, and counted the minutes until 5.00 p.m., the time scheduled for the execution of three men condemned to death for the rape of a young girl, Pappoo.

'Now that the public has tired of public lashings, will they be fed public hangings? Is this the prelude for Bhutto's public assassination?' I asked my diary.

That evening it was announced that four of the five accused in the ZAB case had filed appeals to the Supreme Court. ZAB is waiting for his advocate Yahya Bakhtiar to return. 'Sad, sad day for Pakistan – or what is left of it,' I lamented in my diary, and ended the entry with a quote by Sir Walter Raleigh: 'The world itself is but a large prison, out of which some are led daily to execution.'

I attended a dinner that night at the Pakistan Administrative Staff College, given by the principal Masrur Hasan Khan (former CS Punjab). I had given lectures there on Personnel Management and Financial Accounting. Most of the other teachers and the Foreign Office trainees were present. For some reason, the Principal decided that we should play 20 questions. The first question – Mickey Mouse – was guessed by Mushahid Hussain Syed in five attempts. The second was Satyajit Ray. That took longer. But it was the third challenge which upset Shahnaz and me equally. The Principal asked the trainees to guess the name he circulated amongst us – Pappoo, the murdered girl. I was horrified at his selection. As each question was lobbed and each incorrect reply greeted with derision, I felt sicker and sicker. I hated myself for being too polite to leave in protest.

Dinner was announced immediately after this charade. A bureaucrat trainee came to me as we entered the dining room, and asked: "Would you like the see the television, sir? They are showing the hangings."

I did not need to. The Pakistan Day issue of The Pakistan Times carried on its front page an image of Quaid–e-Azam M.A Jinnah saluting the nation, and below him at his feet, a photograph of the bodies of the three murderers, their necks broken, hanging from the scaffold. The same page carried the news that Mrs. Nusrat Bhutto had visited Mr. Bhutto for the first time since his conviction, and that various Arab leaders – Hafez Assad of Syria, the Emir of Kuwait, the Emir of Bahrain, Sudanese president Jaffar Nimeri, and Egyptian president Anwar Sadat – had sent personal appeals to Ziaul Haq to exercise clemency.

Embedded in an article on '25 years of Pakistan' lay this caveat: Since political comment is banned, the writer has not gone beyond 1971.

I recorded in my diary General Zia's work schedule. I noted that on 26 March, he attended a Cricket Board meeting in the morning, Aitchison College prize-giving in the afternoon (at which he teasingly withheld the award from the young recipient, who looked as bewildered as the PNA Opposition at being denied their prize), and in the evening a Medical Association dinner.

A few days later, General Chishti merged from behind Zia's throne. He announced that he would discuss the formation of a National Government as the CMLA was 'too busy'. In the papers, I read that some of Zia's pressing engagements had been to attend a puppet show in Islamabad. He had been so impressed that he gave the organisers a grant. In Sindh, he gave a sum of Rs 10 lakhs to the already fattened custodians of the Shah Bhitai shrine, and then gave Rs 1,000 to a lady-official who declared that as non-one had molested her in the interior of Sindh, the situation there had to be 'calm and peaceful'.

In April, General Zia made a trip to Saudi Arabia. He took with him an entourage of 24, out of which 18 were members of his family. He returned from the tour he described as 'successful beyond expectations'. According to him, he did not discuss Bhutto's case with King Khaled: 'It was too minor a problem.' A wit from The Pakistan Times published his account of the Saudi visit on 21 April. His piece read:

> 'Love needs no interpreter for expression. You see it in each other's eyes." The Chief Martial Law Administrator, General Mohammad Zia-ul-Haq, on his return from Saudi Arabia last night, narrated to newsmen here this message of his chat with a Saudi dignitary whom he did not identify.
>
> He told the Saudi dignitary: "It's a pity that you can't make love through an interpreter (because) one cannot express (himself) fully."

The CMLA said that he had a very good interpreter in his Adviser Mustafa Gokal, who explained the point to the Saudi dignitary. The Saudi's reply was: "When making love, you don't need an interpreter...you see it in each other's eyes, and eyes say and speak, and that is a true reflection."

The Saudi dignitary, addressing General Zia, further observed: "I hope you see a lot of love in our eyes because I see a lot in yours."'

That, I supposed was, what John F. Kennedy meant (in a different, less romantic situation) as being 'eyeball to eyeball'.

Talks between Zia and the PNA continued well into April 1978. After some hesitation, the PNA agreed to form a National Government. The National Democratic Party[2] under Sherbaz Khan Mazari wanted to reserve the right to say 'No' when it had tired of saying 'Yes'; Asghar Khan almost missed the bus 'due to some misunderstanding'. Salmaan Taseer told me that he expected Asghar Khan to perform a hat-trick – after having ousted Ayub Khan and then Bhutto, his next victim would be General Zia.

By the end of May, Bhutto's case had moved to the Supreme Court. It has been said that a lawyer who conducts his own case has a fool for a client. Bhutto was a greater fool to allow a fellow lawyer like Yahya Bakhtiar to represent him. At the Supreme Court, Yahya Bakhtiar demanded that the approver Masood Mahmood's 'secret evidence' should be disclosed in court. The sealed envelope was opened and out popped the revelation that ZAB had ordered the murder not only of Ahmed Raza Kasuri but also those of his own PPP loyalists Mustafa Khar *and* Jam Sadiq Ali. 'Some envelopes are better left untouched,' I noted in my diary. 'Certainly, no whiskey bottle has been left untouched in the Punjab Club where every evening Bhutto's defence team pour themselves pegs instead of poring over precedents.'

Changes with the arrival of another General – this time General Habibullah – in the Ministry of Production prepared me for changes there. Sure enough, on 17 April, RHB gave me the news that Awan sahib had been removed as Secretary Production. Majid Mufti took over from him. The semi-somnolent but sharp Allauddin Ahmed has been promoted to become Secretary Industries, in place of N.N.A. Qureshi, who having reached the age

---

[2] A resurrection of the National Awami Party (Wali Group).

of 60 has been declared obsolete.

Ghafoor Mirza (DS, MoP), confirmed this news. He told me Mr. Awan had handed over charge and been made OSD - Officer on Special Duty, a euphemism within the service for temporary redundancy.

Mr. Awan's departure, sad though it was for me personally (he had been extremely supportive ever since our first meeting in 1974), proved fortuitous for me career-wise. Some days earlier, Awan sahib during one our meetings in Islamabad, had asked me whether I had any permanent connections with Lahore. "There is a possibility of a change," he said, "an improvement, and I wanted to put your name up for it." He didn't elaborate, beyond a cryptic, "You will be the first to know." Ten days later, Ghafoor Mirza called to say that I was being tipped for the post of Director Finance of either PIDC or Pakistan Steel Mills. He described the manner in which my name came up during the selection process. I wrote in my dairy:

> 'He told me that he happened to be sitting in Awan sahib's room with Habeeb Husain (there as no one else) when HH passed a list of CAs working in the BIM sector to Awan sahib.
>
> "Who do you think is the brightest?" Awan sahib asked HH.
>
> "Oh! Aijazuddin, without a doubt!" GM claims to have replied.
>
> "I told you so," Awan sahib told HH.'

I heard nothing more about it, and then Awan sahib left the Ministry. His high opinion of me was interred with him.

Such compliments were flattering but they did not pay the bills. I confided to my diary, that after four years in the NFC:

> 'My basic salary is Rs 4,500 per month.[3] The increment I received for 1977 was wiped out by the recent professional tax. I cannot prevent the Telephone Department from diverting my number to some-one else's instrument so that a stranger came make free calls at my expense. I cannot prevent cars on two successive days from ramming into mine at the J & M Convent during the early morning crush. I meet the overflow of our expenditure from the money I receive from the sale of

---

[3] As I had been provided accommodation and a car with a driver, these were non-cash benefits. There was a subsidy for utilities such as electricity and telephones, but these were subject to a limit.

PP & SP. After settling with OUP, I should have Rs 23,290 and 116 unsold copies left. Apart from this overdue return on the efforts of my youth, I have no other sources of income, and no prospects ahead either.' The silver lining came with the news from New Delhi that the copies OUP had ordered of *PP & SP* had been sold out at the Delhi Book Fair on the first day.

The prospects of the public sector were no brighter. There were rumours of mergers between corporations, and of taken-over industries being handed back to their previous owners. Nowshera Engineering had already been returned. A decision was taken to hand LEFO back with the authority to retrench half its work force. The Chief Secretary heard of this and warned the CMLA that such an action would lead to 'a Law & Order situation.' I presume he meant 'Lawlessness & Disorder'. General Habibullah, now in position to rectify Bhutto's vindictive wrongs, remained keen on having his beloved Ghandhara Industries restored to him. Cannily, he waited until precedents had been established before proffering his own claim. 'Exactly what the industrial policy is, no one knows. The wind has been taken out the public sector. The few gusts that blow are not enough to propel it forward. Meanwhile professionals like me are left to cope, like mahouts astride a dead elephant, with its decomposing carcass.'

Rumours multiplied every day, fuelled by changes such as the suspension of Mr. Mazhar Ali[4] as Chairman State Cement Corporation of Pakistan in June and then a month later the resignation of Mr. Osman Ali from the Governorship of the State Bank of Pakistan. He was replaced by Mr. A.G.N. Kazi who had been in turn replaced as Secretary General Finance by Ghulam Ishaq Khan, then Governor State Bank. I heard from RHB that the Ministry of Production was itself likely to be wound up. The announcement was expected in the Budget speech. To give the impression that Zia's government decided on crucial issues after obtaining a broad consensus, someone came up with the idea that he should invite sixty-six people to Islamabad for a pre-Budget discussion. The attendees were broken into four sub-groups with the avowed aim of including the recommendations of each in

---

[4] Mr. Mazhar Ali had been Joint Secretary Finance before being selected by Dr. Mubashir Hasan, ZAB's Finance Minister.

the Budget. 'Ridiculous!' I noted. 'As if anything anyone says will alter or improve a Budget that is to be presented in 5 days.'

'The Government is in as topsy-turvy a state as our domestic situation is.[5] The Budget is a fiasco, with price increases which will hit the common man in common places. Aftab Ahmad Khan as Secretary Finance makes the classic evasion when, on being asked about the Budget he had just presented, replied glibly: "Oh, it is not my Budget. It is the Government's."

Zia has tried to teach the PNA a lesson by substituting his Council Advisors by a Council of Ministers, including such luminaries as Ch. Zahur Elahi as Labour Minister and Javed Hashmi (the perennial student leader) as Minister of State for Youth Affairs. Poor Zia. He is extremely sincere but unlike Ayub Khan, he has no potential for political maturity. He takes simple, childish steps and falls too often to be endearing anymore.

The case against ZAB is an example. I have heard from RHB (who happens to be working with the Chief Justice on the National Pay Commission) that there is every possibility that the Supreme Court may refer the case back to the Lahore High Court. This would in itself be an admission of the superficiality of the first trial. If this were to happen, the CJ fears that the Army would by-pass the judiciary altogether, particularly after cases have been admitted recently in High Courts against military personnel acting under Martial Law.'

General Habibullah as Minister continued to dominate if not regulate his ministry. He has had his revenge on Bhutto. Now he wanted to enjoy being a cat amongst the bureaucratic pigeons. Why else should he, in a high level meeting attended by the Secretary Additional Secretary Finance Asad Ahmed, have said bluntly: "Gentlemen, we have to clear this *lidh* (horse manure) left behind by the previous government."

"How do I record this in the minutes?" a disconcerted Deputy Secretary asked me in a low whisper.

"Write: The organic fertiliser production of the previous regime..."

---

[5] Our maid had gone on holiday and the new cook was learning at our expense. Shahnaz was quite literally left holding our two babies.

I was reminded of an occasion when SBA received a letter addressed to the Chairman, *Natural* Fertiliser Corporation of Pakistan. SBA stormed into my room with it. "You write and tell them," he exploded, "that we are the *National* Fertiliser Corporation of Pakistan."

"Just be grateful," I consoled him. "He could have used another four letter word for Urea."

Now that I think about it, I am surprised that whereas we were meticulous in holding board meetings of our subsidiaries after every quarter, the NFC as a body corporate had not held its own since its incorporation in 1974. Until then, the review meetings with the Ministry of Production were deemed enough as a quasi-corporate control mechanism. A Board of Directors had been constituted and its five directors[6] met for the first time on 16 May. Habeeb sahib turned quisling: "You see, Awan sahib never wanted the Corporation Boards to function as such.'

Interference by the military increased and soon political recommendations replaced those from politicians. One case I recall vividly. The NFC Karachi office rang me the news that a Brigadier had been appointed there. I checked with Islamabad. It transpired that the ML authorities had assumed that the NFC had a factory at Karachi and therefore must need a retired Brigadier.

Syed Babar Ali on his trips home would call and ask either Aftab or myself or both to come over for a chat. He felt, that after having had a book published by Sotheby Parke Bernet, I stood qualified to write one on Aitchison College, his alma mater and mine. I deflected his proposal with a question: "Why do you want a book on a stud farm that produces only mules?"[7]

A more serious proposal he made addressed primarily to Aftab consisted of his intention to set up a milk processing plant. On one of his trips to India, he had seen and been deeply impressed by the Milk Cooperative Scheme in Gujarat. He knew that we were one of the largest producers of milk in the world, and yet treated it as a cottage industry. This idea of his was to become Milk-Pak Limited and later after Nestlé bought into it, as Nestlé Milkpak.

---

[6] RHB as Chairman, the ubiquitous Habeeb Hussain, Manzoor Ahmed (Additional Secretary Agriculture), Abdul Jabbar (Member Finance) and Mahmood Ahmed, Chairman FCCL.
[7] The arrogance of youth! I did finally write the Centenary volume of Aitchison College's history in 1986 and later as its Principal wrote another to commemorate its 125th anniversary in 2011.

My interest in art, now given a boost by the publication of one book and with another in the offing, thrust me into prominence. I was invited to give a lecture at the National Museum of Pakistan in Karachi and (grudgingly) by the Lahore Museum. The one at the Lahore Museum included in its audience its former Director Malik Shams. He had left under the cloud of a suspicion that miniatures had been pilfered by him. That charge was never proven, nor one of him buying personally antiques offered to the Museum and then trading in them. Malik felt that the main purpose of my catalogue had been consummated, that the inventory of the LM collection was intact and that he had not misappropriated any miniatures.

During this early part of 1978, my association with the Sikhs deepened. In May, Bill caught me off guard by telling me that he had bought in auction on my behalf[8] a pencil drawing of Rani Jindan by George Richmond, done in 1863. When I saw a photograph of the sketch I realised that it must be in fact the preparatory drawing for the study in oils in the Princess Bamba collection which I had mistaken to be work of August Schoefft. This new attribution came too late for inclusion in my book but we were able to clip in the drawing.[9]

I was able to show this sketch to a Sikh *jatha* that called on me at the NFC office. They were understandably objects of curiosity to the junior staff, many of whom had never seen live Sikhs before.

Our social circle in Lahore remained constricted to family and close friends. Occasionally we would be invited to something special like a dance performance (*mujra* would be too strong a word) given by the then rage of Lahore, Saeena Chowdhry. Young, talented and unselfconsciously nubile, she had been invited to perform by Hafeezullah Hassan, the film producer.[10] He had organised it not at his own home but at Naseem and Sehyr Saigol's sumptuous and centrally air-conditioned home in GOR I. "These singers refuse to sing in rooms that have wall-air conditioners," he explained.

Saeena – all too aware of her appeal – looked disappointed at the weak turnout. Her audience comprised Naseem's in-laws and a motley collection of noisy friends. Hafeez took credit for being able to bring Saeean at the old rate ('Because of her high regard for me!' HH boasted), rather than the Rs 15,000

---

[8] Bill paid for it out of the royalties of *PP&SP*, which he received on my behalf.
[9] See my *Sikh Portraits by European Artists* (1979), page 65 for the drawing and Colour Plate V for the sketch in oils.
[10] He also happened to be the uncle of my sister-in-law Sumayra.

she normally commands per performance. Her singing was desultory. She was asked to dance and went through gyrations that she thought would arouse the elders lolling in front of her. I noticed the classical singer Salamat Ali sitting amongst them. She paid him homage repeatedly as her *ustad*. "She has learned everything she knows from him," Naseem felt bound to explain, adding with a leer: "And I mean *everything*."

My reading at the time reflected my deepening interest in India. I devoured Paul Theroux's *The Great Indian Railway Bazaar*, Mark Bourke-White's recollections (I noted Gandhi merited three pages, Jinnah only one), Ved Mehta's irreverent de-frocking (does one defrock a *dhoti?*) of Gandhi in his brilliant exposé *Mahatma Gandhi and his Apostles* (1977).

On 28 July, I recounted in my diary 'the turmoil of trying to arrange a trip to India':

'First of all, it was not clear whether the UNDP had accepted my nomination to attend the seminar organised by the Bureau of Public Enterprises at Hyderabad (Andhra Pradesh). From some accounts, it appears that every *mohajir* Hyderabadi in government service is jockeying to have his name included. Eventually the permission came through. The next hurdle was to obtain an endorsement on my passport for India. The Lahore Passport office where I applied for three of us – Shahnaz, her sister Lalarukh and myself – needed to refer our cases to Islamabad. I flew there in pursuit, got the Joint Secretary concerned to clear it, and was about to have the permission typed when the clerk asked me my father's name. 'Waheeduddin'. That did it. I knew I would be hoisted on Ayaz's poniard. The Section Officer checked the 'Wanted' list in his files. He found Ayaz's name on the Exit Control List. He refused to issue the permission until I obtained a clearance from the Sindh government. That took a few more days. On 26th I presented myself again at Islamabad and the obtained the vital endorsement, thanks to the verbal orders of the helpful JS. From there I went to the Indian High Commission. Mr. Dutt (the Visa officer) was prepared to issue a visa to me but baulked at giving one to Shahnaz and Lalarukh. The timely production of my *PP & SP* did the trick. Visas were stamped and we were ready to go.

It would be my first trip to India post-1947. I was all too aware of the simmering hostility between our two countries, expressed at various levels and in many petty ways. One example appeared in the newspapers a few days prior to my departure. Pakistan had asked the World Bank for its assistance to procure a million tonnes of wheat from India. 'India would prefer Pakistan making a direct approach for the wheat as it would contribute to further improvement in relations between the two countries.' India wanted a genuflection.

Despite the diplomatic and military tension with India, I had read so much about it, learned about it, written about its culture, history and painting, that I felt I knew it like the back of my hand, at least better than the Army's fist.

CHAPTER 17

IN INDIA – HYDERABAD

Flight PK 276 took no longer to reach Mumbai (then Bombay) from Karachi than a journey to Lahore would have done. Within an hour and a half, we were alerted by the announcement that we would soon be landing at our destination. I looked out of the window. Grey clouds obliterated the sky. Below I could see blocks of flats and between them, open areas of sodden earth. The rain had cleared by the time we disembarked.

Pakistani passengers were shepherded towards a separate counter. The eager ones presented their passports there while the more experienced knew that one needed to fill out visa immigration forms in triplicate, using carbon paper. When one set had been processed, the carbons were removed and handed over to another passenger. It was like playing a slow tedious game of tag.

I had been granted a visa for three cities – Bombay, Hyderabad and Delhi. In those days, almost all Indian visas involved police reporting. That required every Pakistani traveller to register at a special office of the Police department in person within 24 hours of arrival in a city, and again within 24 hours before departure. It was tedious but unavoidable. Delays in reporting were referred to the Ministry of Interior in New Delhi. They were regarded as serious infractions tantamount to illegal stay in India.

My companion Abdul Wahab (a GM in PIDC and a Hyderabadi by birth) and I caught a taxi to the PIEM Hotel where our bookings had been made. The long journey into Bombay city was unforgettable. I had seen slums in Karachi often on the doorstep of posh localities but compared to what I saw from the taxi window, our shanties had a refined poverty about them. Bombay's slums reflected degradation not only of the body but of the spirit. Pavements were patterned with coils of excreta, neatly spaced, feet apart as though habit had created its own measure. One image remains with me still – of some young men showering under a leaking sewage pipeline.

The hotel in Cuffe Parade I noted stood within walking distance of 25 Cuffe Parade - the house of the doyen of Indian art and literature, Mulk Raj Anand. Immediately after dinner, I left Wahab at the hotel and traced Mulk's house. Ever since I discovered that his elder brother Hans Raj had been a drinking companion of my father in pre-1947 New Delhi, I referred to him in our correspondence as Uncle Mulk.

I am not sure what I expected Mulk's house to be. Large, perhaps. Well-decorated? Elegant? Certainly. After all, he had been the editor of *Marg* magazine since 1946, bringing out an issue every quarter devoted to every aspect of Indian culture - painting, music, sculpture, textiles, handicrafts, folk art. Yet, when I reached his home and read the address, I was caught off-guard. The house - a property belonging to the Parsi Taraporevala family - had clearly seen better days. Its once elegant façade, the generous porch, and the spacious front verandah echoed a once gracious occupancy. Now, it appeared dank, unlit, run-down.

Mulk and his wife Shirin lived in room at the back of the house. He welcomed me warmly and made me sit opposite him. Above him stretched an awning of thick plastic that sagged with the afternoon's rain. From a kitchen somewhere inside floated the unmistakable odour of spiced fish being fried.

He ignored that crass reality, as he did his run-down surroundings. Instead he talked about his efforts to establish *Marg*, his keenness to visit his birth-city of Peshawar[1] (the actor Dilip Kumar neé Yusuf Khan had also been born there), and of his desire to promote friendly relations between his country and mine. He wanted to donate a complete set of *Marg* issues to any library in Pakistan, if only he could get them past the Customs on both sides. We arranged to meet at the *Marg* offices in the city the next morning before my flight for Hyderabad.

---

[1] I discovered many years after his death that his acute social sensitivity had been activated by an incident during his childhood in Peshawar, when his aunt – at being ostracized by her community for eating with a Muslim – had committed suicide.

The offices were on the third floor of the Army & Navy Building in up-market Kala Ghora district. There, Mulk introduced me to his colleague and companion Dolly Sahiar and some of the staff who helped him produce the finest art journal of its kind. It had siblings – *Rupam, Roopa Lekha*, and *Lalit Kala* – but none matched the innovative, fertile imaginativeness that went into the content and the layout of each *Marg* issue. They became works of art in themselves, collector's items.

The flight from Mumbai to Hyderabad appeared to be a modern extension of the trade route across the Arabian Sea, continued further inland. The flight was crowded with Gulf Arabs in their white *dish-dashes* and coloured *burnooses*, held in place by what a wit had described as a 'black fan-belt.' Each Arab had with him one obviously South Indian Muslim wife, a number of chattering children, and unmanageable hand luggage.

What intrigued me was that each wife wore as much gold as she could carry - bangles and bracelets up to her elbows, festoons of necklaces from her neck to her waist, as many earrings as she could fit into her flexible ear-lobes, and decimals of numerous rings and toe-rings. I was told that gold worn was exempt from duty. That explained the surfeit.

Wahab and I were greeted by our hosts from the local Institute of Public Enterprise, Hyderabad, and taken to the Hotel Deccan Continental in Minister Road.

The programme we had manoeuvred to attend had been organised by the Institute in collaboration with the Bureau of Public Enterprises in New Delhi, under the aegis of the United Nations Asian and Pacific Development Administration Centre (PDAC) located in Kuala Lumpur. It was this affiliation with the UN that qualified Wahab and I to be participants.

The programme given to us the next morning on registration revealed that the next eight days would consist of at least three lectures each day by specialists, academics and practitioners of public sector administration. Two visits were also planned – to the Electronics Corporation of India and to the Hindustan Tools Factory outside Hyderabad.

For the inaugural ceremony, the sponsors had invited Mrs. Sharda Mukherjee, then Governor Andhra Pradesh.[2] She arrived wearing a starched

---

[2] Mrs. Mukherjee was a Maharashtrian and an instance of the commendable aspect of Indian

cotton sari, her white hair framing her face in trained curls. Her mien reminded me of Mrs. Vijayalakshmi Pandit (Nehru's favourite sister). I discovered the connection was more than superficial. Mrs. Mukherjee's uncle was married to Mrs. Vijayalakshmi Pandit.

Following her into the auditorium where all of us participants were assembled was Mr. Prahlad K. Basu, a senior Indian civil servant seconded to PDAC. In time, he would have a distinguished career, rising to become Minister of State, Government of India, & Chairman, Board for Reconstruction of Public Sector Enterprises. Even in those early days, his lips were puckered in the right direction.

That night, the collector Jagdish Mittal whom I had met at the Los Angeles Colloquium, took me home for dinner with his wife Kamla. Jagdish's modest suburban house gave no clue to the treasures of miniatures that he had collected over the years. Rather like the American Parsi dealer Nasli Heeramaneck who built up his collection of Indian art by buying five, selling four and keeping one, Jagdish was known to trade in paintings. He had to do it cautiously though.

The Indian Antiquities and Art Treasures Act of 1972 had unnerved collectors like Jagdish. They were required now to have anything in their possession that was 'antique' (i.e. more than 100 years old) to be documented, photographed and notified to the Government. The targets of this legislation were the former rulers of India's numerous princely states. They had been deprived of their kingdoms by Nehru in 1947 and of their privy purses by his daughter Indira Gandhi in 1971. They retained though heirlooms and treasures they had inherited. The Nizam of Hyderabad's fabulous collection of jewels was an obvious example. In casting its net as wide as possible, the Government hoped to catch whales as well as winnows like Jagdish. Inevitably, such legislation has the opposite effect. Many treasures went underground or abroad. Collectors declared only those objects they could afford to lose. Many were advised to create trusts to which they donated their collections.

The sessions at the IPE took up most of the day. Each lecture fell within the framework of the Aide Memoire issued to us participants. Its preamble read:

---

policy, which dictated that persons from the same state could not be appointed as governors of that state.

Public Enterprises are operating at the commanding heights of the economy of many countries in the Asian and Pacific region. While some of these enterprises have proved to be financial successes, others are reporting losses or meagre returns year after year. One of the main reasons for their poor performance happens to be the lack of professionalism in the management of those enterprises, especially in the area of finance. The Governments of the region are therefore reinforcing their efforts to improve the quality of financial management in their public enterprises with a view to enabling them to generate a reasonable surplus.

Nehru's neo-socialist vision of the state operating at 'commanding heights', controlling and influencing the national economy, had been borrowed by Mr. Bhutto. Nehru's foresaw that the scale and cost at which Indian industrialisation would have to take place could be afforded only by the state. Private enterprise did not have pockets deep enough to support such a mass industrialisation. By comparison, Mr. Bhutto's nationalisation had a more vengeful underside. He wanted to rob rich Peters by pretending that it was to benefit poor Pauls.

In both cases, though, regardless of the way the assets were created or acquired, the problems of day-to-day management remained. The topics of the various sessions covered the gamut of public sector administration – Financial and Capital Structure Planning, Working Capital management, Transfer pricing, Productivity and Efficiency, Measures for improving performance, its corollary Performance Audit, and of course Internal Audit.

Each speaker brought something to the table. The one whose talk interested me the most (I took copious notes during his presentation) was Mr. Bazle Karim, Additional Secretary/ Director-General, Bureau of Public Enterprises. It was certainly the most cogent and informative. He began with genesis – the Industrial Policy Resolutions of 1948 and 1956, and in 1964 the Committee for Public Undertakings, the Indian equivalent of the U.K. Select Committee on Nationalised Industries. He spoke of its composition – 22 members drawn from the Lok Sabha and 4 from the Rajya Sabha – and the advantage this offered the management of public enterprises to present their cases before the legislators directly rather than through the controlling ministry. This committee had issued over 200 reports – on materials, financial and labour management. Audits were conducted not by the Auditor-General but by commercial auditing firms. He mentioned that the BPE measured performance using 20 financial ratios, and that this scrutiny covered efficiency of performance and proprietary audits to assess whether any expenditure had been necessary and economically beneficent. On the basis of all these evaluations, the Committee prepared annual reports for submission to Parliament.

Participants I noticed were expected to ask judicious questions but there appeared to be little encouragement for an exchange of comparative experience. The tone adopted by the Indian speakers bordered on condescension. It was almost as if India did not need to be taught about public sector management, and certainly not by Pakistan. Even its mistakes were better than ours. During one particular session, I challenged as discreetly as I could this worldly-wise big brother attitude. I offered to speak about our own experience in Pakistan, at which Basu could hardly control his sneer. "Yes, let's hear what Mr. Aijazuddin has to say about Pakistan's attempts at nationalisation."

I did not let him daunt me. As Eleanor Roosevelt once said, 'No-one can make you feel inferior without your consent.' I spoke of our own experience, the role of the Board of Industrial Management and its supersession by the Ministry of Production.

Basu remained sceptical of my intelligence until the evening of my lecture on Pahari painting. Karl Khandalavala had organised that I should speak at the Indian Administrative Staff College, once the palatial home of Princess Durru Shehvar.[3] Karl had been in New Delhi and very obligingly he flew to Hyderabad to preside at my lecture. At the end of the lecture, Basu came up to me, eyes aglow with wonder. Dr. Johnson's famous aphorism about women preachers came to mind. Basu seemed surprised not at how much I knew about Pahari painting but that as a Pakistani, I should know anything at all.

After the crowd had thinned following the lecture a grey haired gentleman of obvious and deliberate refinement walked up to me. He introduced himself as Zaheer Ahmed, former Indian Ambassador to Saudi Arabia and the managing trustee of the Mukarram Jah Trust for Education and Learning.[4]

---

[3] Princess Durru Shehvar, the daughter of the last Caliph of Turkey Abdul Majid, was married in 1931 to Prince Azam Jah (1907–1970), the eldest son and heir of the last Nizam of Hyderabad Osman Ali Khan, Asif Jah VII.

[4] For an account of its inauguration by Prince Mukarram Jah in December 1971, see John

"I would like you to see the paintings in the *Purani Haveli*. Perhaps you could identify some of them. Where are you staying?"

I told him.

"I will pick you up from your hotel at 5.00 p.m. tomorrow."

The next evening, a powder blue Mercedes containing Mr. Zaheer Ahmed drove up to the hotel. Shahnaz, Lalarukh and I joined him in it.

Shahnaz and Lalarukh had travelled to Hyderabad, arriving a day after me. Lala, we discovered, had taken extraordinary precautions to hide her foreign currency from the Indian Customs authorities. She rolled her precious dollar notes, put them into layers of polythene wrapping, and then inserted them into a bottle of shampoo. When she unpacked them, she discovered that the shampoo had permeated through the notes. Without telling anyone, Lala washed her currency and then placed the notes under her pillow to dry. The next evening, when she returned to the hotel, the manager handed her the notes which the room boy had found. It took Lala some time to live down jokes about her attempt at money laundering.

As we drove with Mr. Zaheer Ahmed, he talked about his experiences in Saudi Arabia and more recently as the Nizam's trustee. When his car stopped at a traffic light, it was besieged by some beggars. Without looking at them, he said: "I have told these Muslims so many times not to beg. If they cannot afford education, let them develop some skills." And then to show us that he had taken some practical steps to give form to his advice, as we drove into the elongated driveway of the 19th century *Purani Haveli* (one of the Nizam's numerous lesser palaces), he pointed out the lathes and turning machines installed under his instructions in each of the porticos that once housed the Nizam's horses.

"I have these out here so that young Muslim boys should become trained in some sort of skill."

"Do you receive any support from the Andhra Pradesh government?"

"Quite the reverse. I am constantly questioned why I have set up such facilities only for Muslims. I tell them that this is for anyone who belongs to the backward and under-privileged classes. It just so happens that here in

Zubrzycki, *The Last Nizam: An Indian Prince in the Australian Outback* (Australia, 2006), p. 248.

Hyderabad, Muslims are the ones who are the most under-privileged."

Zaheer Ahmed escorted us though the interior of the *Purani Haveli*, once the official residence of the Nizam. We strolled through the musty, dusty rooms, with their once rich now faded curtains and expensive upholstery now frayed and threadbare, the silver in the large mirrors oxidising into blackness. The oil paintings (mainly European copies) were nothing to write to report to the authorities about. They may have been old, a few of them even antique, but none of them were of any appreciable value or significance.

He walked us through *Ayina Khana* (Mirror House) and the *Chini Khana* (Chinese House), and finally along the extended length of the Nizam's dressing chamber — two storeys of wooden cupboards – said to be the longest wardrobe in the world.

At the end of the tour, he told us that his wife was expecting us for tea. We drove up to a promontory in the exclusive Banjara Hills. We entered the house, were received by Mrs. Zaheer Ahmed – a charming lady with discreet manners - and then taken into the library that had on one side a view across the city towards the Hussain sagar lake.

On a shelf I noticed a framed studio photograph of a young woman.

"Who is this?" I asked Zaheer sahib.

"She is my wife's grand-daughter. Why?"

"She happens to be my sister-in-law. My elder brother Ayaz's wife."

This link proved to be one of the many coincidences I encountered and continued to experience on this and many future trips to India.

One of the excursions organised by our hosts - – a trip to Nagarjuna sagar dam - took up the whole of a Sunday. The dam (the largest masonry dam in the world) spanned the Krishna river. It also spanned two generation of prime ministers - Pandit Nehru laid its foundation stone in 1955 and his daughter Mrs. Indira Gandhi commissioned it twelve years later in 1967.

From its 400 foot height, I could see the vastness of the Deccan plateau and through it sense the geophysical vastness of India. It is one thing to see it splayed on a map, and quite another to look and know that the horizon is not the limit. I got the same feeling standing on the tip of the Ngorongoro crater in Tanzania. Each in its own way made me aware that I was standing not in a country but in a continent.

We were reminded of the dam and its vulnerabilities when we saw Raj Kapoor's latest release *Satyam Shivam Sundaram*. The story was as weak as the dam in it, which broke under the first pressure of incessant monsoon rains. The purpose of the film was to introduce RK's latest find — the voluptuous Zeenat Aman. In it, Ms Aman has a disfigured face so hideous that even she cannot bear to see her reflection in a mirror. Her voice though is as sweet as Lata Mangeshkar's (in fact it was Lata's). A near-sighted engineer (Shashi Kapoor) hears her sing, falls madly in love with her, marries her without once wanting to see the rest of her face.

Buying tickets for the film made me aware of the cultural and linguistic divide between us Pakistani and Indians. I asked the counter teller what was the price of a ticket. He pointed to the inscriptions scrawled above his grilled window. I told him I could not read it.

"Wah, sahib," he exclaimed. "*Hindi bol layte ho magar parhte nahin.* [You speak Hindi but cannot read it.]

"No," I replied. "I am speaking to you in Urdu. You call it Hindi."

During that week, the BPE people arranged a visit to Golconda Fort (Aurangzeb's lofty Waterloo). Looking up at it, I could understand how if adequately provisioned its occupants could withstand a siege of eight long, sodden months. It fell as most of the Deccani forts did during Aurangzeb's final campaign not by military strategy but by a judicious bribe.

We were taken also to see the Salar Jung Museum about which I had heard so much. The museum housed what remained of the countless objêts d'art collected by Nawab Mir Yusuf Ali Khan Salar Jung III (1889–1949), the former Prime Minister of the seventh Nizam of Hyderabad. We were told that he had spent thirty-five years assembling the collection. The guide was very keen that we should admire the marble statue of the *Veiled Rebecca* by G.B. Benzoni, sculpted in 1876, and a good (or bad example) of Victorian melodramatic art.

I went back to the Salar Jung Museum later during the week, the second time to give a lecture (again organised by the ever-considerate Karl) on the Guler *Devi Mahatmya* series. It was a reprise of the one I gave at the Los Angeles Colloquium in 1977, which Karl had attended.

Dr. M.L. Nigham, the Museum's director, introduced me, after which I gave my slide lecture. I thought I had make it clear that the original set of the *Devi Mahatmya* contained 57 folios, which had been dispersed. The slides I intended to show were those in the Lahore Museum. I would make the connections between the pictures and the poem with a linking narrative.

My lecture took about 40 minutes, after which the chairperson (a prominent Hyderabadi lawyer with a prominent *tilak*) rose to express what I assumed would be the customary thanks. Instead, he took a deep breath and opened with the dismissive remark: "One really cannot expect someone like Mr. Aijazuddin [i.e. a Muslim] to understand the significance that the *Devi Mahatmya* has in our lives. I read it reverently every day. In fact, I read it this very afternoon before I came to this lecture. The *Devi Mahatmya* is a message of universal relevance to all of mankind. I cannot exhort you young Indians in the audience strongly enough. Read the *Devi Mahatmya*. Understand its message. Live your life according to its principles. I do, and so should you."

His oration lasted longer than this quotation. I have paraphrased it so that my blood does not boil at having to repeat it.

I waited until he had finished. I stood up and asking Dr. Nigham's permission, I said that I will take the unusual step of responding to a vote of thanks that was both unexpected and unconventional. I explained again to the audience why I could not show a complete set of illustrations. Then I moved into a higher gear: "I am a Muslim and therefore at one remove from such texts that are sacred to Hindus. I have studied many of the *Upanishads*, all of the *Bhagavad Gita*, parts of *Brahma Sutra*, all the books of the *Bhagavata Purana*, some of the *khandas* of the *Ramayana*, and the *Markandeya Purana* of which the *Devi Mahatmya* is the core. I completely agree with my learned friend that each of them contains messages that are universally applicable to all mankind. In which case, I do not understand why he has to be so possessive of something that belongs to all mankind. And further, if the *Devi Mahatmya* is the repository of universal truth, then why is the only translation available in English done by an Englishman E.G. Pargiter and that too in 1899?"

The chairperson looked at me as if he had not heard or understood a word I had said, and then attaching his palms, he left with an air of injured superciliousness. "I am so glad you took him on," Dr. Nigham whispered to me when we said our own private goodbyes. "He is such a relic. He always does this – to every speaker."

For me, such encounters were the price one paid for the unalloyed pleasure of sitting with Jagdish Mittal in his home and savouring folio after folio of the most exquisite miniature paintings. Like every passionate collector, he had a story to accompany each picture. He narrated them softly and tended to swallow his own punch-lines before we could hear them. That did not prevent him from enjoying them himself.

Among the hundred or so he showed us on this our only visit to his home, there was not one I did not covet. Looking at them, I cursed myself for having succumbed to an interest in Indian art that could not be assuaged other than through such rare visits.

Recently, some forty years after that last meeting in Hyderabad, Jagdish paid a belated visit to my home in Lahore, or should I say his paintings did. A set of the two catalogues of the Pahari paintings and Drawings he and more passively his wife Kamla had amassed over the years arrived in the post.[5] They were sent by John Seyller who had collaborated with Jagdish on them. Browsing through the pages and recognising familiar paintings was like being reunited with old friends at some collegiate reunion.

Jagdish introduced us to Col Raj Tandan, a retired army officer who had the singular good fortune of acquiring a Basohli *Ragamala* set of thirty-six paintings.[6] He took us to his home and brought them out for us to admire (and envy). Shahnaz wrote an entertaining account of that encounter in her book *Lost from View*.[7]

At the farewell dinner, one of the guests – Mrs. Roda Mistry, Minister of Culture, AP Government – startled Shahnaz and Lalarukh by smoking a cigar with an almost masculine assertion. I read many years later that she (I presume it was the same Roda Mistry) had established a social NGO and had been arrested in 2001 for arranging children for inter-country adoption without a licence.

[5] John Seyller and Jagdish Mittal, *Pahari Drawings in the Jagdish and Kamla Mittal Museum of Indian Art* (Hyderabad, 2013) , and its companion volume also by John Seyller and Jagdish Mittal, *Pahari Paintings in the Jagdish and Kamla Mittal Museum of Indian Art* (Hyderabad, 2014).
[6] These were the subject of a monograph published in 1980 as *The Ragamala Paintings from Basohli* (Lalit Kala Series Portfolio No.20).
[7] Shahnaz Aijazuddin, 'Another Monsoon', *Lost from View* (Lahore, 1994), pp. 36-38.

My official programme at the Bureau of Public Enterprises ended on 10 August. I settled the bill for my lunches – Rs 100, an absurdly low price for such delicious delicacies as *bagare baingan* (spiced aubergines) and other Hyderabadi specialities.

I made the obligatory trip to the police station the day before we left Hyderabad to register our departure and to have our visa form stamped in evidence.

The three of us – Shahnaz, Lalarukh, and I - flew out to New Delhi on 11 August.

CHAPTER 18

DELHI & CHANDIGARH

I must have been five or six years old the last time I had seen New Delhi. My parents lived for a while in a flat near Chandni Chowk. My recollections of those days are fleeting – playing with tortoises my brother had brought home, our pet dogs Tiny (a terrier) and Laddy (a tolerant Alsatian), and of the Jesus & Mary Convent. I doubt whether my name would appear anywhere in its records (boys were admitted in a separate but linked kindergarten). It did interest me to learn recently from its recent website that its alumni included Aung San Suu Kyi (the Burmese political activist), the singer Kavita Krishnamurti, Sheila Dikshit (Chief Minister of Delhi for fifteen years), and Ms. Priyanka Gandhi (daughter of Rajiv and Sonia Gandhi).

Ms. Gandhi must have been admitted the year I returned to New Delhi. Her great-grandfather Pandit Jawaharlal Nehru and her grandmother Mrs. Indira Gandhi between them had occupied the prime ministerial office for twenty-eight years. By 1978, Mrs. Gandhi had been out of office for a year, having been voted out in the general elections she had called to endorse her actions under the unpopular Emergency.

Morarji Desai – once her former Deputy Prime Minister – defected from Congress, joined the Janata Dal Party and became prime minister. He instituted a series of investigations against her. The most prominent amongst became the Shah Commission set up to determine excesses committed during the Emergency. At first, Mrs. Gandhi refused to appear before the Commission, rejecting its very legality. She did finally relent and was grilled for almost three days by the counsel representing the Indian Government – our friend Karl Khandalavala.

I asked him whether she had been cooperative.

"No. But I persisted."

"Did she hold it against you?"

"Why should she? She knew I was doing my job. She was polite but kept her distance. Her grouse was against Morarji, not me."

Dom Moraes, in his perceptive biography of Mrs. Indira Gandhi which hurt her more than he hoped would help him, made this comparison between the two adversaries:

'Basically it was an unavoidable quarrel: not so much because they were politically different, but because as people they were so far apart. Mrs. Gandhi, who has a flexible mind, probably understood Desai, but that inflexible Calvinist certainly did not understand her. Years later, on a quiet Sunday afternoon, I asked her what her opinion was of Desai. Had it changed over the years? She was vehement, for her; she compressed her lips and said in a whisper more penetrating than a scream. "I have always felt the same about Mr. Desai. He hates people. You can see it in his face. We (by which she meant the Nehrus) are not like that. No," she repeated, "we are not like that."'[1]

Everyone in New Delhi seemed more obsessed with Morarji Desai's conviction about the benefits of urine therapy. He drank a glass of his own fluid every morning. That released any number of ribald jokes. I remember a couple of them. The more innocent had someone offering Desai a Scotch. He replies: "No thanks, I drink my own." A wittier cartoon showed him returning from a foreign trip, and advising his Cabinet colleagues: "Now, you all go home and have a drink. Me, I am going home to get pissed."

Shahnaz, Lalarukh and I checked in at Hotel Janpath, close to Connaught Place. It had all the amenities – just. An air-conditioner, but one that leaked in the room, soaking the carpet which then gave off a dank, stale smell. Its advantage lay in its location. One walked out into a mini-Tibet of stalls selling all sorts of printed Indian cottons, pseudo-amber necklaces, and mementos for the lower income foreign tourist.

Some of the six days we would spend in New Delhi would be used in official obligations – police registration, and a visit to the concerned office to

---

[1] Dom Moraes, *Mrs. Gandhi* (London, 1980), p.141.

have endorsements made on our passports to enable us to visit Dr. Randhawa at Chandigarh and Dr. Ashok Das at Jaipur. We could not get permission for Udaipur as we knew no-one there.

Most of that week we spent was divided between Mughal Delhi and Lutyen's New Delhi. We made the obligatory trips to the tombs of Humayun and Akbar, the Qutb Minar and the necropolis that has been resurrected as the verdant Lodi Gardens. Technically, we needed a visa to go to Agra but as one could do the trip in a day, we took the risk. So much has been written about the Taj that there is probably nothing novel left to say that would do justice to its ineffable beauty. Gazing at it, I felt the same awareness of divinity that I did when seeing Michelangelo's *Pieta* for the first time in St Peter's. It seemed inconceivable that Man unaided should have been able to produce something so perfect out of inert stone.

What did intrigue me was why Shah Jahan had not made provision for his own grave beside that of his beloved Mumtaz Mahal. She lies in the centre, while his – an after-thought, if ever there was one – destroys the symmetry - 'the strict bilateral symmetry with emphasis of the features of a central axis'[2] - that is the hallmark of Mughal architecture. There are of course stories perpetuated by breathless guides of his plans to have a tomb entirely in black marble on the opposite side of the Jamuna river.

Another mystery that has intrigued me is why in all the examples that exist of Imperial and Provincial Mughal painting, there should not have been any accurate contemporary depiction of the construction of the royal tombs or palaces. Even the paintings of durbar scenes set in specific locations such as in the Red Fort in Agra[3] and at Lahore Fort[4] cannot be readily matched with what is visible there today. It is almost as deliberately secretive as the impenetrable veil drawn by the ancient Egyptians on the way they constructed tombs for their Pharaohs.

For us, discovering Lutyen's New Delhi took us into a different empyrean, one inhabited by the living elite. Madhukar Shah (the former

---

[2] Ebba Koch, *Mughal Architecture: An outline of Its History and Development* (1526-1858, (Munich, 1991), p.98.
[3] See M.C. Beach & Ebba Koch, *King of the World: The Padshahnama, an Imperial Mughal manuscript from the Royal Library, Windsor Castle* (London, 1997), plate 19, p.56.
[4] J. P. Losty & Malini Roy, and others, *The Mughals: Life, Art and Culture* (New Delhi, 2103), p.24.

Maharaja of Orchha) arranged for us to see first Hyderabad House on Rajpath. Lutyens had designed it for Nizam Osman Ali Khan of Hyderabad (then the largest state in British India) in the 1920s. The palaces of the Nizams we had seen in Hyderabad reflected their caprices and foibles, as much as The Royal Pavilion in Brighton did the nascent orientalism of the Prince Regent, later George IV. The palace designed Lutyens had nothing to do with Hyderabad or its effete culture; instead it was his advice to the Deccani ruler on the advantages of controlled extravagance. Not surprisingly, the Nizam felt a stranger in a palace that was not of his own choice. In 1947, he donated the house to the Indian Government. It is now used by the Ministry of External Affairs for official functions.

Hyderabad House's companions belonged to the maharajahs of Bikaner, Patiala, Baroda, and Jaipur. Some of them were designed by Lutyens. Even the most modest of them Bikaner House is still commandingly monumental. Today, these affirmations of fealty to King-Emperor George V have been adapted to more plebeian purposes. Bikaner House is used by the Rajasthan Government as its foothold in Delhi. Patiala House became the Delhi High Court and then degenerated into the Delhi District courts. Baroda House (designed, it is said, by Lutyens while travelling on a train) has fulfilled his subconscious prescience by becoming the Zonal headquarters of Northern Railway. And Jaipur House (occupying one corner of the former Prince's Place) has become the home of the National Gallery of Art.

After a tour of Hyderabad House, Madhukar Shah took us into the precincts of Rashtrapati Bhavan. We collected the A.D.C. to the President - at the time Neelam J. Reddy (he happened to be on tour). By this time there were four of us. With the driver, that made it five, six if one included the A.D.C.. Considering the grandeur of our surroundings, it would not have been inappropriate for one of us to have ridden postilion. Instead, we tested the capacity of Madhukar's Ambassador car by folding and bending ourselves to fit into it.

We drove up the Raisina hill, the innocent incline that had become such a *casus belli* between Lutyens and his collaborator Sir Herbert Baker. Lutyens had wanted the Viceregal House to appear on the crest of the hill, visible to everyone on the plain below. Baker insisted that it should be set back and visible fully only after one had ascended the slope. Lutyens complained to Baker that 'the view of [his] Government House "would be obliterated," the palace dome and Jaipur column "awkwardly truncated", and Secretariat towers [Baker's design] so high as to be almost outside one's field of vision'. Baker 'insisted that a steep slope (found at the Agra Fort and many Rajput citadels) was essential at Delhi to express the spirit of a raised and privileged sanctuary.' Baker argued that 'at both Athens and the Capitol in Rome, the crowning building dominate its environs, then disappeared altogether as one mounted a steep approach; Baker envisaged his Secretariats as a worthy propyleum to Lutyen's Parthenon.[5]   Eventually, after years of argument and relentless appeals by Lutyens to two Viceroys (Viscount Hardinge and later Lord Chelmsford), Lutyens was overruled. The two wings of Baker's Secretariat flanking the sloping approach are the first sight one has of the complex. It has been said that the difference between having a house designed by an architect and designing it oneself is the choice between living with the architect's mistakes or with one's own. British Viceroys had, and now Indian presidents have, a choice between living with Baker's mistakes or with Lutyen's.

Only the last Viceroy Lord Mountbatten found a use for the endless steps of the steps that led up to the main building. In the last days of his Viceroyalty, he had his family (wife and two daughters) photographed with over two thousand staff and servants who supported them. And even then there was room to spare for at least five hundred more on either side of the stacks.

It took some time, but we were able to see all the State apartments as well as the private apartments available. Familiar with Lutyen's often quirky attention to detail[6], I sought out the staircase with its roof open to the sky, so that at night stars twinkled in the inky-blue canopy over the space; the tennis courts with its design of circles resembling tennis balls; the carved elephant with a pedestal of a row of flowers in which one is missing, held in its trunk by the mischievous elephant; the Mughal gardens with their elegant, ordered symmetry; and the Vicereine's bathroom, with its (for the 1920s avant garde) shower booth, with three shower heads, one ahead and two on the sides. The guide informed us very seriously: "This is the suite that H.M. Queen Elizabeth

---

[5] Robert G. Irving, *Indian Summer: Lutyens, Baker and Imperial Delhi* (Yale University Press, 1981), pp.154-5.

[6] After completing such a massive project at New Delhi, Lutyen's was prevailed upon by Princess Marie Louise (King George V's cousin) to design a Doll's House for Queen Mary. Three feet tall and built on a scale of 1:12, It is perfect in every detail and completely functional. It is on view at Windsor Castle, U.K.

II stayed in, and this is the bathroom she used."

"Now we know how she washes her armpits", one of us commented.

We visited the National Museum where I was keen on meeting Dr. Grace Morley[7], whose book on *Indian Sculpture* had been my introduction to the subject. The Museum had a superb collection of sculptures, miniatures and historic objects but suffered as such museums do from bureaucratic rigor mortis. The main attraction for me was its collection of folios of the famous *Bhagavata Purana* set, upon which Dr. M.S. Randhawa had published a monograph for the National Museum in 1960. Seeing the originals made one realise how much could be lost even with the most attentive and assiduous of coloured reproduction.

The next stop naturally had to be the National Gallery of Art (formerly Jaipur House). There, the vapid Bengal School water-colours led into the more 'virile' modernists, pre-eminent amongst whom was the Hungarian-Sikh painter Amrita Sher-Gil. Amrita had a talent as fervid as her sex-life. Karl Khandalavala who knew her and written a book about her never admitted to me that he had been one of the beneficiaries of her favours. The British writer Malcolm Muggeridge certainly had been. He confessed in his memoirs to fleeing from Shimla, exhausted by her demands. Her sexual appetite was well-known, and documented. It would not be doing her memory a disservice to say that when Amrita was good, she was very, very good; when she was bad, she was a nymphomaniac.

Amrita Sher-Gil died in December 1941, it is said, of a botched abortion, in her home at Lahore. She was twenty-eight years old. Her paintings occupy one wing of the National Gallery, a reflection of the posthumous reverence with which her work is regarded in India.

The other icon on our list was Mahatma Gandhi. We traced Birla House to see where Gandhi had been assassinated by Nathuram Godse. His footsteps were petrified in red sandstone, leading to the place the spot where he fell while on his way to lead his daily session of non-denominational prayers. His sparse outer room in the otherwise grand mansion owned by the millionaire Birla contained his signature spinning wheel. Gandhi lived in what Juvenal described as 'a state of ambitious poverty'.[8] As an exasperated Sarojini Naidu pointed

---

[7] Founding Director of the NMI.
[8] Juvenal, *Satires*, III, I, 182.

out once, 'It costs us a lot to keep Gandhi in poverty.' Gandhi obviously preferred to live at someone else's expense.

As a student, I had been greatly influenced by Gandhi's writings. His self-abnegation, his determination to control the natural impulses of his body (sometimes a little too publically), his political activism, his ability to articulate his thoughts into a convincing credo, and his espousal of the causes of the poor put him in my eyes at a level higher than many men I admired. Gradually, as I read more *about* him rather than *by* him, cracks began to appear in that image. The idol I had been shown had the feet of a wily, unscrupulous politician. The more I read about the simmering confrontation between Gandhi and Jinnah, I found myself admiring Jinnah more and Gandhi less. My sympathies gravitated towards the mongoose, rather than the snake. We visited also the site of Gandhi's cremation at Raj *ghat*, the spot commemorated with a solid slab of sandstone the colour of faded blood.

Coming from Lahore, the visit to the Red Fort and to the Jamia Masjid in Old Delhi reminded me forcibly of Lahore's provincialism when compared to Delhi's imperialism. Lahore is not at fault. It had been the capital of Mughal empire for only thirteen years, compared to the centrality of Delhi to a dynasty that lasted like the Romanovs in Russia, for over three hundred years. Lahore's fort had been built more as a royal residence than as a daily reminder of imperial presence. It has the same features – a *Diwan-e-Am* (Hall of Public Audience) where the emperor would receive his subjects; a *Diwan-e-Khas* (Hall of Private Audience) to which he would repair when he was bored of listening to public appeals; the *zenana-khana* where, when he was tired of his nobles, he could gratify himself with his wives and concubines; and the private bedroom or *khawabgah* where he could escape when his ears could no longer bear the cacophony of the harem.

The connection between the two forts was evidenced by two gates – the eastern one in Lahore fort facing Delhi and therefore called the Delhi gate, and the western one in the Delhi Fort called the Lahori gate. This was more than just a convenient signpost for would-be travellers. It signified the almost umbilical relationship between the two citadels, as symbols of central authority and provincial regency.

Almost fifteen years separate the Jamia Masjid in Delhi (1644-58) from its younger sibling the Badshahi Mosque in Lahore. The Mughal emperor

Aurangzeb, having deposed his father Shah Jahan, completed the Delhi mosque, and in 1673-74 had one built for himself - a marginally smaller one - at Lahore.

As we walked through Delhi's Red fort, it was difficult to recreate in our minds the grand assemblies that the English envoy Sir Thomas Roe had witnessed at the court of Jahangir or the French jeweller Bernier at that of Aurangzeb. Instead, the shabbiness, the state of decrepitude and neglect reminded me of the vivid description left by the Russian prince Alexis Saltykov when he visited Delhi in 1842, during the reign of the last Mughal Bahadur Shah Zafar II. One evening, he saw the royal procession go past and in the torch light recognised the emperor: 'He looked like an embalmed corpse, as dark as a mummy and decorated with tinsel.' The very next morning, Saltykov was summoned for an audience with the potentate who less than fifteen years later would be the last of his dynasty. 'His face was withered, dark and emaciated, as were his hands. He had an aquiline nose, hollow cheeks, few teeth, and a thin beard dyed reddish black, almost violet. His eyes were darkened with antimony (kohl). This aged man whom I saw on the throne was Bahadur Shah, the descendant of Timurlane.'

Saltykov made the necessary obeisance to the king: 'I expressed my appreciation by handing three more pieces of gold to the emperor who was pleased to receive them. Upon this a brilliant diadem of precious stones was brought to him which he attached with his own hands to my turban while I remained in a respectful position. Finally he placed a collar of pearls around my neck, and invested me with a sword of honour. After each of these gifts I slid a piece of gold politely into the imperial palm, as one does to doctors in England, and he appeared satisfied, poor man, though he seemed like an automaton.'[9] On examining the royal gifts, Saltykov discovered to his disappointment that the brilliant diadem and the collar of pearls were made of glass.

I felt a similar sense of deflation after touring the fort and later Humayun's tomb at Sikandra. These once grand edifices now appeared to be in a state of decline.

We toured the old city and in the evening we were taken for dinner to a

[9] Prince Alexis Saltykov, in H.L.O. Garrett (ed.), *The Punjab a Hundred Years Ago, as described by V. Jacquemont (1831) & A. Soltykoff (1842)*, Lahore, 1935), p. 127.

haveli converted into a restaurant with typical Mughlai/Muslim food. To emphasise its ethnicity, a group of *qawwals* performed at one end of the *haveli*. Their lead singer had hair as long as the Pakistani *qawwal* Ghulam Farid Sabri, except that here his Indian counterpart was a woman. I suppose having seen female singing *qawwalis* on screen in films like *Mughal-e-Azam* and *Pakeeza*, I should not have been surprised. It did come as a shock, though, just later on this trip we were startled to see in Indian Punjab, women in saris or shalwar / kameezes riding motor scooters astride.

We had been advised by Karl that while we were in Delhi, we had to meet Chote Lal Bharany, the son of the late Radha Krishna Bharany, in his day the most famous jeweller cum antique dealer in Delhi. He operated from a shop in Sunder Nagar market. Not only had we been told but so had Kirk Douglas the film actor. We arrived at Bharany's shop and found Mr. Douglas and his blonde wife Anne browsing among Bharany's shelves. Our first instinct was to go up to him and to tell him how much pleasure his films had brought us. His *Spartacus* had been a favourite of both Shahnaz and Lalarukh. When Kirk Douglas saw three determined looking Pakistanis gravitating towards him, he recoiled like someone who had lost an Oscar. Chote Lal noticed this. His invitation to see his private collection of atrtefacts over dinner at his house may have had something to do with that moment.

All I remember now of the dinner at Chote Lal's house is the feeling of envy that all collectors feel on coveting some-one else's acquisitions, and a large framed photograph of an Afro-haired Satya Sai Baba, Chote Lal's guru,[10] and another over-large image, this one a frontal view of his knobbly toes. For some reason, I was reminded of Graham Sutherland's study of Christ's feet which he made while preparing his design of the tapestry in Coventry Cathedral. Sutherland had anticipated that when the tapestry would be hung, only Christ's toes would be in line with the eyes of the pilgrims.

On 19 August, the night before we left for Chandigarh, Ravi Dayal and his wife Mala (Khushwant Singh's daughter) invited us for dinner. Among his guests, Ravi had included Salman Haidar, a friend of Ravi's from their

---

[10] Satya Sai Baba claimed to be the incarnation of Sai Baba of Shirdi. His ability to materialise objects such as rings, watches and ash which he would then distribute to followers earned him both followers and detractors. He built up a very well-endowed charitable foundation and had achieved such stature that when he died in 2011, his funeral was attended by half a million followers, including prime minister Manmohan Singh, Mrs. Sonia Gandhi, Narendra Modi, and Sachin Tendulkar.

Cambridge University days. Salman, being a very senior official in the Ministry of External Affairs,[11] maintained a formal but clearly demarcated distance between himself as an Indian diplomat and us as informed ingratiating Pakistanis. By the end of the evening, he had relaxed sufficiently to talk around but not about his work.

For us, the star of that warm August evening was the writer Ved Mehta, who happened to be in New Delhi that summer. We had missed him in New York in 1977. Ravi indulged us by ensuring that we could meet him over dinner. Shahnaz and I knew him through his moving autobiographical account of his early years *Face to Face* (1957) and brilliant collage *Portrait of India* (1970). He and the poet Dom Moraes had made a trip together to India in the summer of 1959. Each wrote his recollection of account of it. Dom's came out first, in 1960, under the title *Gone Away: An Indian Journal*. I had noticed a copy of it in the W.H. Smith bookstall at Victoria Station soon after its release. I opened it and read this sentence: 'Then I fished your photograph out of my case and stood you among the roses. I looked at you a long time and decided that we both seemed a little lost. So I put you under my pillow instead'. Captivated by Dom's lyricism,[12] I finished the book in one sitting.

Ved's version of the same trip – *Walking the Indian Streets* - appeared in 1963, three years after Dom's. They were so strikingly different that many a reader wondered which of them to believe. Ved – by then a staff writer on the *New Yorker* – felt impelled to reinforce the accuracy of his recollections. When a revised version of his book was published in paperback in 1975, Ved added a lengthy corrective Introduction captioned: *A Bummy Holiday Revisited*. Dom left his version unchanged.[13]

Ravi, by nature gentle and inclusive, ensured as the host common to all of us that the conversation flowed across borders and cultural boundaries. We talked about art, literature, politics, and occasionally lapsed into personalities.

---

[11] He rose to become the Foreign Secretary of India (1995-1997), and then briefly India's High Commissioner to the UK in 1998.

[12] Dom had won the Hawthornden prize for poetry at the age of nineteen.

[13] Dom, in his autobiography *My Son's Father* (London, 1968), mentioned the journey in passing. However, his perceptive assessment of Ved revealed a poet's power over prose: 'Ved was stocky and dapper, dressed always in suits of excellent cut. His closed eyes and slow, deliberate movements gave him a sleepy air which misled those who met him for the first time; he was in fact exceptionally acute, reacting and observing always, and had a rather waspish line of wit.' [p.198]

Shahnaz asked Ved if she could take his handprint. He held out his palm to her. She applied lipstick to it and then took an impression on a sheet of white paper. Later, after our return, she wrote to him from Lahore to apologise for having bothered him. He wrote back:

> 'Dear Shahnaz
>
> My hand still tingles with the memory of the time you and your sister fondled it. I wish I could have my handprint taken every day under such conditions. How can you call it tedious, when, because of the "process", as much as anything, I have set my cap towards Pakistan and Lahore.'[14]

Delhi in those days suffered from periodic power outages. Towards the end of the evening, when it returned yet again, Ved said: "That's the third time tonight." Someone asked him how he could tell. "From the fans." And then, just as we were leaving Ravi's flat, the room became dark once more. Ved put his arm into Shahnaz's and steered her through the furniture towards the front door. Suddenly, we were disadvantaged and he was in his element. He led us through the dark with the intuitive expertise that only blind persons acquire after years of mishaps.

We left for Chandigarh by bus the next morning. For me, the air-conditioned bus represented the emerging Indian middle class which had money, wanted comfortable mobility, and an expectation to be entertained. The bus was equipped with a TV screen upon which they showed relays of Indian films. One of them had a dramatic car chase sequence with sudden swerves and twisting turns. Sitting in the darkened bus, its curtains drawn, one felt as though the bus itself was careering off the road.

On the way, the bus made a pit stop at the factory outlet of the Amul milk plant. There, a range of milk products were available, such as *lassi* (we had entered after all Eastern Punjab), and snacks amongst which were prosaic boiled eggs labelled 'Ram ke gole.' Literally translated I suppose that would read Ram's balls. Even the most pious of the passengers would have difficulty swallowing those.

Dr. M.S. Randhawa and his wife Iqbal Kaur (known to all and now to

---

[14] In my next letter to Ved, I added a postscript: 'The next time we meet, I shall remember to hold your *other* hand.'

us also as Beji) picked us up from the Government guest house where we had been accommodated. He had arranged for us to be declared State guests of the Punjab government.[15] He drove us through the city he as Chief Commissioner had helped create. He had a staccato manner of speaking, which some would have described as brusque and curt. Dr. Randhawa did not like to waste his time and discouraged others from wasting his. He was economical with his time and his words.

"These trees," he said, "pointing to those planted along a road, "when they blossom will be all yellow." And when we took a turning, he added: "Those will bloom a month later and will be all red." Standing by the lake, he told us: "I had this tree planted all around the perimeter of the lake, so that it could provide shade to the visiting public."

Every roundabout was a mini-rose garden. He mentioned that one day he noticed someone climb into a roundabout and pluck a rose from a bush. "I told the driver to stop. I got out and immediately got hold of the culprit. And do you know who it was? Mulk Raj Anand!" He chuckled at the recollection.

Dr. Randhawa had arranged for me to give a lecture on Pahari painting at the Punjab University Chandigarh, where Brijen was Head of the Fine Arts Department. I was surprised to find that the projection would be against the wall rather than a screen. The off-white wall being slightly curved gave each picture a sort of Cinemascope effect. The students did not appear to mind. Dr. Randhawa did, and mumbled to me afterwards his annoyance that a screen had not been arranged.

I had structured my lecture in three sections – Subject, Patron, and Artist. Using examples primarily from the Lahore Museum, I talked about the initial supremacy of subject matter, examples being religious texts such as the Jaina *Kalpa Sutra* and secular narratives such as the *Akbarnama*. Gradually, the patron assumed importance. He had the resources to commission such expensive works of art and also the vanity to demand to be identified with them. In time, the artist emerged out of his self-effacing anonymity, and overshadowed both the patron and the subject. This three-layered approach appealed to Brijen who commented on this structure in his speech of thanks

---

[15] Because of this formality, we had in attendance the Secretary Culture Sardar Man Mohan Singh, a dashing erudite and gifted IAS officer. Before we left, he gave us an inscribed copy of his second book *A Dome of Many-Coloured Glass: 25 Essays on Life, War & Poetry* (Delhi,1977). On our subsequent visit to India, we learned of his untimely death.

after the lecture was over.

Dr. Randhawa's son worked as the manager of the Pinjore Gardens, a Mughal retreat designed by Fidai Khan who had built the Badshahi Mosque in Lahore. The gardens like its counterparts in Lahore and Srinagar consisted of a number of layered terraces, through which water cascaded like God's benevolence from the highest to the lowest levels. Over the centuries, the gardens had fallen into disrepair until they were rescued by Maharaja Yadavindra Singh of Patiala (a former Aitchisonian).

We walked down from terrace to terrace. Shahnaz, Lalarukh, Beji and Dr. Randhawa's son walked ahead. He and I followed.

Suddenly, he asked me: "Kaka, do you know who he is?"

"Yes, he is your son."

"No, Kaka. He is my natural son. You, you are my *spiritual* son."

Pinjore gardens lay in Haryana state. The state governor happened to be Harcharan Singh Brar, Babar Ali's close friend since their student days at Aitchison College. Dr. M. S. Randhawa did not share Babar's enthusiasm for him but nevertheless he took us to Governor's House to have tea with him and Brar's wife Rano. Both were staunch supporters of Mrs. Indira Gandhi, especially so now that she was not in power. They knew that she would return.

Sunday 20 August was our last day in Chandigarh. Dr. Randhawa invited us to have lunch with him at his home in Kharar, some fifteen kilometres west of Chandigarh. A single tack road led us to Garden House, whose name I had written countless times on envelopes addressed to him since our correspondence began in 1967.

Garden House like its owner was modest to a fault. Red brick, utilitarian, and spartan in its comforts. Dr. Randhawa preferred to eat on the verandah, with his back to the refrigerator. He showed me his study upstairs – again very simple. His only extravagance was the use of exquisitely embroidered Chamba *rumals* (in which hill brides from that state kept their dowries) as wrappers for the manuscripts he was working on. His bathroom contained no water heater: simply an immersion rod suspended in a steel bucket.

Over lunch, he said: "Everything you are eating has been grown here.", and pointed as proof at a bush of green chillies. He told me how he had bought this plot and built the house out of the IRs 90,000 he had received on retirement from the Indian Civil Service. I am not sure whether he received any remuneration as Vice Chancellor of the Punjab Agricultural University that he founded at Ludhiana or from the various posts he held after retirement. I did not want to ask.

Sitting on the verandah that afternoon, talking to him in Punjabi, he imparted such a sense of calm in me. When his burnished head caught the sun, it reminded me of the bronze bust of him on display in the library of the Chandigarh Museum & Art Gallery.

We left him and Beji with regret. Later on returning to Pakistan, I sent him this letter of thanks:

My very dear Dr. Randhawa

As we said goodbye to you and Beji, I thought for a moment our hearts would break. Suddenly, even though one was in company and in the midst of activity, one felt an acute sense of loneliness and desolation. All obligations were out of focus and one wished that the car, everything transient would stop to let us continue without the hindrance of pre-planned schedules and programmes, the wholesome purity of that brilliant morning. As I saw you standing beneath the vines, I wanted to communicate to you a part of the searing pleasure and pain I was feeling. Rarely have I felt the impact of a personality with such a permanent effect on my being as I did during those halcyon days at Chandigarh. The pleasure was pure an intense, and the ache as sharp. For a long time, neither Shahnaz, Lalarukh, nor I could speak lest we murmur incoherent and inadequate thoughts about the occasion. The same feeling of deliberate silence restrained me from writing to you during the last hectic week of our departure, lest I convey to you an imperfect recollection of our mood and feelings.

Whatever I say to you, even now, in the tranquility of my own room, whatever I say cannot express the immense gratitude we three have felt to you for the attention and love with you showered on us. Personally, I can only reaffirm a commitment to you, a voluntary bondage to your tutelage which is all the more resilient for being unsolicited.'

My letter, dated 1 September 1978, elicited this response from Dr.

Randhawa a fortnight later:

> Dear Aijazuddin
>
> We are glad to learn from your letter dated 1 September 1978 that you all reached Lahore safely. You have left a fragrance behind you at Chandigarh and Garden House. People whom you met will ever remember you.
>
> I felt that visit to the garden was all too brief. There were so many things to discuss. In all that hurry I forgot to give you a small booklet I had compiled, viz. *Great Thoughts*. I will send it though somebody. It will be a real help in difficult moments of life which we all face.
>
> On 18 August our cook burnt his leg. He thrust his foot in a pail of boiling water, which another helpmate was carrying. I asked Iqbal whether we should bring some cooked food from a restaurant in Chandigarh for our lunch. She said "No, this is not the way we serve such affectionate friends." She started work at 6.00 a.m. and by 11.30 a.m., all that delicious food was ready. She was in tears after your departure and also felt very tired. It is thus – hard work and total unconcern about her own comfort – she has won my respect!
>
> Shahnaz is a charming person and she is devoted to you. You have just the type of wife who assists a husband in work, which is not done by ordinary people. I had long talks with Lalarukh. She is very bright and has an awakened mind. She should go into study of art books seriously.
>
> I regard you as a son, a friend, and a disciple. Long may you live to complete your studies!

CHAPTER 19

RAJASTHAN & MUMBAI

We returned to Delhi from Chandigarh by bus. Ravi Dayal had arranged a dinner at his flat in Sujan Singh Park. It lay on the ground floor opposite that of Khushwant Singh, whose father had built this complex in what in his day must have been the outskirts of Delhi. Today, it is probably half way between the centre of Delhi – if one takes Connaught Place as its commercial epicentre – and Gurgaon, its provincial satrap. Khan Market opposite the block of flats had just opened and both the India International Centre and Lodhi gardens were within walking distance.

Ravi took us across to meet Khushwant before dinner, for he knew that Khushwant went to bed early. Khushwant met us with effusive warmth, speaking in Punjabi about his affection for Pakistan, his birthplace of Hadali (near Khushab), and the great friendship he enjoyed with Manzur Qadir. "That curtain which has *ayats* from the Holy Quran was given to me by Manzur." Above his book cases, he had framed specimens of calligraphy. Occasionally, his wife – a still strikingly handsome lady with a powerful presence – would come into the room, say a few words to us, and then leave Khushwant to his practised repertoire.

I told him of my forthcoming book – *Sikh Portraits by European Artists* – which covered the same post-Ranjit Singh period of Punjabi history that he had written about in his book *The Fall of the Kingdom of the Punjab* (1962). He told me, after finishing his magnum opus – a two volume work on *The History of the Sikhs* - he had considerable material left over. He converted it into this smaller volume. It was not well received because it described the collapse of the Ranjit Singh's empire, a debacle Sikhs preferred to forget. I asked him whether he had a copy of his book to spare. Generously, he found a paperback version which he presented to me, inscribing it 'To Aijazuddin. With much affection, Khushwant Singh, 21 August 1978.'

Dr. Randhawa had arranged that I should give my Pahari lecture in New Delhi, at the Lalit Kala Akademi auditorium Rabindra Bhavan. I felt strange speaking in the Akademi with which I was familiar from Lahore through its journal – a poorer version of *Marg* but slightly classier than *Roopa Lekha*.[1]

We checked in with the Police Registration on arrival, and again within twenty-four hours of departure. Time consuming, but unavoidable.

We had a visa to go to Jaipur but not Udaipur. In those days, Indian Airlines ran a hop, skip and jump flight from New Delhi, to Jaipur, Udaipur, Aurangabad and then Mumbai. The temptation to visit Udaipur was irresistible, so we decided to take a risk and stop at Udaipur. It meant juggling the police reporting timings.

The flight left Delhi early in the morning. We checked in our hotel from where we contacted Asok Das. Having him as a guide made the visit to the City Palace Museum all the more meaningful. He walked us through the various enclosed courtyards, their walls embellished with exquisite and vivid tile-work. This being Rajasthan, carved peacocks and stone elephants abounded. Only with him could we have walked into the normally inaccessible royal apartments. He led us through narrow staircases behind the filigreed *Hawa mahal* façade. From it we could see the busy road outside and in the secluded calm within, two elderly ladies in magenta and green saris cleaning a tray of lentils. "Those are the last surviving widows of Maharaja Sawai Madho Singh II. He died in 1922. They must have been very young then. They are allowed to live here in the palace, as they have nowhere else to go."

Asok's responsibility was to document and preserve the Jaipur royal collection. Some objects were on display in the Mubarak Mahal, a stand-alone structure opposite the entrance gate. My particular interest was to see the illustrated manuscript of the *Razmnama* (the Persian translation of the *Mahabharata*), commissioned by the emperor Akbar.[2] It was completed by 1586. The manuscript because of its value and its fragility had been not been

---

[1] Published by the All India Arts and Crafts Society.
[2] Almost thirty years later, Asok published the manuscript as *Paintings of the Razmnama: The Book of War* (Ahmedabad, 2006).

ordinarily accessible. Asok made an exception and opened its world of vivid, compressed action to us.

We did, as tourists do, the Jaipur Palace, the Jantar Mantar, and the following day trip to see Amber fort. Like the sanctuary at Assisi, the fort was built on a promontory. It stand like a stone diadem on the brow of high hill, overlooking Moata lake. For those who prefer to ride rather than walk, transport is available on caparisoned elephants that lumber their way up and down the long treads that zigzag to the fort. Being a fortress, it paid less attention to the comfort of the occupants and more to the defences it could install and safeguard. While at school at Berkhamsted, I had read a book in its library on Indian royalty. It was called *India of the Princes* by Rosita Forbes, published in 1939. From what I can remember, it contained a glamourised account of how the treasures of the Jaipur maharaja was secreted in the bowels of Amber fort, and safeguarded by hereditary retainers. Only they knew how to access it, and when any maharaja wished to see it, he would be blindfolded first and then led through a maze of tunnels (some led nowhere) to the inner sanctum. He could choose one piece, no more. He would be blindfolded again and led out.

The compulsory registration of antiquities, Mrs. Gandhi's abolition of the privy purses, and her unspeakable animus against Maharani Gayatri Devi of Jaipur dispelled such mystique about Indian royalty.

We registered our departure from Jaipur with the police in the morning of 25August. That meant technically we had to leave within 24 hours. We decided to fly to Udaipur that afternoon, spent the day of the 26th and night there, and then catch the shuttle flight to Mumbai on 27th and report to the police there on 28th morning. It was a risk, but one well worth taking. To be on the safe side, in case someone overheard us, Shahnaz and I decided that we should call each other Sudhir and Prabha. We hoped that because of her clothes, she would be taken as someone from Indian Punjab. Throughout our stay, she and Lalarukh wore shalwar / kameezes. In Hyderabad, women would ask them whether they come from north India. In New Delhi they would ask which part of Indian Punjab they came from, and in Chandigarh the question would inevitably be: "Which part of Pakistan do you come from?"

We stayed at a nondescript hotel near the fort, too modest to enquire where we came from. They did not even ask us for our passports.

This ploy enabled us to spend a glorious day at Udaipur, touring the fort and the curio shops before crossing in a motor boat to the Lake Palace Hotel, in Pichola Lake. The Taj Hotel group had taken over management of the hotel in 1971, added more rooms, and refurbished it to a maharana's standards. There were very few guests there that August. It had yet to become unaffordable to plebeians like us. All we could afford was a margarita each, which we sipped sitting in one of the marble cupolas on the lakeside. A carpet of lotuses floated towards us and in the distance we could see thunder clouds and occasional flashes of lightning. One understood from where Rajasthani miniature painters obtained their inspiration and their reverence for nature.

I resolved that when I died, I would ask God to allow me to haunt the Lake Palace. One could spend eternity there without having to spend the fortune it costs to stay there now, even for a night.[3]

We sneaked out of Udaipur the next day, passing on our way to the airport a sight I had never seen before: two female Jain monks, walking on wooden elevated *chappals* (to minimise their contact with the earth), and dressed in white, with a muslin mask over their noses and mouths, to prevent them accidentally inhaling a living insect. I had lived with Malde and his cousins in London. They were Jains, albeit non-orthodox ones. Later I met more in his extended family in Nairobi. I had never seen a Jaina in ascetic 'uniform', as it were.

We caught the same Delhi-Jaipur-Udaipur shuttle. Its next stop was Aurangabad, before continuing to Mumbai. En route, the stewardess announced that due to bad weather, the plane would not land at Aurangabad. The French tourist in the seat next to me had been reading notes in her guide book on the famous caves at Ajanta and Ellora at Aurangabad. Without a flicker of disappointment, she turned the pages of her guide book to Mumbai.

Mumbai was as we had left it, except for the fresh rosettes of excrement. Karl had asked us to spend our days in Mumbai with him and his wife Mehri in their house – 63, Worli Sea Face. I was surprised to discover that the house – beautifully located overlooking the Arabian Sea - did not belong to them but to a pair of old Parsi sisters. They lived upstairs, and seemed to spend most of their day looking out of the window to watch passers-by or to keep an eye on Karl's house guests. All they must have seen would have been an occasional

---

[3] Today, the Grand Palace Suite costs IRs 92,000 per night.

fisher-woman without a blouse washing her second sari and then spreading it to dry on the boulders that prevented the sea from inundating the houses.

Karl and Mehri were childless. He was devoted to her and fretted over her, responding to her every whim. They lived a frugal existence, attended to by an aged retainer. Sea breezes wafted unimpeded through their ground-floor room. The curtains were of white cotton, bunched on two horizontal wires.

It did not take Shahnaz and Lalarukh long to melt Mehri's reserve.

"I like your friends," Mehri told Karl, over dinner that first night.

"I told you that you would," he replied.

When we returned to our room after dinner, Shahnaz and Lala collapsed on the bed with a fit of the giggles. Suppressing their laughter, they told me between gasps that after what Karl had told them about the seriousness of Mehri's illnesses, they had not expected her to last even through dinner.

The next morning Karl took us to the police department to effect our registration. The officer wanted me to explain the missing twenty-fours between checking out of Jaipur on 25th and checking in at Mumbai on 28th.

"Seventy two-hours gap. Why?"

I could explain 48 hours, but the unexplained 24 hours?

Karl came to my rescue.

"Sir, it was raining very heavily yesterday and so I could not bring them to your office."

Grudgingly, the police officer accepted Karl's explanation. Aft the registration was over, I waited for Karl outside. When he returned, he told me that he had stayed behind to have his driver's challan cancelled.

"I told them it was my fault. I ordered him to go into a one-way street."

"Doesn't he know who you are?" I asked Karl. He was after all one of the leading lawyers in Mumbai.

"Yes," he replied, with a self-effacing smile. "I do work for the police now and again. They are therefore very kind to me."

I did not want to inconvenience Karl and so we hired a taxi to take us around Mumbai. The Sikh driver took us up and down Marine Drive, to Quaid-e-Azam's magnificently located house on Malabar Hill, and the Parsee

Tower of Silence. The *Chor* or Thief's bazaar lay in a warren of congested streets. While we were trying to manoeuvre our way out of a traffic snarl-up, a funeral cart passed us in the rain, the thin corpse enveloped in a white muslin shroud that clung to the body with decidedly less appeal than Zeenat Aman's in Raj Kapoor's wet-porn film *Satyam, Shivam, Sundaram*.

To be in the heart of what would later be termed Bollywood and not see a film would have been sacrilegious. The three of us bought tickets from the touts outside the cinema at twice the normal rates. It saved having to queue and run the risk of being disappointed. Someone once described money as compressed time. Nowhere truer than outside an Indian cinema hall. The film Shahnaz and Lala wanted to see was the blockbuster *Sholay*, a brilliantly improbable story about two hired guns Amitabh Bachchan and Dharmendra who come to the rescue of a remote village harassed by the villain Amjad Khan and his cronies. It could be described as a *chapati* eastern in contrast to the spaghetti western. The only thing missing in it was Clint Eastwood.

The script by the Salim-Javed duo contained as many quotable lines as Shakespeare's *Hamlet*. (It was said that a member of the audience was once overheard leaving a performance of *Hamlet*, commenting: "Nice play, but riddled with quotations!")

We had seats behind a party of young Mumbai girls. One in particular just in front of me had obviously seen the film a number of times. She knew the script by heart. Before each punch-line of dialogue, she would recite it loudly to her companion. I tolerated this for about half an hour (the film lasts over three hours). When I could take no more of her predictive rendition of the script, I tapped her on the shoulder and said:

"Miss, we have paid black market rates to listen to the actors, not to you."

"Hai, ketla burra manas che,"[4] she muttered to her friend in Gujrati.

We did not have time or the contacts to visit any film set or witness shooting. We did the next best thing, which was to drive around the residences of the film stars. The Sikh taxi driver seemed to know the location of all. "This house belonged to Madhubala" or "This is where Ashok Kumar lives." Shahnaz's favourite Indian actor at that time was Rajesh Khanna. The drive took us to the wooden gate of the actor's house – *Aashiwaad*.

---

[4] "What a bad man he is!"

During the journey there, the driver talked about some guru whose devotees vied to drink water wrung from his dhotis. With a straight face, I asked the sardar whether we could have some of the water in which Rajesh's clothes had been rinsed.

My lecture in Mumbai had been organised by Karl at the then Prince of Wales Museum. (It now has the impossibly long name: Chhatrapatī Shivaji Mahārāj Vastu Saṅgrahālay (CSMVS), formerly Prince of Wales Museum of Western India.)

After it, we were invited by the Singhania family (friends of Babar Ali) to dinner in the penthouse of their twenty-six storey block of flats, overlooking Marine Drive. Each of the guests had a waiter in attendance behind each diner. At the conclusion, our host wanted to show us the collection his father had accumulated over years of foreign travel. It was heartbreaking to see two floors filled with showcases crammed with souvenirs from every place he had visited around the globe. None of them were worth looking at but I do recall a small porcelain commode with the message: "Please drop in on Brighton."

When it was time to leave, Mr. Singhania and his wife accompanied us to the lift. There we noticed the waiters, dressed in their own clothes, their white uniforms folded and secured in their armpits waiting patiently for the lift to come. The moment the lift doors opened, they filed in along with us. Had it been Pakistan, I remarked to Shahnaz afterwards, the host would have made his staff wait for the next lift or sent them down 26 floors by the stairs.

On the last evening we spent with Karl, he took out some of miniatures from his superb collection.[5] He had assisted Sir Dorab Tata and Sir Cowasji Jehangir expand their collections, buying at a time that important paintings could still be had and at prices he could afford. It was an unalloyed joy to sit with him and to savour the company of old friends like Raja Balwant Singh of Jasrota.

I never saw Karl again. Gradually, first Mehri and after her death Karl began to spend more time in their own home in Pune. He and I maintained our correspondence through letters or latterly through New Year cards. The last one in his own handwriting showed that he was as combative as ever.

---

[5] The Karl and Meherbai collection contained amongst other valuable objects many superb examples of Chola bronzes (Karl's specialty). After Karl's death in 1995, the collection was bequeathed by him to the CSMVS Museum.

"Dear Aijaz

Not heard from you since you last sent the charming family photos. Hope you are all well. Any chance of a visit to Bombay?

Festival of India[6] catalogues have been coming out with some Pahari paintings therein. I am reviewing all of them - the USA catalogues, including Goswamy's in *Lalit Kala* no.23. Will send you a copy. I've not been too kind!

There has been a furore here about sending irreplaceable treasures of art out of the country, but still it goes on with some exceptions, because I and a few others created a strong opposition for which of course I am regarded as a thorn in the side of the Govt. because I flayed Mrs. Pupul Jayakar (the Head of the Festival business) right and left in the press. Most of these exhibitions are dismally attended, except for the first few days, unlike the Chinese, the Tutankhamen and the Persian exhibitions or even the Silk Route and Search for Alexander. I cannot understand why?"

---

[6] Held in various London galleries simultaneously in 1992.

CHAPTER 20

VIENNA & VED MEHTA

Within a month of returning from India, I found myself on a plane again, this time westwards. I had been nominated to attend a UNIDO Workshop on Regional Co-operation in Vienna, convened in the first week of September 1978.

On 6 September, I reached Karachi airport, checked in and had my passport stamped by the immigration, when suddenly a young voluble Sindhi approached me. He clutched a register which he opened and then ran his finger down the alphabetical index.

"Are you Fakir Syed Ayazuddin?"

"No. He is my brother."

"Do you know he has left the country without permission?"

"No. I have not spoken to him today. He may have gone abroad. He runs an airline agency. He comes and goes. Anyway, isn't it your job to stop him, not mine?"

"You're right," he agreed. "Three persons have already been suspended because of him. Whoever catches him when he returns will get a promotion."

The Sindhi official took my passport, disappeared into an office, reappeared about ten minutes later and said: "You are cleared." Then, in a low voice, he confided: "These Martial law people do not know whom they want to stop and whom they want to let go. Sometime ago, Faiz Ahmed Faiz was going abroad. The plane he was in had already taken off when we received orders to off-load him. We recalled the plane even though it was in the air. By the time it had landed and taxied back, we were told he could proceed abroad.

Some days later, an enquiry was held to find who had given permission for him to board."

Mine was an early morning flight. I was too tired to care about Faiz sahib's trials. My fellow passengers on this KLM flight consisted of a surfeit of sunburned Dutch holiday-makers returning to Holland from Indonesia, the luggage racks heavy with wooden carvings and vivid orchids, wrapped in polythene to protect them from a Viennese winter.

The flight reached Vienna at 5.30 a.m., in a biting wind. At the Austrian Customs, an Alsatian dog was allowed to roam among the passengers, sniffing each person. The dog then jumped on to the conveyor belt and after sniffing a suitcase, would leap over it to the next one, and the next. The moment he reached mine, he seemed to go wild. He slobbered over and around it. The Customs officials pounced on my suitcase. I could not have disowned it even if I had been tempted to. Its matching hand-carrier with unmistakable red and green bands lay at my feet.

A Customs official summoned me and asked me for my passport. By this time, the other passengers had retrieved their luggage and passed me on their way out. I could glean their thoughts: "Yes, yet another Pakistani trying to smuggle drugs into our country."

The officer opened my suitcase and painstakingly checked each item of clothing. Fortunately, it was a soft bottomed suitcase and so he satisfied himself by padding it with open palms. What had triggered off the response from the sniffer dog had been a packet of innocuous shelled pine nuts that I was taking to London for Bill Archer. The moment the official put the packet in front of the dog, it lost interest.

"You can go now."

My cheeks burned with the mark of the Pakistani star and crescent.

My pride was slightly assuaged when I alighted at the air terminal.

"Hilton, sir?" the porter asked.

"Nein," I replied, "but thank you for asking." I walked across the park to the Hotel Roemischer Kaiser in Annagasse 16. Its onion-skin letter head described it as a 'Baroque-style Palais, situated in the very heart of Vienna between the Opera-House and St Stephen's Cathedral.' Central, it certainly was. Its amenities were minimal but adequate. A bed, a window, and a small shower cubicle in the room itself.

After a quick bath and calls to UNIDO and OPEC to register my arrival, I walked to the Kunsthistorisches Museum building in Ringstrasse. I had made an appointment to see Dr. Egger to find out whether he had any information about the Austro-Hungarian painter August Schoefft and the exhibition of his works in Vienna in 1855. Dr. Egger brought out some of the folios of the *Hamza-nama* paintings that had been commissioned by the Mughal emperor Akbar. Painted on cloth for portability, they were technically too large to qualify as 'miniatures', yet they conformed to the tradition of such manuscript illustrations. The Kunsthistorisches Museum possessed the largest collection of folios and handling some of them, I was intrigued to learn that they had been used as curtain hangings once.

As I had time available, I scoured some the antiquarian bookshops and then called on Mr. Abdul Sattar, our Ambassador in Vienna. He and his homely wife lived in a rather grand building in Gloriettastrasse. I sat at the table with him and shared his lunch - a bowl of soup. His wife, insulated from the Viennese winter in a thick tartan plaid shirt, watched over him solicitously. Except for the occasional UNIDO meetings, there was little business to keep Mr. Sattar's highly intelligent mind absorbed. He seemed to be marking time until his return within a few months to Pakistan for a higher position.[1]

From Vienna, I rang Bill Archer and also Philip Wilson who to my relief confirmed that he had received the final manuscript of my *Sikh Portraits by European Artists*.

On this trip, I tried to eat as frugally as I could, so that I could save enough money to buy the water-colours of Lahore I had seen at Giles Eyre's gallery. Breakfast was never more than coffee and rolls that tasted like cotton wool, a sandwich for lunch and a cup of soup for dinner. My only indulgence was to tour the art galleries. The Hofburg was closed, so I went to the Handschrift collection of the Bibliotek and to the Albertina where for me the attraction was not David Hockney's work but a superb drawing by Michelangelo and of a pheasant's wing by Albert Dürer.

My abstinence did not pay off. When I phoned Giles to ask if the William Simpson water-colour of the interior of Jahangir's tomb was still

---

[1] Mr Sattar rose to be Foreign Minister, first briefly in 1993, and later 1999-2002.

available, to my chagrin I learned that it had been sold a few days earlier to the travel writer Paul Theroux. Some years later, when I wanted a transparency of it for inclusion in my book *Lahore: Illustrated Views of the 19th Century*,[2] he generously sent me one, asking for nothing more in return than the pen with which I had written to him.

I felt gratified that my book *Pahari Paintings* had reached the bookshops in Vienna. I found it in Wolfrom's, rubbing covers with Bill's two volumes.

The UNIDO Experts Working Group meeting was convened on the 7th floor of the UNIDO building, in a small committee room. I found my name card placed between Qidwai of SAFCO and a Mr. Oyekan from Nigeria. M.B. Verghese (India's Secretary Fertilisers) took the chair and later took us out for lunch at the Rathauskeller (located in the cellar of the Rathaus). It being Ash Wednesday, the Christian faithful were invited to order cold boiled herring. For once Islam came to my rescue. I indulged myself by ordering Schnitzel Holstein surrounded little islets of vegetables and fruit. My companion General Kassim (an Indonesian Zia look-alike) copied me and thanked me afterwards.

Satiated we returned for the second session. Meerhaus from the IBRD asked me: "Did UNIDO pay for the meal?"

"No, we did – as member countries."

The second day dragged, retarded by Verghese's lack-lustre chairmanship. The Director-General Khane came into the room, detected the Lethe-like atmosphere and then slipped out at a discreet moment. Understandably, Verghese wanted to promote the Indian viewpoint and whenever he could he would invite the India representative Dr. Mukherjee to pontificate on the strides the Indian fertiliser industry had made over the past thirty years.

Over lunch, one day, Dr. Mukherjee discussed the possibility of a joint venture between India and Pakistan using Pakistan's gas as feedstock. India would invest 40% equity and guarantee a minimum off-take of 40% of the finished product. Verghese who could never get my name right (*Ajimuddin, Ajamuddin, Aijamuddin, Aijazazuddin*) murmured encouragement from his end of the table.

---

[2] See Aijazuddin, *Lahore: Illustrated Views of the 19th Century* (Ahmedabad, 1991), pl.9.

I sensed a trap. Sure enough, as soon as we had returned to the committee room, Verghese announced that one of the projects UNIDO could assist in would be the joint venture that Pakistan and India had agreed to set up.

I waited to a decent interval to elapse before asking for the floor. For once, Verghese yielded with alacrity, hoping that I would endorse his coup. "While I always relish the company of my colleague from India, especially over lunch," I intoned, "I should nevertheless clarify that the establishment of a joint venture is more properly the subject of bilateral discussions between our two governments."

Verghese made a hasty retreat. He did not need to mispronounce my name again. I was not invited to speak after that.

It became clear to us invitees that the UNIDO staff did not know what to do with us. They had invited enough participants to complete a quorum, without any regard to which regions were likely to welcome integration, or what role UNIDO could perform as a facilitator. Those like me who came from third world countries were handed an allowance of AS 4,650 as a sop. Those from developed countries or IFIs like the World Bank were compensated by the distractions Vienna had to offer.

One morning, I noticed scribbled on a pad left overnight by one of the World Bank attendees: 'Shall I chat up one of the secretaries tonight?'

Beneath it, his IBRD colleague had scrawled: 'Perhaps she has a friend?'

As I happened to arrive that morning before anyone else, I added a postscript: 'Perhaps she is really a he, from the KGB!'

I took my place seat and watched with some *schadenfreude* the two IBRD men enter, settle in their seats, read my addition, and then blush furiously.

By the end of the three day workshop, no-one cared about its outcome. I happened to go backstage to get some photocopying done and overheard Verghese say to Richard Lines (a UNIDO staff member): "You are not going to put down all that bullshit we have just heard, are you?" And in that one remark, I understood the expensive futility of the UN and all its over-staffed agencies and over-paid employees.[3]

---

[3] Two of the advertisements in the UNIDO canteen caught my eye: 'For sale- Mercedes 380' and 'Household effects – settee, tape-recorder and various chandeliers.'

Mr. Oyekan and I travelled to London together. When we landed at Heathrow, he insisted that I should accompany him in his official car. We waited, and waited. Eventually, after forty-five minutes, a Nigerian chauffeur with rings on each finger and a gold bracelet on each wrist drove up without a word of explanation. When Oyekan asked me where I would like to be dropped, I said 'Chalk Farm'. I noticed the chauffeur grimace.

I left the hospitable Oyekan and his surly driver to each other and instead caught the Piccadilly line from the new Heathrow Terminal. Bill received me at 18 Provost Road with the same warmth that he always exhibited. Bill looked well but it was clear that he had not recovered from the trauma of the car accident he had some months earlier. While his case was still in court, his licence had been returned to him and so he was permitted to drive again. He fretted however about the outcome of the court hearings and the effect this accident would have on his insurance policy, unblemished until now.

On my first morning in London, Bill insisted on driving Tim-bibi and myself to the new India Office Library premises in Waterloo Road. Tim had her own cataloguing work to do but she took the trouble of ferreting out some interesting sketches of Lahore done by Ambrose Oldfield, a doctor attached to the British troops who were posted to the Lahore Durbar in 1846, following the First Sikh War. Less appealing though historically equally relevant were sketches by Bellasis and Ainslie. She showed me a copy of *Original Sketches of the Punjaub* by a Lady (1854). I had seen folios on display in the Punjab Archives but had never seen a bound copy.

I was able to see Giles in his Duke Street shop. He brought out the three water-colours he had of Lahore – one by William Simpson dated 1864 of Wazir Khan's Mosque, and two done by an anonymous artist of the Lahore Fort ramparts in September 1846. We had earlier agreed over the phone from Vienna that he could let me have the Simpson for £250. With the two additional pictures, the total came to £450.

"I can give you £425. But I do not need the frames."

'In which case let us settle at £400," Giles said. He was as keen on shedding this dead stock (no collectors were interested in Lahore) as I was on acquiring it.

"Would you keep an eye open for *Original Sketches*, should you come across a copy?"

"I wish you had told me earlier. I have just sent a copy to Christie's for sale in their next auction."

The next morning, on 14 September, my last day in London, Bill received in the post a letter from his insurance company informing him that his policy would not be subject to any conditions. He reacted as if he had been granted a last-minute reprieve from the gallows.

Before leaving Bill for the airport, I tied an *imam zamin*[4] on his upper arm. He was deeply touched, so much so that he attributed the good news from the insurance company as entirely due to my presence, compounded by the influence of the *imam zamin*.

I reached Heathrow well in time and learned that two PIA aircraft had been grounded in New York because of blizzards. I made use of the delay by going back to the India Office Library to examine some old 19th century photographs by William Baker, James Craddock and Samuel Bourne.

Bill came to pick us up and then insisted on dropping me in St James's, close to Giles's shop where Giles had kept the copy of *Original Sketches* that he had retrieved from Christie's. I clutched it as securely as Bill had his letter from the insurance company and took the tube to Heathrow to catch the PIA flight to Karachi.

I was not sure how I would explain these latest indulgences of mine to Shahnaz. She had enjoyed collecting as much as I did, but gradually as our family obligations increased, she would have preferred me to spend on more domestic things, mundane but necessary.

I arrived in the pristine soft-snow flaked September of Vienna and returned to the cage of Zia's puritan penitentiary. Zia's rightist leanings became manifest in many ways. The most obvious impact on us at the NFC came with the appointment of Professor Ghafoor Ahmed (Secretary-General of the PNA) as the new Minister of Production. We obtained an insight into the Professor's priorities when he announced that he would be coming to Lahore, not to review the NFC or the SCCP, but to preside over the swearing-in ceremony of the National Bank of Pakistan Officers' Association.

Majid Mufti who took over as Secretary replacing Awan sahib was no better. I had not seen him for over three months at a stretch, and met him only

---

[4] A talisman favoured by Shias.

once before that. I was told that he was preoccupied heading a committee to review all the appointments made in public sector enterprises between 1 January 1972 and 5 July 1977. Anyone earning a consolidated salary of more than Rs 600 had to be included on the list. And that list had to be provided in *ten* sets.

Just before the end of the year, on 24 December 1978, Majid Mufti visited the NFC offices. He asked to see us separately in our rooms, I suspect to see for himself the 'luxurious style' with which our offices were decorated. He came to my room accompanied by Riyaz Bokhari. He noticed the worn furniture, the ragged carpet, and must have felt reassured that public money was being spent on projects rather than lavishly furnished headquarters.

"I knew your father in Bahawalpur," Mufti said, to establish a connection. He was extremely polite, and even more so when we met again with other NFC management personnel in the Board room. The NFC is doing well, he told us, without going into specifics. He noted the production capacity of Pak-Arab and Pak-Saudi, the likely dates of commercial production. Then, he closed his diary and was ready for lunch. Javed Talat, back in the Ministry after a stint in exile as Managing Director of Ittehad Chemicals, accompanied Majid Mufti. I invited him to sit in what had once been his room, now mine, while our meeting with the Secretary took place. At lunch I ensured that he was shown due deference, not that it mattered to him.

Someone in the Ministry had an idea that the BIM should formulate standard service rules for the public sector enterprises. A meeting was convened on 16 October. A lazy Assistant Secretary disinterred some rules that had been framed earlier, changed a few clauses reclassifying peons and daftaris and presented them at the meeting. I gently sabotaged the meeting by suggesting that as the BIM had the service rules of all the corporations and their subsidiaries, the BIM might first like to compare these, amalgamate them, and then identify those differences that needed resolution. I drove the point home by asking whether the committee wanted service rules for the BIM, or the holding corporations, or their operational subsidiaries, or for all three categories. No one in the BIM or the Ministry of Production could answer.

Gradually, the strict control that Rafi Raza and Awan sahib had instituted of quarterly review meetings with each corporation and its units slackened and then disappeared. At NFC, we continued to hold these review meetings internally but under the guise of Board meetings.

In Pak-Arab at Multan, in October an initial run yielded some ammonia and urea from the new plant. In November, the five-day test run of the Ammonia plant was conducted successfully, much to our relief and to the delight of the ADNOC directors.

Pak-Saudi continued to suffer from the determined incompetence of its managing director Dr. Wahab. At the end of October I was sent to Mirpur Mathelo to quell a Young Turks rebellion by his engineers, led by a Senior Manager Zahid Aziz. Every attempt by us at NFC to persuade him to delegate authority evoked a brittle response from him. One exchange I still recall. He asked me to find him a Finance Manager.

"What should be his qualifications?" I asked him.

"I don't care," he replied. "All I want is that he should be able to stand up to you."

The third major project - the Chinese funded Haripur Urea Fertiliser project - lumbered silently forward like some Asian water-buffalo. Try as hard we could, we could not obtain a delivery schedule from the Chinese. We explained that we needed to know that dimensions of large storage tanks, for example, so that we could check whether these could pass under bridges or through tunnels on the way from Karachi to Haripur Hazara. The Chinese officials at the Embassy would listen to us impassively and then reply that we would be informed when each shipment left Shanghai. Sure enough, in time, we began receiving packets bound in shiny red ribbon, which contained the bills of lading.

The Chinese maintained their own vocabulary. They spoke in repetitive platitudes or predictable clichés. For example, when I invited the Economic Counsellor Mr. Chang (in effect the officiating Ambassador) and his wife for tea at our home, he bemoaned the lack of progress in China, holding the Gang of Four responsible for impeding his country's industrialisation. With a frightening conviction, he insisted that a Third World War was inevitable.

"They can be sure of it," Shahnaz said after they had left, "because they are the ones who will start it."

During this period, at the fag end of 1978, the public sector had to endure yet another committee on its re-organisation. There had been the

Uqaili Commission, the Utra Commission, the Jafarey Commission, and most recently the Beg Commission, headed by H.U. Beg. The Secretary to the Beg Commission, I discovered, happened to be Ghafoor Mirza, whom I had met earlier when he was still trying to obtain justice from the Government. His case seemed too incredible to be untrue. According to him, in 1972, he had been Assistant Commissioner Income Tax. His wife had an argument with a teacher who reported her to Mrs. Nusrat Bhutto. She in turn complained to Dr. Mubashir Hasan, then Finance Minister. Ghafoor Mirza was removed from service peremptorily and languished for almost six years before being reinstated with Rs 1.25 lakhs in back pay and having his seniority restored. As can only happen in Pakistan, he became the Secretary of the potent Beg Committee.

The Beg Committee began by inviting various industrialists like Razak Dawood (MD of Dawood Hercules) and disgruntled ones like R. Latif (whose company BECO had been forcibly nationalised) to appear before it. Having heard them out, it formulated its recommendations. To be more accurate, Ghafoor Mirza drafted its final report and had it endorsed by the Committee members. I noted in my diary on 6 November his whispered disclosure that:

1. The Ministry of Production would be abolished;
2. A full-time Chairman would be appointed. He would be assisted by two Members, one responsible for controlling process industries (fertilisers, cement, chemicals) and the other basic industries such as light and heavy engineering steel, etc.);
3. The Member Finance would be the Chairman NDFC;
4. Units would be merged and rationalised;
5. Corporations too would be merged and superfluous ones wound up.

Despite Ghafoor Mirza's diligence, the recommendations of the Beg Committee began to collect dust even before copies of it could be distributed within the Government.

At the national level, Zia and his government blundered with all the artlessness of novices. A diary entry for October 1978 read:

'Political scene – a disaster. A government of PNA parrots and Fauji crested cranes – without policy, aim or direction – united in their determination to acquire and retain power for as long as possible. If

ZAB's cabinet had been one dominated by lawyers, Zia's is a conclave of religious clerics, aided by such false gurus as A.K. Brohi and malevolent Aleister Crowleys as Sharifuddin Pirzada.

Brohi explains the constitutional position of the president as:

- The president during Bhutto's time [Fazal Elahi Chaudhry] was merely a figurehead. He had no power under the Constitution. He was bound to act on the advice of the PM. As the CMLA is the *de facto* PM, he might as well be president as well. For one thing, it saves another person's salary; for another, if we had put someone else there, there would have been at least five other contending generals who would have been disappointed at being left out.

- Concentration of power? Oh no, Brohi explained. We could not elect the president as there are no Legislative Assemblies. CMLA has assumed power under the Doctrine of Necessity.[5] To exercise power as president, he needs Assemblies. As there are no Assemblies, there can be no concentration of power.

A joke doing the rounds in those days described a *kachehri* held by Ziaul Haq to receive plaints from different animals.

First a delegation of cockerels applies for a NOC to go abroad.

"Why?" the CMLA asks.

"Well, ever since the maulvis wake up the public with the azan every morning, there is no work left for us to do."

"Ah, I see. NOC granted."

The next batch was a pack of dogs.

"Ever since the introduction of the *Nizam-e-Mustafa*, there are no robbers for us to bark at."

"OK. NOC granted."

The final contingent was a drove of donkeys.

"And why do all of you asses want a NOC?"

---

[5] Oliver Cromwell had justified his own assumption of powers when in 1654, he said: 'Necessity hath no law. Feigned necessities, imaginary necessities … are the greatest cozenage that man can put upon the Providence of God., and make pretences to break known rules by.'

"Well, those of us who could become ministers have already joined your Cabinet. So, the remainder want to go abroad."

On 13 October, I devoted almost a page to Zia's errancy:

'Ziaul Haq is getting carried away with the sound of his own verbosity. He is making the most inane pronouncements and issuing banal instructions. One letter received from him records that during a spot tour of government offices, amongst other 'appalling' things, he found 'ashtrays choke-full of cigarette butt ends, which had fallen on the floor.' The Secretary Production inscribed in the margins of this *farman*: 'We should discuss this important letter.'

Today's news is that Zia has had an inspiration (if he tries hard enough, he will start having revelations) that he should create a Women's Division. While inaugurating a seminar by the Business & Professional Women's Club in Karachi (in the words of The Pakistan Times reporter) 'the President dressed in a General's uniform, quietly left the Banquet Hall, accompanied by members of his entourage. As there was no one in the congregation to lead the prayers, the President was requested to lead the prayers. He accepted.

Poor man. He seems condemned to filling up a vacuum in leadership.

His ministers are floundering, each making pronouncements on subjects outside his own ministerial remit – Ghafoor Ahmed on the textile industry, Farooqi on labour, and Ch. Zahur Elahi on everything else.'

To me, the similarity between Oliver Cromwell (a confirmed regicide) and Zia (a potential regicide) became clearer by the day. Many years later, I wrote an article for *The Nation* titled 'General Ziaul Haq - Our Chief of Men' in which I compared the lives and careers of Oliver Cromwell and Ziaul Haq. Researching it, I was startled at the continuous parallels that continued even after their death and dismemberment.[6]

Zia used the Supreme Court judges to commit what can only be described as 'a judicial murder'. Many disagreed with me at the time that Zia would not hang Bhutto. I remained convinced that he would. But before then, he would ensure that Mr. Bhutto suffered a thousand deaths.

---

[6] Reprinted in my book *The Armless Queen & Other Essays* (Lahore, 1994), pp. 273-276.

On 18 December, Mr. Bhutto made an appearance before the Supreme Court.[7] I wrote about it in my dairy.

> 'The newspapers gave prominent coverage to all the dramatic aspects of his public appeal – his insistence that 'not only his life but his honour, the honour of his family, his potential career and the future of Pakistan were at stake,' his dizziness 'because he had been in a death cell which was 10 x 7 feet,' and his humble admission of the power the Supreme Court could exercise over him and how dependent he realized he was upon their goodwill.
>
> What a historic trial for Pakistan! How right Bhutto is to connect his own future with that of this country. No single individual after Quaid-e-Azam could have dared to make such a claim; none had the credentials. Just as the Quaid's death in 1948 released a flotsam and jetsam of political dead-wood and opportunists, Bhutto's murder will release a sewer of corrupt decomposing matter to swill across our political future.
>
> Personally, I feel extremely sorry for ZAB. He has been punished enough by the sheer humiliation of being punishable at all. He is conscious of his stature and political ability. Everyone is convinced of it but somehow this emasculated nation is too much of a eunuch to react.'

The following day, Bhutto flailed at his tormentors. 'ZAB has begun swinging blows now that he has regained the use of his muscles. He swiped at the Supreme Court, saying that 'an illegitimate child could not be legitimized,' to which the Chief Justice replied lamely: "That issue was decided in the Nusrat Bhutto case."

A few days later, the irony of Mr. Bhutto's situation and that of Mrs. Indira Gandhi hit me. 'The two signatories to the Shimla Agreement who bargained and haggled over 90,321 POWs and CUPCs should today find themselves behind bars – ZAB in Rawalpindi and Mrs. IG in Delhi.'

While many of us discussed the Bhutto case in the privacy of our homes, it was wise to keep our opinions to ourselves, or better still to one's diary. That

---

[7] It was during this appearance that Mr. Bhutto called the approver Masood Mahmood 'a congenital liar.'

explains why this poem I composed on a PNA leaders*fatwa* that self-immolation was un-Islamic remained in my diary until now:

> Self-burning's un-Islamic,
>> an authority explains.
>> Discuss but don't become
>>> a burning issue, he maintains.
>
> You mustn't kill yourself, he says,
>> for no suicide attains
> Salvation. You'll surely end up in Hell
>> leaving charred remains.
>
> These inflammable dissidents,
>> rejecting worldly gain,
> Roasting meat on pavements
>> cooking chops, joints and brains
>
> Will ruin Lahore's restaurants,
>> where everyone entertains
> Their friends to a tandoori meal
>> on plates with fatty stains.
>
> Just ask yourself, Muslim
>> carnivore, will anyone take the pains
> To verify your kabab's origins? No? Then become
>> A vegetarian pacifist who abstains.

Perhaps no incident provided as cruel an insight into the naïve incompetence, the hypocrisy of the rightist parties as the behaviour of Prof. Ghafoor Ahmed. As Minister of Production, he ordered public sector employees to hear him speak on Quaid-e-Azam. Despite it being an official holiday, we were summoned to be present at WAPDA auditorium. I wrote a longish account of it in my diary:

'The irony was not lost on anyone. A Jamaat-e-Islami minister talking on the Quaid.

The Minister, Secretary Production and the three Lahore-based Chairmen sat on the stage. The programme started promptly at 10.00 a.m. A lengthy *qirat* was followed by an even lengthier translation. Next came a rather pompous poem composed by a finance man from the Cement Corporation in honour of Quaid. He contended that by adding the name 'Ali' to his name, Jinnah had improved upon his credentials as Muslim. Clearly no one had told the earnest poet that the courts had yet to adjudicate on whether Jinnah died a Shia or a Sunni.

When it was Prof Ghafoor Ahmed's turn, he spoke on Quaid's ideals for exactly one minute, and then launched into a blistering critique of the public sector and of its managers. Not only were they inefficient but they were not even patriotic. To prove this latter point, he recalled a meeting with some 'salt of the earth' in Hyderabad who assured him that they did not want imported cement but preferred their own, local, national, Pakistani cement.

"Don't look for material rewards," he exhorted us. "You should be content with the joy of service. Be like a gardener who prepares the ground, sows the seed, watches the plant grow and the buds emerge. The joy the gardener feels when the bud burst into bloom is something only he can experience. Be like that gardener."

The scheduled speeches finished by 10.35 a.m. As the Minister had time available before his next appointment – a meeting with the chairmen of the corporations on the Beg Committee report – he invited members of the audience to take the floor.

One ill-clad, unshaven stranger took the microphone. "I was a fellow worker of the Quaid's", he began. The audience murmured its acknowledgment. "I have come to honour him who was a *kafir*, an atheist, a non-Muslim, a drunkard. I have come to honour him," he continued, in a stronger voice, "whose party, of which I was a two-anna paying member, is now being torn to shreds by you and your government..."

Needless to say, after this outburst, the meeting was quickly adjourned.

"That mad old coot," I overheard a NFC staff member say. "Bless him. If it had not been for him, we would have been there for hours."'

The antidote to such mind-numbing functions lay in my other persona. Shahnaz and I agreed to lend our lithographs for exhibition linked to the British Council collection of rare books on Pakistan. The exhibition opened in Lahore on 5 October, was displayed in Islamabad and then taken to Karachi. The slim catalogue became the crucible of an expanded book I compiled some years later - *Historical Images of Pakistan*.

Soon after this exhibition had been inaugurated at Lahore, I received a call from someone in Indian Airlines[8] inviting Shahnaz and myself to meet their Managing Director Sarin and his wife over dinner. The next night, we discovered why. My diary reads:

> 'Sarin's wife is Ved's sister Nirmala!! Apparently she had been given our names by Ved and the IA office had been trying to trace us. Shahnaz extremely excited and in a way also apprehensive that Nimmi may not live up to the image Ved had conveyed though his writings.[9]

We dumped our children at Barque's next door and went to Room 311 of the Intercontinental hotel. A motley crowd for drinks – Justice Yaqub Ali, lofty and reticent; Satnam Mahmood, high but for different reasons; Bapsi Sidhwa, fellow author and as ignorant of my books as I am of hers; Salim Malik FCA, knocking back free whiskies.

Sarin extremely surprised that I should know that he had been in Hindustan Aeronauticals, State Trading, etc. before joining Indian Airlines.

"How do you know so much about me?"

"I read books other than by Ved Mehta."

---

[8] Indian airlines had just opened their new offices in Faletti's hotel.
[9] Ved Mehta had written about them in his book *Face to Face* (1957).

A larger crowd gathered for the late dinner. We stay on with Nimmi and Sarin while Malika Pukhraj's driver went to her home to bring some tapes they had asked for. When they arrived finally at 10.30, she obligingly signed them for the Sarins.'

Some days after the Sarins left, I wrote an account of their visit to Lahore and of our 'discovery' of his father's house in Temple Road where Ved grew up. I quote an extract from my letter to him of 21 October 1978:

'Our very dear Ved …

Yesterday morning, taking our two children along even though they did not know what to expect, we visited 11 Temple Road. One or two false turnings and then suddenly we drove slowly past a house with the name 'Dr. Amolak Mehta' etched black letters on a white marble slab, set in new grey cement.

We entered the gate, turned left into a small garden with a water-tank, child-high, set against a front wall, and then walked the ten or so steps onto the front verandah. The house has been divided. Partitioned would be a better word. The portion which contained your rooms is now occupied by two doughty old ladies, sisters of Dr. Mubashir Hasan, the former Finance Minister of Mr. Bhutto's government and now Secretary-General of the Pakistan People' Party. He lives elsewhere with his wife who is a pathologist, but often spends his Fridays with his two lonely sisters.

We sat in the drawing room, Shahnaz on the sofa and I on the bay window-sill, while we talked to the ladies about the state of the house when they took it over and their meetings with your father when he came after 1947 to collect your books [.]

Would it seem odd to you, Ved, you whom we have met for only one evening of our lives and God knows may never meet again, that for the long still moment that we stood at the entrance to your rooms, we felt deeply for and with you? It was not just a matter of checking the room against your description of it or recognising obvious features. It was something far more than that. We were not standing on the threshold of your past but in some subtle way of our own as well. It was ours because both Shahnaz and I together felt it acutely [.]

Nirmala's presence in Lahore, so soon after our own meeting with you in New Delhi, must be a sign from someone, that there are finer things to come. We repeat even more vehemently now, our invitation for you to come to Pakistan, to Lahore and to your own home.'

During that last quarter of 1978, we met the new Indian Ambassador Shankar Bajpai and his wife Meera on a number of occasions, either in Lahore or in Islamabad. Shankar had been given the thorny task of re-establishing diplomatic relations between his government which was loath to do business with yet another military dictator and his Pakistani hosts who craved acknowledgement of the new regime. One excuse was provided by the cricket Test match. I happened to be returning to Lahore on the same flight as Mr. Rajinder Dutt, the Indian First Secretary. He was en route to Multan where the teams were playing one of the matches. His luggage contained 'lubricants' for the Indian players. The baggage handlers, with neighbourly malice, deliberately dropped the crates and tried to look apologetic.

A few days later, Shankar invited me over to his suite in the Hilton hotel for drinks. It surprised me when I discovered that I would be the only Pakistani. He wanted me to meet Narindar Saroop, an Indian-born bigwig in the Conservative Party and its candidate for the seat at Reading.[10] Saroop narrated an anecdote told to him by his friend who worked in Coutt's (bankers to the Royal Family, and therefore also to Saroop). Whenever the Duke of Windsor would come to London, he would lunch with his Coutt's banker at the Ritz Hotel. The waiter, after having served them over the years, mentioned that he would be migrating to the Bahamas.

"Whom will you be working for?" the Duke asked him. The waiter gave a name. "Don't know him."

"Were you in the Bahamas, sir?" the waiter asks the Duke.

"Didn't you know that I was once the Governor of the Bahamas, during the war?"

The waiter shook his head.

"Let me try again. Did you know that I was once the King-Emperor of India?"

---

[10] He lost in the 1979 general elections.

The cricket match played between the Indian and the Pakistan teams in Lahore on 1 November was fraught with tension. To the delight of the Lahori crowd, Zaheer Abbas and Asif Iqbal played magnificently and won the game.

That evening Bajpai had given a dinner in honour of both teams. I arrived, sandwiched between one lift-load of players and the second. Rajinder Singh Bedi, soft-palmed and despondent; Zaheer Abbas, given a hero's welcome. Bajpai expressed relief that Pakistan had won. "Imagine the embarrassment if India had won – in Lahore!"

The German Ambassador agreed: "I feel most strongly for my colleague in London when the World Cup football series is played. If God forbid our team wins, he has to board up our Embassy in case the shutters are torn down by irate Londoners!"

Ziaul Haq, exuberant at Pakistan's victory, even though it was only the first of three matches, declared a national holiday in celebration.

December 25, 1978, Shahnaz and I shared Christmas greetings with our Christian brethren but in an unexpected way. I heard from our servant Zaman who heard from our neighbour Khokhar's servant that the television set that had been stolen from Khokhar's house in early October had been recovered and was in Model Town police station.

Our house had also been burgled that same night. On 5 October, early in the morning, our maid Zulaikha burst into our bedroom, beating her chest and wailing that she had been violated. I went with her to the store room where she kept her small tin trunk and discovered that during the night, thieves had entered our house from the drawing room window, broken the lock of the store, and rifled anything they thought valuable. Zulaikha's savings were the smallest part of the booty. The thieves took Shahnaz's silk sheets, unstitched cloth, etc.

As fate would have it, that was the one night that I had shifted the sofa away from the window. Normally it blocked the window, preventing it from being opened inwards. I felt so vulnerable. Perhaps the most distressing moment for me was the see the foot prints of the robbers clearly imprinted in the morning dew. It was as if they had just escaped, moments earlier.

Hearing of the possible recovery of our belongings almost three months after the theft, Shahnaz and I drove with the girls to Model Town police station. The SHO sat on a chair with three shivering culprits squatting at his feet.

"Did you steal from their house as well?" he asked them.

They could hardly remember. They had broken into every house in our road, jumping over walls to gain access.

"Put them against heater," he ordered his subordinate. I was about to compliment him on his innate humanity when he stopped me short: "These bastards. If you put them close to heater, they wilfully scorch themselves and then complain before the magistrate that we have tortured them. No, we use the heater to burn the soles of their feet."

At this, I suggested Shahnaz should take the girls to the car.

On getting no response or admission of guilt from these hapless crooks, the SHO asked for a bamboo.

He belaboured them with it, careful not leave any marks. At this, Shahnaz left us and returned to the car.

After a few minutes, I joined her.

"What were they doing now?" she asked me.

"The SHO asked for some red chillie powder. That was my breaking point."

Before we left, the SHO asked us to identify our belongings from an array displayed on a table top. Shahnaz's silken sheets had already been sold or recycled, and her cut pieces adorning some stranger's body. To my surprise, I found a tweed jacket that I had bought in Austin Reed in 1964, had worn in London and in Nairobi where it was stolen and then recovered, and now, stolen again and recovered yet again.

Just as we were leaving, the SHO picked up a weather-beaten copy of the *Kama Sutra* that Shahnaz's mother had discovered hidden atop an almirah of an octogenarian relative. We had left it on the verandah with some other books we intended to throw away. The thieves had grabbed it on their way out.

"Is this yours?" he asked.

"No." I replied. "You can keep it." I knew it would not be of any interest to him. It contained no illustrations.

CHAPTER 21

HANGING FIRES

Could any year in this decade have started with a greater sense of foreboding than 1979?

On the first day of the year, the Shah of Iran found himself being despatched into exile, for a second time[1], ostensibly for medical treatment abroad. He would never return to power, or to Iran, even for burial.

During most of the first month of that fateful year, Zulfikar Ali Bhutto found himself in the dock of a Pakistani court. He too would never return to power, but would be allowed to return to his home town Larkana, only for burial.

Anyone who could discern a pattern in Zia's behaviour since he took control in July 1977 would have traced an adamantine determination to ensure that Zulfikar Ali Bhutto had to be eliminated. From informal sources, one learned that Zia, having become privy to secrets known only to Bhutto and his accomplices, convinced himself that Bhutto had to be hanged, if not for the accidental death of Ahmed Raza Kasuri's father, then certainly for far more heinous crimes which Zia chose not to reveal to the public.

There was something of the stricken gladiator about Mr. Bhutto. Nattily dressed in his well-cut suits yet naked to his enemies, armed with the formidable power of oratory yet defenceless against the jeers of his opponents on the bench, courageous but outnumbered by his adversaries, he knew that even if he succeeded in combat, his life was in the hands a tin-hat Caesar who

---

[1] The Shah had been forced into exile once before in 1953 by his prime minister Mohammad Mosaddegh.

would decide his fate with a twist of the thumb.

Gradually, everything turned against Bhutto. Even *Time* magazine, upon whose cover he had tried desperately to appear while in office, mentioned his trial, but in an inside page. Had he been allowed to read it, he would have been mortified to see that he had to share the space with Mrs. Indira Gandhi, and perhaps for him the unkindest cut, the reporter reproducing Bhutto's impassioned, death-defying speech before the Supreme Court bench found fault with Bhutto's grammar.

On the morning of 6 February, I noticed armoured cars patrolling outside our offices in Alfalah Building. I called Wadoud 'Woody' Afridi (our man in Islamabad) and asked him to check what was happening at the Supreme Court there.

"It has been cordoned off."

"Post someone to stand on the perimeter of the cordon."

At 11.30 a.m., he called back. "The verdict is against him. Two judges have dissented."

By lunchtime, the Urdu papers had issued flash supplements. I learned later (to my disappointment) that Air Marshal Asghar Khan had attended the Supreme Court hearing. It was a petty act of revenge for all the humiliations he had suffered at Bhutto's hands.[2]

The actual verdict had been a 4:3 split – Justices Haleem, Safdar Shah and Dorab Patel had dissented. There could not have been a clearer, as the BBC was quick to point out, Punjabi vs. non-Punjabi divide.

On 1 March, Zia felt it necessary to make an announcement at Lahore airport of all places that he would abide by the verdict of the Supreme Court. I wrote in my diary that his pronouncement was 'an exhortation intended to fortify the waning confidence of the Supreme Court. He seems determined to hang him. Obviously an earlier effort to involve the Military Council and the PNA through the Cabinet has backfired. No-one wants to be party to the decision. Slowly every conspirator is moving away.'

On 22 March, the Indian Ambassador Shankar Bajpai invited Shahnaz

---

[2] One particular insult the Air Marshal could not have relished was to be called an 'aloo' or potato by Bhutto.

and myself, along with some other guests, to meet B. K. Nehru.[3] On meeting me, BKN expressed surprise at my age: "But you are so young! I expected someone much older. Perhaps with a long white beard."

I replied: "I shaved it off for you."

He laughed: "But how have you managed to become an expert on Pahari painting at your age? Dr. Randhawa described you as one."

Bajpai had gone to Amritsar for the day, presumably to brief his Foreign Secretary on the Bhutto case.

"Do you think there will be a reaction if they hang Mr. Bhutto?" Bajpai asked me as I was leaving.

"No. Not immediately."

"I agree," he replied.

That month, the rumour mills went into override. On 23 March, the news spread that a special barrack was being constructed at Rawalpindi jail as lodgings for a VIP lifer.

The Supreme Court announced that it would give its verdict on the admissibility of Bhutto's appeal at 10.00 a.m. on 23th March. Zia for his part distracted the public with an announcement that general elections would be held on 17 November. Meanwhile, copies of Bhutto's testament *If I am Assassinated* published in India began to circulate here in Pakistan. 'Vintage ZAB,' I noted, 'although perhaps the last drops from the bottle.'

The Supreme Court rejected Bhutto's appeal on 24 March. The notes of dissent hinted to the Executive that a liberal exercise of the inherent power of clemency might be appropriate. Justice Safdar Ali Shah explained what his note of dissent meant to the BBC correspondent Mark Tully as they (in the quaint words of *The Pakistan Times*) 'strolled down a road in Islamabad.' Safdar's disclosure was an attempt to counteract the Government's contention that the SC decision had been unanimous. By law, the sentence would have to be carried out within seven days.

The impact of this decision on NFC forced a cancellation of the inauguration of Pak-Arab in Multan, scheduled for 25 March. 'Everyone at Multan crushed; RHB at the point of tears. The decision to cancel was, I suspect, less to do with any resolve on Zia's part than indecision on the part of our amenable sycophantic Secretary Majid Mufti. Five years of effort, endeavour, and frustrations have led to the crescendo of this disappointment.'

Our daughter Mubarika's third birthday's fell on 1 April. We celebrated it, but inevitably the overtones of the Bhutto case permeated into our home. I noted that 'our neighbour overheard Shaheen Ramay announce at a coffee party in the morning that ZAB had been hanged at 4.00 a.m., and that his body had been handed over to his relatives. The BBC said otherwise. Picking up a cue from Hafeez Pirzada's statement (by the way, in the heat of this crisis, HP has whipped up enough passion to marry his school-teacher mistress), Mark Tully mentioned that during his last interview with Zia, Zia had asked Mark why Bhutto's family had not appealed for clemency. Mark Tully believed that Zia wanted them to appeal so that he had grounds for commuting the sentence, yet he sought the appeal as an admission by Bhutto of his guilt. The longer Zia delays, the more detrimental it will be for him. It is now a war of nerves, with ZAB fighting magnificently for his life with nothing more potent than an eloquent silence. If only he could have been as quiet when in power.'

On 3 April, I recorded:

'Strong rumours that the hanging has taken place, that it is taking place on 10th, or on the 4th, or that it will not take place at all. Pakistan Television Corporation (PTV) announced that "top secret papers had been discovered in ZAB's in Larkana and Karachi". As if a PM could be expected to have less than top secret papers in his possession! Really, the naïve diversionary tactics being used by General Mujeeb[4] who according to Mushahid Hussain is one of the few experts on psychological warfare in the army.'

The following day, 4 April, I wrote in my diary:

'A black, monstrous day for Pakistan. We have hanged our un-saintly Billy.[5] An early morning supplement rushed to the stands by Nawa-i-Waqt announced that Bhutto had been hanged this morning. Tremendous security at Lahore airport as I left to attend an ADP meeting in Islamabad. Our flight was delayed as Islamabad airport

---

[4] Lt. General (Retd), Mujeeb-ur-Rehman, then Secretary Information.
[5] The allusion was to the book by Robert Graves, THEY HANGED MY SAINTLY BILLY: The Life and Death of Dr. William Palmer (1957).

was closed. They were flying his body to Larkana for burial. I had to pass Rawalpindi jail on my way to Islamabad. Not a soul to be seen outside its walls. At 11.00 a.m., pockets of persons grouped outside each Secretariat building, congregating around anyone who had a radio or was reading the special supplements brought out by the Urdu dailies. Inside, the ADP Priorities Committee continued its deliberations without a word of regret or sympathy at the passing of the man who had once been their prime minister and had now died as a common criminal.

Later in the day, Mumtaz Bhutto and Hafeez Pirzada led a public *namaz-e-janaza* in Liaquat Bagh, attended by a thousand persons. A *thousand* persons!

"He did not have a friend in the world," Awan-sahib said later, as we drive home for lunch. "But that did not mean that no one cared for him. He was too important a person to be ignored. He broke the bureaucrats, ridiculed the politicians, emasculated the judiciary, but he was nevertheless the prime minister. These wooden-heads have no sense. They cannot see beyond the ends of their noses!"

Dinner that evening for the Chinese Economic Counsellor. I suggested to RHB that it should be cancelled. At first he agreed but then changed his mind, sensing I suspect that someone may construe the cancellation as a pro-Bhutto expression of remonstrance. So we sat in the Rawalpindi Intercontinental with 11 Chinese construction engineers who spoke no English, and pretended that nothing of consequence had occurred that morning.'

I remained in Rawalpindi for meetings with the Chinese on the plant site at Hazara. On 5 April, I noted:

'Banner headline in the paper slipped under my door, ZULFIKAR ALI BHUTTO HANGED, and accompanying it his official photograph as PM. The description of the hanging was harrowing, as usual with the government's inept handling of the case, they have tried to refute something and made themselves look ridiculous. The BBC reported last night that Bhutto's last words were: "*Ya Allah, mujhe ma'af kar. Main begunah hun.*" [Ya Allah, forgive me. I am innocent.] *The Pakistan Times* of course had to refute this. 'Actually, he wrote something twice instead.'

Throughout the day on the site I remained apprehensive that someone from the Chinese team would mention Bhutto's name. They seemed more intent on stuffing me with a twelve course meal. From Beijing, however, came a statement that Mr. Bhutto had been the last foreign dignitary to meet Chairman Mao before his death, and that he was a personal friend of Premier Zhou Enlai. Read that A.K. Brohi is being sent abroad. He was shown carrying an overcoat. He will need more than that to counteract the chilly reception he is likely to get in foreign capitals.'

Both Shahnaz and I felt deeply about the tragedy. I recorded my indignation in my dairy:

'So that is that! We have destroyed the finest, most brilliant mind Pakistan had created. I do not mean to imply that he was not corrupt or arrogant or vindictive. He was all this and worse. He had more vices than versatility itself; he had used and abused them to the full. But that is not the true measure of the man. He was the most *significant* man in Pakistan.

I was not a Bhutto fan. I was too sickened by the sight of the splattering blood of his victims to rejoice at his own bloodless, brutal murder. It is not even an assassination, which might have yielded him the aura of martyrdom. He has been murdered, slowly, viciously, with malice afore-thought. '*Ba shauq e-sagan, shikar-e-sheran kardand*' (For their sport, curs have hunted down lions.) Now that they have done with him, they must go fight among themselves.

What I deplore is this crimson flow in the mainstream of our politics. This is a bad augury, not only for the destruction it portends, but because it is an unnatural, unnerving departure from our traditional method of doing away with our political hot potatoes. After Liaquat Ali Khan's assassination, when the killing of Gandhi was still fresh in the minds of our politicos, there has been no murder like this one. Ayub Khan loathed Ayub Khuhro to the point of wanting him dead; Yahya hated Mujibur Rahman but could not bring himself to have him killed; Bhutto disliked Ayub Khan but let nature take its revenge. This Cromwell [Zia] has perverted the pattern of our history. He has misshapen its future. By committing regicide, he will forfeit his own head.

The most obvious outcome, once the shock wears off, will be the sacrifice of the executioner himself. This was a decision Zia had to take on his own. He was forced to. He wanted the Judiciary to do it for him. In the last resort, they backed out leaving a plea for clemency, albeit in fine print. He turned to the Military Council, but they politely returned the pen and gripped their barrels more tightly. He sought the support of the PNA through the Cabinet but they reminded him collectively that it could not be a joint decision but an individual one, and one that only he as president could make. If Zia had any doubt about the loneliness of his position, Maulana Mufti Mahmud delineated it by gloating the day before Bhutto's execution that 13 crore Muslims had been avenged.

Queen Elizabeth I vacillated for fourteen years before finally signing the death warrant of her cousin and rival Mary Queen of Scots. Zia dithered for twenty-one months. Elizabeth spent her remaining years regretting her decision, even though she made someone else a scapegoat. In Zia's case, *he* is the scapegoat.'

Ziaul Haq's closest civilian associate (and after his death his successor as president) was Ghulam Ishaq Khan, more a pickled than a seasoned bureaucrat. He had been appointed Governor State Bank of Pakistan by Bhutto in 1971, and in 1975 recalled to Islamabad to become Secretary Defence. It proved to be a decision Bhutto would have cause to regret.

Ghulam Ishaq Khan 'assisted' in the military takeover in July 1977. Zia appointed him as Secretary Finance to control the financial situation of the country while he tackled its political turbulence. In time, Ghulam Ishaq would take over as president after Zia's death in 1988.

My first encounter with him occurred during a review session convened on 13 January 1979. All the BIM corporations were summoned to Islamabad. Whoever had scheduled an hour for a comprehensive review of 10 corporations had not reckoned on Mr. Ghulam Ishaq Khan's temperament. By 12.30 p.m., three hours after the meeting started, only one corporation – the innocuous amoeba of PIDC – had been examined. RHB and I thought we could use our time productively by holding the 3rd NFC Board meeting. We had hardly begun when we received a summons.

'The meeting opened the moment GIK returned from the President's court. A strong Pathan accent, a mandarin's fingers. Strongly anti-PPP. Incapable of identifying priorities. Spent as much time on LCFF's production as on Pak-Arab's which was more than ten times its size. GIK complimentary about NFC. "One of the better run Corporations. You have good professional management." GIK suddenly lost interest after he detected a mistake in Pak-Arab's figures.'

The struggle for control in Pak-Saudi between Wahab and Sherwani continued to cause RHB a headache. It turned into a migraine after Bokhari visited Mirpur Mathelo. He had what amounted to a showdown with Dr. Wahab, He returned fuming, livid with Dr. Wahab.

"I want to change him. But who can I replace him with?" he complained to me. "What are your own plans?"

I gave him my reasons why I thought Sherwani was better qualified to become MD, PSFL.

On 7 April, too soon after Mr. Bhutto's hanging, a fire occurred in the tall prilling tower at Pak-Saudi. All the polypropylene filling was incinerated, a loss of a crore of rupees. We were able to assess the damage ourselves when on 23 April Bokhari and I convened a Board meeting at the plant site. The confrontation between Wahab and Sherwani could be summarised in the following monosyllabic exchange:

Wahab: "Yes."   Sherwani: "No."

Wahab: "No."   Sherwani: "Yes."

On the overnight train back, I wrote in my diary that Dr. Wahab's attitude to the NFC's review meetings was akin to the Victorian marm's attitude to sex: 'Something essentially distasteful but unavoidable, and therefore to be endured with an expression of resignation resembling a feigned headache.'

Wahab's confrontation with me came to a head when Bokhari nominated both of us to go to Milan to negotiate with FAVRA International. I phoned Wahab and was told by him that he would inform me whether we would be going at all. When I heard nothing from him, I called again. He came on the line to tell me that we would be leaving for Milan that evening. When I asked him why he had not informed me earlier, he replied: "I forgot." That was too much for me. I shot off a letter to him immediately explaining why I could not accompany him. Seeing his foreign trip in jeopardy, he tried contacting me on the phone. I refused his calls. He then showed up at my office. We had a long amiable chat, during which he tried to disarm me by narrating some nauseating anecdotes about himself. He tried hard to pressurise me into withdrawing my letter. I remained adamant.

RHB phoned a while later, and expressed surprise that I was not on my way to Milan. Thinking that I was at fault, he asked for my reasons in writing. I told him that I had already given them in writing to Dr Wahab. His copy was on its way to the Chairman's office.

In July, Bokhari took the decision he ought to have done months earlier. He replaced Dr. Wahab by Sherwani, and at Pak-Arab in Multan, he rewarded Zahur Ahmed Khan for his efforts as Project Manager of such a large project by appointing him as MD in place of Aftab Ahmed.

It seemed appropriate to introduce Zahur as the new MD to NFC's co-shareholders in the Multan project. The ADNOC directors were very keen that a Board meeting should be held in Abu Dhabi. On 5th August, a team led by RHB, with Aftab, Zahur, Fawzia Najm (PFL's Finance Manager) and Waqar its Company Secretary flew to Abu Dhabi. No soon had we entered the arrivals lounge than we were informed that the following day was the 13th anniversary of H.H. Sheikh Zayed's accession. The Board meeting would therefore be held on 7th.

Once again, I found myself incarcerated in the constricting comfort of the Abu Dhabi Hilton. On a previous occasion, in 1975, our delegation's visit had coincided with the death of one of Sheikh Zayed's uncles. We had gone to ask ADNOC to increase its capital stake in Pak-Arab to help meet the project's over-runs. Nothing could be transacted until the four day period of mourning had been completed. On that occasion, we were driven to Al Ain, to Dubai and taken around Abu Dhabi. When eventually, Babar Ali was invited to meet Sheikh Tahnoun (Chairman ADNOC and the ruler's son-in-law) at Al Ain, the interview lasted half an hour. Shaikh Tahnoun spent 20 minutes admiring the expensive falcon we had selected as a gift for him, five minutes complimenting the Shikarpuri *halwa* we had brought for him which he shared with those attending his majlis, and the last five minutes asking how much money we needed.

"$ 20 million," Babar told him, hat in hand and heart in mouth.

"Done," the generous sheikh replied, and then went back to stroking the falcon and savouring the *halwa*.

Before leaving on this 1979 visit, we called on our Ambassador Riffat Pasha Sheikh (Javed Talat's uncle) - pompous and boastful about how much he knew about the Pak-Arab project, except that his information was at least a year out of date. He stressed that Zia's government should be pragmatic, less arrogant: "After all, they should not think that they can get away with murder!!" He blushed. "I have said the wrong thing, haven't I?"

Although he had been in Abu Dhabi for some months, he had not been invited to present his credentials. Sheikh Zayed had been a personal friend of Bhutto's. He had been invited by Bhutto to attend the Islamic Summit in 1974. He had sent a plea for clemency, which Zia had spurned. Sheikh Zayed was in no mood to humour Zia with diplomatic niceties.

Travelling abroad on such trips gave me the opportunity of phoning my friends in London. It had become a habit to dial 722 2713 and to hear Bill Archer's voice answer. This time I knew that he would not be there, for on 10 March I learned that Bill had passed away. I conveyed my feelings to my diary:

> 'Only last night, I dreamed about him and Tim-bibi. The dream was still vivid in my mind when I reached the office. My PA's room was before mine in the corridor, and so I sat at his typewriter and wrote a letter to Bill, asking him to come to Lahore for a few weeks. He had been complaining about the treacherous cloudy winter and the cold. In one of his last letters he mentioned that he had not seen the sun for almost three months. Having completed the letter, I went to my own room and found on my desk, a telex from Philip Wilson saying that Bill had died on Wednesday, 6 March. There was no further information other than that the funeral would take place next week, to be followed by a memorial service.
>
> I felt crushed. I returned home and sat in the room Bill and Tim had occupied when they stayed with us in 1976. I wept uncontrollably. I tried to phone Tim-bibi but there was no response. She must have

gone to stay with her son Michael in Dedham.

Felt dull and empty the whole day, tearful at the sight of anything that reminded me of him. What a dear friend and mentor he had been! Generous, considerate and unrestrained in his love. More than a father. I used to joke about being his 'adopted' son. He would counter that with a phrase from his, in which he described the various putative sons of Ranjit Singh tactfully, as his 'accepted' progeny. How I shall miss his friendship and his fun!

I tried to call Dr. Randhawa the following day but his Kharar number appeared to be out or order. I managed to speak to him on the 12th. He took the news stoically, almost as though he had been expecting it. I then spoke to Brenda, Tim-bibi's daily help. She told me that Bill had taken his own life. Stunned at hearing that. Shahnaz however had suspected that for some time.

It was only when I was able to speak to Tim-bibi at Michael's that the full sequence became known. She told me she had gone to the India Office Library and in the late afternoon, as usual she waited for him to pick her up. When he did not appear, she assumed that he must have had another accident. She caught the tube home and found him in bed, with a note telling her that while he loved her, he did not feel that he wanted to live anymore.

"He felt that as his creative process had dried up," she said, "there was nothing left to live for, but there was us all, wasn't there, Aijaz?" My heart broke. "You will keep in touch, won't you?" she added.[6]

Bill had talked about 'doing away' with himself when we stayed with him in London in 1977. Tim-bibi had told me then about a dear friend of theirs who had supplied them with a number of fine Daniells and Hodges prints. He decided that he did not want to face the deterioration that old age would bring. He walked into his garden and hanged himself. According to Tim, that death had affected Bill deeply. It provided him with a sort of precedent which he felt impelled to follow.

---

[6] We did keep in touch with her, visiting her once at her house in Dedham. She died on 4 February 2005.

I had been aware for the past year and a half that Bill, particularly after the publication of his magnum opus on Pahari painting, had felt a gnawing lack of purpose, a gradual erosion of his peace of mind. No amount of coaxing by Tim-bibi or reminders of his place in the Archer family as its pater familias, or expressions of support from his numerous friends across the globe could convince him that he was needed. He decided that he did not need himself anymore, and quit.

Inevitably in such a situation, when one partner wilfully departs, the residual burden falls on the survivor. Tim-bibi will have to alter her ordered pattern of life completely.'

Bill died before the appearance of my book *Sikh Portraits by European Artists* that he and I had such fun working on. In a sense I am glad he did not have to witness the traumas I had to endure with its difficult birth.

It had not been a difficult book to write. Once I had formulated its structure in my mind – two sections, the first biographies of Ranjit Singh and family and the second an analysis of the large Schoefft panorama of the Lahore Darbar – the actual writing took less than six weeks. I had sent PWP the final manuscript in September. It took a little while to compose. Anne Jackson, my editor, sent me a note saying that the galley proofs would be ready by 17 January and the page proofs by 17 April.

The galley proofs were brought to Lahore by one of our NFC engineers Taqdees Khan. I corrected them as quickly as I could. Fortuitously, just as I was trying to find a way of having them carried to London, someone from Oxford University Press came to see me with a visitor from London. He would be too happy to carry the packet of proofs for me. It was too good to be true. It was.

A couple of days later, I happened to call Charles Lewis (the MD of OUP at Karachi) to chat about the exhibition of our lithographs. At the end, almost as an afterthought, he told me that Mr. Conibear (the OUP courier) had lost my proofs.

Fortunately I had a photocopy of the proofs. I re-did the corrections and again fortuitously, someone (this time from the publishers Longmans) was leaving for London on 15th. He would be happy to take them. These did reach PWP.

The page proofs came on 1 April. I corrected those swiftly (PWP was strict about deadlines) and arranged for a pilot in PIA known to Agha Ikram to carry them to London. On 17th I learned that the corrected page proofs were lying with the doorman of the Royal Garden Hotel, where the PIA crew stayed, and could I have them collected?

My trials did not end there. When I rang Anne from Abu Dhabi in August, she told me that the first copies of Sikh Portraits would be ready by Friday. She had made arrangements with Charles Lewis who happened to be visiting London that she would send some copies through him. As a precaution, I asked her to give the six author's copies to Mian Tajammul Hussain, a banker friend of my uncle Amjad Ali visiting London at the time.

Tears come to my eyes as I re-read my account of what happened to that first consignment:

'After all the efforts I made from Abu Dhabi to arrange the safest and speediest dispatch of my book, everything went wrong. Tajammul Hussain who was supposed to bring the books arrived on 18 August via Jeddah. "The books are in his luggage which will follow in a few days,' someone from his office assured me. His luggage arrived on 20th. He was not available to open it. Eventually, this morning I learned that he had been given two packets by PWP - one small one and another larger one. I feared the worst. Sure enough, Tajammul had brought the small packet which contained Tim-bibi's latest book British Portraiture in India and left behind the larger one containing my six author's copies.

I cannot record my unspeakable chagrin and grief at Tajammul's mistake, especially when I had emphasized to him repeatedly that the books were not for me but by me. I had planned that these books should reach me before Eid so that I could send Dr. Randhawa's copy to him via someone leaving for Chandigarh. Above all, I wanted it for the children. [The book was dedicated to them.] It will probably mean nothing to them, but it will mean a great deal to me giving it to them.

In time, I suppose, my frustration and temper inflamed by these disappointments will like death itself lose their sting. For the moment though I feel very very low, dejected and very alone.'

Had I been more mature or more philosophical, I would have taken solace from the news that my *Pahari Paintings* had been a success. By mid August 1979, PWP informed me that they had only 150 copies left and might consider a reprint.[7] Had I been a better physical condition (public sector demands are heavier on the brain and the buttocks than on one's brawn), I would not have suffered a slipped disc from picking up a bucket of water at the wrong angle. Lying supine on a hard bed for about a fortnight gave me the opportunity of making notes from all the books I had on Sikh history to supplement the material I had retrieved from the Punjab Archives. And had I been less determined, I would have quickly lost heart and not persisted in accumulating much material about my ancestors, the triad of three Fakir brothers who had served Maharaja Ranjit Singh and his successors with such distinction.[8]

My forays into authorship I knew could never support me financially. My pocket belonged to the NFC, or to any higher bidder. Zia's determination to undo everything that Bhutto had done extended to the public sector. Suddenly, the justifications for expanding public ownership or of making the public sector an engine of growth (it had yet to be decided whether it would be at the front of the train pulling or at the back of it pushing) were being questioned and discarded. Interestingly, the very same bureaucrats who had promoted nationalisation became its pall-bearers.

By September 1979, I had spent four years in the NFC – four exciting, creative and productive years that had enabled me to exercise and demonstrate my intellectual potential. As Babar Ali wanted to have a lean team at Head Office, I handled four portfolios – Planning, Finance, Commercial and Personnel. The demands of Finance were obvious. I had to arrange financing for the three major projects at Multan, Mirpur Mathelo and Hazara. The projects looked to us, and we at the NFC had to look to the Government. The government did not want to deal with individual units clamouring like hungry chicks for sustenance. As the interlocutor, I found myself negotiating for foreign exchange with the Saudis, the World Bank, the Asian Development Bank, and the OPEC Special Fund. For local currency, the only source was the Government for long-term financing and commercial banks for working capital. Towards the end of my stay at NFC, I had to organise the conversion

---

[7] My optimism was short-lived. It remained at its original print-run of 1,500 copies.
[8] The product of this research took shape almost thirty-five years later in my book *The Resourceful Fakirs: Three Muslim brothers at the Sikh Court of Lahore* (New Delhi, 2014).

of funds given to us over the years through ADP allocations into equity and interest bearing debentures.

The Commercial department in NFC acted as a coordinator, aggregating and fulfilling the import requirements of the operating units at Multan, Daudkhel, Faisalabad and Jaranwala for rock phosphate from Jordan and sulphur from Morocco.

Personnel management proved to be quite a challenge. It took me some time to establish a centralised cadre of executives whom we could deploy to operating units and to projects according to their needs. The logical companion to this had to be a uniform pay scale. It took me some months and a little arm-twisting to achieve this. In those days, liberated by Bhutto's promises of egalitarianism, the unions had acquired more muscle. Each of our units had a separate collective bargaining agent with agreement that expired on different dates. The implication was obvious. No sooner had the first agreement been concluded than the next union expected to use that as platform from which to demand increases. The only solution was to call a caucus of all the unions and to make them accept one agreement applicable to all.

In time the unions hit back by circulating a pamphlet ridiculing me as the *Shahzada-e-NFC* (Prince of NFC). This of course found its way to the desks of the Ministry of Production. No one there mentioned it when I next visited the ministry. I could detect the change in atmospherics from the evasive look in the eyes of Habeeb Husain's PA. Sure enough, while I was sitting with HH, the offensive document was brought in and wordlessly placed on HH's desk. I knew this would be used as an excuse to delay my overdue promotion as Director Finance.

The Ministry itself underwent a change of ministership. In June 1979 Lt. General Ghulam Hassan Khan (formerly Minister Petroleum) replaced Prof Ghafoor Ahmed. Our first review meeting with him took place on 12 September. Dressed in full uniform, the general opened the meeting with a condemnation of the public sector. After an hour, his interest began to flag. His yawns became noticeably more frequent. His ennui became infectious. Within the half hour, he had us yawning in sympathy.

A fortnight or so later, Majid Mufti called me to Islamabad. He asked me whether I would head a resurrected BIM. I spent about twenty minutes with him, taking care initially to analyse the defects in the public sector organisations and demonstrating to him that I was exactly the person he needed to rectify its ills. Having massaged him, I then threw iced water on his hopes by telling him that I could not accept his offer, even though it would have catapulted me to the level of a Chairman. The bankruptcy of policy within the government became more apparent day by day. Agreeing to his offer would have been as infructuous as accepting a post-dated cheque, as M.K. Gandhi once said in a different context, on a bank that was failing.

In 1979, I had reached the age of thirty-seven. I had been working on and off for twenty years ever since I joined Maurice Apple & Co. as a green articled clerk in 1959. At the NFC, I had gained a reputation of professionalism and competence which I wanted to accrue to my personal advancement. During 1978 and 1979, I received a number of offers of employment. The most lucrative – one that would have doubled my NFC salary of Rs 7,000 per month – came from Premier Tobacco. Its disadvantage, apart from the nature of its business, lay in relocation to Karachi.

Another came from the Dada group, co-shareholders with NFC in Lyallpur Chemicals and Fertilisers Ltd. Ahmed Dada invited me to become partners with them in the fertiliser import business. They wanted to use my expertise in the fertiliser industry and my contacts within government.

Babar Ali, whenever he returned from his frequent trips abroad, would make fresh offers each time – once to join his friend Naseeruddin in Nigeria, another to work with someone (he would not specify who) somewhere abroad, a third to head the IT company he planned to incorporate, and a fourth to be part of his team to establish a milk plant.

Another mentor – S.B. Awan – who had been relegated to the O & M Division (the equivalent of the human appendix in the body corpus of government) wanted me to join him as his Director-General. Flattering but as insecure a posting as his own position there was.

The offer I did accept came suddenly and from an unexpected source.

CHAPTER 22

FAREWELL TO LAHORE

What was I doing in mid September 1979 looking at a glittering red silk codpiece with black lace trimmings in Dubai?

I noticed it in the lingerie shop window opposite the Al Futtaim offices, where I had gone to meet Uncle Rahmat Ali Khan.[1] He had retired from Pakistan Burmah Shell and gone abroad, as many other senior executives had done, to the Gulf where he joined the Al Futtaim Group as Group Personnel Director.

Dubai seemed to most congenial destination. It was even then the most cosmopolitan among the newly emerging emirates, a commercial hub and one not too fastidious about whether its expatriate employees could speak Arabic or not. For that, Dubai businessmen employed Syrians or Egyptians. They avoided requiting Palestinians for political reasons, just as for the same reason Abu Dhabi gave them refuge.

Uncle Rahmat's invitation came as a surprise to me. He called during Ramazan (the month of fasting) and asked me to send my CV to his man Ghani (also ex-PBS) in Karachi. I heard nothing more for some weeks until a letter arrived, inviting me to spend a weekend in Dubai, at Al Futtaim's expense. Within a day a PTA for a first class ticket arrived at the PIA offices, and three days later I was on my way to Karachi en route for Dubai.

Sultan Khan (ex-United Bank and now General Manager Bank of Oman, also an Al Futtaim subsidiary) was on the same flight. At first I resented his inquisitiveness until I realised that he could tell me more about

---

[1] Son of Khan Qurban Ali Khan.

the AF group that I myself might be able to glean over a weekend. He suggested that I should not commit myself until I had spoken to him first. He had something else in mind for me. Even in the day or so I spent in transit at Karachi, two other offers came up – from OUP to take over from Charles Lewis and from my friend Fareed Khan to join a firm making plastic containers for the pharmaceutical industry. Suddenly a third cropped up from another friend M. Hanafi – that I should join Grindlays Bank and take over from him as Regional Manager North at Lahore.

I discussed the options in my diary:

'Out of all these possibilities, the Al Futtaim appears the most attractive. Not simply because of the money. I have no idea how much they propose to offer me. It seems to have the widest avenue for growth. Majid Al Futtaim has emerged as one of the leading businessmen in Dubai, securing such lucrative agencies as Toyota, National, Sanyo, Wimpey, etc. He has a number of specialised divisions trading within Dubai and some companies abroad. His personal interest though lies in real estate. He has built property on prime locations in Dubai but he has his eye on real estate outside the Gulf.

Dubai operates at its own pace and according to its own time-scale. The fact that Al Futtaim has the Seiko watch agency can be misleading. Their observance of timing and the pace of business is so elastic one might as well throw one's wristwatch into the creek and go by the sun instead. Work at AF commences at 8.00 a.m. and continues until 1.00 p.m. It resumes at 4.00 p.m. for another two hours in the afternoon. It is a crazy life, explicable only when one meets the people themselves. Sudden wealth has made them ultra-confident. Many I know have become soft and indolent. There are some who have held out, clinging to their Bedouin reserve and reticence. Majid appears to be one of them.

He is the only one who matters in his vast sprawling group. Just as the sun dominates the working hours of the commercial community in Dubai, Majid's polyglot empire rotates around him. To see top executives who held the most senior positions in Pakistan – Iradat

Husain[2], Naziruddin Mahmood, Humayun Mufti – sit outside Majid's office and wait to be summoned is a measure of his control over them, and of their submission to the power of the petro-dirham. None of them can go abroad or even on leave without his express permission. It is true he never withholds it. By having to ask, they are reminded that they are his vassals.

He recruits very cautiously and selectively. He had reason to be careful. His first batch – Egyptians – began to undermine him and enrich themselves out of his pockets. To control them, he brought in white expatriates – from Britain, even Australia. When he calculated how much they cost him and what little he received in return, he cast his net over India. Shoals of professionals came, until he discovered their herd instinct - his head of IT had recruited practically half the population of his village in Kerala. As an antidote to the Indians, he turned towards Pakistan. Qualitatively, his haul came from a higher level of professionals. Competent, acquiescent and diligent, their defect was an inability to see any other Pakistani excel.

Majid in a way reminded me of Maharaja Ranjit Singh. The Sikh couldn't, Majid wouldn't read any paper placed before him. His sharp mind enabled him to retain every scrap of pertinent information. He knew more about his businesses than his British Group Finance Director Mr. Bean.

I had the opportunity of meeting Majid Al Futtaim himself. He had with him Bean (an English Chartered Accountant junior to me and a bit of mediocrity) and Dr. Al Shash, the cherubic Syrian managing director of the AF Real Estate company for which I was being considered.

Uncle Rahmat was of course terrified that I might somehow misbehave and bring discredit to him as my sponsor. After an interview he would mull over each word said in my favour: "Bean gave you an excellent chit."

Before I left Dubai on13th, I was asked to see Dr. Shash. He told me that he thought I fitted the bill and that both he and Majid felt that I

---

[2] Formerly of United Bank Limited, and then MD of Futtaim's Middle East Bank Ltd.

would be an asset to the organisation. He wanted me to join by 1ˢᵗ
November. I told him that it could not be earlier than 30 November
as I owed an obligation to my present employers to serve out my notice
period. He seemed genuinely pleased at my response. "I admire you
all the more for it."

While in Dubai I called on Humayun Mufti for dinner. With him as
guide, I explored the labyrinth of the AF group. Later, I wondered
why he had joined AF. Within Pakistan, everyone in the BIM had the
most outlandish explanations. In fact, finding himself out on a limb in
the altered environment of the BIM, he joined AF because he had no
other alternative.

"Didn't Majid Al Futtaim know of his reputation in the BIM?" I asked
Uncle Rahmat.

He replied: "Yes, Majid told him: *I know you have a reputation in
Pakistan. Don't bring it here.*"

"And Mufti joined despite that?"

Al Futtaim had arranged accommodation at the Dubai Sheraton – an
architectural caprice that looked from the creek like the head of a
hooded falcon. In the restaurant, one evening, I encountered Dr. Aziz
Kurtha[3] dining with M.F Husain. Aziz very insistent that I should
visit his home that evening, an invitation he underlined when he
learned that Sotheby's were publishing my second book. He is quite
indiscriminate in dropping names and often drops yours in your own
lap.

On hearing my regret, he said: "But we may not see each other for
another six years?"

"Not if you try hard enough."

I left the cool pink and magenta splendour of the Sheraton, boarded
the flight for Karachi, settled in my first class seat, and prayed that
this was not a mirage.

Before I left for Abu Dhabi, Shahnaz and I had been able to host Ved

[3] Dr. Aziz Kurtha had rather controversial career subsequently in cases involving the author
Jeffery Archer and disputed ownership of de Souza's paintings.

Mehta in Lahore. He had sent me a message from New York that he wanted to come to Lahore from New Delhi, and if possible also visit Rawalpindi and Murree. I left a detailed account in my diary of the anxieties that led up to his visit:

'21 August: Great excitement of the past few days have subsided leaving a dark ring of disappointment to mark the high level of our expectations. It all started with a telegram from Ved indicating that he might be coming to Pakistan later this month. He would be reaching Delhi on 13th and wanted to fly to Lahore, and also visit Rawalpindi and Murree if possible. There was a flurry of messages from me to him, sent through couriers travelling to Europe so that I could catch him before he left New York and simultaneously through others going eastwards to India. Arrangements and bookings were made exactly in accordance with his final programme, which was to arrive in Lahore on 20th by Indian Airlines, travel to Rawalpindi and Murree on 21st, and then after spending the 22nd in Lahore, to fly back to New Delhi on 23rd. With almost proprietary selfishness, Shahnaz and I (armed with Ved's autobiography Face to Face) planned to have dinner with him, take him to his former home 11 Temple Road, and then after our return from Rawalpindi, to take him to the Emerson School for the Blind, where we had unearthed his enrolment record.

Imagine our surprise when on 19th evening we heard from Smith of the American Consulate that he would like to have us over for dinner tomorrow to meet Mr. Ved Mehta. I was incensed. Here I had taken the trouble of organizing Ved's programme and now I was being invited by someone who did not even know him to have dinner with my guest. What horrified me was the prospect that on Ved's first night in Lahore – the city of his birth and of his poignant childhood – he would have to spend it amongst curious fellow-Americans wanting to view him. It seemed from Mr. Smith's message that Ved had agreed to the dinner, and so we were left with no option but to accept.

The following evening, barely an hour before Ved's expected arrival, we received a message from Smith telling us that Ved had fallen ill in New Delhi and that his visit had been postponed. But could we come for dinner anyway, as there was a mountain of food to be demolished.

Hoping against hope, Shahnaz and I went to the airport nevertheless to meet the Indian Airlines flight. No sign of Mr. Mehta. We returned home disconsolate, to discover yet another message from Mr. Smith that his mother had died in the U.S. and therefore his dinner stood cancelled.

29 August: Shahnaz and I returned from Islamabad on 26th, just in case Ved decided to come to Lahore on 27th. Quite by chance, a spot scrutiny of the passengers list at the India Airlines office yielded his name for the 27th. A call from the Ford Foundation in New Delhi confirmed Ved's plans.

As the time of Ved's flight drew closer, Shahnaz began to feel ill. By 5.00 p.m., an hour before the IA aircraft was due to land, Shahnaz was writing in agony. The penicillin injection she had been given in the morning had not controlled the infection. The intense pain made her cry out aloud. At 5.30 p.m., she was given another injection and with it an intravenous dose of Novalgin as a sedative. I brought her home to rest. Suddenly she vomited and within seconds brightened up, insisting that she was now well enough to go the airport and receive Ved. She dressed in a jiffy, doused herself with cologne, and accompanied me to the airport. I asked out servant Yusuf to sit on the back seat of the car in case Shahnaz collapsed on the tarmac.

The Indian Airlines aircraft taxied to a halt. The hatch opened. Datta (the IA manager) appeared and gave me the thumbs up sign. A moment Ved appeared.

Shahnaz met him first. I embraced him and shouted "Welcome Home" above the roar of the fuelling truck's engine. Immigration did not take long, and neither did Customs. Ved had only a battered leather briefcase which he insisted on carrying himself and a black Indian Airlines overnight bag.

"Anything to declare?" the Customs officer asked Ved.

The temptation was irresistible. "Tell him that like Oscar Wilde, you have nothing to declare but your genius!"

I had parked our car near a large tree that provided shade to cabbies during the day and shelter to twittering birds after sunset.

"What a lovely welcome to receive on returning to Lahore!" Ved exclaimed.

On the way to the Intercontinental hotel, I described as naturally as I could the various sights we passed – Fortress Stadium, Aitchison College, etc. We accompanied him to Room 406. I showed him the bed, the location of the writing table, and the door leading into the bathroom.

"The light switch is on the left," I said by force of habit. I could have bitten my tongue off.

Ved, without a moment's pause, switched the light on and closed the door behind him.

I wasn't sure that Shahnaz would be up to accompanying us to 11 Temple Road. She was. We took Ved down the Mall towards Regal Chowk, turned into Temple Road, and parked outside No 11.

Shahnaz and Ved walked up to its gate. He ran his fingers across the marble plaque which bore his father's name –Dr. Amolak Ram – and then gently pushed open one of the wooden gates. I rang the bell.

Through the window, I could see Dr. MH's two sisters in the drawing room, lying in untidy disarray. One of them - the round-faced one – came to the door, peered through the gauze at us and then cautiously opened the door halfway.

"We had come to see you the other day. You remember?" but before I could say anything further, she interrupted me with: "No, I cannot remember seeing you. No one has ever been to this house."

Shahnaz steeped forward with a fuller explanation. She then introduced Ved. At this, the tone of the harridan changed.

"Come in," she said, expansively. She settled Ved in one of the carved chairs closest to the door. She spoke to him about the time he and his family had lived this house. As common link between them, apart from the house itself, was Sheikh Jamil who had 'helped' the Mehta obtain a water-pipe connection and later occupied their home and according to the harridan, also rifled it contents. She deplored his misbehaviour loudly, as if he could still hear her, and followed that with a tirade at her misfortune at having lost all her belongings in 1947 in their old house in Panipat. "Auctioned the lot for Rs 2!" she complained with vehemence.

Try as hard we could, we could not staunch the forward flow of her belated recriminations. The fact that there was someone sitting in front of her who had lost as much as she had did not occur to her. Her recollections arched over the past 32 years and would have continued had we not risen from our chairs and more or less demanded that we show Ved the rest of the house.

I took him first to the room on the right – his father's dressing room.

"Wasn't there a corridor here?" Ved asked, "Leading off to the left." We entered it and then stood in the dining room facing the fire place still with its original magenta-coloured tiles. Ved recalled the cupboards set in the walls, the location of the doors lading out on to the verandah. The room opposite the dining room used to be his mother's bedroom. Now it was crowded with charpoys.

Soon we were on the verandah, close to Ved's room. He moved forward, down two steps and turned right, stopping before a doorway.

"This used to be your room," the round faced sister said. "We now use it for prayers."

"Then perhaps I should not enter."

I took him in nevertheless. He walked in it for a few minutes. I thought he might touch the cupboard handles or pass his hands over the window panes. Overtly he showed no interest but it was clear to Shahnaz and myself that Ved was deeply affected.

Ved's memory was unerringly accurate. The slightest modifications were exposed by his searing questions. Never testy or difficult, always sharp and accurate.

The ladies decided to take us upstairs to the part of the house Shahnaz and I had not seen on our last visit.

"I won't go," the moon faced one demurred. "I have a heart condition."

The slimmer sister led us up the stairs.

"That must be Pom's room, straight ahead," Ved asked. "See if there is a staircase leading up from the driveway."

From the first floor to the roof, a flat area open to the skies, one had a commanding view of the dome and the spire of St Patrick's Cathedral, silhouetted against the evening sky. At one end of the roof lay a small covered chamber in which the Mehta family could repair if it began to rain while they were sleeping outdoors in the summer. This was the roof from which Ved would scamper foolhardily when fly kites during Basant.'[4]

My diary entry stops here. I left blank pages after it in the hope that I would complete the narrative. I never did. The memory of that trip is still fresh in my mind and I will try to recall its essential details.

We took Ved to his old school – the Emerson School for the Blind – in Sheranwala Gate, inside the old city. Mr. Baqir, the teacher who had caused him so much pain and grief, was still teaching there. He of course did not recognise Ved among the hundreds of blind boys who had passed through and suffered at his calloused hands.

Ved had been particularly keen on going to Rawalpindi. He could not remember address of the house his family had lived in, other than it was located somewhere behind the house of Sardars Mohan Singh and Sohan Singh. That grand house in a garden the size of a public park had become President's House under Ayub Khan and Yahya Khan, then Prime Minister's House under Bhutto, and now Ziaul Haq's secretariat. He mentioned in his book *Face to Face* that although dilapidated, the house was surrounded by an acre of open land.

We drove along the road behind the presidency, first once and then again. It was only when we noticed a gate adjacent to a house that been constructed obviously after 1947 that we suspected that might be the entrance to Ved's house. Sure enough, we drove in and after a minute or so, the house came into view. The modern house that had blocked it from the main road had been built in its ample garden.

The car stopped. Ved steeped out on the gravel and said affirmatively: "Yes, this is the house. When you enter, it will have a central corridor with rooms leading off it. " We asked the occupants whether we could go around

---

[4] Shahnaz has given a brilliantly evocative and amusing account of this visit in an article 'The Many Ways of looking at Lahore', reprinted in her book *Lost From View* (Lahore, 1994), pp.101-3.

the house. It had remained unchanged since Ved had lived there in 1945. Being government property even then, it had never been altered or improved.

Ved walked to the area behind the house. "This is where I reassembled my brother Om's bicycle." He made it sound so simple. In fact, he not only taught himself how to make the bicycle functional, he learned to ride it unaided. On one occasion he described how, unbeknownst to his sisters he followed them, 'taking directions from their voices' to their school – Presentation Convent. Not knowing the way back alone, he waited outside the school until his sisters emerged in the afternoon.[5]

Ved's father used to take him to Murree. We drove there, lurching along the winding road. He had little recollection of Murree, other than the bracing air and the fragrance of pines.

The return flight to Lahore hit a patch of bad weather. The Fokker aircraft seemed to bounce. I sensed Ved's nervousness and held his hand. He would have preferred Shahnaz's.

His letter sent on 14 September after his return to New York said as much:

> My dear Shahnaz and Aijaz
>
> In recent years I had come to think of Pakistan with dread. The houses in which I'd grown up had become in my memory shells and labyrinths to which I could never return and, even if I did, I could never find my way back into them.
>
> Then I had a chance meeting with you two (or rather three[6]) and part of my reluctance to go to the dinner of Ravi's was that I did not want to stoke the fires of memory. I realized after our meeting that I would never feel the same about Pakistan, that in fact it was a real place with real people whom I could love and care about as I do my family.
>
> My visit to Pakistan – I should really say to Lahore, to Rawalpindi, to Murree, or rather to 11 Temple Road, to 10 Civil Lines, to Pindi Point – has strengthened that feeling even more than I could have imagined.

---

[5] See *Face to Face*, pp.44-45.
[6] My sister-in-law Lalarukh Agha whom Ved had met in 1978.

I've thought about both of you – and Auntie and the girls – often. I keep on marvelling at your capacity for friendship. Aijaz, when you have the time, send me your impressions of the schools and houses we visited. By the way, my grandfather's house was the third one from the corner [in Mehta Galli], which makes me think that the house of the lawyer we walked into on my first night was the correct house [...]

Finally, Aijaz, at the risk of offending you, I do have to say that holding hands with Shahnaz was much more exciting than holding hands with you...

In 1983, Ved married Linn Cooper. In time they had two lovely daughters Sage and Natasha. Sage came to stay with us in Lahore and of course we took her on 'a pilgrimage' to her grandfather's house 11 Temple Road. That first meeting with Ved in New Delhi in 1978 and his visit to Pakistan a year later has ripened into a deep and satisfying friendship between our families that remains until today. Whenever any one of us goes to New York we make it a point of calling on him and Linn at their flat on 79th Street, bought as Ved told me in 1980 out of 'some windfall profits.' On one occasion, after lunch, we talked as Ved preferred to in Punjabi. He asked me whether I was a practising Muslim.

"Sort of," I replied. "Something I do find disturbing is that the Holy Quran is compiled in a sequence from the longest to the shortest *ayats*, instead of in the chronological order of revelation."

Ved fell silent for a moment, and then floored me with this response: "Why should you expect God to follow a man-made chronology?"

Ved's visit to Lahore, the trip to Dubai to meet Al Futtaim, and the simmering crisis within the country and the NFC brought me to the end of September. I waited for a letter of offer from Al Futtaim's. Suddenly, at 11.00 a.m., on 20 September, I was called by the Chairman's PA to take a call from Dubai. Uncle Rahmat Ali Khan came on the line. He told me that AF confirmed its offer of employment. Could he regard my acceptance as confirmed? I sounded casual in my response.

The formal letter arrived in the post a week later. I signed the copy and then called my PA Butt to take some dictation. I began by dictating my letter of resignation from NFC. Butt could hardly hold his pencil straight. Then I dictated a letter of acceptance to Al Futtaim. His face broke out into a smile that stretched from Lahore to Dubai.

The NFC Board meeting held on 30 September settled any qualms I may have had about leaving the NFC. Only two directors attended – Bokhari as Chairman and Habeeb Husain who looked for every opportunity to get away from Islamabad. Two directors were a hardly a quorum but no one in the government seemed to care. This lack of seriousness towards the business of the public sector became symbolic of the attitude of the Ministry of Production. Unclear in its motives, it began issuing order which involved changes they had not thought through. The latest order reconstituted the Boards of the subsidiaries, inducting persons with no credentials. Until then, the internal corporate structure had been a pyramid. NFC as the holding company appointed its Chairman, Technical Director, and its Finance & Personnel Director on the Board of each subsidiary. They were common to each to ensure uniformity. With the new order, the only common link between the NFC and its subsidiaries would be the Chairman. I could predict what would happen. Board meetings would become mere formalities, held if at all then once a year. The role of the Corporation would be superfluous.

The altered mood in the Ministry impinged upon me more directly. Before leaving for Vienna to attend the Experts' Workshop, RHB whispered to me that someone (he did not specify who) had been filling the Minister's ear with propaganda against me. It had reached an extreme in which the failure of Pak-Arab at Multan to achieve full production had been not the fault of the plant management but singularly *mine*. RHB also mentioned that my requests to call on the minister were interpreted as attempts to 'clear' myself.

As the Secretary Majid Mufti happened to be Lahore on that day, I thought I would meet him here rather than wasting a day waiting for him between his appointments. I went to Chamba House where he was staying. He feigned illness and sent a message of regret that he could not receive me. I then drove to the airport at 3.45 p.m. and waited until 4.35 p.m. for him to arrive. As I had anticipated, he tried to avoid discussing my case. I unloaded whatever I had on my chest, as politely and as firmly as I could. I knew he would be too cowardly to convey my words to the minister.[7] To be honest, I could not care anymore. The worst the ministry could do would be to refuse to accept my resignation, or withhold my end of service dues.

---

[7] Once the winter residence of the Rajas of Chamba, one of the Punjab hill states.

At the political level, Zia rode a tide of success. He fooled the public into holding local bodies' elections instead of at the national level. 'By sheer accident,' I noted in my diary, 'or by the failure or collapse of those around him, Zia has gained a sort of hollow stature. Out of the persons who looked down on him when he ousted Bhutto, the Shah of Iran is himself out, Daud in Afghanistan and even his successor Taraki have both been removed, Morarji Desai has gone and Charan Singh is going. Zia has begun talking about Islamic democracy.' The choice, as a friend put it, is between siding with a Shia Iran or a Wahabi Saudi Arabia. One thing became clear: both the General and the PNA were determined to keep the PPP out of the game.

I happened to meet Col. Siddiq Salik, Zia's PRO, at the Chinese National day celebrations on 30 September. He invited me to meet him at PM's house in Rawalpindi the following day. I reached Gate no 2.

"Your name?"

"Aijazuddin?"

"Col. Aijazuddin?"

"No. *Mr.* Aijazuddin. I am *not* an Army officer." Not that I would have been mistaken for one. There was enough tinkling brass there any way.

SS's PA told me that a cabinet meeting was in progress. SS came as soon as he was free. His main reason was to rail against OUP for neglect of his book *Witness to Surrender*, its reluctance to pay him royalties, and other just complaints that I shared.

"It is not for nothing," I consoled him, "that Taufiq Rafat and I have re-christened the man at OUP. Instead of Mascarehnas, we call him 'Ascarehnas.'

I waited until he had vented his spleen against OUP, before asking him about Zia.

"Does he realise that Asghar Khan is plotting his hat-trick?"[8]

"He knows it. He is sitting on a volcano. We all are but ... the view from the top is so good that one forgets."

I told my diary:

---

[8] Air Marshal Asghar Khan was given credit for removing Ayub Khan and then Zulfikar Ali Bhutto.

'Zia has no intention of transferring power. Every morning, he must be viewing his reflection and asking:

Magic mirror on the wall,

To whom should I transfer power,

If at all.

Zia may be sitting on a volcano but he feels secure enough. Although the all-too-public dissensions within the political parties may accrue to his benefit, the economic situation is not stable. Ghulam Ishaque Khan's nomination for the Secretary-Generalship of the Islamic Conference has been routed. Prices are now phenomenally high and rising daily.

Almost everyone is of the opinion that elections will be held, but not this November but in March 1980. Shankar Bajpai insists that he heard Zia say during a speech at Quetta (during which he made the now famous remark that nowhere in the Holy Quran did he find any mention of 17 November) that the elections would be in March. Bajpai thought it might have been a slip of the tongue.

A slip or not, the results of the Local Bodies' elections have fortified his resolve to stay in power. Almost 80% of the candidates were former PPP stalwarts. Abida is one such turncoat. As soon as she was declared winner at Jhang, her cousin Iftikhar Bukhari filed a petition against her and obtained a stay order blocking her result.

We met her for dinner soon after the result. Each guest – the Fullers (US Consul General), Bajpai, the Riazuddin Ahmads, the Mazhar Ali Khans – were collared separately and informed of Ifi's caddish behaviour. Shahnaz is right. Everyone invited to *Al Greevaz* is expected to be absorbed by what Chandi is doing.'

Zia postponed the elections. He made the announcement in a television broadcast. Like all his predecessors after they discovered television, he appeared flanked by the Pakistan flag and a portrait of the long-suffering Quaid.

"Where is Mr. Bhutto?" Momina asked me. "Won't he appear on

television again?" adding what we all felt, "I don't like this man."

During his speech, Zia gave a predictable justification for the action he proposed to take. He cited disunity among the politicians; their selfishness. He reiterated his eagerness to come to terms with them. But alas! He regretted that there appeared to be solution in sight. Therefore postponement was unavoidable.

Having declared his intent, Zia made the nation bite his bullet. "Now," he leered, "you will understand what Martial Law is really like!"

Sure enough, some days afterwards, public lashings took place in Rawalpindi, Lahore, Faisalabad, and other cities. Any crime committed was announced and with it the exemplary punishment awarded by the Summary Military Court. The type of crime did not bother the censors. Never in its history had *The Pakistan Times* carried so often news reports of unnatural offences against minor boys. Perhaps the most frightening example of this public exhibition of intent to rule by terror is the condemnation to death by a Summary Military Court of the five socialites who had robbed and then raped Shabnam, the film actress. The day after this announcement, the families of the convicted boys were shown pleading with Shabnam for mercy. Zia meanwhile confirmed the death sentence.

Any doomed offenders who harboured any hopes of clemency had only to look at the front page of *Nawa-i-Waqt* of 6 November. Five photographs showed the dead body of Syed Hassan, the hijacker who had been executed that morning.

'Oh, Cromwell – what in the name of God are you doing. Worse, what are you doing in the name of God?'

Events that November precipitated with a vehemence none of us had anticipated. On 19 November, the Iranians stormed the US Embassy in Tehran. Carter retaliated by blocking all Iranian assets in US jurisdiction. The stalemate continued.

On 21 November, I tuned in to the BBC at 7.15 a.m. and heard to my horror that the Holy Ka'aba had been attacked yesterday by terrorists. At 1.15 p.m., I passed the *Nawa-i-Waqt* office off Queen's Road. I noticed the *zamima* or news-sheet being sold by young street hawkers. Within the hour, by 2.15 p.m., a crowd could be seen collecting. They chanted slogans which at first sounded anti-Khomeini but soon changed to 'Carter *murdabad*.' By 2.30 p.m. or so, the American Centre on Queen's Road was under attack. Within an hour, smoke was billowing from the incinerating Centre. A damaged fire truck lay immobile in the middle of the road. Police were trying to haul it away as if it was some dead Spanish bull.

I drove past the Centre at 5.00 p.m. Smoke still spouted from the debris. The letter 'C' hung from its hinges. Police were everywhere, urging drivers not to slow down as they drove past the smouldering ruins. I returned home to learn that the U.S. Consulate had also been attacked.

I immediately phoned the Fullers. Understandably they were not at home.

That afternoon, students attacked the US Embassy in Islamabad. Two staff members were killed. The other 140 managed to take shelter in a bunker and survived. It was reported that Ziaul Haq had been cycling through Rawalpindi bazaar when this occurred. He appeared on television, this time to inform the public that he had spoken to King Khaled. Zia asked everyone in Pakistan to pray for the release of the Holy Ka'aba. God, he opined, could be relied upon to look after His own house.

In Lahore, the protests continued. At about 12.00 a.m., a large procession of about 200 students, many on motorbikes, congregated on Shahrah-e-Quaid-e-Azam. They moved en masse towards Faisal Square. Armed police blocked their progress, preventing them from flowing down to Queen's Road and upstream to the Punjab Assembly building (now the DMLA Secretariat). The students were organised. There was no doubt about that. Two or three leaders (one of them shirtless) exhorted the mob towards the police. The moment they saw two truck-loads of Army personnel, the demonstrators parted. They let the trucks pass through them and then closed ranks to confront the police again.

In an ill-advised attempt to follow the crowd, I narrowly missed having a brick thrown through my windshield.

During these days, Babar Ali called me to his office to give me a copy of a book – *Yadgar-e-Fakir* - which he commissioned on my father. He wrote an inscription on a sheet of paper and handed it to me: 'To check its English, not its content.' He left on another of his journeys abroad, this time to Tanzania. He asked me to deliver a copy of the book to Ch. Zafrulla.

On 11 December, Shahid Attaullah (a relation) took me to see Ch. sahib. We arrived at 4.30 p.m., and were shown into a profusion of Byzantine gold lame and gilt furnishings. His former wife Badr Begum[9] has a Midas weakness for anything golden. I sat on a sofa nearest the fireplace.

"That is Ch. Sahib's chair."

Ch. Zafrulla entered, walking slowly but firmly. He was 86 years old. He had his two acolytes – Ch. Bashir Ahmed and Sh. Ijaz Ahmed - in tow. Ch. Sahib's ignored any newcomer for a while before tossing a question at him, casually but with the intention of testing the freshman's responses.

Today, his remark to me was: "How does your height compare with that of your father?"

Shades of Azizuddin's diplomacy passed through my mind. "His stature was such," I replied, "that I could never dare comparing myself with him."

He smiled. "I asked that question not in the metaphorical sense but in the physical one."

This time I gave him a straight reply: "I was three inches taller than him."

We talked about the present situation while his two cronies listened with deference. His community of Ahmadis has embalmed him into some sort of living lama, imbued with super-human attributes, one of them being a phenomenal memory. When, for example, I asked Ch sahib whether he might like to read my *Sikh Portraits* book, Sh. Ijaz piped up: "Ch. sahib is a very fast reader. In three days, he finished a book of over 900 pages!"

"No," Ch. sahib corrected him mildly: "It was only 700 pages."

I asked him where I should deliver it.

"Come tomorrow. I am expecting your uncle Amjad. Your presence will dilute the meeting."

The next morning, I collected Lalla Amjad and drove him to Ch. Zafrulla's cottage, built in the spacious gardens of Badr Begum's estate near

---

[9] After her divorce from Ch Zafrulla, Badr Begum married Ch Shahnawaz, a wealthy businessman with the Mercedes Benz dealership and the Shezan chain of restaurants.

Cavalry Ground. Chairs had been placed for us in the garden.

Ch. sahib came and seated himself in the sun, ignoring the shade of the garden umbrella. He and Lalla Amjad bantered, sometimes on weighty matters such as America's reference to the International Court of Justice over Iran's occupation of its embassy in Teheran ('It has no relevance. Iran has never accepted the jurisdiction of the ICJ.'), and then on banal topics as their eating habits.

"I have no lunch," Ch. Z. explained, "but have an early dinner."

"I have a heavy lunch," Lalla Amjad countered. "Only a light salad at about 7.00 p.m. By 8.00 p.m., I am in bed," adding with twinkle "at least when I am in Pakistan."

CZ retorted mischievously: "Knowing you, as I do, Amjad, I am sure you go to bed at 8.00 p.m. when you are abroad also, but not to sleep..."

Lalla Amjad, a septuagenarian, blushed like a debutante.

I met Ch. Zafrulla again by chance. I had gone to Lalla Amjad's to collect the proofs of his book and discovered Ch. Sahib there. He had come to condole the death of Akhtar Ahsan (Lalla Amjad's cousin and also brother-in-law).

"Did you get my message?" he asked me.

"The one through Naazish?" He had called to tell her his pleasure at meeting me.

He nodded. "I enjoyed and am still enjoying your book."

Sh. Ijaz added: "You have exceeded your father's achievements in this field."

"That is not high praise," Ch. Sahib interjected.

"But Col. sahib wrote a number of books."

"I know. I say that bearing those in mind," CZ said with finality.

He asked me to meet him the next day as he had a book to present to me. A fortnight later, on 22 December, I took Shahnaz with me to meet Ch. Zafrulla. We had to wait our turn as he had a succession of visitors, all Ahmadis, one from Hyderabad, another from Demark. He gave me a copy of his translation of the Holy Quran and also a volume of Bashir Ahmad's writings which had just arrived from London. This version did not have Ch.

sahib's introduction. I had found an earlier edition of the same work (with Ch. sahib's Introduction) in a second-hand bookshop for five rupees some weeks earlier.

I told him that we were leaving Lahore for Dubai shortly.

"Would you mind if I wrote to you?" I asked him.

"Please do. That would be nice. Your letters will come as literature."

The last weeks of December 1979 became a blur of packing and farewell dinners given by friends. We reciprocated with a large party at 13-C Ghalib Road. The house was almost empty. Our belongings had been packed in cartons and sent to Karachi.

We had invited all our friends. The arrangements for dinner had been made in the garden. The inside of the house had been converted into a dance floor, with music organised by Masood Hasan. To our relief, everything went off well – the food, the music, the dancing, and the lubricating punch. Just when we thought no one had the energy to dance any more, a young actress named Rouhani Bano (who had acted with Shahnaz in Imtiaz Ali Taj's play *Anarkali*) decided to give an impromptu solo. She loaded her tape and to the music of an Indian film song, she cavorted, gyrated and shimmied with such abandon that Aitzaz Ahsan couldn't help commenting: "She seems to be less *Rouhani* Bano and more *Jismani* Bano."

The NFC's farewell dinner for us at the Pak-Arab Dak house evoked a rare compliment from RHB. He commented that my departure would have the effect of removing the 'F' from NFC.

Shahnaz and I left for Karachi where I had already deposited the children with Aunty Nayyar. We were touched to see at the airport Babar Ali and his wife Perwin, Shahnaz's cousin Anis and his wife Amti, Shahid and Naazish, and Mushahid Hussain Syed.

We stopped overnight at Multan, from where caught the connecting train to Karachi. The train to Karachi arrived twelve hours late, twelve precious hours that I had hoped I would spend with the girls. The PIA fight to Dubai on 28th returned from the runaway. Our luggage was off loaded. I noticed the traces on my suitcase had been broken. When we reached home and checked it, I discovered that one of the baggage handlers had stolen my father's Gold Rolex watch. I saw the loss as a libation to the travel jinx.

I left finally for Dubai the next day, on 29 December. It had been almost exactly eight years since Shahnaz and I had got married during the 1971 war.

INDEX